# First Person Past

## *American Autobiographies*
### *Volume I*

# First Person Past

*American Autobiographies*
*Volume I*

*Second Edition*

EDITED BY

**MARIAN J. MORTON**
and
**RUSSELL DUNCAN**

**BRANDYWINE PRESS** · St. James, New York

ISBN: 1-881089-07-X

Copyright © 1994, 2003 by Brandywine Press

2nd Printing 2003

*Telephone Orders:* 1-800-345-1776

Printed in the United States of America

*In gratitude for generous financial and technical support, we would like to dedicate* First Person Past *to John Carroll University.*

# CONTENTS

# INTRODUCTION

*First Person Past* lets some fascinating people speak for themselves, men and women who participated in, shaped, and observed many of the most exciting and important events of United States history.

They wrote about that past and their own lives in a unique kind of historical literature, autobiography. This literary form is a retrospective account of its author's life, which begins with childhood and describes in narrative a significant portion of that life. The novelist William Dean Howells described autobiography as "the most democratic" of American literary genres. This is an overstatement since most Americans have not had the inclination, the time, or the literary skills to write their life stories. Nevertheless, because most autobiography does not claim to be high culture, it has offered a voice to groups like women, African-Americans, native Americans, and immigrants, whose writings have sometimes been excluded from the literary canon.

From the hundreds of American autobiographies, the editors have chosen twelve for Volume I of *First Person Past* because they are interesting history and good literature. We have tried to preserve their literary and historical virtues as we edited them for inclusion in this single volume.

# AUTOBIOGRAPHY AS HISTORY

The autobiographers in this volume reveal much about the private sides of American life. Anne Bradstreet wrote of childbirth; Benjamin Franklin of childhood. Franklin spoke honestly of his own premarital sexual adventures. Frederick Douglass and Harriet Jacobs told of the sadistic lust of Southern slaveholders, while Elizabeth Ashbridge, Davy Crockett, and Elizabeth Cady Stanton interpreted marriage and family quite differently. Olaudah Equiano and Black Hawk saw Anglo-American culture from their own marginalized positions.

These autobiographers also provide their personal perspectives on public events. Their first-hand accounts dramatize and authenticate much of the American story from the colonial period through Reconstruction.

The religious intensity of Puritanism, expressed in the mid-seventeenth century by Anne Bradstreet, drove these English colonists to the New World. They established in Massachusetts Bay their "city on a hill," tightly-knit, patriarchal, and dedicated to the preservation and promulgation in the wilderness of their own faith and way of life.

In 1659 Massachusetts Bay colony hanged the bold Quaker missionary Mary Dyer; a century later, when Elizabeth Ashbridge recorded her life story, Quakers were firmly and safely established in several colonies, especially Pennsylvania and the Jerseys. The Quaker settlements reflected the growing religious and ethnic heterogeneity of the colonial population. Indentured servitude filled the crying need for workers in an economy where land was plentiful and labor in short supply. Tens of thousands of servants, like Ashbridge, came to the New World in search of opportunity; many, however, came involuntarily.

The American colonies were built upon another form of servitude, that of Africans, kidnapped—like Olaudah Equiano—from their homeland. Slavery existed in all the English colonies and flourished because it made profits for both slave owners and slave traders.

An unwilling participant himself in the slave trade, Equiano was an enthusiastic partisan in the wars between the British, French, and Spanish for control of the New World. Those bloody and continual conflicts on land and sea ended with the French defeat in 1763, leaving the British the major colonial power in North America.

Still a loyal British colonist, Benjamin Franklin aided the British in their last battle against the French. His autobiography tells of the growing friction between the colonies and the mother country, foreshadowing the American Revolution in which he also played a key role.

The American bid for independence succeeded in part because the colonies already had independent political institutions such as the colonial assembly where Franklin held his first political post. These institutions provided leadership and direction during and after the Revolution. The colonists had also developed a viable commercial economy, built upon the needs of growing cities like Franklin's home town, Boston, and his adopted city, Philadelphia.

During the first decades of the nineteenth century, the pace of economic change accelerated. In the 1830s the textile mills of Lowell, Massachusetts, harbingers of the country's full-blown industrialization, created a new work force of women and children. Harriet Robinson described the ways in which industrialization changed their lives.

The American defeat of the British had also opened up western lands. Land speculators, hunters, and farmers swarmed across the Appalachian Mountains into Tennessee, Kentucky, and the Northwest Territory. Their rugged frontier settlements expanded the geographical and the political boundaries of the new United States. As property qualifications for voting were eliminated, politicians like Andrew Jackson and Davy Crockett who styled themselves "common men" began to outpoll the older political elites.

Crockett's political success—like Jackson's—rested in good measure on his reputation as an Indian fighter, for native Americans did not willingly give up their homelands. The surrender of Black Hawk in the war that bears his name, and the slaughter of Indian women and children by federal soldiers, illustrated the deadly price that Indians would pay throughout the nineteenth century for white "progress."

Although the Northern economy had begun to industrialize, the South remained agricultural, ever more dependent on cash crops like cotton and the "peculiar institution" of slavery. Frederick Douglass and Harriet Jacobs revealed that slavery was far more than an economic institution; it was an oppressive social system which brutalized blacks and dehumanized whites.

By the 1830s slavery had begun to offend the small but vocal group of American abolitionists who later encouraged Douglass and Jacobs to write their stories. The movement to abolish the evil of slavery was part of the larger impulse to reform many aspects of American life and behavior from diet to education. The poet and philosopher Ralph Waldo Emerson exclaimed, "What a fertility of projects for the salvation of the world!" Both Tunis Campbell and Elizabeth Cady Stanton supported temperance and abolitionism, and Stanton's chief project became the cause of women's rights.

By 1868 voters had established the tradition of celebrating American military victories by sending generals to the White House. President Ulysses S. Grant, head of the Union forces during the Civil War, followed soldier-presidents George Washington, Andrew Jackson, and William Henry Harrison. Grant's defeat of the Confederate troops at Shiloh and Vicksburg and around Richmond dramatized the huge cost in human life of this tragic war in which Americans killed Americans.

The fighting ended in 1865, but the conflict between the North and the South continued another dozen years while Congress tried to rebuild the nation and reconstruct the South. Campbell's imprisonment for trying to aid the freedmen illustrates the difficulties of that reconstruction.

# AUTOBIOGRAPHY AS LITERATURE

Autobiography lives halfway between fact and fiction. Claiming that his or her story is a factual account of the past, the autobiographer puts that story together using some of the imaginative strategies of fiction.

The personal nature of autobiography means that many of its author's statements, unlike those of the historian, cannot be corroborated. The autobiographer's "facts" often exist only in his or her memory, a memory always selective and not always reliable. By necessity, the autobiographer has greater freedom and license to create and "make up" the past—in short, to write fiction.

The autobiographer also has greater freedom than the historian to make the story come out right. (Writing the story of your life may be the only way to live it over again without the mistakes or the boring parts.) The narrative usually takes the form of a journey: a journey through time, through space, or through spiritual travail. Bradstreet's very short story combined all three. In both religious and secular autobiography, there is often a conversion experience which moves the plot forward.

Few of us like to appear naked in public, and neither does an autobiographer, who disguises his or her nakedness by creating someone to play his or her part throughout the story. This invented self—or persona—tells us how the autobiographer wishes to be perceived. Most authors construct a persona which is acceptable to their time and place. Reflecting the different expectations of their culture, men and women often portray themselves differently: men as solitary individuals, women as family members or maternal figures.

Part of the autobiographer's disguise is the voice in which the author speaks, the language that is employed. Douglass's thundering oratory advertised his emancipation from slavery; Robinson's sentimental prose defined her as a genteel lady. Black Hawk symbolically spoke only through a white translator.

Even the most skillful writer of fiction, however, can get tripped up by reality. The "real," or historically determined, self may appear naked on the pages of the book. Even that great master of illusion, Franklin, occasionally lets his disguise drop. Sometimes an author's life contradicts his life story. Douglass insisted that slavery was always utterly destructive; his personal triumph suggested otherwise. Sometimes the author's voice does not ring true: Crockett's down-home twang was a political pose.

Autobiography's plot is often predictable. Knowing how the journey has ended in the present, the author will predetermine its direction in the past. There are no surprises, no accidents, no chance happenings in Elizabeth Cady Stanton's story.

In no other historical genre are history and literature so intimately interwoven as in autobiography. Informative as fact and intriguing as fiction, autobiography challenges its readers to distinguish between them and to understand and enjoy both.

*Marian Morton*
*Russell Duncan*
John Carroll University

# First Person Past

*American Autobiographies*
*Volume I*

# ANNE BRADSTREET
## 1612?–1672

*America's "Tenth Muse" was born to Puritan gentry, Thomas and Dorothy Dudley, and encouraged by her father, received an extraordinary education for a young woman of her time. At age 16, she married Simon Bradstreet, a Puritan and a member of the joint stock company which settled Massachusetts Bay. The Bradstreets and the Dudleys migrated to the colony in 1630 on the ship "Arabella" with its future governor, John Winthrop.*

*Despite her privileged status, Anne Bradstreet's life was filled with trials. The New World was a shock to any gently reared Englishwoman (one of her shipmates, Dorothy Bradford, drowned herself rather than face a life in the wilderness). The young wife was often left at home with her growing family, for Simon Bradstreet was busy with the political and economic affairs of the fledgling colony.*

*Writing itself was a struggle, for she had to overcome both the Puritan distrust of poetry and her own conviction that a woman probably should not write at all ("I am obnoxious to each carping tongue who says my hand a needle better fits"). Her work has survived only because her brother-in-law had her verses published in London in 1650. Bradstreet carefully crafted some verses imitating her favorite poets, Sir Walter Raleigh and Guillarme Du Bartas, but far more powerful and enduring are her poems about her own life. These expressed her deep love for her husband and children and her grief at the deaths of friends and family, including two infant grandchildren, as well as the insular domestic life of this seventeenth-century woman. "To My Dear Children," addressed to her eight offspring, was inspired by the travail of another childbirth, which might bring her own death.*

*This classic spiritual autobiography gives eloquent testimony to still another struggle, Bradstreet's life-long effort to resign herself—as a good woman and a good Puritan—to God's will. At the heart of Puritanism was the belief in the intimate relationship between God and worshipper. Bradstreet's autobiographical fragment reveals that the relationship was not always a happy or tranquil one, for the brief narrative recounts her troubled journey as she wrestled with Satan and heresies until convinced of the power and truth of her Puritan God.*

Several Poems Compiled with Great Variety of Wit and Learning. Full of Delight. *Boston: John Foster, 1678. Reprinted in* A Woman's Inner World: Selected Poetry and Prose of Anne Bradstreet, *edited by Adelaide P. Amore. Washington, D.C.: University Press of America, 1982.*

## TO MY DEAR CHILDREN

This book by any yet unread,
I leave for you when I am dead,
That being gone, here you may find
What was your living mother's mind.
Make use of what I leave in love
And God shall bless you from above.

A. B.

My dear children,—

I, knowing by experience that the exhortations of parents take most effect when the speakers leave to speak, and being ignorant whether on my death bed I shall have opportunity to speak to any of you much less to all, thought it the best whilst I was able to compose some short matters (for what else to call them I know not) and bequeath to you, that when I am no more with you, yet I may be daily in your remembrance (although that is the least in my aim in what I now do) but that you may gain some spiritual advantage by my experience. I have not studied in this you read to show my skill, but to declare the Truth, not to set forth my self, but the Glory of God. If I had minded the former it had been perhaps better pleasing to you, but seeing the last is the best, let it be best pleasing to you.

The method I will observe shall be this—I will begin with God's dealing with me from my childhood to this day.

In my young years, about 6 or 7 as I take it, I began to make conscience of my ways, and what I knew was sinful as lying, disobedience to parents, etcetera, I avoided it. If at any time I was overtaken with the like evils, it was a great trouble. I could not be at rest 'till by prayer I had confessed it unto God.

I was also troubled at the neglect of private duties, though too often tardy that way. I also found much comfort in reading the Scriptures, especially those places I thought most concerned my condition, and as I grew to have more under-standing, so the more solace I took in them.

In a long fit of sickness which I had on my bed, I often communed with my heart, and made my supplication to the most high who set me free from that affliction.

But as I grew up to be about 14 or 15 I found my heart more carnal, and sitting loose from God, vanity and the follies of youth take hold of me.

About 16, the Lord laid his hand sore upon me and smote me with the small pox. When I was in my affliction, I besought the Lord, and confessed my pride and vanity and he was entreated of me, and again restored me. But I rendered not to him according to the benefit received.

After a short time I changed my condition and was married and came into this country, where I found a new world and new manners, at which my heart rose. But after I was convinced it was the way of God, I submitted to it and joined to the church at Boston.

After some time I fell into a lingering sickness like a consumption, together with a lameness, which correction I saw the Lord sent to humble and try me and do me good: and it was not altogether ineffectual.

It pleased God to keep me a long time without a child which was a great grief to me, and cost me many prayers and tears before I obtained one, and after him gave me many more, of whom I now take the care, that as I have brought you into the world, and with great pains, weakness, cares, and fears brought you to this, I now travail in birth again of you till Christ be formed in you.

Among all my experiences of God's gracious dealings with me I have constantly observed this, that he hath never suffered me long to sit loose from him, but by one affliction or other hath made me look home, and search what was amiss—so usually thus it hath been with me that I have no sooner felt my heart out of order, but I have expected correction for it, which most commonly hath been upon my own perosn, in sickness, weakness, pains, sometimes on my soul, in doubts and fears of God's displeasure, and my sincerity towards him. Sometimes he hath smote a child with sickness, sometimes chastened by losses in estate, and these times (through his great mercy) have been the times of my greatest getting and advantage, yea I have found them the times when the Lord hath manifested the most love to me. Then have I gone to searching, and have said with David, Lord search me and try me, see what ways of wickedness are in me, and lead me in the way everlasting: and seldom or never but I have found either some sin I lay under which God would have reformed, or some duty neglected which he would have performed. And by his help I have laid vows and bonds upon my soul to perform his righteous commands.

If at any time you are chastened of God, take it as thankfully and joyfully as in greatest mercies. For if ye be his, ye shall reap the greatest benefit by it. It hath been no small support to me in times of darkness, when the Almighty hath hid his face from me, that yet I have had abundance of sweetness and refreshment after affliction and more circumspection in my walking after I have been afflicted. I have been with God like an untoward child, that no longer than the rod has been on my back (or at least in sight) but I have been apt to forget him and my self too. Before I was afflicted I went astray, but now I keep thy statutes.

I have had great experience of God's hearing my prayers, and returning comfortable answers to me, either in granting the thing I prayed for, or else in satisfying my mind without it; and I have been confident it hath been from him, because I have found my heart through his goodness enlarged in thankfulness to him.

I have often been perplexed that I have not found that constant joy in my pilgrimage and refreshing which I supposed most of the servants of God have, although he hath not left me altogether without the witness of his Holy Spirit, who hath oft given me his word and set to his seal that it shall be well with me. I have sometimes tasted of that hidden manna that the world knows not, and have set up my Ebenezer, and have resolved with my self that against such a promise, such tastes of sweetness, the gates of Hell shall never prevail. Yet have I many sinkings and droopings, and not enjoyed that felicity that sometimes I have done. But when I have been in darkness and seen no light, yet have I desired to stay my self upon the Lord. And, when I have been in sickness and pain, I have thought if the Lord would but lift up the light of his countenance upon me, although he ground me to powder, it would be but light to me. Yea, often have I thought were it Hell itself and could there find the love of God toward me, it would be a Heaven. And, could I have been in Heaven without the love of God, it would have been a Hell to me. For, in Truth, it is the absence and presence of God that makes Heaven or Hell.

Many times hath Satan troubled me concerning the verity of the Scriptures, many times by atheism. How could I know whether there was a God if I never saw any miracles to confirm me, and those which I read of, how did I know, but they were feigned. That there is a God my reason would soon tell me by the wondrous works that I see, the vast frame of the Heaven and the earth, the order of all things, night and day, summer and winter, spring and autumn, the daily providing for this great household upon the earth, the preserving and directing of all to its proper end. The consideration of these things would with amazement certainly resolve me that there is an Eternal Being.

But how should I know he is such a God as I worship in Trinity, and such a Saviour as I rely upon? Though this hath thousands of times been suggested to me, yet God hath helped me over. I have argued thus with my self. That there is a God I see. If ever this God hath revealed himself, it must be in his word, and this must be it or none. Have I not found that operation by it that no humane invention can work upon the soul? Hath not judgements befallen diverse who have scorned and contend it? Hath it not been preserved through all ages maugre all the heathen tyrants and all of the enemies who have opposed it? Is there any story but that which shows the beginnings of times, and how the world came to be as we see? Do we not know the prophecies in it fulfilled which could not have been so long foretold by any but God himself?

When I have got over this block, then have I another put in my way. That admit this be the true God whom we worship, and that be his word, yet why may not the popish religion be the right? They have the same God, the same Christ, the same word. They only interpret it one way, we another.

This hath sometimes stuck with me, and more it would, but the vain fooleries that are in their religion, together with their lying miracles, and cruel persecutions of the saints, which admit were they as they term them, yet not so to be dealt withall.

The consideration of these things and many the like would soon turn me to my own religion again.

But some new troubles I have had since the world has been filled with blasphemy, and sectaries, and some who have been accounted sincere Christians have been carried away with them, that sometimes I have said, "Is there faith upon the earth?" And I have not known what to think; but then I have remembered the words of Christ that so it must be, and that, if it were possible, the very elect should be deceived. "Behold," saith our Saviour, "I have told you before," that hath stayed my heart, and I can now say, "Return, O my soul, to thy rest, upon this rock Christ Jesus will I build my faith, and if I perish, I perish." But I know all the powers of Hell shall never prevail against it. I know whom I have trusted, and whom I have believed, and that he is able to keep that I have committed to his charge.

Now to the King, immortal, eternal, and invisible, the only wise God, be honor and glory for ever and ever. Amen.

This was written in much sickness and weakness, and is very weakly and imperfectly done; but if you can pick any benefit out of it, it is the mark which I aimed at.

# ELIZABETH ASHBRIDGE
## 1713–1755

*It would be hard to imagine a woman less like Anne Bradstreet than Eliza-beth Ashbridge—lower-class, estranged from family, childless, unhappily married, and a Quaker. Yet there are similarities in the stories of these two women.*

*Ashbridge was born Elizabeth Sampson in Middlewich, Cheshire County, in England. Her father was a barber, frequently away from home plying his trade on shipboard. At age fourteen, Elizabeth ran away from her family to marry her sweetheart, who died five months later. After her father disowned her, she fled to the American colonies. Like thousands of others, she became an indentured servant to pay for her trans-Atlantic passage, selling herself for four years to a master who became abusive. After purchasing her freedom, she married an itinerant schoolteacher, taken with her youthful singing and dancing. The couple wandered from New York to New England to Pennsylvania to New Jersey, one or both of them teaching in village schools. When she found herself drawn to the Quakers, her husband ridiculed her pious behavior and beat her. He died in 1740, leaving her to repay his considerable debts. In 1746 she married another Quaker, Aaron Ashbridge. She became a prominent member of her church and a public Friend (licensed preacher). She wrote this auto-biography before she left on a missionary trip in 1753 to Ireland, where she died in 1755. Aaron Ashbridge edited the extant version of her autobiog-raphy, which was published in 1774.*

*Elizabeth Ashbridge's story is full of worldly adventures, many of which pitted her against men in authority. Yet like Bradstreet's, this is primarily a spiritual autobiography. At its very beginning, Ashbridge fore-shadowed her later calling—wishing, she says, that she could have been born a man so that she could have become a minister. The crucial events in the narrative are her encounters with—and rejections of—various churches from Anglicans to Presbyterians to Baptists to Roman Catholics—until she found her home with the Quakers. Like Bradstreet, Ashbridge wrestled with the Devil as well as her personal demons, even contemplating suicide. In the end, she found the freedom and egalitarianism of Quakerism conge-nial to her restless spirit. Quakers believed that both men and women expe-rienced the divine Inner Light, which allowed them to be saved and to preach salvation. Within Quakerism she also found an acceptable public role and a compelling voice with which to speak out in this manuscript as well as in the Quaker meetings.*

Some Account of the Fore-Part of the Life of Elizabeth Ashbridge. *Nantwich, England, 1774. Reprinted in* The Norton Anthology of American Literature, *Third edition, Volume 1. New York: WW Norton and Co. 1989.*

My life being attended with many uncommon occurrences, some of which I brought upon myself, which I believe were for my good, I have therefore thought proper to make some remarks on the dealings of Divine Goodness with me, having often had cause with David, to say, "It is good for me that I have been afflicted" [Psalm 119:71]; and I most earnestly desire that whosoever reads the following lines may take warning and shun the evils that through the deceitfulness of Satan I have been drawn into.

I was born in Middlewich, in Cheshire [England], in the year 1713, of honest parents. My father's name was Thomas Sampson, he was a surgeon; my mother's name was Mary. My father was a man that bore a good character, but [not] so strictly religious as my mother, who was a pattern of virtue to me. I was the only child of my father, but my mother had a son and a daughter by a former husband. Soon after my birth my father took to the sea, and followed his profession on board a ship many long voyages, till I was twelve years old, about which time he settled at home; so that my education lay mostly on my mother, in which she discharged her duty by endeavoring to instill into me the principles of virtue during my tender age, for which I have since had cause to be thankful to the Lord, that he blessed me with such a parent tho' her good advice and counsel have been as cast upon the water, etc. In short, she was a good example to all about her, and beloved by most that knew her, tho' not of the same religious persuasion I am now of. But oh! alas, when the time came that she might reasonably have expected the benefit of her labor, and have had comfort from me, I left her, of which I shall mention in its proper place.

In my very infancy I had an awful regard for religion and a great love for religious people, particularly the ministers, and sometimes grieved at my not being a boy and therefore could not be one, as I thought they were good men, and beloved of God. I also had a great love for the poor, remembering I had read they were blessed of the Lord; this I took to mean such as were poor in this world, and often went to their poor cottages to see them, and if I had any money or other things, I used to give them some, remembering that saying, that they that give to the poor lend to the Lord, and I had when very young an earnest desire to be beloved of him. I used also to make remarks on those called gentlemen, and when I heard them swear it would grieve me much; for my mother had informed me that if I used any naughty words, God would not love me. As I grew up I took notice that there were several different religious societies, wherefore I often went alone and wept, desiring that I might be directed to the right. Thus my young years were attended with such like tender desires, tho' I was sometimes guilty of those things incident to children, but then I always found something in me that made me sorry for what I did amiss. Till I arrived at the age of fourteen years, I was as innocent as most children, about which time my sorrows began, and have continued most part of my life, through my giving way to a foolish passion, in setting my affections on a young man, who became a suitor to me, without my parents' consent, till I suffered myself (I may say with sorrow of heart) to be carried off in the night, and to be married before my parents found me; altho' as soon as they missed me all possible search was made after me, but all in vain, till too later to recover me.

This precipitate act plunged me into a vast scene of sorrow, for I was soon smote with remorse for thus leaving my parents, who had a right to have disposed of me, or at least their approbation ought to have been consulted in the affair, for I was soon chastised formy disobedience. Divine Providence let me see my error, and in five months I was stripped of the darling of my soul, and left a young and disconsolate widow.

I had then no home to fly to. My father was so displeased that he would do nothing for me, but my dear mother had some compassion toward me, and kept me amongst the neighbors for some time, till by her advice I went to Dublin, to a relation of hers, in hopes that absence would help to regain my father's affection. But he continued inflexible and would not send for me, and I dared not to return without his permission.—This relation with whom I lived was one of the people called Quakers. His conduct was so different from the manner of my education, which was in the way of the Church of England, that it made my situation disagreeable; for tho', as I said, I had a religious education, yet I was allowed to sing and dance, which my cousins were against, and I having a great vivacity in my natural disposition could not bear to give way to the gloomy scene of sorrow, and conviction gave it the wrong effect, and made me more wild and airy than before, for which I was often reproved. But I then thought, as a great many do now, that it was the effect of singularity and therefore would not be subject to it.

I having at that time a distant relation in the west of Ireland, I left Dublin, and went there, where I was entertained, and what rendered me disagreeable in the former place was quite pleasing to the latter. Between these two relations I spent 3 years and 2 months. While I was in Ireland I contracted an intimacy with a widow and her daughter, who were Papists, with whom I used to discourse about religion, they in defense of their faith, and I of mine; and altho' I was then very wild, it made me very thoughtful. The old woman would tell me of such mighty miracles done by their priests that I began to be disturbed in my mind, and thought that if those things were so, they must be the Apostle's successors. The old woman perceiving it one day, said in rapture, that if I, under God, can be instrumental to convert you to the holy Catholic faith, all the sins that ever I committed will be forgiven me. In a while it go so far that the priests came to converse withme, and I being young and my judgment weak was ready to believe what they said. And tho' wild as I was, it cost me many a tear with desires that I might be rightly directed. For some time I frequented their place of worship, but none of my relations knew I had any intention of going with them. At length I concluded never to be led darkly into their belief, and thought to myself—if their articles of faith are good, they will not be against my knowing them. Therefore the next time I had an opportunity with the priest, I told him I had some thoughts of becoming one of his flock, but I did not like to join with them, till I knew all I was to agree to, and therefore desired to see their principles. He answered I must first confess my sins to him, and gave me till next day to consider of them. I was not much against that, having done nothing that any person could hurt me, and if, thought I, what the man says be true, it will be for my good. So when he came again, I told him all I could remember, which I thought bad enough; but he thought me, as he said, the most innocent creature that ever made confession to him. When he had done he took a book out of his pocket, and read all which I was to swear to, if I joined with them.

Tho' I was but young, I made my remarks as he went on, but I do not think it worth my writing, nor the reader's hearing. It was a great deal of ridiculous stuff. But what made me sick of my new intention was (I believe I should have swallowed the rest), I was to swear, "I believed the Pretender to be the true heir to the crown of England, and that he was King James' son, and also, that whosoever died out of the pale of the church were damned." As to the first, I did not believe it essential salvation, whether I believed it or not, and to take an oath to any such thing would be very unsafe; and the second I saw struck directly against charity, which the Apostles preferred before all other Graces. And besides, I had a religious mother who was out of that opinion. I therefore thought it would be wicked in me to believe she was damned. I therefore concluded to consider about it, but before I saw him again a sudden turn took hold of me, which put a final end to it.

My father still keeping me at so great a distance, I thought myself quite shut out of his affections, and therefore concluded, since my absence was most agreeable he should have it, and getting acquaintance with a gentlewoman lately from Pennsylvania, who was going back again, where I had an uncle, my mother's brother, I soon agreed with her for my passage, and being ignorant in the nature of an indenture consented to be bound. As soon as this was over, she invited me to go and see the vessel we was to sail in, [to] which I readily consented, not knowing what would follow. When I came on board I found a young woman, who I afterwards understood was of a good family and had been deluded away by this creature. I was extremely glad to think I should have such an agreeable companion, but while we were in discourse, our kidnapper left us, and went ashore, and when I wanted to go was not permitted. I was kept there near three weeks, in which time the young woman's friends found her and fetched her away, by which means my friends found me, and went to the water bailiff, who brought me on shore, and our gentlewoman was obliged to conceal herself, or she would have been laid fast. My friends kept me close for two weeks, but at least I found means to get away, for my thoughts being full of going to America, I was determined to proceed with my intention, and one day meeting with the captain, I inquired of him when they sailed, and entered on board the same ship that I was on board before, and I have since thought there was [a] Providential hand in it. . . .

In nine weeks from the time I left Dublin we arrived at New York, viz. on the 15 of the 7th month, 1732. Now those to whom I had been instrumental to preserve life proved treacherous to me.—I was a stranger in a strange land.

The captain got an indenture and demanded of me to sign it, at the same time threatening me if I refused it. I told him I could find means to satisfy him for my passage without being bound, but he told me I might take my choice; either to sign that or have the other in force which I signed in Ireland. By this time I had learned the character of the before-mentioned woman, by which she appeared to be a vile person, and I feared if ever I was in her power she would use me ill on her brother's account. I therefore in a fright signed the latter, and tho' there was no magistrate present it proved sufficient to make me a servant for four years. In two weeks time I was sold, and were it possible to convey in characters a scene of the sufferings of my servitude, it would affect the most stony heart with pity for a young creature who had been so tenderly brought up. For tho' my father had no great estate yet he lived well, and I had been used to little but the school, tho' it had been better for me now if I had been brought up to greater hardships.

For a while I was pretty well used, but in a little time the scale turned, which was occasioned by a difference between my master and me, wherein I was innocent; but from that time he set himself against me, and was so inhuman that he would not suffer me to have clothes to be decent in, making me to go barefoot in the snowy weather, and to be employed in the meanest drudgery, wherein I suffered the utmost hardships that my body was able to bear. . . .

I had to one woman and no other discovered the occasion of this difference, and the nature of it, which two years before had happened betwixt my master and me, and by that means he heard of it, and tho' he knew it to be true, he sent for the town whipper to correct me for it, and upon his appearing, I was called in and ordered to strip, without asking whether I deserved it or not, at which my heart was ready to burst, for I could as freely have given up my life, as suffer such ignominy. And I then said, if there be a God, be graciously pleased to look down on one of the most unhappy creatures, and plead my cause, for thou knowest what I have said is the truth, and had it not been from a principle more noble than he was capable of, I would have told it before his wife. Then fixing my eyes on the barbarous man, in a flood of tears, I said to him, Sir, if you have no pity on me, yet for my father's sake spare me from this shame (for before this he had heard of my father several ways), and if you think I deserve such punishment do it yourself. He then took a turn about the room and bid the whipper go about his business, so I came off without a blow, which I thought something remarkable.

I know began to think my credit was gone, for they said several things of me, which (I bless God) were not true; and here I suffered so much cruelty that I knew not how to bear it, and the enemy immediately came in and put me in a way how to get rid of it all, by tempting me to end my miserable life, which I joined with, and for that purpose went into the garret in order to hang myself, at which time I was convinced there was a God, for as my feet entered the place, horror seized me to that degree that I trembled much, and while I stood in amazement, it seemed as tho' I head a voice say, "There is a hell beyond the grave," at which I was greatly astonished and convinced of an Almighty Power, to whom I prayed, saying "God be merciful and enable me to bear whatsoever thou of thy providence shall bring or suffer to come upon me for my disobedience." I then went downstairs but let none know what I had been about.

Soon after this I had a dream, and tho' some may ridicule dreams, yet this seems very significant to me, therefore I shall mention it.—I thought somebody knocked at the door, which when I had opened there stood a grave woman, holding in her right hand an oil lamp burning, who with a solid countenance fixed her eyes on me, and said, "I am sent to tell thee, that if thou wilt return to the Lord thy God, he will have mercy on thee, and thy lamp shall not be put out in obscure darkness;" upon which the light flamed from the lamp in a very radiant manner and the vision left me. But oh! alas, I did not give up to join with the heavenly vision, as I think I may call it; for, after all this, I was near being caught in another snare, which if I had, would probably have been my ruin, from which I was also preferred.

I was accounted a fine singer and dancer, in which I took great delight, and once falling in company with some of the stage players, then at New York, they took a great fancy to me, as they said, and persuaded me to become an actress amongst them, and they would find means to get me from my servitude, and that I should live like a lady. The proposal took with me, and I used much pains to qualify myself for the stage, by reading plays, even when I should have slept, but after all this I found a stop in my mind, when I came to consider what my father would think when he heard of it, who had not only forgiven my disobedience in marriage, but had sent for me home, tho' my proud heart would not suffer me to return in so mean a condition I was then in, but rather chose bondage.

When I had served three years I bought the remainder of my time, and got a genteel maintenance by my needle, but alas! I was not sufficiently punished by my former servitude but got into another, and that for life; for a few months after this, I married a young man, who fell in love with me for my dancing—a poor motive for a man to choose a wife, or a woman to choose a husband.

As to my part I fell in love for nothing I saw in him, and it seems unaccountable, that I, who had refused several offers, both in this country and in Ireland, should at last marry a man I had no value for.

In a week after we were married, my husband, who was a school-master, removed from New York, and took me along with him to New England, and settled at a place called Westerley, in Rhode Island government. With respect to religion, he was much like myself, without any; for when he was in drink he would use the worst of oaths. I don't mention this to expose my husband, but to show the effect it had upon me, for I now saw myself ruined, as I thought, being joined to a man I had no love for, and who was a pattern of no good to me. I therefore began to think we were like two joining hands and going to destruction, which made me conclude that if I was not forsaken of God, to alter my course of life. But to love the Divine Being, and not to love my husband, I saw was an inconfidency, and seemed impossible; therefore I requested, with tears, that my affections might increase towards my husband, and I can say in truth that my love was sincere to him. I now resolved to do my duty towards God, and expecting that I must come to the knowledge of it by reading the Scriptures, I read them with a strong resolution of following their directions, but the more I read the more uneasy I grew, especially about baptism, for altho' I had reason to believe I was sprinkled in my infancy, because at the age of fourteen I passed under the bishop's hands for confirmation, as it is called, yet I could not find any precedent for that practice, and upon reading where it is said, he that believes and is baptized, etc., I observed that belief went before baptism, which I was not capable of when I was sprinkled, at which I grew very uneasy, and living in a neighborhood that were mostly Seventh Day Baptists, I conversed with them, and at length thinking it to be really my duty, I was baptized by one of their teachers, but did not join strictly with them, tho' I began to think the seventh-day the true sabbath, and for some time kept it as such. My husband did not yet oppose me, for he saw I grew more affectionate to him, but I did not yet leave off singing and dancing so much, but I could divert him whenever he desired it. . . .

We stayed several weeks at Boston, and I remained still dissatisfied as to religion, tho' I had reformed my conduct so as to be accounted by those that knew me a sober woman. But that was not sufficient; for even then I expected to find the sweets of such a change, and though several thought me religious, I dared not to think myself so, and what to do to be so, I seemed still an utter stranger to. I used to converse with people of all societies, as opportunity offered, and, like many others, had got a deal of head knowledge, and several societies thought me of their opinion, but I joined strictly with none, resolving never to leave searching till I found the TRUTH. This was in the 22d year of my age.

While we were at Boston, I went one day to the Quakers' meeting, not expecting to find what I wanted, but from a motive of curiosity. At this meeting there was a woman spoke, at which I was a little surprised, for I had never heard one before. I looked on her with pity for her ignorance, and in contempt of her practice said to myself, 'I am sure you're a fool, for if ever I should turn Quaker, which will never be, I could not be a preacher." In these and such like thoughts I sat while she was speaking. After she had done, there stood up a man, which I could better bear; he spoke well, as I thought, from good Joshua's resolutions, viz., "As for me and my house we will serve the Lord." After a time of silence he went to prayer, which was attended with something so aweful and affecting that I was reduced to tears, yet a stranger to the cause.

Soon after this we left Boston, for my husband was given to ramble, which was very disagreeable to me, but I must submit. We went to Rhode Island, where he hired a place to keep a school. . . .

Soon after this my husband hired a place further up the island, where we were nearer a Church of England, to which place I used to go, for tho' I disliked some of their ways, yet I approved of them the best. . . .

For one night as I lay in my bed, my husband by me asleep, bemoaning my miserable condition, I had strength to cry, "O my God, had thou no mercy left? Look down I beseech thee for Christ's sake, who has promised that all manner of sin and blasphemy shall be forgiven. Therefore Lord, if thou wilt graciously please to extend this promise to me, an unworthy creature, trembling before thee, there is nothing thou shalt command, but I will obey." In an instant my heart tendered and dissolved into a flood of tears, abhorring my past offenses, and admiring the mercies of God; for I was made to hope in Christ my redeemer, and enabled to look upon him with an eye of faith, and saw fulfilled what I believed when the priest lent me his book, that if ever my prayers would be acceptable to God, I should be enabled to pray without form, and so used it no more. Nevertheless I thought to join with some religious society, but met with none that I liked in everything. Yet the Church of England seemed nearest, upon which I joined with them and received the Sacrament, so called, and can say in truth that I did it with reverence and fear.

Being thus released from deep distress, I seemed like another creature, and went often alone without fear and tears flowed abundantly from my eyes; and once as I was abhorring myself, in great humility of mind, I heard a gracious voice say, "I will not forsake thee, only obey what I shall make known unto thee." I then entered into covenant, saying, "My soul doth magnify thee the God of mercy; if thou will vouchsafe thy Grace, the rest of my days shall be devoted to thee, and if it be thy will that I beg my bread, I will be content and submit to thy Providence."

I now began to think of my relations in Pennsylvania, whom I had not yet seen, and having a great desire to see them, I got leave of my husband to go, and also a certificate from the priest, in order that if I made any stay, I might be received as a member wherever I came. Then setting out, my husband bore me company to the Blazing Star Ferry, saw me safe over, and then returned. In the way near a place called Maidenhead, I fell from my horse and was disabled from traveling for some time, and abode at the house of an honest Dutchman, who with his wife was very kind to me, and tho' they had much trouble in going to the doctor and waiting upon me, for I was several days unable to help myself, yet would have nothing for it, which I thought very kind, and charged me if ever I came that way again to call and lodge there.

I arrived next at Trent town [Trenton, New Jersey], Ferry, where I met with no small mortification upon hearing that my relations were Quakers, and what was worst of all, my aunt was a preacher. I was sorry to hear of it, for I was exceedingly prejudiced against those people, and I have often wondered with what face they could call themselves Christians; and I began to repent my coming, sometimes having a mind to return back without seeing them. At last I concluded to go see them since I was so far on my journey, tho' I expected little comfort from my visit. But see how God brings unforeseen things to pass, for by my going there I was brought to the knowledge of the TRUTH.

I went from Trent town to Philadelphia by water, and thence to my uncle's on horseback, where I met with a very kind reception; for tho' my own uncle was dead and my aunt married again, yet both she and her husband received me in a very kind manner. I had not been there 3 hours before I met with a shock, and my opinion began to alter with respect to these people; for seeing a book lie on the table, and being much given to reading, I took it up, which my aunt observing, said, "Cousin, that is a Quaker's book, Samuel Crisp's *Two Letters*," and I suppose she thought I should not like it, at perceiving that I was not one. I made her no answer, but thought to myself. What can these people write about, for I have heard that they deny the Scripture, and have no other bible but George Foxe's *Journal,* and that they deny all the holy Ordinances; for I resolved to read a little, and had not read two pages before my very heart burned within me, and tears came into my eyes, which I was afraid would be seen. I therefore walked with the book into the garden, and the piece being small, read it through before I went in, and sometimes uttering these involuntary expressions: "My God, if ever I come to the true knowledge of the truth, must I be of this man's opinion, who has fought thee as I have done, and join with these people that I preferred the Papists to, but a [few] hours ago. Oh! Thou the God of my salvation and of my life, who hast in an abundant manner manifested thy long-suffering and tender mercy in redeeming me as from the lowest hell, a monument of thy grace. Lord my soul beseeches thee to direct me in the right way, and keep me from error; and then according to my covenant, I'll think nothing too near to part with for thy name's sake, if these things be so. Oh! happy people thus beloved of God."

After I came a little to myself I washed my face, lest any in the house should perceive I had been weeping. At night I got very little sleep, for the old enemy began to suggest that I was one of those that wavered and was not steadfast in the faith, advancing several texts of Scripture against me, and them that mention, in the latter days there shall be those that will deceive the very elect, and these people were them, and that I was in danger of being deluded. Here the subtle serpent transformed himself so hiddenly that I verily thought this to be a timely caution from a good angel, so resolved to beware of these deceivers, and for some weeks did not touch any of their books.

The next day being the first of the week, I wanted to have gone to church, which was distant about four miles, but being a stranger and having nobody to go with me was forced to give it up, and as most of the family was going to meeting, I went with them. But with this conclusion: not to like them. And so it was; for as they sat in silence, I looked over the meeting, thinking within myself, how like fools these people sit, how much better were it to stay at home and read the Bible, or some good book, than to come here and go to sleep; for I being very sleepy thought they were no better than me. Indeed, at length I fell asleep and had like to have fallen down, but this was the last time I ever fell asleep in a meeting, tho' often assaulted with it.

I now began to be lifted up with spiritual pride, and thought myself better than they, but through mercy this did not last long, for in a little time I was brought low, and saw that they were people to whom I must join. It may seem strange that I, who had lived so long with one of this society in Dublin, should yet be so great a stranger to them. In answer, let it be considered, that during the time I was there, I never read one of their books or went to one meeting, and besides, I had heard such ridiculous stories of them as made me think they were the worst of any society of people. But God that knew the sincerity of my heart looked with pity on my weakness, and soon let me see my error; for in a few weeks there was an afternoon's meeting held at my uncle's to which came that servant of the Lord, William Hammons, who was then made instrumental in convincing me of the TRUTH more perfectly, and helping me over some great doubts, tho' I believe no one did ever sit in greater opposition than I did when he first stood up. But I was soon brought down, for he preached the Gospel with such power that I was forced to give up and confess it was the TRUTH. . . .

All this while I did not let anybody know the condition I was in, nor did appear like a Friend, and feared a discovery. I now began to think of returning to my husband, but found a restraint to stay where I was. I then hired a place to keep a school, and hearing of a place for him wrote desiring him to come to me, but let him know nothing how it was with me.

I loved to go to meetings, but did not like to be seen to go on weekdays, and therefore to shun it used go go from my school through the woods to them. But notwithstanding all my care, the neighbors that were not Friends soon began to revile, calling me Quaker, saying they supposed I intended to be a fool and turn preacher. I then received the same censure that I, a little above a year before, had passed on one of the handmaids of the Lord at Boston, and so weak was I, alas, I could not bear the reproach, and in order to change their opinions got in to greater excess in apparel than I had freedom to wear for some time before I became aquainted with Friends. In this condition I continued till my husband came, and then began the trial of my faith. Before he reached me he heard I was turned Quaker, at which he stamped saying, I had rather have heard she had been dead, well as I love her, for if so all my comfort is gone; he then came to me, and had not seen me for four months; I got up and met him, saying, "My dear, I am glad to see thee," at which he fell in a great passion, and said, "The devil THEE thee, don't THEE me." I used all the mild means I could to pacify him, and at length got him fit to go and speak to my relations, but he was alarmed, and as soon as he got alone he said, "So I see your Quaker relations have made you one." I told him they had not, which was true, nor had I ever told them how it was with me. But he would have it that I was one, and therefore should not stay amongst them, and having found a place to his mind, hired it, and came directly back to fetch me, and in one afternoon walked near thirty miles to keep me from meeting, the next day being the first-day, and on the morrow took me to the aforesaid place, hired lodgings at a Church-man's house, who was one of the wardens, and a bitter enemy to Friends, and would tell me a great deal of ridiculous stuff. But my judgment was too clearly convinced to believe. I still did not appear like a Friend, but they all believed I was one. When my husband and him used to be making their diversions and revilings, I used to sit in silence, but now and then an involuntary sigh would break from me, at which he would say to my husband, "There, did not I tell you your wife was a Quaker, and she will be a preacher soon," upon which my husband once in a great rage came up to me, and striking his hand over me said, "You had better be hanged on that day." I then, Peter like, in a panic denied my being a Quaker, at which great horror seized upon me, and continued for near three months, so that I again feared that by denying the Lord who brought me the heavens were shut against me; for great darkness surrounded me, and I was again plunged in despair.

I used to walk much alone in the woods, where no eye saw, or ear heard me, and there lamented my miserable condition, and have often gone from morning till night without breaking my fast, with which I was brought so low that my life was a burden to me. The devil seemed to vaunt [that although] the sins [of] my youth were forgiven, yet now he was sure of me, for that I had committed the unpardonable sin, and hell would inevitably be my portion, and my torments would be greater than if I had hanged myself at the first.

In this doleful condition I had now to bewail my misery, and even in the night, when I could not sleep, under the painful distress of my mind. And if my husband perceived me weeping he used to revile me for it. At last, when he and his friends thought themselves too weak to overset me, tho' I feared it was already done, he went to the priest at Chester to advise what to do with me. This man knew I was a member of the Church, for I had shown him my certificate. His advice was to take me out of Pennsylvania, and find some place where there was no Quakers, and there my opinion would wear off. To this my husband agreed, saying he did not care where he went, if he could but restore me to that liveliness of temper I was naturally of, and to that Church of which I was a member. I, on my part, had no spirit to oppose their proposals, neither much cared where I was; for I seemed to have nothing to hope for, but daily expected to be made a spectacle of Divine Wrath, and I was possessed it would be by thunder.

The time of removal came and I was not suffered to bid my relations farewell. My husband was poor and kept no horse, so I must travel on foot. We came to Wilmington, 15 miles thence to Philadelphia, by water; here he took me to a tavern, where I soon became a spectacle and discourse of the company. My husband told them his wife was turned Quaker, and that he designed, if possible, to find out some place where there was none. Oh, thought I, I was once in condition of deserving that name, but now it was over with me. Oh, that I might, from a true hope, once more have an opportunity to confess to the TRUTH, tho' sure of all manner of cruelties yet I would not regret it. These were my concerns while he was entertaining the company with my story, in which he told them that I had been a good dancer, but now he could neither get me to dance nor sing; upon which one of the company starts up, saying, "I'll go fetch my fiddle and we'll have a dance," at which my husband was pleased. The fiddle came, the sight of which put me in a sad condition, for fear, if I refused,my husband would be in a great passion. However I took up this resolution not to comply whatever might be the consequence. He came to me and took me by the hand, saying, "Come my dear, shake off that gloom, let's have a civil dance, you would now and then, when you were a good Church-woman and that is better than a stiff Quaker." I, trembling, desired to be excused. But he insisted on it, and knowing his temper to be exceeding cholenc, I durst not say much, but would not consent. He then pulled me round the room till tears affected my eyes, at sight of which the musician stopped, and said, "I'll play no more, let your wife alone," of which I was glad. There was also a man in [this] company who came from Freehold, in West Jersey, who said, "I see your wife is a Quaker, but if you'll take my advice, you need not go so far (for my husband designed to go to Staten Island), come and live amongst us and we'll soon cure her from her Quakerism, and we want both a school-master and mistress." To which he agreed. . . .

Hence we set forward for Freehold, and coming through Stony Brook, my husband turning towards me said tauntingly. "There's one of Satan's Synagogues, don't you want to be in it? I hope I shall see you carried off [by] this new religion." I made no answer but went on. In a little time we came to a large run of water, over which was no bridge, and we being strangers knew no way to get over. But through we was obliged to go. My husband carried our clothes, which we had in bundles, and I pulled off my shoes and waded through in my stockings, which served somewhat to prevent the chill of the water from [freezing] me, it being very cold and a fall of snow, in the 12th month. My heart was concerned in prayer that the Lord would sanctify all my afflictions to me, and give me patience to bear whatsoever should be suffered to come upon me.

We walked most part of a mile before we came to a house, which proved to be a sort of tavern. My husband called for some spirituous liquors, but I got some cider mulled, which when I had drank of't, the cold being struck to my heart made me extremely sick, insomuch, that when we were a little past the house I expected I should have fainted, and not being able to stand, fell down under a fence. Which my husband observing, tauntingly said, "What's the matter now, what are you drunk? where's your religion now?" He knew better, and at that time I believed he pitied me, yet was suffered grievously to afflict me. In a little time I grew better, and going on came to another tavern at which place we lodged. The next day I was indifferent well, and as we proceeded on our journey a young man with an empty cart overtook us, and I desired my husband to ask the young man to let us ride, which he did and it was readily granted. I now thought myself well off, and took it as a great favor, for my proud heart was humbled, and I did not regard the looks of it, tho' the time had been that I would not have been seen in a cart. This cart belonged to a man at Shrewsbury and was to go through the place that we were going to, so we rode on. We soon had the care of the team to ourselves, from a failure in the driver, to the place where I was intended to have been made a prey on. But see how unforeseen things are brought to pass by a Providential hand. It is said and answered, Shall we do evil that good may come? God forbid. Yet hence good came to me. Here my husband would fain have me stay, while he went to see the team safe at home, but I told him no, since he had led me through the country like a vagabond, I would not stay behind him; so we went on, and lodged that night at the man's house who owned the cart. Next day on our return to Freehold, we met a man riding full speed, who stopped, and said to my husband, Sir, are you a school-master? and was answered yes. I came to tell you, replied the stranger, of two new school houses, and each want a master and are two miles apart. How this stranger came to hear of us, who came but the night before, I never knew, but I was glad he was not one called a Quaker, lest my husband should have thought it had been a plot. I said to my husband: My dear, look on me with pity. If thou hast any affections left for me, which I hope thou hast, for I am not conscious of having done anything to alienate them here, here is, continued I, an opportunity to settle us both, and I am willing to do all in my power towards an honest livelihood.

My expression took place, and after a little pause he consented to the young man's directions and made towards the place, and in our way we came to the house of a worthy Friend, whose wife was a preacher, tho' we did not know it. I was surprised to see the people so kind to us who were strangers. We had not been long in the house before we were invited to lodge there that night, it being the last of the week. I said nothing, but waited to hear my master speak. He soon consented, saying, My wife has had a tedious travel, and I pity her, at which kind expressions I was greatly affected, for they were now very seldom used to me.

The Friends' kindness could not have proceeded from my appearing in the garb of a Quaker, for I had not yet altered my dress; but the woman of the house, after we had concluded to say, fixed her eyes on me and said, I believe thou hast met with a deal of troubles, to which I made but little answer. My husband observing they were of that sort of people he had so much endeavored to shun would give us no opportunity for any discourse that night, but the next morning I let the Friend know a little how it was with me. Meeting time came, to which I longed to go, but durst not ask my husband leave, for fear of disturbing him, till we were settled, and then thought I, If ever I am favored to be in this place, come life or death. I'll fight through, for my salvation is at stake. The Friends, getting ready for meeting, asked my husband if he would go, saying they knew who were to be his employers, and if they were at meeting, they would speak to them. He then consented to go. Then said the woman, Friend, and wilt thou let thy wife go? to which he denied, making several objections, all which she answered so prudently, that he could not be angry and at last he consented. With joy I went, for I had not been at one for near 4 months, and an heavenly meeting it was to me. I now renewed my covenant, and saw the word of the Lord made good, that I should have another opportunity to confess to his name, for which, "My soul did magnify the Lord, and my spirit did rejoice in the God of my salvation," who had brought strange things to pass. May I ever be preserved in humility, never forgetting his tender mercies to me.

Here according to my desire we settled, my husband got one school and I the other. We took a room at a Friend's house, a mile from each school, and 8 miles from the meeting-house. Before the next first-day we were got to our new settlement, and now I concluded to let my husband see that I was determined to join with Friends. When the first-day came I directed myself to him in this manner: "My dear, art thou willing to let me go to meeting?" at which he fell into a rage, saying, "No, you shan't." I then drew up a resolution and told him that as a dutiful wife ought, so was I ready to obey all his commands, but where they imposed on my conscience I no longer durst, for I had already done it too long, and had wronged myself by it, and tho' he was near and I loved him as a wife ought, yet God was nearer than all the world to me, and had made me sensible this was the way I ought to go, which I assured him was no small cross to my own will. Yet I had given up my heart, and hoped he that had called for it would enable me the residue of my life to keep it steadily devoted to him whatever I suffered, adding I hoped not to make him any worse a wife for it. But all I could say was in vain. I had not put my hand to the plow and resolved not to look back, so went without leave, but expected to be immediately followed and forced back. He did not follow me as I expected, so I went to a neighbor's and got a girl to show me the way; and then went on rejoicing and praising God in my heart who had thus far given me power, and another opportunity to confess to the TRUTH.

Thus for some time I had to go 8 miles on foot to meeting, which I never thought hard. My husband now bought a horse, but would not let me ride him, neither when my shoes were wore out would he let me have a new pair, thinking by that means to keep me from meetings. But this did not hinder me, for I have taken strings and tied round to keep them on. He now finding no hard usage could alter my resolution, neither threatening to beat me, nor denying it, for he several times struck me with sore blows, which I endeavored to bear with patience, believing the time would come when he would see I was in the right, which accordingly [he] did. He once came up to me and took out his penknife, saying, "If you offer to go to meeting to-morrow, with this knife I'll cripple you, for you shall not be a Quaker." I made him no answer but when morning came I set out as usual, and he was not suffered to hurt me.

In despair of recovering me himself, he now fled to the priest for help, and told him that I had been a very religious woman in the way of the Church of England, was a member of it, and had a good certificate from Long Island, but now as bewitched and turned Quaker, which almost broke his heart. He therefore desired, as he was one who had the care of souls, he would come and pay me a visit, and use his best endeavors to reclaim me, and he hoped by the blessings of God it would be done.

The priest consented to come, and the time was fixed, which was to be that day two weeks, for he said he could not come sooner. My husband came home extremely pleased, and told me of it, at which I smiled and said I hope to be enabled to give a reason for the hope that is in me, at the same time believing the priest would never trouble me nor he never did. Before this appointed time came it was required of me in a more public manner to confess to the world what I was, and to give up in prayer at the meeting. The fight of which and the power that attended it made me tremble, and I could not hold myself still. I now again desired death and could have freely given up my natural life as ransom. And what made it harder for me, I was not taken under the care of friends; and what kept me from requesting it was for fear I should be overcome, and bring a scandal on the Society. I begged to be excused till I was joined, and then I would give up freely, to which I received this answer, as tho' I had heard a distinct voice, "I am a covenant-keeping God, and the words that I spoke to thee when I found thee in distress, even that I would never leave thee, nor forsake thee, if thou wouldst be obedient to what I should make known to thee, which I will assuredly make good; but if thou refuse, my Spirit shall not always strive. Fear not, I will make way for thee through all thy difficulties, which shall be many, for my name's sake, but be faithful, and I will give thee a crown of life." I then being sure it was God that spoke, said, "Thy will, O God, be done, I am in thy hand, do with me according to thy word." And I gave up, but after it was over the enemy came in like a flood, telling me I had done what I ought not, and should now bring dishonor to this people. But this shock did not last long.

This day, as usual, I had gone on foot. My husband, as he afterwards told me, lying on the bed, these words ran through him, "Lord where shall I fly to shun thee," at which he arose, and seeing it rain, got the horse and came to fetch me, and coming just as the meeting broke up, I got on horseback as quick as possible, lest he should hear what had happened. Nevertheless he had heard, and as soon as we were got into the woods he began, saying, What do you mean thus to make my life unhappy? could you not be a Quaker without turning fool after this manner? I answered in tears, saying, My dear, look on me with pity, if thou hast any; can'st thou think that I in the bloom of my days would bear all that thou knowst of, and a great deal which thou knowest not of, if I did not believe it to be my duty? This took hold of him, and he taking my hand said, Well, I'll even give you up, for I see it don't avail to strive. If it be of God, I cannot overthrow it, and if it be of yourself it will soon fall, and I saw the tears stand in his eyes, at which my heart was overcome with joy, and I would not have changed conditions with a queen. I already began to reap the fruit of my obedience, but my trials did not end here. The time being up that the priest was to come, but no priest appeared, my husband went to fetch him, but he would not come, saying he was busy and could not, which so displeased my husband that he'd never go near him more, and for some time went to no place of worship. . . .

Friends had not been to talk with me, nor did they know what to do till I had appeared again, which was not for some time, when at the monthly meeting, four Friends came to pay me a visit, which I was glad of, and gave them such satisfaction that they left me well satisfied. I then joined with Friends, my husband went to no place of worship. One day he said, I'd go to meeting, only I'm afraid I shall hear your clack, which I cannot bear. I used no persuasions, yet when meeting-time came he got the horse, and took me behind him and went to meeting. But for several months, if he saw me offer to rise, he would go out, till one time I got up before he was aware, and then, as he afterwards said, was ashamed to do it, and from that time never did nor hindered me from going to meeting, and tho' he, poor man, could not take up the Cross, yet his judgment was convinced, and sometimes in a flood of tears would say, My dear, I've seen the beauty there is in the TRUTH, and that thou art in the right, and I pray God preserve thee in it, but as for me the Cross is too heavy, I cannot bear it. I told him I hoped he that had given me strength would also favor him. Oh! said he, I can't bear the reproach thou dost to be called turn-coat, and become a laughing stock to the world. But I'll no longer hinder thee from it; which I looked on as a great favor that my way was thus far made easy, and a little hope remained that my prayers would be heard on his account.

In this place he had got linked in with some that he was afraid would make game of him, which indeed they already did, asking him when he designed to commence preacher, for that they saw he intended to turn Quaker, and seemed to love his wife better since she did than before. We were now got to a little house by ourselves, which tho' mean, and little to put in it, our bed being no better than chaff, yet I was truly content, and did not envy the rich their riches. The only desires Inow had was my own persuasion, and to be blessed with the reformation of my husband. These men used to come to our house and there provoke my husband to sit up and drink sometimes till near day, while I have been sorrowing in a stable. As I once sat in this condition I heard my husband say to his company, I cannot bear any longer to afflict my poor wife in this manner, for whatever you may think of her, I do believe she is a good woman, upon which he came to me, and said, Come in, my dear, God has given thee a deal of patience, I'll put an end to this practice. And so he did, for this was the last time they sat up at nights. My husband now thought if he was in any place where it was not known that he had been so bitter against Friends he could do better than here, but I was much against his moving, fearing it would turn out to his hurt, having been for some months much altered for the better, establishing me in the TRUTH, and therefore would not have him be afflicted about that, and according to the measure of Grace received did what I could both by example and advice for his good, and my advice was for him to fight through it here, fearing he would grow weaker, and the enemy gain advantage over him, if he thus fled. But all I could say did not prevail against his moving, and hearing of a place at Burdon Town [Bordentown], [he] went there. But that did not suit. He then moved to Mount Holy [Holly], and there we settled. He got a good school and so did I, and here we might have done very well. We got our house pretty well furnished for poor folks. I now began to think I wanted but one thing to complete my happiness, viz, the reformation of my husband, to which also I had too much reason to doubt, for it fell out according to my fears, and he grew worse here, and took to drinking, so that it seemed as tho' my life was to be a continual scene of sorrow, and most earnestly I prayed to Almighty God, to endue me with patience to bear my afflictions, and submit to his providence, which I can say in truth I did without murmuring, or even uttering an unsavory expression, to the best of my knowledge, except once when my husband coming home a little in drink, in which frame he was very fractious, and finding me at work by a candle, came to me, put it out, and fetching me a box on the ear said, You don't earn your light, which unkind usage—for he had not struck me of two years before—went hard with me, and I uttered these [sic] rash expressions, "Thou art a vile man," and was a little angry, but soon recovered and was sorry for it. He struck me again, which I received without so much as a word in return, and [he] went on in a distracted manner, uttering several rash expressions that bespoke despair, as that he now believed he was predestined to damnation, and he did not care how soon God would strike him dead and the like. I durst say but little, but at length I broke out in these words, "Lord look down on my afflictions, and deliver me by some means or other." I was answered I should soon be, and so I was, but in such a manner as I verily believed it would have killed me.

In a little time he went to Burlington, where he got in drink, and enlisted for a common soldier to go to Cuba, anno dom. 1740. I had drank many bitter cups, but this seemed to exceed them all; for indeed my very senses seemed shaken. I now a thousand times blamed myself for making such an undevised request, fearing I had displeased God by it, and tho' he had granted it, it was in displeasure and suffered to be in this manner to punish me. But I can say I never desired his death more than my own, nay not so much. I have since had cause to believe his mind was benefited by the undertaking, which hope makes up for all I have suffered from him, being informed that he did in the army what he could not do at home, viz. suffer for the testimony of TRUTH. When they came to an engagement he refused to fight, for which he was whipped, and brought before the general, who asked him why he enlisted, if he would not fight. I did it, said he, in a drunken frolic, when the devil had the better of me, but my judgment is convinced, that I ought not, neither will I, whatever I suffer. I have but one life and you may take that if you please, but I'll never take up arms. They used him with much cruelty to make him yield, but could not, by means whereof he was so disabled that the general sent him to the hospital at Chelsea, near London, where in nine months he died, and I hope made a good end, for which I prayed both night and day, till I heard of his death.

Thus I thought it my duty to say what I could in his favor, as I have been obliged to say so much of his hard usage to me, all which I hope did me good, and altho' he was so bad yet had several good properties, and I never thought him the worst of men. He was one I loved, and had he let religion have its perfect work, I should have thought myself happy in the lowest state of life, and I have cause to bless God who enabled me in the station of a wife to do my duty, and now a widow, to submit to his will, always believing every thing he doth to be right. May he in all stations of life so preserve me by the arm of Divine Power, that I may never forget his tender mercies to me, the remembrance whereof doth often bow down my soul in humility before his throne, saying, Lord, what was I, that thou should'st have revealed to my soul the knowledge of the TRUTH, and done so much for me, who deserved thy displeasure rather. But in me thou hast shown thy long-suffering and tender mercy. May Thou, O God, be glorified, and I abased, for it is thy own works that praise thee, and, of a truth, to the humble soul makest everything sweet.

# OLAUDAH EQUIANO
## 1745–1797

*Olaudah Equiano and Benjamin Franklin were almost contemporaries; indeed, Equiano probably visited Philadelphia while Franklin lived there. The stories they tell have some remarkable similarities. Yet the lives of the two men—one white and free, the other black and enslaved for much of his life—are diametrically different.*

*Equiano rejected the New World, contrasting its barbarities with the culture of his African homeland. Captured as a young boy by an enemy tribe, Equiano served several African masters until he was sold to a British slaver. His* Interesting Narrative of the Life of Olaudah Equiano, or Gustavus Vassa, The African *described in shocking detail the dread middle passage between Africa and the New World, and his subsequent visits to the British colonies in the West Indies, Virginia, and Georgia gave graphic evidence of the cruelty of slavery as it took hold in the British colonies. After his emancipation in 1766, Equiano left the Americas, returning only briefly some years later.*

*Like Franklin's, this autobiography is a success story in many respects. Equiano learned to read and write and became a skillful sailor on his master's ships, which ironically often carried slaves. He also earned enough money to buy his freedom. As a free man, he continued his voyages around the world from the Mediterranean Sea to the North Pole.*

*After his retirement from the sea, Equiano became an abolitionist and an advocate for the African people. He contemplated going to Africa as a missionary for the Church of England but was denied permission by the Bishop of London. He received a government appointment to assist in the colonization of Sierra Leone, but lost the position after exposing graft in the operation. Equiano never returned to his homeland. In 1792 he married Susanna Cullen and died in 1797.*

*His autobiography was the most important testimony against slavery until Frederick Douglass's* Narrative of the Life of Frederick Douglass. *It was first published in England in 1789 and then in 1791 in the United States, appearing thereafter in several editions.*

*Equiano's* Narrative *tells of maritime and spiritual journeys. It is full of adventure on the high seas: dramatic battles between the British and the French as the two empires fought to conquer the New World, terrific storms, devastating shipwrecks, and hair-breadth escapes. Villains capture and abuse slaves; heroes befriend and rescue them. Equiano's wanderings reflected more than his seafaring skills or his love of adventure. Although*

*he joined the Church of England, his pursuit of salvation was more compli-
cated than Bradstreet's; his pursuit of perfection more difficult than
Franklin's. What Equiano sought was his elusive identity as a black man
among whites, an African in an English culture.*

The Life of Olaudah Equiano, or Gustavus Vassa the African
Written by Himself. *London: 1789. Reprint, New York: Negro Universi-
ties Press, 1969.*

I believe it is difficult for those who publish their own memoirs to escape the
imputation of vanity; nor is this the only disadvantage under which they labor: it
is also their misfortune, that what is uncommon is rarely, if ever, believed, and
what is obvious we are apt to turn from with disgust, and to charge the writer with
impertinence. People generally think those memoirs only worthy to be read or
remembered which abound in great or striking events; those, in short, which in a
high degree excite either admiration or pity: all others they consign to contempt
and oblivion. It is therefore, I confess, not a little hazardous in a private and
obscure individual, and a stranger too, thus to solicit the indulgent attention of the
public; especially when I own I offer here the history of neither a saint, a hero, nor
a tyrant. I believe there are few events in my life, which have not happened to
many: it is true the incidents of it are numerous; and, did I consider myself an
European, I might say my sufferings were great: but when I compare my lot with
that of most of my countrymen, I regard myself as a *particular favorite of heaven,*
and acknowledge the mercies of Providence in every occurrence of my life. If,
then, the following narrative does not appear sufficiently interesting to engage
general attention, let my motive be some excuse for its publication. I am not so
foolishly vain as to expect from it either immortality or literary reputation. If it
affords any satisfaction to my numerous friends, at whose request it has been
written, or in the smallest degree promotes the interests of humanity, the ends for
which it was undertaken will be fully attained, and every wish of my heart gratified. Let it therefore be remembered, that, in wishing to avoid censure, I do not
aspire to praise.

That part of Africa, known by the name of Guinea, to which the trade for
slaves is carried on, extends along the coast above 3400 miles, from Senegal to
Angola, and includes a variety of kingdoms. Of these the most considerable is the
kingdom of Benin, both as to extent and wealth, the richness and cultivation of
the soil, the power of its king, and the number and warlike disposition of the
inhabitants. It is situated nearly under the line, and extends along the coast about
170 miles, but runs back into the interior part of Africa to a distance hitherto, I
believe, unexplored by any traveller; and seems only terminated at length by the
empire of Abyssinnia, near 1500 miles from its beginning. This kingdom is divided
into many provinces or districts: in one of the most remote and fertile of which, I
was born, in the year 1745, situated in a charming fruitful vale, named Essaka.
The distance of this province from the capital of Benin and the sea coast must be
very considerable: for I had never heard of white men or Europeans, nor of the
sea; and our subjection to the king of Benin was little more than nominal; for
every transaction of the government, as far as my slender observation extended,
was conducted by the chief or elders of the place. The manners and government

of a people who have little commerce with other countries, are generally very simple; and the history of what passes in one family or village, may serve as a specimen of the whole nation. My father was one of those elders or chiefs I have spoken of, and was styled Embrenche; a term, as I remember, importing the highest distinction, and signifying in our language a *mark* of grandeur. This mark is conferred on the person entitled to it, by cutting the skin across at the top of the forehead, and drawing it down to the eye-brows: and while it is in this situation applying a warm hand, and rubbing it until it shrinks up into a thick *weal* across the lower part of the forehead. Most of the judges and senators were thus marked; my father had long borne it: I had seen it conferred on one of my brothers, and I also was *destined* to receive it by my parents. Those Embrenche or chief men, decided disputes and punished crimes; for which purpose they always assembled together. The proceedings were generally short: and in most cases the law of retaliation prevailed. I remember a man was brought before my father, and the other judges, for kidnapping a boy; and, although he was the son of a chief or senator, he was condemned to make recompense by a man or woman slave. Adultery, however, was sometimes punished with slavery or death; a punishment which I believe is inflicted on it throughout most of the nations of Africa: so sacred among them is the honor of the marriage bed, and so jealous are they of the fidelity of their wives. Of this I recollect an instance—a woman was convicted before the judges of adultery, and delivered over, as the custom was, to her husband, to be punished. Accordingly he determined to put her to death: but it being found, just before her execution, that she had an infant at her breast; and no woman being prevailed on to perform the part of a nurse, she was spared on account of the child. The men, however, do not preserve the same constancy to their wives, which they expect from them; for they indulge in a plurality, though seldom in more than two. Their mode of marriage is thus:—both parties are usually betrothed when young by their parents (though I have known the males to betroth themselves.) On this occasion a feast is prepared, and the bride and bridegroom stand up in the midst of all their friends, who are assembled for the purpose, while he declares she is henceforth to be looked upon as his wife, and that no other person is to pay any addresses to her. This is also immediately proclaimed in the vicinity, on which the bride retires from the assembly. Some time after, she is brought home to her husband, and then another feast is made, to which the relations of both parties are invited: her parents then deliver her to the bridegroom, accompanied with a number of blessings, and at the same time they tie round her waist a cotton string of the thickness of a goose-quill, which none but married women are permitted to wear: she is now considered as completely his wife; and at this time the dowry is given to the new married pair, which generally consists of portions of land, slaves, and cattle, household goods, and implements of husbandry. These are offered by the friends of both parties; besides which the parents of the bridegroom present gifts to those of the bride, whose property she is looked upon before marriage; but after it she is esteemed the sole property of her husband. The ceremony being now ended, the festival begins, which is celebrated with bonfires, and loud acclamations of joy, accompanied with music and dancing.

We are almost a nation of dancers, musicians and poets. Thus every great event, such as a triumphant return from battle, or other cause of public rejoicing, is celebrated in public dances, which are accompanied with songs and music suited to the occasion. The assembly is separated into four divisions, which dance either

**OLAUDAH EQUIANO**

apart or in succession, and each with a character peculiar to itself. The first division contains the married men, who in their dances frequently exhibit feats of arms, and the representation of a battle. To these succeed the married women, who dance in the second division. The young men occupy the third: and the maidens the fourth. Each represents some interesting scene of real life, such as a great achievement, domestic employment, a pathetic story, or some rural sport; and as the subject is generally founded on some recent event, it is therefore ever new. This gives our dances a spirit and variety which I have scarcely seen elsewhere. We have many musical instruments, particularly drums of different kinds, a piece of music which resembles a guitar, and another much like a stickado. These last are chiefly used by betrothed virgins, who play on them on all grand festivals.

As our manners are simple, our luxuries are few. The dress of both sexes is nearly the same. It generally consists of a long piece of calico, or muslin, wrapped loosely round the body, somewhat in the form of a highland plaid. This is usually dyed blue, which is our favorite color. It is extracted from a berry, and is brighter and richer than any I have seen in Europe. Besides this, our women of distinction wear golden ornaments, which they dispose with some profusion on their arms and legs. When our women are not employed with the men in tillage, their usual occupation is spinning and weaving cotton, which they afterwards dye, and make into garments. They also manufacture earthen vessels, of which we have many kinds. Among the rest, tobacco pipes, made after the same fashion, and used in the same manner, as those in Turkey.

Our manner of living is entirely plain; for as yet the natives are unacquainted with those refinements in cookery which debauch the taste: bullocks, goats, and poultry, supply the greatest part of their food. . . .

As we live in a country where nature is prodigal of her favors, our wants are few and easily supplied; of course we have few manufactures. They consist for the most part of calicoes, earthen ware, ornaments, and instruments of war and husbandry. But these make no part of our commerce, the principal articles of which, as I have observed, are provisions. In such a state, money is of little use; however, we have some small pieces of coin, if I may call them such. They are made something like an anchor; but I do not remember either their value or denomination. We have also markets, at which I have been frequently with my mother. These are sometimes visited by stout mahogany-colored men from the south-west of us: we call them *Oye-Eboe,* which term signifies red men living at a distance. They generally bring us fire-arms, gunpowder, hats, beads, and dried fish. The last we esteemed a great rarity, as our waters were only brooks and springs. These articles they barter with us for odoriferous woods and earth, and our salt of wood ashes. They always carry slaves through our land; but the strictest account is exacted of their manner of procuring them before they are suffered to pass. Sometimes indeed, we sold slaves to them, but they were only prisoners of war, or such among us as had been convicted of kidnapping, or adultery, and some other crimes, which we esteemed heinous. This practice of kidnapping induces me to think, that, notwithstanding all our strictness, their principal business among us was to trepan our people. I remember too, they carried great sacks along with them, which not long after, I had an opportunity of fatally seeing applied to that infamous purpose.

Our land is uncommonly rich and fruitful, and produces all kinds of vegetables in great abundance. We have plenty of Indian corn, and vast quantities of cotton and tobacco. Our pine apples grow without culture; they are about the size of the largest sugar-loaf, and finely flavored. We have also spices of different kinds, particularly pepper; and a variety of delicious fruits which I have never seen in Europe; together with gums of various kinds, and honey in abundance. All our industry is exerted to improve these blessings of nature. Agriculture is our chief employment; and every one, even the children and women, are engaged in it. Thus we are all habituated to labor from our earliest years. Every one contributes something to the common stock; and, as we are unacquainted with idleness, we have no beggars. The benefits of such a mode of living are obvious. The West India planters prefer the slaves of Benin or Eboe, to those of any other part of Guinea, for their hardiness, intelligence, integrity, and zeal. Those benefits are felt by us in the general healthiness of the people, and in their vigor and activity; I might have added, too, in their comeliness. Deformity is indeed unknown amongst us, I mean that of shape. Numbers of the natives of Eboe now in London, might be brought in support of this assertion: for, in regard to complexion, ideas of beauty are wholly relative. I remember while in Africa to have seen three negro children who were tawny, and another quite white, who were universally regarded by myself, and the natives in general, as far as related to their complexions, as deformed. Our women, too, were in my eye at least, uncommonly graceful, alert, and modest to a degree of bashfulness; nor do I remember to have heard of an instance of incontinence amongst them before marriage. They are also remarkably cheerful. Indeed, cheerfulness and affability are two of the leading characteristics of our nation.

Our tillage is exercised in a large plain or common, some hours' walk from our dwellings, and all the neighbors resort thither in a body. They use no beasts of husbandry; and their only instruments are hoes, axes, shovels, and beaks, or pointed iron, to dig with. Sometimes we are visited by locusts, which come in large clouds, so as to darken the air, and destroy our harvest. This, however, happens rarely, but when it does, a famine is produced by it. I remember an instance or two wherein this happened. This common is often the theatre of war; and therefore when our people go out to till their land, they not only go in a body, but generally take their arms with them for fear of a surprise; and when they apprehend an invasion, they guard the avenues to their dwellings, by driving sticks into the ground, which are so sharp at one end as to pierce the foot, and are generally dipt in poison. From what I can recollect of these battles, they appear to have been irruptions of one little state or district on the other, to obtain prisoners or booty. Perhaps they were incited to this, by those traders who brought the European goods I mentioned, amongst us. Such a mode of obtaining slaves in Africa is common; and I believe more are procured this way, and by kidnapping, than any other. When a trader wants slaves, he applies to a chief for them, and tempts him with his wares. It is not extraordinary, if on this occasion he yields to the temptation with as little firmness, and accepts the price of his fellow creatures' liberty, with as little reluctance as the enlightened merchant. Accordingly he falls on his neighbors, and a desperate battle ensues. If he prevails and takes prisoners, he gratifies his avarice by selling them; but, if his party be vanquished, and he falls into the hands of the enemy, he is put to death; for, as he has been known to foment their quarrels, it is thought dangerous to let him survive, and no ransom can save him, though all other prisoners may be redeemed. We have fire-arms, bows and arrows, broad two-edged swords and javelins: we have shields also which cover a man from head to foot. All are taught the use of these weapons;

even our women are warriors, and march boldly out to fight along with the men. Our whole district is a kind of militia: on a certain signal given, such as the firing of a gun at night, they all rise in arms and rush upon their enemy. It is perhaps something remarkable, that when our people march to the field a red flag or banner is borne before them. . . .

I have already acquainted the reader with the time and place of my birth. My father, besides many slaves, had a numerous family, of which seven lived to grow up, including myself and a sister, who was the only daughter. As I was the youngest of the sons, I became, of course, the greatest favorite with my mother, and was always with her; and she used to take particular pains to form my mind. I was trained up from my earliest years in the art of war: my daily exercise was shooting and throwing javelins; and my mother adorned me with emblems, after the manner of our greatest warriors. In this way I grew up till I was turned the age of eleven, when an end was put to my happiness in the following manner:—generally when the grown people in the neighborhood were gone far in the fields to labor, the children assembled together in some of the neighboring premises to play; and commonly some of us used to get up a tree to look out for any assailant, or kidnapper, that might come upon us—for they sometimes took those opportunities of our parents' absence, to attack and carry off as many as they could seize. One day as I was watching at the top of a tree in our yard, I saw one of those people come into the yard of our next neighbor but one to kidnap, there being many stout young people in it. Immediately on this I gave the alarm of the rogue, and he was surrounded by the stoutest of them, who entangled him with cords, so that he could not escape till some of the grown people came and secured him. But, alas! ere long it was my fate to be thus attacked, and to be carried off, when none of the grown people were nigh. One day, when all our people were gone out to their works as usual, and only I and my dear sister were left to mind the house, two men and a woman got over our walls, and in a moment seized us both, and, without giving us time to cry out, or make resistance, they stopped our mouths, and ran off with us into the nearest wood. Here they tied our hands, and continued to carry us as far as they could, till night came on, when we reached a small house, where the robbers halted for refreshment, and spent the night. We were then unbound, but were unable to take any food; and, being quite overpowered by fatigue and grief, our only relief was some sleep, which allayed our misfortune for a short time. The next morning we left the house, and continued travelling all the day. For a long time we had kept the woods, but at last we came into a road which I believed I knew. I had now some hopes of being delivered; for we had advanced but a little way before I discovered some people at a distance, on which I began to cry out for their assistance; but my cries had no other effect than to make them tie me faster and stop my mouth, and then they put me into a large sack. They also stopped my sister's mouth, and tied her hands; and in this manner we proceeded till we were out of sight of these people. When we went to rest the following night, they offered us some victuals, but we refused it; and the only comfort we had was in being in one another's arms all that night, and bathing each other with our tears. But alas! we were soon deprived of even the small comfort of weeping together. The next day proved a day of greater sorrow than I had yet experienced; for my sister and I were then separated, while we lay clasped in each other's arms. It was in vain that we besought them not to part us; she was torn from me, and immediately carried away, while I was left in a state of distraction not to be described. I cried and grieved continually; and for several days did not eat any thing but what they forced into my mouth. At length, after many days travelling, during which I had often changed masters, I got into the hands of a chieftain, in a very pleasant country. This man had two wives and some children, and they all used me extremely well, and did all they could to comfort me; particularly the first wife, who was something like my mother. Although I was a great many days' journey from my father's house, yet these people spoke exactly the same language with us. This first master of mine, as I may call him, was a smith, and my principal employment was working his bellows, which were the same kind as I had seen in my vicinity. They were in some respects not unlike the stoves here in gentlemen's kitchens, and were covered over with leather; and in the middle of that leather a stick was fixed, and a person stood up, and worked it in the same manner as is done to pump water out of a cask with a hand pump. I believe it was gold he worked, for it was of a lovely bright yellow color, and was worn by the women on their wrists and ankles. I was there I suppose about a month, and they at last used to trust me some little distance from the house. This liberty I used in embracing every opportunity to inquire the way to my own home; and I also sometimes, for the same purpose, went with the maidens, in the cool of the evenings, to bring pitchers of water from the springs for the use of the house. I had also remarked where the sun rose in the morning, and set in the evening, as I had travelled along; and I had observed that my father's house was towards the rising of the sun. I therefore determined to seize the first opportunity of making my escape, and to shape my course for that quarter; for I was quite oppressed and weighed down by grief after my mother and friends; and my love of liberty, ever great, was strengthened by the mortifying circumstance of not daring to eat with the free-born children, although I was mostly their companion. . . .

**[He was sold several times.]**

Thus I continued to travel, sometimes by land, sometimes by water, through different countries and various nations, till, at the end of six or seven months after I had been kidnapped, I arrived at the sea coast. It would be tedious and uninteresting to relate all the incidents which befell me during this journey, and which I have not yet forgotten; of the various hands I passed through, and the manners and customs of all the different people among whom I lived—I shall therefore only observe, that in all the places where I was, the soil was exceedingly rich; the pumpkins, eadas, plaintains, yams, &c. &c. were in great abundance, and of incredible size. There were also vast quantities of different gums, though not used for any purpose, and every where a great deal of tobacco. The cotton even grew quite wild, and there was plenty of red-wood. I saw no mechanics whatever in all the way, except such as I have mentioned. The chief employment in all these countries was agriculture, and both the males and females, as with us, were brought up to it, and trained in the arts of war.

The first object which saluted my eyes when I arrived on the coast, was the sea, and a slave ship, which was then riding at anchor, and waiting for its cargo. These filled me with astonishment, which was soon converted into terror, when I was carried on board. I was immediately handled, and tossed up to see if I were sound, by some of the crew; and I was now persuaded that I had gotten into a world of bad spirits, and that they were going to kill me. Their complexions, too, differing so much from ours, their long hair, and the language they spoke, (which was very different from any I had ever heard) united to confirm me in this belief. Indeed, such were the horrors of my views and fears at the moment, that, if ten thousand worlds had been my own, I would have freely parted with them all to have exchanged my condition with that of the meanest slave in my own country. When I looked round the ship too, and saw a large furnace of copper boiling, and a multitude of black people of every description chained together, every one of their countenances expressing dejection and sorrow, I no longer doubted of my fate; and, quite overpowered with horror and anguish, I fell motionless on the deck and fainted. When I recovered a little, I found some black people about me, who I believed were some of those who had brought me on board, and had been receiving their pay; they talked to me in order to cheer me, but all in vain. I asked them if we were not to be eaten by those white men with horrible looks, red faces, and long hair. They told me I was not: and one of the crew brought me a small portion of spirituous liquor in a wine glass, but, being afraid of him, I would not take it out of his hand. One of the blacks, therefore, took it from him and gave it to me, and I took a little down my palate, which, instead of reviving me, as they thought it would, threw me into the greatest consternation at the strange feeling it produced, having never tasted any such liquor before. Soon after this, the blacks who brought me on board went off, and left me abandoned to despair.

I now saw myself deprived of all chance of returning to my native country, or even the least glimpse of hope of gaining the shore, which I now considered as friendly; and I even wished for my former slavery in preference to my present situation, which was filled with horrors of every kind, still heightened by my ignorance of what I was to undergo. I was not long suffered to indulge my grief; I was soon put down under the decks, and there I received such a salutation in my nostrils as I had never experienced in my life: so that, with the loathsomeness of the stench, and crying together, I became so sick and low that I was not able to eat, nor had I the least desire to taste any thing. I now wished for the last friend, death, to relieve me; but soon, to my grief, two of the white men offered me eatables; and, on my refusing to eat, one of them held me fast by the hands, and laid me across, I think the windlass, and tied my feet, while the other flogged me severely. I had never experienced any thing of this kind before, and although not being used to the water, I naturally feared that element the first time I saw it, yet, nevertheless, could I have got over the nettings, I would have jumped over the side, but I could not; and besides, the crew used to watch us very closely who were not chained down to the decks, lest we should leap into the water; and I have seen some of these poor African prisoners most severely cut, for attempting to do so, and hourly whipped for not eating. This indeed was often the case with myself. In a little time after, amongst the poor chained men, I found some of my own nation, which in a small degree gave ease to my mind. I inquired of these what was to be done with us? they gave me to understand, we were to be carried to these white people's country to work for them. I then was a little revived, and thought, if it were no worse than working, my situation was not so desperate; but still I feared I should be put to death, the white people looked and acted, as I thought, in so savage a manner; for I had never seen among any people such instances of brutal cruelty; and this not only shown towards us blacks, but also to some of the whites themselves. One white man in particular I saw, when we were permitted to be on deck, flogged so unmercifully with a large rope near the foremast, that he died in consequence of it; and they tossed him over the side as they would have done a brute. This made me fear these people the more; and I expected nothing less than to be treated in the same manner. I could not help expressing my fears and apprehensions to some of my countrymen; I asked them if these people had no country, but lived in this hollow place? (the ship) they told me they did not, but came from a distant one. 'Then,' said I, 'how comes it in all our country we never heard of them?' They told me because they lived so very far off. I then asked where were their women? had they any like themselves? I was told they had. 'And why,' said I, 'do we not see them?' They answered, because they were left behind. I asked how the vessel could go? they told me they could not tell; but that there was cloth put upon the masts by the help of the ropes I saw, and then the vessel went on; and the white men had some spell or magic they put in the water when they liked, in order to stop the vessel. I was exceedingly amazed at this account, and really thought they were spirits. I therefore wished much to be from amongst them, for I expected they would sacrifice me; but my wishes were vain—for we were so quartered that it was impossible for any of us to make our escape.

While we stayed on the coast I was mostly on deck; and one day, to my great astonishment, I saw one of these vessels coming in with the sails up. As soon as the whites saw it, they gave a great shout, at which we were amazed; and the more so, as the vessel appeared larger by approaching nearer. At last, she came to an anchor in my sight, and when the anchor was let go, I and my countrymen who saw it, were lost in astonishment to observe the vessel stop—and were now convinced it was done by magic. Soon after this the other ship got her boats out, and they came on board of us, and the people of both ships seemed very glad to see each other. Several of the strangers also shook hands with us black people, and made motions with their hands, signifying I suppose, we were to go to their country, but we did not understand them.

At last, when the ship we were in, had got in all her cargo, they made ready with many fearful noises, and we were all put under deck, so that we could not see how they managed the vessel. But this disappointment was the least of my sorrow. The stench of the hold while we were on the coast was so intolerably loathsome, that it was dangerous to remain there for any time, and some of us had been permitted to stay on the deck for the fresh air; but now that the whole ship's cargo were confined together, it became absolutely pestilential. The closeness of the place, and the heat of the climate, added to the number in the ship, which was so crowded that each had scarcely room to turn himself, almost suffocated us. This produced copious perspirations, so that the air soon became unfit for respiration, from a variety of loathsome smells, and brought on a sickness among the slaves, of which many died—thus falling victims to the improvident avarice, as I may call it, of their purchasers. This wretched situation was again aggravated by the galling of the chains, now became insupportable; and the filth of the necessary tubs, into which the children often fell, and were almost suffocated. The shrieks of the women, and the groans of the dying, rendered the whole a scene of horror almost inconceivable. Happily perhaps, for myself, I was soon reduced so low here that it was thought necessary to keep me almost always on deck; and from my extreme youth I was not put in fetters. In this situation I expected every hour to share the fate of my companions, some of whom were almost daily brought upon deck at the point of death, which I began to hope would soon put an end to my miseries. Often did I think many of the inhabitants of the deep much more happy than myself. I envied them the freedom they enjoyed, and as often wished I could change my condition for theirs. Every circumstance I met with, served only to render my state more painful, and heightened my apprehensions, and my opinion of the cruelty of the whites.

One day they had taken a number of fishes; and when they had killed and satisfied themselves with as many as they thought fit, to our astonishment who were on deck, rather than give any of them to us to eat, as we expected, they tossed the remaining fish into the sea again, although we begged and prayed for some as well as we could, but in vain; and some of my countrymen, being pressed by hunger, took an opportunity, when they thought no one saw them, of trying to get a little privately; but they were discovered, and the attempt procured them some very severe floggings. One day, when we had a smooth sea and moderate wind, two of my wearied countrymen who were chained together, (I was near them at the time,) preferring death to such a life of misery, somehow made through the nettings and jumped into the sea: immediately, another quite dejected fellow, who, on account of his illness, was suffered to be out of irons, also followed their example; and I believe many more would very soon have done the same, if they had not been prevented by the ship's crew, who were instantly alarmed. Those of us that were the most active, were in a moment put down under the deck, and there was such a noise and confusion amongst the people of the ship as I never heard before, to stop her, and get the boat out to go after the slaves. However, two of the wretches were drowned, but they got the other, and afterwards flogged him unmercifully, for thus attempting to prefer death to slavery. In this manner we continued to undergo more hardships than I can now relate, hardships which are inseparable from this accursed trade. Many a time we were near suffocation from the want of fresh air, which we were often without for whole days together. This, and the stench of the necessary tubs, carried off many. . . .

At last, we came in sight of the island of Barbadoes, at which the whites on board gave a great shout, and made many signs of joy to us. We did not know what to think of this; but as the vessel drew nearer, we plainly saw the harbor, and other ships of different kinds and sizes, and we soon anchored amongst them, off Bridgetown. Many merchants and planters now came on board, though it was in the evening. They put us in separate parcels, and examined us attentively. They also made us jump, and pointed to the land, signifying we were to go there. We thought by this, we should be eaten by these ugly men, as they appeared to us; and, when soon after we were all put down under the deck again, there was much dread and trembling among us, and nothing but bitter cries to be heard all the night from these apprehensions, insomuch, that at last the white people got some old slaves from the land to pacify us. They told us we were not to be eaten, but to work, and were soon to go on land, where we should see many of our country people. This report eased us much. And sure enough, soon after we were landed, there came to us Africans of all languages.

We were conducted immediately to the merchant's yard, where we were all pent up together, like so many sheep in a fold, without regard to sex or age. As every object was new to me, every thing I saw filled me with surprise. What struck me first, was, that the houses were built with bricks and stories, and in every other respect different from those I had seen in Africa; but I was still more astonished on seeing people on horseback. I did not know what this could mean; and, indeed, I thought these people were full of nothing but magical arts. While I was in this astonishment, one of my fellow-prisoners spoke to a countryman of his, about the horses, who said they were the same kind they had in their country. I understood them, though they were from a distant part of Africa; and I thought it odd I had not seen any horses there; but afterwards, when I came to converse with different Africans, I found they had many horses amongst them, and much larger than those I then saw.

We were not many days in the merchant's custody, before we were sold after their usual manner, which is this:—On a signal given, (as the beat of a drum,) the buyers rush at once into the yard where the slaves are confined, and make choice of that parcel they like best. The noise and clamor with which this is attended, and the eagerness visible in the countenances of the buyers, serve not a little to increase the apprehension of terrified Africans, who may well be supposed to consider them as the ministers of that destruction to which they think themselves devoted. In this manner, without scruple, are relations and friends separated, most of them never to see each other again. I remember, in the vessel in which I was brought over, in the men's apartment, there were several brothers, who, in the sale, were sold in different lots; and it was very moving on this occasion, to see and hear their cries at parting. . . .

**[He was taken to Virginia and sold to Captain Michael Henry Pascal, a commander in the British royal navy, who gave him the name of Gustavus Vassa. In 1757 Equiano began his life of seafaring, shipping out with his master on a ship of war and observing the British victory over the French at Louisburg.]**

We arrived at Cape Breton in the summer of 1758; and here the soldiers were to be landed, in order to make an attack upon Louisburgh. My master had some part in superintending the landing; and here I was in a small measure gratified in seeing an encounter between our men and the enemy. The French were posted on the shore to receive us, and disputed our landing for a long time; but at last they were driven from their trenches, and a complete landing was effected. Our troops pursued them as far as the town of Louisburgh. In this action many were killed on both sides. One thing remarkable I saw this day.—A lieutenant of the Princess Amelia, who, as well as my master, superintended the landing, was giving the word of command, and while his mouth was open, a musket ball went through it, and passed out at his cheek. I had that day, in my hand, the scalp of an Indian king, who was killed in the engagement; the scalp had been taken off by an Highlander. I saw the king's ornaments too, which were very curious, and made of feathers.

Our land forces laid siege to the town of Louisburgh, while the French men-of-war were blocked up in the harbor by the fleet, the batteries at the same time playing upon them from the land. This they did with such effect, that one day I saw some of the ships set on fire by the shells from the batteries, and I believe two or three of them were quite burnt. . . .

It was now between two and three years since I first came to England, a great part of which I had spent at sea; so that I became inured to that service, and began to consider myself as happily situated, for my master treated me always extremely well; and my attachment and gratitude to him were very great. From the various scenes I had beheld on shipboard, I soon grew a stranger to terror of every kind, and was, in that respect at least, almost an Englishman. I have often reflected with surprise that I never felt half the alarm at any of the numerous dangers I have been in, that I was filled with at the first sight of the Europeans, and at every act of theirs, even the most trifling, when I first came among them, and for some time afterwards. That fear, however, which was the effect of my ignorance, wore away as I began to know them. I could now speak English tolerably well, and I perfectly understood every thing that was said. I not only felt myself quite easy with these new countrymen, but relished their society and manners. I no longer looked upon them as spirits, but as men superior to us; and therefore I had the stronger desire to resemble them, to imbibe their spirit, and imitate their manners. I therefore embraced every occasion of improvement, and every new thing that I observed I treasured up in my memory. I had long wished to be able to read and write; and for this purpose I took every opportunity to gain instruction, but had made as yet very little progress. However, when I went to London with my master, I had soon an opportunity of improving myself, which I gladly embraced. Shortly after my arrival, he sent me to wait upon the Miss Guerins, who had treated me with much kindness when I was there before; and they sent me to school.

While I was attending these ladies, their servants told me I could not go to Heaven unless I was baptized. This made me very uneasy, for I had now some faint idea of a future state. Accordingly I communicated my anxiety to the eldest Miss Guerin, with whom I was become a favorite, and pressed her to have me baptized; when to my great joy, she told me I should. She had formerly asked my master to let me be baptized, but he had refused. However she now insisted on it; and he being under some obligation to her brother, complied with her request. So I was baptized in St. Margaret's church, Westminster, in February, 1759, by my present name. . . .

**[During the next four years he sailed to the Mediterranean and witnessed the ongoing war between the French and the British. In 1763 when peace was concluded, Equiano hoped that he would be freed. Instead, he was sold, taken to the West Indies, and sold again to a Quaker merchant, Robert King. King was a good master, but Equiano saw much brutality.]**

I had the good fortune to please my master in every department in which he employed me; and there was scarcely any part of his business, or household affairs, in which I was not occasionally engaged. I often supplied the place of a clerk, in receiving and delivering cargoes to the ships, in tending stores, and delivering goods. And besides this, I used to shave and dress my master when convenient, and take care of his horse; and when it was necessary, which was very often, I worked likewise on board of different vessels of his. By these means I became very useful to my master, and saved him, as he used to acknowledge, above a hundred pounds a year. Nor did he scruple to say I was of more advantage to him than any of his clerks; though their usual wages in the West Indies are from sixty to a hundred pounds current a year.

I have sometimes heard it asserted that a negro cannot earn his master the first cost; but nothing can be further from the truth. I suppose nine-tenths of the mechanics throughout the West Indies are negro slaves; and I well know the coopers among them earn two dollars a day, the carpenters the same, and often times more; as also the masons, smiths, and fishermen, &c. And I have known many slaves whose masters would not take a thousand pounds current for them.

But surely this assertion refutes itself; for, if it be true, why do the planters and merchants pay such a price for slaves? And, above all, why do those who make this assertion exclaim the most loudly against the abolition of the slave trade? So much are men blinded, and to such inconsistent arguments are they driven by mistaken interest! I grant, indeed, that slaves are sometimes, by half-feeding, half-clothing, over-working and stripes, reduced so low, that they are turned out as unfit for service, and left to perish in the woods, or expire on the dunghill.

My master was several times offered, by different gentlemen, one hundred guineas for me, but he always told them he would not sell me, to my great joy. And I used to double my diligence and care, for fear of getting into the hands of those men who did not allow a valuable slave the common support of life. Many of them even used to find fault with my master for feeding his slaves so well as he did; although I often went hungry, and an Englishman might think my fare very indifferent; but he used to tell them he always would do it, because the slaves thereby looked better and did more work.

While I was thus employed by my master, I was often a witness to cruelties of every kind, which were exercised on my unhappy fellow slaves. I used frequently to have different cargoes of new negroes in my care for sale; and it was almost a constant practice with our clerks, and other whites, to commit violent depredations on the chastity of the female slaves; and these I was, though with reluctance, obliged to submit to at all times, being unable to help them. When we have had some of these slaves on board my master's vessels, to carry them to other islands, or to America, I have known our mates to commit these acts most shamefully, to the disgrace, not of Christians only, but of men. I have even known them to gratify their brutal passion with females not ten years old; and these abominations, some of them practiced to such scandalous excess, that one of our captains discharged the mate and others on that account. And yet in Montserrat I have seen a negro man staked to the ground, and cut most shockingly, and then his ears cut off bit by bit, because he had been connected with a white woman, who was a common prostitute. As if it were no crime in the whites to rob an innocent African girl of her virtue; but most heinous in a black man only to gratify a passion of nature, where the temptation was offered by one of a different color, though the most abandoned woman of her species. . . .

**[He became a skillful sailor and acquired some money buying and trading as he traveled around the West Indies with a captain who befriended him.]**

Every day now brought me nearer my freedom, and I was impatient till we proceeded again to sea, that I might have an opportunity of getting a sum large enough to purchase it. I was not long ungratified; for, in the beginning of the year 1766, my master bought another sloop, named the Nancy, the largest I had ever seen. She was partly laden, and was to proceed to Philadelphia; our captain had his choice of three, and I was well pleased he chose this, which was the largest; for, from his having a large vessel, I had more room, and could carry a larger quantity of goods with me. Accordingly, when we had delivered our old vessel, the Prudence, and completed the lading of the Nancy, having made near three hundred per cent by four barrels of pork I brought from Charleston, I laid in as large a cargo as I could, trusting to God's providence to prosper my undertaking. With these views I sailed for Philadelphia. On our passage, when we drew near the land, I was for the first time surprised at the sight of some whales, having never seen any such large sea monsters before; and as we sailed by the land, one morning, I saw a puppy whale close by the vessel; it was about the length of a wherry boat, and it followed us all the day till we got within the Capes. We arrived safe, and in good time at Philadelphia, and I sold my goods there chiefly to the Quakers. They always appeared to be a very honest, discreet sort of people, and never attempted to impose on me; I therefore liked them, and ever after chose to deal with them in preference to any others.

One Sunday morning, while I was here, as I was going to church, I chanced to pass a meeting-house. The doors being open, and the house full of people, it excited my curiosity to go in. When I entered the house, to my great surprise, I saw a very tall woman standing in the midst of them, speaking in an audible voice something which I could not understand. Having never seen any thing of this kind before, I stood and stared about me for some time, wondering at this odd scene. As soon as it was over, I took an opportunity to make inquiry about the place and people, when I was informed they were called Quakers. I particularly asked what that woman I saw in the midst of them had said, but none of them were pleased to satisfy me; so I quitted them, and soon after, as I was returning, I came to a church crowded with people; the church-yard was full likewise, and a number of people were even mounted on ladders looking in at the windows. I thought this a strange sight, as I had never seen churches, either in England or the West Indies, crowded in this manner before. I therefore made bold to ask some people the meaning of all this, and they told me the Rev. Mr. George Whitfield was preaching. I had often heard of this gentleman, and had wished to see and hear him; but I never before had an opportunity. I now therefore resolved to gratify myself with the sight, and pressed in amidst the multitude. When I got into the church, I saw this pious man exhorting the people with the greatest fervor and earnestness, and sweating as much as I ever did while in slavery on Montserrat beach. I was very much struck and impressed with this; I thought it strange I had never seen divines exert themselves in this manner before, and was no longer at a loss to account for the thin congregations they preached to.

When we had discharged our cargo here, and were loaded again, we left this fruitful land once more, and set sail for Montserrat. My traffic had hitherto succeeded so well with me, that I thought, by selling my goods when we arrived at Montserrat, I should have enough to purchase my freedom. But as soon as our vessel arrived there, my master came on board, and gave orders for us to go to St. Eustatia, and discharge our cargo there, and from thence proceed for Georgia. I was much disappointed at this; but thinking, as usual, it was of no use to encounter with the decrees of fate, I submitted without repining, and we went to St. Eustatia. After we had discharged our cargo there, we took in a live cargo, (as we call a cargo of slaves). Here I sold my goods tolerably well; but, not being able to lay out all my money in this small island to as much advantage as in many other places, I laid out only part, and the remainder I brought away with me net. We sailed from hence for Georgia, and I was glad when we got there, though I had not much reason to like the place from my last adventure in Savannah; but I longed to get back to Montserrat and procure my freedom, which I expected to be able to purchase when I returned. . . .

When we had unladen the vessel, and I had sold my venture, finding myself master of about forty-seven pounds—I consulted my true friend, the captain, how I should proceed in offering my master the money for my freedom. He told me to come on a certain morning, when he and my master would be at breakfast together. Accordingly, on that morning I went, and met the captain there, as he had appointed. When I went in I made my obeisance to my master, and with my money in my hand, and many fears in my heart, I prayed him to be as good as his offer to me, when he was pleased to promise me my freedom as soon as I could purchase it. This speech seemed to confound him, he began to recoil, and my heart that instant sunk within me. 'What,' said he, 'give you your freedom? Why, where did you get the money? Have you got forty pounds sterling?' 'Yes, sir,' I answered. 'How did you get it?' replied he. I told him, very honestly. The captain then said he knew I got the money honestly, and with much industry, and that I was particularly careful. On which my master replied, 'I got money much faster than he did; and said he would not have made me the promise he did if he had thought I should have got the money so soon. 'Come, come,' said my worthy captain, clapping my master on the back, 'Come, Robert, (which was his name) I think you must let him have his freedom;—you have laid your money out very well; you have received a very good interest for it all this time, and here is now the principal at last. I know Gustavus has earned you more than a hundred a year, and he will save you money, as he will not leave you.—Come, Robert, take the money.' My master then said he would not be worse than his promise; and, taking the money, told me to go to the Secretary at the Register Office, and get my manumission drawn up. These words of my master were like a voice from heaven to me. In an instant all my trepidation was turned into unutterable bliss; and I most reverently bowed myself with gratitude, unable to express my feelings, but by the overflowing of my eyes, and a heart replete with thanks to God, while my true and worthy friend, the captain, congratulated us both with a peculiar degree of heart-felt pleasure. As soon as the first transports of my joy were over, and that I had expressed my thanks to these my worthy friends, in the best manner I was able, I rose with a heart full of affection and reverence, and left the room, in order to obey my master's joyful mandate of going to the Register Office. As I was leaving the house I called to mind the words of the Psalmist, in the 126th Psalm, and like him, 'I glorified God in my heart, in whom I trusted.' These words had been impressed on my mind from the very day I was forced from Deptford to the present hour, and I now saw them, as I thought, fulfilled and verified. My imagination was all rapture as I flew to the Register Office; and, in this respect, like the apostle Peter, (whose deliverance from prison was so sudden and extraordinary, that he thought he was in a vision,) I could scarcely believe I was awake. Heavens! who could do justice to my feelings at this moment! Not conquering heroes themselves, in the midst of a triumph—Not the tender mother who has just regained her long lost infant, and presses it to her heart—Not the weary hungry, mariner, at the sight of the desired friendly port—Not the lover, when he once more embraces his beloved mistress, after she has been ravished from his arms! All within my breast was tumult, wildness, and delirium! My feet scarcely touched the ground, for they were winged with joy; and, like Elijah, as he rose to Heaven, they 'were with lightning sped as I went on.' Every one I met I told of my happiness, and blazed about the virtue of my amiable master and captain. . . .

**[Although a free man, he continued to sail for King although the vessels bore slaves. In 1767 he departed for London, but soon took to the sea again, sailing to Turkey, Italy, the West Indies, and the North Pole, where he narrowly escaped a frozen death.]**

On the morning of the 6th of October, (I pray you to attend,) all that day, I thought I should either see or hear something supernatural. I had a secret impulse on my mind of something that was to take place, which drove me continually for that time to a Throne of Grace. It pleased God to enable me to wrestle with him, as Jacob did: I prayed that if sudden death were to happen, and I perished, it might be at Christ's feet.

In the evening of the same day, as I was reading and meditating on the 4th chapter of Acts, twelfth verse, under the solemn apprehensions of eternity, and reflecting on my past actions, I began to think I had lived a moral life, and that I had a proper ground to believe I had an interest in the divine favor; but still meditating on the subject, not knowing whether salvation was to be had partly for our own good deeds or solely as the sovereign gift of God;—in this deep consternation the Lord was pleased to break in upon my soul with his bright beams of heavenly light; and in an instant, as it were, removing the veil, and letting light into a dark place, I saw clearly with an eye of faith, the crucified Saviour bleeding on the cross on mount Calvary: the scriptures became an unsealed book, I saw myself a condemned criminal under the law, which came with its full force to my conscience, and when 'the commandment came sin revived, and I died.' I saw the Lord Jesus Christ in his humiliation, loaded and bearing my reproach, sin, and shame. I then clearly perceived that by the deeds of the law no flesh living could be justified. I was then convinced that by the first Adam sin came, and by the second Adam (the Lord Jesus Christ) all that are saved must be made alive. It was given me at that time to know what it was to be born again: John iii. 5. I saw the eighth chapter to the Romans, and the doctrines of God's decrees, verified agreeable to his eternal, everlasting, and unchangeable purposes. The word of God was sweet to my taste, yea, sweeter than honey and the honeycomb. Christ was revealed to my soul as the chiefest among ten thousand. These heavenly moments were really as life to the dead, and what John calls an earnest of the Spirit. (John xvi. 13, 14, &c.) This was indeed unspeakable, and I firmly believe undeniable by many. Now every leading providential circumstance that happened to me, from the day I was taken from my parents to that hour, was then in my view, as if it had but just then occurred. I was sensible of the invisible hand of God, which guided and protected me, when in truth I knew it not: still the Lord pursued me, although I slighted and disregarded it: this mercy melted me down. When I considered my poor wretched state I wept, seeing what a great debtor I was to sovereign free grace. Now the Ethiopian was willing to be saved by Jesus Christ, the sinner's only surety, and also to rely on none other person or thing for salvation. Self was obnoxious, and good works he had none, for it is God that worketh in us both to will and to do. Oh! the amazing things of that hour can never be told—it was joy in the Holy Ghost! I felt an astonishing change; the burden of sin, the gaping jaws of hell, and the fears of death, that weighed me down before, now lost their horror; indeed I thought death would now be the best earthly friend I ever had. Such were my grief and joy as I believe are seldom experienced I was bathed in tears, and said. What am I that God should thus look on me, the vilest of sinners? I felt a deep concern for my mother and friends, which occasioned me to pray with fresh ardor; and in the abyss of thought, I viewed the unconverted people of the world in a very awful state, being without God and without hope. . . .

In the spring of 1784, I thought of visiting old ocean again. In consequence of this I embarked as steward on board a fine new ship called the London, commanded by Martin Hopkin, and sailed for New York. I admired this city very much; it is large and well built, and abounds with provisions of all kinds. While we lay here a circumstance happened which I thought extremely singular. One day a malefactor was to be executed on a gallows; but with a condition that if any woman, having nothing on but her shift, married the man under the gallows, his life was to be saved. This extraordinary privilege was claimed; a woman presented herself, and the marriage ceremony was performed.

Our ship having got laden, we returned to London in January, 1785. When she was ready again for another voyage, the captain being an agreeable man, I sailed with him from hence in the spring, March 1785, for Philadelphia. On the 5th of April, we took our departure from the lands-end, with a pleasant gale; and about nine o'clock that night the moon shone bright, and the sea was smooth, while our ship was going free by the wind, at the rate of about four or five miles an hour. At this time another ship was going nearly as fast as we on the opposite point, meeting us right in the teeth, yet none on board observed either ship until we struck each other forcibly head and head, to the astonishment and consternation of both crews. She did us much damage, but I believe we did her more; for when we passed by each other, which we did very quickly, they called to us to bring to, and hoist out our boat, but we had enough to do to mind ourselves; and in about eight minutes we saw no more of her. We refitted as well as we could the next day, and proceeded on our voyage, and in May arrived at Philadelphia.

I was very glad to see this favorite old town once more; and my pleasure was much increased in seeing the worthy Quakers freeing and easing the burdens of many of my oppressed African brethren. It rejoiced my heart when one of these friendly people took me to see a free school, they had erected for every denomination of black people, whose minds are cultivated here, and forwarded to virtue; and thus they are made useful members of the community. Does not the success of this practice say loudly to the planters, in the language of scripture—'Go ye and do likewise.'. . .

I have only therefore to request the reader's indulgence and conclude. I am far from the vanity of thinking there is any merit in this narrative: I hope censure will be suspended, when it is considered that it was written by one, who was as unwilling, as unable, to adorn the plainness of truth by the coloring of imagination. My life and fortune have been extremely chequered, and my adventures various. Even those I have related are considerably abridged. If any incident in this little work should appear uninteresting and trifling to most readers, I can only say, as my excuse for mentioning it, that almost every event of my life made an impression on my mind, and influenced my conduct. I early accustomed myself to look for the hand of God in the minutest occurrence, and to learn from it a lesson of morality and religion; and in this light, every circumstance I have related, was to me, of importance. After all, what makes any event important, unless by its observation we become better and wiser, and learn 'to do justly, to love mercy, and to walk humbly before God?' To those who are possessed of this spirit, there is scarcely any book or incident so trifling, that does not afford some profit, while to others the experience of ages seems of no use; and even to pour out to them the treasures of wisdom is throwing the jewels of instruction away.

# BENJAMIN FRANKLIN
## 1706–1790

*Famous in his lifetime and in ours as a scientist, inventor, diplomat, printer, educator, philanthropist, philosopher, patriot, and social icon, Benjamin Franklin was the most prominent American of the eighteenth century. He helped create the new Republic by being the only person to sign its four great founding documents: the Declaration of Independence (1776), the Franco-American Alliance (1778), the Treaty of Paris (1783), and the U.S. Constitution (1787). Franklin also wrote the nation's first great book and with it introduced the genre of autobiography.*

*He did all this with only two years of formal education, dropping out of school for good at the age of ten. Born the fifteenth of seventeen children of a soap and candle maker in Boston, Franklin rose to personify national and individual success stories of rags to riches. Franklin and the country grew up together in power, wealth, and fame. That story is at the center of his autobiography, which concludes in 1759. Franklin wrote it between 1771 and 1790, the first part addressed to his son.*

*By 1757, and with the French and Indian War in progress, Franklin had made a fortune as a printer and as author of* Poor Richard's Almanack, *a colonial bestseller. He retired from business and threw himself completely into public affairs. Franklin understood that a community could achieve advantages for all its people only by pooling resources. Even before entering the public arena full time, his ideas on social responsibility were instrumental in founding the nation's first public library, fire company, and public hospital. He organized the American Philosophical Society and started an academy that became the University of Pennsylvania. Franklin was a competitive individualist whose belief in the hard work and virtue of the "Protestant Ethic" promoted capitalism.*

*For nearly twenty years, until 1775, Franklin represented Pennsylvania's interests in London and at home. Just prior to the American Revolution, he returned to Philadelphia and served as a delegate to the Second Continental Congress. Thereafter, he went to Paris to win French military and financial support in the fight against the British. The seventy-year-old Franklin charmed the French with his anecdotes, homilies, extraordinary mind, homespun clothes, and wigless head. He often wore a fur skin hat, bifocals of his own invention and carried a walking stick made of apple wood. Fashionable women and freemasons joined others in what became a cult following. Franklin advertised Americans as a people and America as a country that rewarded merit and despised hereditary aristocracy.*

*While Puritan Anne Bradstreet, Quaker Elizabeth Ashbridge, and missionary Tunis Campbell looked spiritually to God for deliverance, Deist Franklin helped develop Enlightenment ideas of self-made men bettering the world through good works of human initiative. Like Ashbridge, Franklin rejected the class stratification and Christianity of the Puritans; unlike Ashbridge, Franklin's gender was not a handicap to his aspirations.*

*Nor was his race. While Olaudah Equiano rejected an America that enslaved him, Franklin exemplified the American dream of success. His autobiography provides part of the story and can only be understood as part of the mosaic of distinct portraits and experiences informed by Bradstreet, Ashbridge, Equiano, Black Hawk, Crockett, and others. With the possible exception of Frederick Douglass's* Narrative, *Franklin's work remains the most influential and widely read autobiography in United States history and literature.*

*The reason is clear. One of Franklin's contemporaries, John Adams, once remarked that the American Revolution was not the war. The Revolution ended before the war commenced and was the change in sentiments in the hearts and minds of the people. Franklin was a life model of this development—the American revolutionized by the colonial experience—a "new man" in a New World.*

Autobiography. *1817. Reprint, London: J. M. Dent & Sons, Ltd., 1908.*

Having emerged from the poverty and obscurity in which I was born and bred, to a state of affluence and some degree of reputation in the world, and having gone so far through life with a considerable share of felicity, the conducing means I made use of, which with the blessing of God so well succeeded, my posterity may like to know, as they may find some of them unsuitable to their own situations, and therefore fit to be imitated.

That felicity, when I reflected on it, has induced me sometimes to say, that were it offered to my choice, I should have no objection to a repetition of the same life from its beginning, only asking the advantages authors have in a second edition to correct some faults of the first. So I might, besides correcting the faults, change some sinister accidents and events of it for others more favourable. But though this were denied, I should still accept the offer. Since such a repetition is not to be expected, the next thing most like living one's life over again seems to be a recollection of that life, and to make that recollection as durable as possible by putting it down in writing.

Hereby, too, I shall indulge the inclinations so natural in old men, to be talking of themselves and their own past actions; and I shall indulge it without being tiresome to others, who, through respect to age, might conceive themselves obliged to give me a hearing, since this may be read or not as any one pleases. And, lastly (I may as well confess it, since my denial of it will be believed by nobody), perhaps I shall a good deal gratify my own *vanity*. Indeed, I scarce ever heard or saw the introductory words, *'Without vanity I may say,'* etc., but some vain thing immediately followed. Most people dislike vanity in others, whatever share they have of it themselves; but I give it fair quarter wherever I meet with it, being persuaded that it is often productive of good to the possessor, and to others that are within his sphere of action; and therefore, in many cases, it would not be altogether absurd if a man were to thank God for his vanity among the other comforts of life.

And now I speak of thanking God, I desire with all humility to acknowledge that I owe the mentioned happiness of my past life to His kind providence, which led me to the means I used and gave them success. My belief of this induces me to *hope,* though I must not *presume,* that the same goodness will still be exercised toward me, in continuing that happiness, or enabling me to bear a fatal reverse, which I may experience as others have done; the complexion of my future fortune being known to Him only in whose power it is to bless to us even our afflictions. . . .

My grandfather Thomas, who was born in 1598, lived at Ecton till he grew too old to follow business longer, when he went to live with his son John, a dyer at Banbury, in Oxfordshire, with whom my father served an apprenticeship. There my grandfather died and lies buried. We saw his gravestone in1758. His eldest son Thomas lived in the house at Ecton, and left it with the land to his only child, a daughter, who, with her husband, one Fisher, of Wellingborough, sold it to Mr. Isted, now lord of the manor there. My grandfather had four sons that grew up, viz.: Thomas, John, Benjamin and Josiah. I will give you what account I can of them, at this distance from my papers, and if these are not lost in my absence, you will among them find many more particulars.

Thomas was bred a smith under his father; but, being ingenious, and encouraged in learning (as all my brothers were) by an Esquire Palmer, then the principal gentleman in that parish, he qualified himself for the business of scrivener; became a considerable man in the county; was a chief mover of all public-spirited undertakings for the county or town of Northampton, and his own village, of which many instances were related of him; and much taken notice of and patronized by the then Lord Halifax. He died in 1702, January 6, old style, just four years to a day before I was born. The account we received of his life and character from some old people at Ecton, I remember, struck you as something extraordinary, from its similarity to what you knew of mine. 'Had he died on the same day,' you said, 'one might have supposed a transmigration.'

John was bred a dyer, I believe of woolens. Benjamin was bred a silk dyer, serving an apprenticeship at London. He was an ingenious man. I remember him well, for when I was a boy he came over to my father in Boston, and lived in the house with us some years. He lived to a great age. His grandson, Samuel Franklin, now lives in Boston. He left behind him two quarto volumes, MS., of his own poetry, consisting of little occasional pieces addressed to his friends and relations, of which the following, sent to me, is a specimen. He had formed a short-hand of his own, which he taught me, but, never practising it, I have now forgot it. I was named after this uncle, there being a particular affection between him and my father. He was very pious, a great attender of sermons of the best preachers, which he took down in his short-hand, and had with him many volumes of them. He was also much of a politician; too much, perhaps, for his station. There fell lately into my hands, in London, a collection he had made of all the principal pamphlets relating to public affairs, from 1641 to 1717; many of the volumes are wanting as appears by the numbering, but there still remain eight volumes in folio, and twenty-four in quarto and in octavo. A dealer in old books met with them, and knowing me by my sometimes buying of him, he brought them to me. It

**BENJAMIN FRANKLIN**

seems my uncle must have left them here when he went to America, which was about fifty years since. There are many of his notes in the margins.

This obscure family of ours was early in the Reformation, and continued Protestants through the reign of Queen Mary, when they were sometimes in danger of trouble on account of their zeal against popery. They had got an English Bible, and to conceal and secure it, it was fastened open with tapes under and within the cover of a joint-stool. . . .

Josiah, my father, married young, and carried his wife with three children into New England, about 1682. The conventicles having been forbidden by law, and frequently disturbed, induced some considerable men of his acquaintance to remove to that country, and he was prevailed with to accompany them thither, where they expected to enjoy their mode of religion with freedom. By the same wife he had four children more born there, and by a second wife ten more, in all seventeen; of which I remember thirteen sitting at one time at his table, who all grew up to be men and women, and married; I was the youngest son, and the youngest child but two, and was born in Boston, New England. My mother, the second wife, was Abiah Folger, daughter of Peter Folger, one of the first settlers of New England, of whom honorable mention is made by Cotton Mather, in his church history of that country, entitled *Magnalia Christi Americana*, as 'a godly, learned Englishman,' if I remember the words rightly. I have heard that he wrote sundry small occasional pieces, but only one of them was printed, which I saw now many years since. It was written in 1675, in the homespun verse of that time and people, and addressed to those then concerned in the government there. It was in favor of liberty of conscience, and in behalf of the Baptists, Quakers, and other sectaries that had been under persecution, ascribing the Indian wars, and other distresses that had befallen the country, to that persecution, as so many judgments of God to punish so heinous an offense, and exhorting a repeal of those uncharitable laws. The whole appeared to me as written with a good deal of decent plainness and manly freedom. . . .

My elder brothers were all put apprentices to different trades. I was put to the grammar-school at eight years of age, my father intending to devote me, as the tithe of his sons, to the service of the Church. My early readiness in learning to read (which must have been very early, as I do not remember when I could not read), and the opinion of all his friends, that I should certainly make a good scholar, encouraged him in this purpose of his. My uncle Benjamin, too, approved of it, and proposed to give me all his short-hand volumes of sermons, I suppose as a stock to set up with, if I would learn his character. I continued, however, at the grammar-school not quite one year, though in that time I had risen gradually from the middle of the class of that year to be the head of it, and farther was removed into the next class above it, in order to go with that into the third at the end of the year. But my father, in the meantime, from a view of the expense of a college education, which having so large a family he could not well afford, and the mean living many so educated were afterwards able to obtain— reasons that he gave to his friends in my hearing—altered his first intention, took me from the grammar-school, and sent me to a school for writing and arithmetic, kept by a then famous man, Mr. George Brownell, very successful in his profession generally, and that by mild, encouraging methods. Under him I acquired fair writing pretty soon, but I failed in the arithmetic, and made no progress in it. At ten years old I was taken home to assist my father in his business, which was that of a tallow-chandler and sope-boiler; a business he was not bred to, but had assumed on his arrival in New England, and on finding his dying trade would not maintain his family, being in little request. Accordingly, I was employed in cutting wick for the candles, filling the dipping mold and the molds for cast candles, attending the shop, going on errands, etc.

I disliked the trade, and had a strong inclination for the sea, but my father declared against it; however, living near the water, I was much in and about it, learnt early to swim well, and to manage boats; and when in a boat or canoe with other boys, I was commonly allowed to govern, especially in any case of difficulty; and upon other occasions I was generally a leader among the boys, and sometimes led them into scrapes. . . .

I think you may like to know something of [my father's] person and character. He had an excellent constitution of body, was of middle stature, but well set, and very strong; he was ingenious, could draw prettily, was skilled a little in music, and had a clear pleasing voice, so that when he played psalm tunes on his violin and sung withal, as he sometimes did in an evening after the business of the day was over, it was extremely agreeable to hear. He had a mechanical genius too, and, on occasion, was very handy in the use of other tradesmen's tools; but his great excellence lay in a sound understanding and solid judgment in prudential matters, both in private and publick affairs. In the latter, indeed, he was never employed, the numerous family he had to educate and the straitness of his circumstances keeping him close to his trade; but I remember well his being frequently visited by leading people, who consulted him for his opinion in affairs of the town or of the church he belonged to, and showed a good deal of respect for his judgment and advice; he was also much consulted by private persons about their affairs when any difficulty occurred, and frequently chosen an arbitrator between contending parties. At his table he liked to have, as often as he could, some sensible friend or neighbor to converse with, and always took care to start some ingenious or useful topic for discourse, which might tend to improve the minds of his children. By this means he turned our attention to what was good, just, and prudent in the conduct of life; and little or no notice was ever taken of what related to the victuals on the table, whether it was well or ill dressed, in or out of season, of good or bad flavor, preferable or inferior to this or that other thing of the kind, so that I was brought up in such a perfect inattention to those matters as to be quite indifferent what kind of food was set before me, and so unobservant of it, that to this day if I am asked I can scarce tell a few hours after dinner what I dined upon. This has been a convenience to me in travelling, where my companions have been sometimes very unhappy for want of a suitable gratification of their more delicate, because better instructed, tastes and appetites.

My mother had likewise an excellent constitution: she suckled all her ten children. I never knew either my father or mother to have any sickness but that of which they dyed, he at 89, and she at 85 years of age. They lie buried together at Boston. . . .

From a child I was fond of reading, and all the little money that came into my hands was ever laid out in books. Pleased with the *Pilgrim's Progress,* my first collection was of John Bunyan's works in separate little volumes. I afterward sold them to enable me to buy R. Burton's *Historical Collections;* they were small chapmen's books, and cheap, 40 or 50 in all. My father's little library consisted chiefly of books in polemic divinity, most of which I read, and have since often regretted that, at a time when I had such a thirst for knowledge, more proper books had not fallen in my way, since it was now resolved I should not be a clergyman. Plutarch's Lives there was in which I read abundantly, and I still think that time spent to great advantage. There was also a book of De Foe's, called an *Essay on Projects,* and another of Dr. Mather's called *Essays to do Good,* which perhaps gave me a turn of thinking that had an influence on some of the principal future events of my life.

This bookish inclination at length determined my father to make me a printer, though he had already one son (James) of that profession. In 1717 my brother James returned from England with a press and letters to set up his business in Boston. I liked it much better than that of my father, but still had a hankering for the sea. To prevent the apprehended effect of such an inclination, my father was impatient to have me bound to my brother. I stood out some time, but at last was persuaded, and signed the indentures when I was yet but twelve years old. I was to serve as an apprentice till I was twenty-one years of age, only I was to be allowed journeyman's wages during the last year. In a little time I made great proficiency in the business, and became a useful hand to my brother. I now had access to better books. An acquaintance with the apprentices of booksellers enabled me sometimes to borrow a small one, which I was careful to return soon and clean. Often I sat up in my room reading the greatest part of the night, when the book was borrowed in the evening and to be returned early in the morning, lest it should be missed or wanted. . . .

When about 16 years of age I happened to meet with a book, written by one Tryon, recommending a vegetable diet. I determined to go into it. My brother, being yet unmarried, did not keep house, but boarded himself and his apprentices in another family. My refusing to eat flesh occasioned an inconveniency, and I was frequently chid for my singularity. I made myself acquainted with Tryon's manner of preparing some of his dishes, such as boiling potatoes or rice, making hasty pudding, and a few others, and then proposed to my brother, that if he would give me, weekly, half the money he paid for my board, I would board myself. He instantly agreed to it, and I presently found that I could save half what he paid me. This was an additional fund for buying books. But I had another advantage in it. My brother and the rest going from the printing-house to their meals, I remained there alone, and, despatching presently my light repast, which often was no more than a bisket or a slice of bread, a handful of raisins or a tart from the pastry-cook's, and a glass of water, had the rest of the time till their return for study, in which I made the greater progress, from that greater clearness of head and quicker apprehension which usually attended temperance in eating and drinking.

And now it was that, being on some occasion made ashamed of my ignorance in figures, which I had twice failed in learning when at school, I took Cocker's book of Arithmetick, and went through the whole by myself with great ease. I also read Seller's and Shermy's books of Navigation, and became acquainted with the little geometry they contain; but never proceeded far in that science. . . .

My brother had, in 1720 or 1721, begun to print a newspaper. It was the second that appeared in America, and was called the *New England Courant.* The only one before it was the *Boston News-Letter.* I remember his being dissuaded by some of his friends from the undertaking, as not likely to succeed, one newspaper being, in their judgment, enough for America. At this time (1771) there are not less than five-and-twenty. He went on, however, with the undertaking, and after having worked in composing the types and printing off the sheets, I was employed to carry the papers through the streets to the customers.

He had some ingenious men among his friends, who amused themselves by writing little pieces for this paper, which gained it credit and made it more in demand, and these gentlemen often visited us. Hearing their conversations, and their accounts of the approbation their papers were received with, I was excited to try my hand among them; but, being still a boy, and suspecting that my brother would object to printing anything of mine in his paper if he knew it to be mine, I contrived to disguise my hand, and, writing an anonymous paper, I put it in at night under the door of the printing-house. It was found in the morning, and communicated to his writing friends when they called in as usual. They read it, commented on it in my hearing, and I had the exquisite pleasure of finding it met with their approbation, and that, in their different guesses at the author, none were named but men of some character among us for learning and ingenuity. I suppose now that I was rather lucky in my judges, and that perhaps they were not really so very good ones as I then esteemed them.

Encouraged, however, by this, I wrote and conveyed in the same way to the press several more papers which were equally approved; and I kept my secret till my small fund of sense for such performances was pretty well exhausted, and then I discovered it, when I began to be considered a little more by my brother's acquaintance, and in a manner that did not quite please him, as he thought, probably with reason, that it tended to make me too vain. And, perhaps, this might be one occasion of the differences that we began to have about this time. Though a brother, he considered himself as my master, and me as his apprentice, and, accordingly, expected the same services from me as he would from another, while I thought he demeaned me too much in some he required of me, who from a brother expected more indulgence. Our disputes were often brought before our father, and I fancy I was either generally in the right, or else a better pleader, because the judgment was generally in my favor. But my brother was passionate, and had often beaten me, which I took extremely amiss; and, thinking my apprenticeship very tedious, I was continually wishing for some opportunity of shortening it, which at length offered in a manner unexpected.

One of the pieces in our newspaper on some political point, which I have now forgotten, gave offense to the Assembly. He was taken up, censured, and imprisoned for a month, by the speaker's warrant, I suppose, because he would not discover his author. I too was taken up and examined before the council; but, though I did not give them any satisfaction, they contented themselves with admonishing me, and dismissed me, considering me, perhaps, as an apprentice, who was bound to keep his master's secrets. . . .

**[At age 17, he broke with his brother and went to Philadelphia where he found work in a printing shop.]**

I believe I have omitted mentioning that, in my first voyage from Boston, being becalmed off Block Island, our people set about catching cod, and hauled up a great many. Hitherto I had stuck to my resolution of not eating animal food, and on this occasion I considered, with my master Tryon, the taking every fish as a kind of unprovoked murder, since none of them had, or ever could do us any injury that might justify the slaughter. All this seemed very reasonable. But I had formerly been a great lover of fish, and, when this came hot out of the frying-pan, it smelt admirably well. I balanced some time between principle and inclination, till I recollected that, when the fish were opened, I saw smaller fish taken out of their stomachs; then thought I, 'If you eat one another, I don't see why we mayn't eat you.' So I dined upon cod very heartily, and continued to eat with other people, returning only now and then occasionally to a vegetable diet. So convenient a thing is it to be a *reasonable creature,* since it enables one to find or make a reason for every thing one has a mind to do. . . .

> **[He courted Deborah Read, went to England and spent eighteen months working in two printing houses before returning to Philadelphia in 1726 to work in the mercantile store and printing shop owned by Wygate Keimer. In his absence, Read married a man who deserted her.]**

Before I enter upon my public appearance in business, it may be well to let you know the then state of my mind with regard to my principles and morals, that you may see how far those influenced the future events of my life. My parents had early given me religious impressions, and brought me through my childhood piously in the Dissenting way. But I was scarce fifteen, when, after doubting by turns of several points, as I found them disputed in the different books I read, I began to doubt of Revelation itself. Some books against Deism fell into my hands; they were said to be the substance of sermons preached at Boyle's Lectures. It happened that they wrought an effect on me quite contrary to what was intended by them; for the arguments of the Deists, which were quoted to be refuted, appeared to me much stronger than the refutations; in short, I soon became a thorough Deist. . . .

I grew convinced that *truth, sincerity* and *integrity* in dealings between man and man were of the utmost importance to the felicity of life; and I formed written resolutions, which still remain in my journal book, to practice them ever while I lived. Revelation had indeed no weight with me, as such; but I entertained an opinion that, though certain actions might not be bad *because* they were forbidden by it, or good *because* it commanded them, yet probably these actions might be forbidden *because* they were bad for us, or commanded *because* they were beneficial to us, in their own natures, all the circumstances of things considered. And this persuasion, with the kind hand of Providence, or some guardian angel, or accidental favorable circumstances and situations, or all together, preserved me, through this dangerous time of youth, and the hazardous situations I was sometimes in among strangers, remote from the eye and advice of my father, without any willful gross immorality or injustice, that might have been expected from my want of religion. I say willful, because the instances I have mentioned had something of *necessity* in them, from my youth, inexperience, and the knavery of others. I had therefore a tolerable character to begin the world with; I valued it properly, and determined to preserve it.

We [Franklin and a business partner] had not been long returned to Philadelphia before the new types arrived from London. We settled with Keimer, and left him by his consent before he heard of it. We found a house to hire near the market, and took it. To lessen the rent, which was then but twenty-four pounds a year, though I have since known it to let for seventy, we took in Thomas Godfrey, a glazier, and his family, who were to pay a considerable part of it to us, and we to board with them. We had scarce opened our letters and put our press in order, before George House, an acquaintance of mine, brought a countryman to us, whom he had met in the street inquiring for a printer. All our cash was now expended in the variety of particulars we had been obliged to procure, and this countryman's five shillings, being our first-fruits, and coming so seasonably, gave me more pleasure than any crown I have since earned; and the gratitude I felt toward House has made me often more ready than perhaps I should otherwise have been to assist young beginners.

There are croakers in every country, always boding its ruin. Such a one then lived in Philadelphia; a person of note, an elderly man, with a wise look and a very grave manner of speaking; his name was Samuel Mickle. This gentleman, a stranger to me, stopt one day at my door, and asked me if I was the young man who had lately opened a new printing-house. Being answered in the affirmative, he said he was sorry for me, because it was an expensive undertaking, and the expense would be lost; for Philadelphia was a sinking place, the people already half-bankrupts, or near being so; all appearances to the contrary, such as new buildings and the rise of rents, being to his certain knowledge fallacious; for they were, in fact, among the things that would soon ruin us. And he gave me such a detail of misfortunes now existing, or that were soon to exist, that he left me half melancholy. Had I known him before I engaged in this business, probably I never should have done it. This man continued to live in this decaying place, and to declaim in the same strain, refusing for many years to buy a house there, because all was going to destruction; and at last I had the pleasure of seeing him give five times as much for one as he might have bought it for when he first began his croaking.

I should have mentioned before, that, in the autumn of the preceding year, I had formed most of my ingenious acquaintance into a club of mutual improvement, which we called the JUNTO; we met on Friday evenings. The rules that I drew up required that every member, in his turn, should produce one or more queries on any point of Morals, Politics, or Natural Philosophy, to be discussed by the company; and once in three months produce and read an essay of his own writing, on any subject he pleased. Our debates were to be under the direction of a president, and to be conducted in the sincere spirit of inquiry after truth, without fondness for dispute, or desire of victory; and, to prevent warmth, all expressions of positiveness in opinions, or direct contradiction, were after some time made contraband, and prohibited under small pecuniary penalties. . . .

Our first papers made a quite different appearance from any before in the province; a better type, and better printed; but some spirited remarks of my writing, on the dispute then going on between Governor Burnet and the Massachusetts Assembly, struck the principal people, occasioned the paper and the manager of it to be much talked of, and in a few weeks brought them all to be our subscribers.

Their example was followed by many, and our number went on growing continually. This was one of the first good effects of my having learnt a little to scribble; another was, that the leading men, seeing a newspaper now in the hands of one who could also handle a pen, thought it convenient to oblige and encourage me. Bradford still printed the votes, and laws, and other publick business. He had printed an address of the House to the governor, in a coarse, blundering manner, we reprinted it elegantly and correctly, and sent one to every member. They were sensible of the difference: it strengthened the hands of our friends in the House, and they voted us their printers for the year ensuing. . . .

I now opened a little stationer's shop. I had in it blanks of all sorts, the correctest that ever appeared among us, being assisted in that by my friend Breintnal.

I had also paper, parchment, chapmen's books, etc. One Whitemash, a compositor I had known in London, an excellent workman, now came to me, and worked with me constantly and diligently; and I took an apprentice, the son of Aquila Rose.

I began now gradually to pay off the debt I was under for the printing-house. In order to secure my credit and character as a tradesman, I took care not only to be in *reality* industrious and frugal, but to avoid all appearances to the contrary. I drest plainly; I was seen at no places of idle diversion. I never went out a fishing or shooting; a book, indeed, sometimes debauched me from my work, but that was seldom, snug, and gave no scandal; and, to show that I was not above my business, I sometimes brought home the paper I purchased at the stores through the streets on a wheelbarrow. Thus being esteemed an industrious, thriving young man, and paying duly for what I bought, the merchants who imported stationery solicited my custom; others proposed supplying me with books, and I went on swimmingly. In the mean time, Keimer's credit and business declining daily, he was at last forced to sell his printing-house to satisfy his creditors. He went to Barbadoes, and there lived some years in very poor circumstances.

His apprentice, David Harry, whom I had instructed while I worked with him, set up in his place at Philadelphia, having bought his materials. I was at first apprehensive of a powerful rival in Harry, as his friends were very able, and had a good deal of interest. I therefore proposed a partnership to him, which he, fortunately for me, rejected with scorn. He was very proud, dressed like a gentleman, lived expensively, took much diversion and pleasure abroad, ran in debt, and neglected his business; upon which, all business left him; and, finding nothing to do, he followed Keimer to Barbadoes, taking the printing-house with him. There this apprentice employed his former master as a journeyman; they quarrelled often; Harry went continually behindhand, and at length was forced to sell his types and return to his country work in Pennsylvania. The person that brought them employed Keimer to use them, but in a few years he died.

There remained now no competitor with me at Philadelphia but the old one, Bradford; who was rich and easy, did a little printing now and then by straggling hands, but was not very anxious about the business. However, as he kept the post-office, it was imagined he had better opportunities of obtaining news; his paper was thought a better distributer of advertisements than mine, and therefore had many more, which was a profitable thing to him, and a disadvantage to me; for, though I did indeed receive and send papers by the post, yet the publick opinion was otherwise, for what I did send was by bribing the riders, who took them privately, Bradford being unkind enough to forbid it, which occasioned some resentment on my part; and I thought so meanly of him for it, that, when I afterward came into his situation, I took care never to imitate it.

I had hitherto continued to board with Godfrey, who lived in part of my house with his wife and children, and had one side of the shop for his glazier's business, though he worked little, being always absorbed in his mathematics. Mrs. Godfrey projected a match for me with a relation's daughter, took opportunities of bringing us often together, till a serious courtship on my part ensued, the girl being in herself very deserving. The old folks encouraged me by continual invitations to supper, and by leaving us together, till at length it was time to explain. Mrs. Godfrey managed our little treaty. I let her know that I expected as much money with their daughter as would pay off my remaining debt for the printing-house, which I believe was not then above a hundred pounds. She brought me word they had no such sum to spare; I said they might mortgage their house in the loan-office. The answer to this, after some days, was, that they did not approve the match; that, on inquiry of Bradford, they had been informed the printing business was not a profitable one; the types would soon be worn out, and more wanted; that S. Keimer and D. Harry had failed one after the other, and I should probably soon follow them; and, therefore, I was forbidden the house, and the daughter shut up.

Whether this was a real change of sentiment or only artifice, on a supposition of our being too far engaged in affection to retract, and therefore that we should steal a marriage, which would leave them at liberty to give or withhold what they pleased, I know not; but I suspected the latter, resented it, and went no more. Mrs. Godfrey brought me afterward some more favorable accounts of their disposition, and would have drawn me on again; but I declared absolutely my resolution to have nothing more to do with that family. This was resented by the Godfreys; we differed, and they removed, leaving me the whole house, and I resolved to take no more inmates.

But this affair having turned my thoughts to marriage, I looked round me and made overtures of acquaintance in other places; but soon found that, the business of a printer being generally thought a poor one, I was not to expect money with a wife, unless with such a one as I should not otherwise think agreeable. In the mean time, that hard-to-be-governed passion of youth hurried me frequently into intrigues with low women that fell in my way, which were attended with some expense and great inconvenience, besides a continual risque to my health by a distemper which of all things I dreaded, though by great good luck I escaped it. A friendly correspondence as neighbors and old acquaintances had continued between me and Mrs. Read's family, who all had a regard for me from the time of my first lodging in their house. I was often invited there and consulted in their affairs, wherein I sometimes was of service. I pitied poor Miss Read's unfortunate situation, who was generally dejected, seldom cheerful, and avoided company. I considered my giddiness and inconstancy when in London as in a great degree the cause of her unhappiness, though the mother was good enough to think the fault mroe her own than mine, as she had prevented our marrying before I went thither, and persuaded the other match in my absence. Our mutual affection was revived, but there were now great objections to our union. The match was indeed looked upon as invalid, a preceding wife being said to be living in England; this could not easily be proved, because of the distance; and, though there was a report of his death, it was not certain. Then, though it should be true, he had left many debts, which his successor might be called upon to pay. We ventured, however, over all these difficulties, and I took her to wife, September 1st, 1730. None of the inconveniences happened that we had apprehended; she proved a good and faithful helpmate, assisted me much by attending the shop; we throve together, and have ever mutually endeavoured to make each other happy. Thus I corrected that great erratum as well as I could.

About this time, our club meeting, not at a tavern, but in a little room of Mr. Grace's, set apart for that purpose, a proposition was made by me, that, since our books were often referred to in our disquisitions upon the queries, it might be convenient to us to have them altogether where we met, that upon occasion they might be consulted; and by thus clubbing our books to a common library, we should, while we liked to keep them together, have each of us the advantage of using the books of all the other members, which would be nearly as beneficial as if each owned the whole. It was liked and agreed to, and we filled one end of the room with such books as we could best spare. The number was not so great as we expected; and though they had been of great use, yet some inconveniences occurring for want of due care of them, the collection, after about a year, was separated, and each took his books home again.

And now I set on foot my first project of a public nature, that for a subscription library. I drew up the proposals, got them put into form by our great scrivener, Brockden, and, by the help of my friends in the Junto, procured fifty subscribers of forty shillings each to begin with, and ten shillings a year for fifty years, the term our company was to continue. We afterwards obtained a charter, the company being increased to one hundred: this was the mother of all the North American subscription libraries, now so numerous. It is become a great thing itself, and continually increasing. These libraries have improved the general conversation of the Americans, made the common tradesmen and farmers as intelligent as most gentlemen from other countries, and perhaps have contributed in some degree to the stand so generally made throughout the colonies in defence of their privileges.

*Mem°.* Thus far was written with the intention expressed in the beginning and therefore contains several little family anecdotes of no importance to others. . . .

**[What follows was written many years after in compliance with the advice contained in these letters, and accordingly intended for the public. The affairs of the Revolution occasioned the interruption. Franklin established the first colonial public library in Philadelphia by taking subscriptions and donations.]**

This library afforded me the means of improvement by constant study, for which I set apart an hour or two each day, and thus repaired in some degree the loss of the learned education my father once intended for me. Reading was the only amusement I allowed myself. I spent no time in taverns, games, or frolicks of any kind; and my industry in my business continued as indefatigable as it was necessary. I was indebted for my printing-house; I had a young family coming on to be educated, and I had to contend with for business two printers, who were established in the place before me. My circumstances, however, grew daily easier. My original habits of frugality continuing, and my father having, among his instructions to me when a boy, frequently repeated a proverb of Solomon, 'Seest thou a man diligent in his calling, he shall stand before kings, he shall not stand before mean men,' I from thence considered industry as a means of obtaining wealth and distinction, which encouraged me, though I did not think that I should ever literally *stand before kings,* which, however, has since happened; for I have stood before *five,* and even had the honour of sitting down with one, the King of Denmark, to dinner.

We have an English proverb that says, '*He that would thrive, must ask his wife.*' It was lucky for me that I had one as much disposed to industry and frugality as myself. She assisted me cheerfully in my business, folding and stitching pamphlets, tending shop, purchasing old linen rags for the paper-makers, etc., etc. We kept no idle servants, our table was plain and simple, our furniture of the cheapest. For instance, my breakfast was a long time bread and milk (no tea), and I ate it out of a two-penny earthen porringer, with a pewter spoon. But mark how luxury will enter families, and make a progress, in spite of principle: being called one morning to breakfast, I found it in a China bowl, with a spoon of silver! They had been bought for me without my knowledge by my wife, and had cost her the enormous sum of three-and-twenty shillings, for which she had no other excuse or apology to make, but that she thought *her* husband deserved a silver spoon and China bowl as well as any of his neighbors. This was the first appearance of plate and China in our house, which afterward, in a course of years, as our wealth increased, augmented gradually to several hundred pounds in value.

I had been religiously educated as a Presbyterian; and though some of the dogmas of that persuasion, such as *the eternal decrees of God, election, reprobation, etc.,* appeared to me unintelligible, others doubtful, and I early absented myself from the public assemblies of the sect, Sunday being my studying day, I never was without some religious principles. I never doubted, for instance, the existence of the Deity; that he made the world, and governed it by his Providence; that the most acceptable service of God was the doing good to man; that our souls are immortal; and that all crime will be punished, and virtue rewarded, either here or hereafter. These I esteemed the essentials of every religion; and, being to be found in all the religions we had in our country, I respected them all, though with different degrees of respect, as I found them more or less mixed with other articles, which, without any tendency to inspire, promote, or confirm morality, served principally to divide us, and make us unfriendly to one another. This respect to all, with an opinion that the worst had some good effects, induced me to avoid all discourse that might tend to lessen the good opinion another might have of his own religion; and as our province increased in people, and new places of worship were continually wanted, and generally erected by voluntary contribution, my mite for such purpose, whatever might be the sect, was never refused.

Though I seldom attended any public worship, I had still an opinion of its propriety, and of its utility when rightly conducted, and I regularly paid my annual subscription for the support of the only Presbyterian minister or meeting we had in Philadelphia. He used to visit me sometimes as a friend, and admonish me to attend his administrations, and I was now and then prevailed on to do so, once for five Sundays successively. Had he been in my opinion a good preacher, perhaps I might have continued, notwithstanding the occasion I had for the Sunday's leisure in my course of study; but his discourses were chiefly either polemic arguments, or explications of the peculiar doctrines of our sect, and were all to me very dry, uninteresting, and unedifying, since not a single moral principle was inculcated or enforced, their aim seeming to be rather to make us Presbyterians than good citizens.

At length he took for his text that verse of the fourth chapter of Philippians, *'Finally, brethren, whatsoever things are true, honest, just, pure, lovely, or of good report, if there be any virtue, or any praise, think on these things.'* And I imagined, in a sermon on such a text, we could not miss of having some morality. But he confined himself to five points only, as meant by the apostle, viz.:

1. Keeping holy the Sabbath day.
2. Being diligent in reading the holy Scriptures.
3. Attending duly the publick worship.
4. Partaking of the Sacrament.
5. Paying a due respect to God's ministers.

These might be all good things; but, as they were not the kind of good things that I expected from that text, I despaired of ever meeting with them from any other, was disgusted, and attended his preaching no more. I had some years before composed a little Liturgy, or form of prayer, for my own private use (viz., in 1728), entitled, *Articles of Belief and Acts of Religion.* I returned to the use of this, and went no more to the public assemblies. My conduct might be blameable, but I leave it, without attempting further to excuse it; my present purpose being to relate facts, and not to make apologies for them.

It was about this time I conceived the bold and arduous project of arriving at moral perfection. I wished to live without committing any fault at any time; I would conquer all that either natural inclination, custom, or company might lead me into. As I knew, or thought I knew, what was right and wrong, I did not see why I might not always do the one and avoid the other. But I soon found I had undertaken a task of more difficulty than I had imagined. While my care was employed in guarding against one fault, I was often surprised by another; habit took the advantage of inattention; inclination was sometimes too strong for reason. I concluded, at length, that the mere speculative conviction that it was our interest to be completely virtuous, was not sufficient to prevent our slipping; and that the contrary habits must be broken, and good ones acquired and established, before we can have any dependence on a steady, uniform rectitude of conduct. For this purpose I therefore contrived the following method.

In the various enumerations of the moral virtues I had met with in my reading, I found the catalogue more or less numerous, as different writers included more or fewer ideas under the same name. Temperance, for example, was by some confined to eating and drinking, while by others it was extended to mean the moderating every other pleasure, appetite, inclination, or passion, bodily or mental, even to our avarice and ambition. I proposed to myself, for the sake of clearness, to use rather more names, with fewer ideas annexed to each, than a few names with more ideas; and I included under thirteen names of virtues all that at that time occurred to me as necessary or desirable, and annexed to each a short precept, which fully expressed the extent I gave to its meaning.

### 1. Temperance
Eat not to dullness; drink not to elevation.

### 2. Silence
Speak not but what may benefit others or yourself; avoid trifling conversation.

### 3. Order
Let all your things have their places; let each part of your business have its time.

### 4. Resolution
Resolve to perform what you ought; perform without fail what you resolve.

### 5. Frugality
Make no expense but to do good to others or yourself; *i.e.,* waste nothing.

### 6. Industry
Lose no time; be always employed in something useful; cut off all unnecessary actions.

### 7. Sincerity
Use no hurtful deceit; think innocently and justly, and, if you speak, speak accordingly.

### 8. Justice
Wrong none by doing injuries, or omitting the benefits that are your duty.

### 9. Moderation
Avoid extremes; forbear resenting injuries so much as you think they deserve.

### 10. Cleanliness
Tolerate no uncleanliness in body, clothes, or habitation.

### 11. Tranquillity
Be not disturbed at trifles, or at accidents common or unavoidable.

### 12. Chastity
Rarely use venery but for health or offspring, never to dulness, weakness, or the injury of your own or another's peace or reputation.

### 13. Humility
Imitate Jesus and Socrates.

My intention being to acquire the *habitude* of all these virtues, I judged it would be well not to distract my attention by attempting the whole at once, but to fix it on one of them at a time; and, when I should be master of that, then to proceed to another, and so on, till I should have gone through the thirteen; and, as the previous acquisition of some might facilitate the acquisition of certain others, I arranged them with that view, as they stand above. Temperance first, as it tends to procure that coolness and clearness of head, which is so necessary where constant vigilance was to be kept up, and guard maintained against the unremitting attraction of ancient habits, and the force of perpetual temptations. This being acquired and established, Silence would be more easy; and my desire being to gain knowledge at the same time that I improved in virtue, and considering that in conversation it was obtained rather by the use of the ears than of the tongue, and therefore wishing to break a habit I was getting into of prattling, punning, and joking, which only made me acceptable to trifling company, I gave *Silence* the second place. This and the next *Order,* I expected would allow me more time for attending to my project and my studies. *Resolution,* once become habitual, would keep me firm in my endeavors to obtain all the subsequent virtues; *Frugality* and Industry freeing me from my remaining debt, and producing affluence and independence, would make more easy the practice of Sincerity and Justice, etc., etc. Conceiving then, that, agreeably to the advice of Pythagoras in his Golden Verses, daily examination would be necessary, I contrived the following method for conducting that examination.

I made a little book, in which I allotted a page for each of the virtues. I ruled each page with red ink, so as to have seven columns, one for each day of the week, marking each column with a letter for the day. I crossed these columns with thirteen red lines, marking the beginning of each line with the first letter of one of the virtues, on which line, and in its proper column, I might mark, by a little black spot, every fault I found upon examination to have been committed respecting that virtue upon that day.

I determined to give a week's strict attention to each of the virtues successively. Thus, in the first week, my great guard was to avoid every the least offence against *Temperance,* leaving the other virtues to their ordinary chance, only marking every evening the faults of the day. Thus, if in the first week I could keep my first line, marked T, clear of spots, I supposed the habit of that virtue so much strengthened, and its opposite weakened, that I might venture extending my attention to include the next, and for the following week keep both lines clear of spots. Proceeding thus to the last, I could go through a course compleat in thirteen weeks, and four courses in a year. And like him who, having a garden to weed, does not attempt to eradicate all the bad herbs at once, which would exceed his reach and his strength, but works on one of the beds at a time, and, having accomplished the first, proceeds to a second, so I should have, I hoped, the encouraging pleasure of seeing on my pages the progress I made in virtue, by clearing successively my lines of their spots, till in the end, by a number of courses, I should be happy in viewing a clean book, after a thirteen weeks' daily examination. . . .

The precept of *Order* requiring that *every part of my business should have its alloted time,* one page in my little book contained the following scheme of employment for the twenty-four hurs of a natural day.

| | | |
|---|---|---|
| THE MORNING | 5 | Rise, wash and address *Powerful* |
| *Question.* | 6 | *Goodness!* Contrive day's business, and |
| What good shall I do this | 7 | take the resolution of the day; prosecute |
| day? | | the present study, and breakfast. |
| | 8 | |
| | 9 | |
| | 10 | Work. |
| | 11 | |
| NOON | 12 | Read, or overlook my accounts, and |
| | 1 | dine. |
| | 2 | |
| | 3 | |
| | 4 | Work. |
| | 5 | |
| EVENING | 6 | Put things in their places. Supper. Music |
| *Question.* | 7 | or diversion, or conversation. |
| What good have I done to- | 8 | Examination of the day. |
| day? | 9 | |
| | 10 | |
| | 11 | |
| | 12 | |
| NIGHT | 1 | Sleep. |
| | 2 | |
| | 3 | |
| | 4 | |

I entered upon the execution of this plan for self-examination, and continued it with occasional intermissions for some time. I was surprised to find myself so much fuller of faults than I had imagined; but I had the satisfaction of seeing them diminish. To avoid the trouble of renewing now and then my little book, which, by scraping out the marks on the paper of old faults to make room for new ones in a new course, became full of holes, I transferred my tables and precepts to the ivory leaves of a memorandum book, on which the lines were drawn with red ink, that made a durable stain, and on those lines I marked my faults with a black-lead pencil, which marks I could easily wipe out with a wet sponge. After a while I went through one course only in a year, and afterward only one in several years, till at length I omitted them entirely, being employed in voyages and business abroad, with a multiplicity of affairs that interfered; but I always carried my little book with me.

My scheme of ORDER gave me the most trouble; and I found that, though it might be practicable where a man's business was such as to leave him the disposition of his time, that of a journeyman printer, for instance, it was not possible to be exactly observed by a master, who must mix with the world, and often receive people of business at their own hours. *Order,* too, with regard to places for things, papers, etc. I found extreamly difficult to acquire. I had not been early accustomed to it, and, having an exceeding good memory, I was not so sensible of the inconvenience attending want of method. This article, therefore, cost me so much painful attention, and my faults in it vexed me so much, and I made so little progress in amendment, and had such frequent relapses, that I was almost ready to give up the attempt, and content myself with a faulty character in that respect, like the man who, in buying an ax of a smith, my neighbour, desired to have the whole of its surface as bright as the edge. The smith consented to grind it bright for him if he would turn the wheel; he turned, while the smith pressed the broad face of the ax hard and heavily on the stone, which made the turning of it very fatiguing. The man came every now and then from the wheel to see how the work went on, and at length would take his ax as it was, without farther grinding. 'No,' said the smith, 'turn on, turn on; we shall have it bright by-and-by; as yet, it is only speckled.' 'Yes,' says the man, *'but I think I like a speckled ax best.'* And I believe this may have been the case with many, who, having, for want of some such means as I employed, found the difficulty of obtaining good and breaking bad habits in other points of vice and virtue, have given up the struggle, and concluded that *'a speckled ax was best';* for something, that pretended to be reason, was every now and then suggesting to me that such extreme nicety as I exacted of myself might be a kind of foppery in morals, which, if it were known, would make me ridiculous; that a perfect character might be attended with the inconvenience of being envied and hatred; and that a benevolent man should allow a few faults in himself, to keep his friends in countenance.

In truth, I found myself incorrigible with respect to Order; and now I am grown old, and my memory bad, I feel very sensibly the want of it. But, on the whole, though I never arrived at the perfection I had been so ambitious of obtaining, but fell far short of it, yet I was, by the endeavor, a better and a happier man than I otherwise should have been if I had not attempted it; as those who aim at perfect writing by imitating the engraved copies, though they never reach the wished-for excellence of those copies, their hand is mended by the endeavor, and is tolerable while it continues fair and legible.

It may be well my posterity should be informed that to this little artifice, with the blessing of God, their ancestor owed the constant felicity of his life, down to his 79th year, in which this is written. What reverses may attend the remainder is in the hands of Providence; but, if they arrive, the reflection on past happiness enjoyed ought to help his bearing them with more resignation. To Temperance he ascribes his long-continued health, and what is still left to him of a good constitution; to Industry and Frugality, the early easiness of his circumstances and acquisition of his fortune, with all that knowledge that enabled him to be a useful citizen, and obtained for him some degree of reputation among the learned; to Sincerity and Justice, the confidence of his country, and the honorable employs it conferred upon him; and to the joint influence of the whole mass of the virtues, even in the imperfect state he was able to acquire them, all that evenness of temper, and that cheerfulness in conversation, which makes his company still sought for, and agreeable even to his younger acquaintance. I hope, therefore, that some of my descendants may follow the example and reap the benefit. . . .

My list of virtues contained at first but twelve; but a Quaker friend having kindly informed me that I was generally thought proud; that my pride showed itself frequently in conversation; that I was not content with being in the right when discussing any point, but was overbearing, and rather insolent, of which he convinced me by mentioning several instances; I determined endeavouring to cure myself, if I could, of this vice or folly among the rest, and I added *Humility* to my list, giving an extensive meaning to the word.

I cannot boast of much success in acquiring the *reality* of this virtue, but I had a good deal with regard to the *appearance* of it. I made it a rule to forbear all direct contradiction to the sentiments of others, and all positive assertion of my own. I even forbid myself, agreeably to the old laws of our Junto, the use of every word or expression in the language that imported a fixed opinion, such as *certainly, undoubtedly,* etc., and I adopted, instead of them, *I conceive, I apprehend,* or *I imagine* a thing to be so or so; or it *so appears to me at present.* When another asserted something that I thought an error, I denied myself the pleasure of contradicting him abruptly, and of showing immediately some absurdity in his proposition; and in answering I began by observing that in certain cases or circumstances his opinion would be right, but in the present case there *appeared* or *seemed* to me some difference, etc. I soon found the advantage of this change in my manner; the conversations I engaged in went on more pleasantly. The modest way in which I proposed my opinions procured them a readier reception and less contradiction; I had less mortification when I was found to be in the wrong, and I more easily prevailed with others to give up their mistakes and join with me when I happened to be in the right.

And this mode, which I at first put on with some violence to natural inclination, became at length so easy, and so habitual to me, that perhaps for these fifty years past no one has ever heard a dogmatical expression escape me. And to this habit (after my character of integrity) I think it principally owing that I had early so much weight with my fellow-citizens when I proposed new institutions, or alterations in the old, and so much influence in public councils when I became a member; for I was but a bad speaker, never eloquent, subject to much hesitation in my choice of words, hardly correct in language, and yet I generally carried my points.

In reality, there is, perhaps, no one of our natural passions so hard to subdue as *pride*. Disguise it, struggle with it, beat it down, stifle it, mortify it as much as one pleases, it is still alive, and will every now and then peep out and show itself; you will see it, perhaps, often in this history; for, even if I could conceive that I had completely overcome it, I should probably be proud of my humility. . . .

In 1732 I first published my Almanack, under the name of *Richard Saunders;*

it was continued by me about twenty-five years, commonly called *Poor Richard's Almanack*. I endeavored to make it both entertaining and useful, and it accordingly came to be in such demand, that I reaped considerable profit from it, vending annually near ten thousand. And observing that it was generally read, scarce any neighborhood in the province being without it, I considered it as a proper vehicle for conveying instruction among the common people, who bought scarcely any other books; I therefore filled all the little spaces that occurred between the remarkable days in the calendar with proverbial sentences, chiefly such as inculcated industry and frugality, as the means of procuring wealth, and thereby securing virtue, it being more difficult for a man in want, to act always honestly, as, to use here one of those proverbs, *it is hard for an empty sack to stand upright.*

These proverbs, which contained the wisdom of many ages and nations, I assembled and formed into a connected discourse prefixed to the Almanack of 1757, as the harangue of a wise old man to the people attending an auction. The bringing all these scattered counsels thus into a focus enabled them to make greater impression. The piece, being universally approved, was copied in all the newspapers of the Continent; reprinted in Britain on a broad side, to be stuck up in houses, two translations were made of it in French, and great numbers brought by the clergy and gentry, to distribute gratis among their poor parishioners and tenants. In Pennsylvania, as it discouraged useless expense in foreign superfluities, some thought it had its share of influence in producing that growing plenty of money which was observable for several years after its publication.

I considered my newspaper, also, as another means of communicating instruction, and in that view frequently reprinted in it extracts from the *Spectator,* and other moral writers; and sometimes published little pieces of my own, which had been first composed for reading in our Junto. Of these are a Socratic dialogue, tending to prove that, whatever might be his parts and abilities, a vicious man could not properly be called a man of sense; and a discourse on self-denial, showing that virtue was not secure till its practice became a habitude, and was free from the opposition of contrary inclinations. These may be found in the papers about the beginning of 1735.

In the conduct of my newspaper, I carefully excluded all libeling and personal abuse, which is of late years become so disgraceful to our country. Whenever I was solicited to insert any thing of that kind, and the writers pleaded, as they generally did, the liberty of the press, and that a newspaper was like a stage-coach, in which any one who would pay had a right to a place, my answer was, that I would print the piece separately if desired, and the author might have as many copies as he pleased to distribute himself, but that I would not take upon me to spread his detraction; and that, having contracted with my subscribers to furnish them with what might be either useful or entertaining, I could not fill their papers with private altercation, in which they had no concern, without doing them manifest injustice. Now, many of our printers make no scruple of gratifying the malice of individuals by false accusations of the fairest characters among ourselves, augmenting animosity even to the producing of duels; and are, moreover, so indiscreet as to print scurrilous reflections on the government of neighboring states, and even on the conduct of our best national allies, which may be attended with the most pernicious consequences. These things I mention as a caution to young printers, and that they may be encouraged not to pollute their presses and disgrace their profession by such infamous practices, but refuse steadily, as they may see by my example that such a course of conduct will not, on the whole, be injurious to their interests. . . .

I had begun in 1733 to study languages; I soon made myself so much a master of the French as to be able to read the books with ease. I then undertook the Italian. An acquaintance, who was also learning it, used often to tempt me to play chess with him. Finding this took up too much of the time I had to spare for study, I at length refused to play any more, unless on this condition, that the victor in every game should have a right to impose a task, either in parts of the grammar to be got by heart, or in translations, etc., which tasks the vanquished was to perform upon honour, before our next meeting. As we played pretty equally, we thus beat one another into that language. I afterwards with a little painstaking, acquired as much of the Spanish as to read their books also.

I have already mentioned that I had only one year's instruction in a Latin school, and that when very young, after which I neglected that language entirely. But, when I had attained an acquaintance with the French, Italian, and Spanish, I was surprized to find, on looking over a Latin Testament, that I understood so much more of that language than I had imagined, which encouraged me to apply myself again to the study of it, and I met with more success, as those preceding languages had greatly smoothed my way. . . .

**[In 1736, his four-year-old son died of smallpox and he got his start in politics as the clerk of the General Assembly.]**

I began now to turn my thoughts a little to public affairs, beginning, however, with small matters. The city watch was one of the first things that I conceived to want regulation. It was managed by the constables of the respective wards in turn; the constable warned a number of housekeepers to attend him for the night. Those who chose never to attend, paid him six shillings a year to be excused, which was supposed to be for hiring substitutes, but was, in reality, much more than was necessary for that purpose, and made the constableship a place of profit; and the constable, for a little drink, often got such ragamuffins about him as a watch, that respectable housekeepers did not choose to mix with. Walking the rounds, too, was often neglected, and most of the nights spent in tippling. I thereupon wrote a paper to be read in Junto, representing these irregularities, but insisting more particularly on the inequality of this six-shilling tax of the constables, respecting the circumstances of those who paid it, since a poor widow housekeeper, all whose property to be guarded by the watch did not perhaps exceed the value of fifty pounds, paid as much as the wealthiest merchant, who had thousands of pounds' worth of goods in his stores.

On the whole, I proposed as a more effectual watch, the hiring of proper men to serve constantly in that business; and as a more equitable way of supporting the charge, the levying a tax that should be proportioned to the property. This idea, being approved by the Junto, was communicated to the other clubs, but as arising in each of them; and though the plan was not immediately carried into execution, yet by preparing the minds of people for the change, it paved the way for the law obtained a few years after, when the members of our clubs were grown into more influence.

About this time I wrote a paper (first to be read in Junto, but it was afterward published) on the different accidents and carelessness by which houses were set on fire, with cautions against them, and means proposed of avoiding them. This was much spoken of as a useful piece, and gave rise to a project, which soon followed it, of forming a company for the more ready extinguishing of fires, and mutual assistance in removing and securing of goods when in danger. Associates in this scheme were presently found, amounting to thirty. Our articles of agreement obliged every member to keep always in good order, and fit for use, a certain number of leather buckets, with strong bags and baskets (for packing and trans- porting of goods), which were to be brought to every fire; and we agreed to meet once a month and spend a social evening together, in discoursing and communi- cating such ideas as occurred to us upon the subject of fires, as might be useful in our conduct on such occasions.

The utility of this institution soon appeared, and many more desiring to be admitted than we thought convenient for one company, they were advised to form another, which was accordingly done; and this went on, one new company being formed after another, till they became so numerous as to include most of the inhabitants who were men of property; and now, at the time of my writing this, though upward of fifty years since its establishment, that which I first formed, called the Union Fire Company, still subsists and flourishes, though the first members are all deceased but myself and one, who is older by a year than I am. The small fines that have been paid by members for absence at the monthly meet- ings have been applied to the purchase of fire-engines, ladders, fire-hooks, and other useful implements for each company, so that I question whether there is a city in the world better provided with the means of putting a stop to beginning conflagrations; and, in fact, since these institutions, the city has never lost by fire more than one or two houses at a time, and the flames have often been extin- guished before the house in which they began has been half consumed.

In 1739 arrived among us from Ireland the Reverend Mr. Whitefield, who had made himself remarkable there as an itinerant preacher. He was at first permitted to preach in some of our churches; but the clergy, taking a dislike to him, soon refused him their pulpits, and he was obliged to preach in the fields. The multi- tudes of all sects and denominations that attended his sermons were enormous, and it was matter of speculation to me, who was one of the number, to observe the extraordinary influence of his oratory on his hearers, and how much they admired and respected him, notwithstanding his common abuse of them, by assuring them they were naturally *half beasts and half devils*. It was wonderful to see the change soon made in the manners of our inhabitants. From being thought- less or indifferent about religion, it seemed as if all the world were growing reli- gious, so that one could not walk through the town in an evening without hearing psalms sung in different families of every street. . . .

I happened soon after to attend one of his sermons, in the course of which I perceived he intended to finish with a collection, and I silently resolved he should get nothing from me. I had in my pocket a handful of copper money, three or four silver dollars, and five pistoles in gold. As he proceeded I began to soften, and concluded to give the coppers. Another stroke of his oratory made me ashamed of that, and determined me to give the silver; and he finished so admirably that I emptied my pocket wholly into the collector's dish, gold and all. At this sermon there was also one of our club, who, being of my sentiments respecting the building in Georgia, and suspecting a collection might be intended, had, by precaution, emptied his pockets before he came from home. Towards the conclusion of the discourse, however, he felt a strong desire to give, and applied to a neighbour, who stood near him, to borrow some money for the purpose. The application was unfortunately [made] to perhaps the only man in the company who had the firmness not to be affected by the preacher. His answer was, '*At any other time, Friend Hopkinson, I would lend to thee freely; but not now, for thee seems to be out of thy right senses. . . .*'

**[Between 1742 and 1744, he invented the stove that bears his name, established the Philosophical Society, organized a 1200-man militia as defense against possible French and Spanish incursions, and established an academy that became the University of Pennsylvania.]**

When I disengaged myself, as above mentioned, from private business, I flattered myself that, by the sufficient though moderate fortune I had acquired, I had secured leisure during the rest of my life for philosophical studies and amusements. I purchased all Dr. Spence's apparatus, who had come from England to lecture here, and I proceeded in my *electrical experiments* with great alacrity; but the publick, now considering me as a man of leisure, laid hold of me for their purposes, every part of our civil government, and almost at the same time, imposing some duty upon me. The governor put me into the commission of the peace; the corporation of the city chose me of the common council, and soon after an alderman; and the citizens at large chose me a burgess to represent them in Assembly. This latter station was the more agreeable to me, as I was at length tired with sitting there to hear debates, in which, as clerk, I could take no part, and which were often so unentertaining that I was induced to amuse myself with making magic squares or circles, or any thing to avoid weariness; and I conceived my becoming a member would enlarge my power of doing good. I would not, however, insinuate that my ambition was not flatted by all these promotions; it certainly was; for, considering my low beginning, they were great things to me; and they were still more pleasing, as being so many spontaneous testimonies of the public good opinion, and by me entirely unsolicited.

The office of justice of the peace I tried a little, by attending a few courts, and sitting on the bench to hear causes; but finding that more knowledge of the common law than I possessed was necessary to act in that station with credit, I gradually withdrew from it, excusing myself by my being obliged to attend the higher duties of a legislator in the Assembly. My election to this trust was repeated every year for ten years, without my ever asking any elector for his vote, or signifying, either directly or indirectly, any desire of being chosen. On taking my seat in the House, my son was appointed their clerk.

The year following, a treaty being to be held with the Indians at Carlisle, the governor sent a message to the House, proposing that they should nominate some of their members, to be joined with some members of council, as commissioners for that purpose. The House named the speaker (Mr. Norris) and myself; and, being commissioned, we went to Carlisle, and met the Indians accordingly.

As those people are extremely apt to get drunk, and, when so, are very quarrelsome and disorderly, we strictly forbad the selling any liquor to them; and when they complained of this restriction, we told them that if they would continue sober during the treaty, we would give them plenty of rum when business was over. They promised this, and they kept their promise, because they could get no liquor, and the treaty was conducted very orderly, and concluded to mutual satis-faction. They then claimed and received the rum; this was in the afternoon: they were near one hundred men, women, and children, and were lodged in temporary cabins, built in the form of a square, just without the town. In the evening, hearing a great noise among them, the commissioners walked out to see what was the matter. We found they had made a great bonfire in the middle of the square; they were all drunk, men and women, quarreling and fighting. Their dark-coloured bodies, half naked, seen only by the gloomy light of the bonfire, running after and beating one another with firebrands, accompanied by their horrid yell-ings, formed a scene the most resembling our ideas of hell that could well be imag-ined; there was no appeasing the tumult, and we retired to our lodging. At midnight a number of them came thundering at our door, demanding more rum, of which we took no notice.

The next day, sensible they had misbehaved in giving us that disturbance, they sent three of their old counselors to make their apology. The orator acknowl-edged the fault, but laid it upon the rum; and then endeavored to excuse the rum by saying, *'The Great Spirit, who made all things, made every thing for some use, and whatever use he designed any thing for, that use it should always be put to. Now, when he made rum, he said, "Let this be for the Indians to get drunk with," and it must be so.'* And, indeed, if it be the design of Providence to extirpate these savages in order to make room for cultivators of the earth, it seems not improb-able that rum may be the appointed means. It has already annihilated all the tribes who formerly inhabited the sea-coast. . . .

**[Franklin helped establish the first public hospital in the colonies and persuaded the Assembly to pave the streets and erect street lights. He became deputy postmaster general for the northern colonies in 1753.]**

In 1754, war with France being again apprehended, a congress of commissioners from the different colonies was, by order of the Lord of Trade, to be assembled at Albany, there to confer with the chiefs of the Six Nations concerning the means of defending both their country and ours. Governor Hamilton, having received his order, acquainted the House with it, requesting they would furnish proper pres-ents for the Indians, to be given on this occasion; and naming the speaker (Mr. Norris) and myself to join Mr. Thomas Penn and Mr. Secretary Peters as commis-sioners to act for Pennsylvania. The House approved the nomination, and provided the goods for the present, and though they did not much like treating out of the provinces; and we met the other commissioners at Albany about the middle of June.

In our way thither, I projected and drew a plan for the union of all the colonies under one government, so far as might be necessary for defense, and other impor-tant general purposes. As we passed through New York, I had there shown my project to Mr. James Alexander, and Mr. Kennedy, two gentlemen of great knowledge in public affairs, and, being fortified by their approbation, I ventured to lay it before the Congress. It then appeared that several of the commissioners had formed plans of the same kind. A previous question was first taken, whether a union should be established, which passed in the affirmative unanimously. A committee was then appointed, one member from each colony, to consider the several plans and report. Mine happened to be preferred, and, with a few amend-ments, was accordingly reported.

By this plan the general government was to be administered by a president-general, appointed and supported by the crown, and a grand council was to be chosen by the representatives of the people of the several colonies, met in their respective assemblies. The debates upon it in Congress went on daily, hand in hand with the Indian business. Many objections and difficulties were started, but at length they were all overcome, and the plan was unanimously agreed to, and copies ordered to be transmitted to the Board of Trade and to the assemblies of the several provinces. Its fate was singular: the assemblies did not adopt it, as they all thought there was too much *prerogative* in it, and in England it was judged to have too much of the *democratic*. The Board of Trade therefore did not approve of it, nor recommend it for the approbation of his majesty; but another scheme was formed, supposed to answer the same purpose better, whereby the governors of the provinces, with some members of their respective councils, were to meet and order the raising of troops, building of forts, etc., and to draw on the treasury of Great Britain for the expense, which was afterwards to be refunded by an act of Parliament laying a tax on America. My plan, with my reasons in support of it, is to be found among my political papers that are printed.

Being the winter following in Boston, I had much conversation with Governor Shirley upon both the plans. Part of what passed between us on the occasion may also be seen among those papers. The different and contrary reasons of dislike to my plan makes me suspect that it was really the true medium; and I am still of opinion it would have been happy for both sides the water if it had been adopted. The colonies, so united, would have been sufficiently strong to have defended themselves; there would then have been no need of troops from England; of course, the subsequent pretence for taxing America, and the bloody contest it occasioned, would have been avoided. But such mistakes are not new; history is full of the errors of states and princes. . . .

[During the French and Indian War, he aided the British and American effort and offered Gen. Braddock advice on the Iroquois style of fighting. Braddock took offense and told Franklin: "These savages may, indeed, be a formidable enemy to your raw American militia, but upon the king's regular and disciplined troops, sir, it is impossible they should make any impression." The Iroquois attacked and killed 714 of Braddock's 1100 men as he marched toward Ft. Duquesne. Colonel Franklin took charge of recruiting militia and establishing forts on the northwestern frontier of Pennsylvania before sailing to London in 1757 to petition the king to side with the Assembly against the Royal Governor in a monetary dispute.]

# DAVID CROCKETT
## 1786–1836

*Davy Crockett had less than 100 days of formal education. Yet his "Narrative" prepared the way for a new style of American literature, Southwestern Humor, with its emphasis on the picturesque setting, localized speech, and tall tales of the backcountry. Optimistic reading audiences of the early republic craved success stories of "man in" or "man over" nature. Crockett provided the secular example of a Southern poorwhite-made-good. Rough to the core, he could triumph over "savages" and aristocrats alike. He could outtalk, outshoot, outdrink, and outstare anybody.*

*Crockett engaged Thomas Chilton, a U.S. Representative from Kentucky, to help him write his story. It is not that Crockett couldn't write himself, he could—and elegantly—but part of Crockett's appeal was the anti-intellectual populist idea: "well, maybe I can't write, but I can shoot and I can think." Crockett became the Whig's counter to Andrew Jackson, who also claimed Tennessee as home. Crockett the Whig was equal to Jackson the Democrat in his ability to represent the common man in rhetoric, if not reality. Crockett was the individualistic natural man in a racoon-tailed cap.*

*Crockett spent his youth moving westward with his family and being hired out by his father to work for neighbors. During the Creek War (part of the War of 1812), he established himself as a proficient Indian killer. He parlayed that fame—and his ability to use metaphor and tall tales—into a political career. In the Age of Jackson, Crockett opposed the Indian Removal Bill (1830) and supported the Bank of the United States. He sat in Congress in 1827, 1829 and 1833; he failed to get a seat in 1825, 1831 and 1835. His autobiography was politically motivated.*

*His political autobiography pulled from the earthy style of Franklin, but he added hillbilly twang to his narrative. Crockett was as far removed from genteel civilization as Franklin was in it. But Crockett was cultured and could fit easily into Congressional discussions and cocktail parties. To be elected to Congress though, he had to make the cork float in Tennessee waters. He had to create myth. Like Franklin, Crockett played up his Americanism as a plain, practical, self-made man. Franklin dressed his part by wearing homespun, Crockett preferred buckskin.*

*Franklin, the scientist, author of "Poor Richard's Almanack," man of the world, and founder of the Republic, was toasted as a hero in Philadelphia and Paris. Crockett, the realist, slave speculator, man of the woods and Indian killer, drank whisky and helped push white America across the Appalachian mountains toward the Mississippi River. He became a legendary figure while he lived. His death alongside others at the Alamo had much to do with stirring up sentiment for the war with Mexico. Like Daniel Boone, Jim Bridger, and Natty Bumpo, he is symbol and reality of the white American frontiersman.*

A Narrative of the Life of David Crockett of the State of Tennessee, Writter by Himself. *Philadelphia: 1834; reprint, New Haven: College and University Press, 1972.*

In the following pages I have endeavoured to give the reader a plain, honest, homespun account of my state in life, and some few of the difficulties which have attended me along its journey, down to this time. I am perfectly aware, that I have related many small and, as I fear, uninteresting circumstances; but if so, my apology is, that it was rendered necessary by a desire to link the different periods of my life together, as they have passed, from my childhood onward, and thereby to enable the reader to select such parts of it as he may relish most, if, indeed, there is any thing in it which may suit his palate.

I have also been operated on by another consideration. It is this:—I know, that obscure as I am, my name is making a considerable deal of fuss in the world. I can't tell why it is, nor in what it is to end. Go where I will, everybody seems anxious to get a peep at me; and it would be hard to tell which would have the advantage, if I, and the "Government," and "Black Hawk," and a great eternal big caravan of *wild varments* were all to be showed at the same time in four different parts of any of the big cities in the nation. I am not so sure that I shouldn't get the most custom of any of the crew. There must therefore be something in me, or about me, that attracts attention, which is even mysterious to myself. I can't understand it, and I therefore put all the facts down, leaving the reader free to take his choice of them.

On the subject of my style, it is bad enough, in all conscience, to please critics, if that is what they are after. They are a sort of vermin, though, that I sha'n't even so much as stop to brush off. If they want to work on my book, just let them go ahead; and after they are done, they had better blot out all their criticisms, than to know what opinion I would express of *them* and by what sort of a curious name I would call *them,* if I was standing near them, and looking over their shoulders. They will, at most, have only their trouble for their pay. But I rather expect I shall have them on my side.

But I don't know of any thing in my book to be criticised on by honourable men. Is it on my spelling? that's not my trade. Is it on my grammar?—I hadn't time to learn it, and make no pretensions to it. Is it on the order and arrangement of my book?—I never wrote one before, and never read very many; and, of course, know mighty little about that. Will it be on the authorship of the book?—this I claim, and I'll hang on to it, like a wax plaster. The whole book is my own, and every sentiment and sentence in it. I would not be such a fool, or knave either, as to deny that I have had it hastily run over by a friend or so, and that some little alterations have been made in the spelling and grammar; and I am not so sure that it is not the worse of even that, for I despise this way of spelling contrary to nature. And as for grammar, it's pretty much a thing of nothing at last, after all the fuss that's made about it. In some places, I wouldn't suffer either the

**DAVID CROCKETT**

spelling, or grammar, or any thing else to be touch'd; and therefore it will be found in my own way.

But if any body complains that I have had it looked over, I can only say to him, her, or them—as the case may be—that while critics were learning grammar, and learned to spell, I, and "Doctor Jackson, L.L.D." were fighting in the wars; and if our books, and messages, and proclamations, and cabinet writings, and so forth, and so on, should need a little looking over, and a little correcting of the spelling and the grammar to make them fit for use, it's just nobody's business. Big men have more important matters to attend to than crossing their *t*'s—, and dotting their *i*'s—, and such like small things. But the "Government's" name is to the proclamation, and my name's to the book; and if I didn't write the book, the "Government" didn't write the proclamation, which no man *dares to deny*!

But just read for yourself, and my ears for a heel tap, if before you get through you don't say, with many a goodnatured smile and hearty laugh, "This is truly the very thing itself—the exact image of its Author." . . .

My father's name was John Crockett, and he was of Irish descent. He was either born in Ireland or on a passage from that country to America across the Atlantic. He was by profession a farmer, and spent the early part of his life in the state of Pennsylvania. The name of my mother was Rebecca Hawkins. She was an American woman, born in the state of Maryland, between York and Baltimore. It is likely I may have heard where they were married, but if so, I have forgotten. It is, however, certain that they were, or else the public would never have been troubled with the history of David Crockett, their son.

I have an imperfect recollection of the part which I have understood my father took in the revoluntionary war. I personally know nothing about it, for it happened to be a little before my day; but from himself, and many others who were well acquainted with its troubles and afflictions, I have learned that he was a soldier in the revolutionary war, and took part in that bloody struggle. He fought, according to my information, in the battle at Kings Mountain against the British and tories, and in some other engagements of which my remembrance is too imperfect to enable me to speak with any certainty. At some time, though I cannot say certainly when, my father, as I have understood, lived in Lincoln county, in the state of North Carolina. How long, I don't know. But when he removed from there, he settled in that district of country which is now embraced in the east division of Tennessee, though it was not then erected into a state.

He settled there under dangerous circumstances, both to himself and his family, as the country was full of Indians, who were at the time very troublesome. By the Creeks, my grandfather and grandmother Crockett were both murdered, in their own house, and on the very spot of ground where Rogersville, in Hawkins county, now stands. At the same time, the Indians wounded Joseph Crockett, a brother to my father, by a ball, which broke his arm; and took James a prisoner, who was still a younger brother than Joseph, and who, from natural defects, was less able to make his escape, as he was both deaf and dumb. He remained with them for seventeen years and nine months, when he was discovered and recollected by my father and his eldest brother, William Crockett; and was purchased by them from an Indian trader, at a price which I do not now remember; but so it was, that he was delivered up to them, and they returned him to his relatives. He now lives in Cumberland county, in the state of Kentucky, though I have not seen him for many years.

My father and mother had six sons and three daughters. I was the fifth son.

What a pity I hadn't been the seventh! For then I might have been, by *common consent,* called *doctor,* as a heap of people get to be great men. But, like many of them, I stood no chance to become great in any other way than by accident. As my father was very poor, and living as he did *far back in the back woods,* he had neither the means nor the opportunity to give me, or any of the rest of his children, any learning.

But before I get on the subject of my own troubles, and a great many very funny things that have happened to me, like all other historians and biographers, I should not only inform the public that I was born, myself, as well as other folks, but that this important event took place, according to the best information I have received on the subject, on the 17th of August, in the year 1786; whether by day or night, I believe I never heard, but if I did, I have forgotten. I suppose, however, it is not very material to my present purpose, nor to the world, as the more important fact is well attested, that I was born; and, indeed, it might be inferred, from my present size and appearance, that I was pretty *well born,* though I have never yet attached myself to that numerous and worthy society. . . .

**[Crockett's family moved thrice within Tennessee and at 12, he helped drive a herd of cattle four hundred miles to Virginia.]**

[I went to] a little country school, which was kept in the neighborhood by a man whose name was Benjamin Kitchen; though I believe he was no way connected with the cabinet. I went four days, and had just began to learn my letters a little, when I had an unfortunate falling out with one of the scholars,—a boy much larger and older than myself. I knew well enough that though the school-house might do for a still hunt, it wouldn't do for *a drive,* and so I concluded to wait until I could get him out, and then I was determined to give him salt and vinegar. I waited till in the evening, and when the larger scholars were spelling, I slip'd out, and going some distance along his road, I lay by the way-side in the bushes, waiting for him to come along. After a while he and his company came on sure enough, and I pitched out from the bushes and set on him like a wild cat. I scratched his face all to a flitter jig, and soon made him cry out for quarters in good earnest. The fight being over, I went on home, and the next morning was started again to school but do you think I went? No, indeed. I was very clear of it; for I expected the master would lick me up, as bad as I had the boy. So, instead of going to the school-house, I laid out in the woods all day until in the evening the scholars were dismissed, and my brothers, who were also going to school, came along, returning home. I wanted to conceal this whole business from my father, and I therefore persuaded them not to tell on me, which they agreed to.

Things went on in this way for several days; I starting with them to school in the morning, and returning with them in the evening, but lying out in the woods all day. At last, however, the master wrote a note to my father, inquiring why I was not sent to school. When he read this note, he called me up, and I knew very well that I was in a devil of a hobble, for my father had been taking a few *horns,* and was in a good condition to make the fur fly. He called on me to know why I had not been at school? I told him I was afraid to go, and that the master would whip me; for I knew quite well if I was turned over to this old Kitchen, I should be cooked up to a cracklin, in little or no time. But I soon found that I was not to expect a much better fate at home; for my father told me, in a very angry manner, that he would whip me an eternal sight worse than the master, if I didn't start immediately to the school. I tried again to beg off; but nothing would do, but to go to the school. Finding me rather too slow about starting, he gathered about a two year old hickory, and broke after me. I put out with all my might, and soon we were both up to the top of our speed. We had a tolerable tough race for about a mile; but mind me, not on the school-house road, for I was trying to get as far the t'other way as possible. And I yet believe, if my father and the schoolmaster could both have levied on me about that time, I should never have been called on to sit in the councils of the nation, for I think they would have used me up. But fortunately for me, about this time, I saw just before me a hill, over which I made headway, like a young steamboat. As soon as I had passed over it, I turned to one side, and hid myself in the bushes. Here I waited until the old gentleman passed by, puffing and blowing, as tho' his steam was high enough to burst his boilers. I waited until he gave up the hunt, and passed back again: I then cut out, and went to the house of an acquaintance a few miles off, who was just about to start with a drove. His name was Jesse Cheek, and I hired myself to go with him, determining not to return home, as home and the school-house had both become too hot for me. . . .

**[He worked his way to Baltimore and back, staying away from home for more than two years.]**

I passed on until I arrived in Sullivan county, in the state of Tennessee, and there I met with my brother, who had gone with me when I started from home with the cattle drove.

I staid with him a few weeks, and then went on to my father's, which place I reached late in the evening. Several waggons were there for the night, and considerable company about the house. I enquired if I could stay all night, for I did not intend to make myself known, until I saw whether any of the family would find me out. I was told that I could stay, and went in, but had mighty little to say to any body. I had been gone so long, and had grown so much, that the family did not at first know me. And another, and perhaps a stronger reason was, they had no thought or expectation of me, for they all had long given me up for finally lost.

After a while, we were all called to supper. I went with the rest. We had sat down at the table and begun to eat, when my eldest sister recollected me: she sprung up, ran and seized me around the neck, and exclaimed, "Here is my lost brother."

My feelings at this time it would be vain and foolish for me to attempt to describe. I had often thought I felt before, and I suppose I had, but sure I am, I never had felt as I then did. The joy of my sisters and my mother, and, indeed, of all the family, was such that it humbled me, and made me sorry that I hadn't submitted to a hundred whippings, sooner than cause so much affliction as they had suffered on my account. I found the family had never heard a word of me from the time my brother left me. I was now almost *fifteen* years old; and my increased age and size, together with the joy of my father, occasioned by my unexpected return, I was sure would secure me against my long dreaded whipping; and so they did. But it will be a source of astonishment to many, who reflect that I am now a member of the American Congress,—the most enlightened body of men in the world,—that at so advanced an age, the age of fifteen, I did not know the first letter in the book.

I had remained for some short time at home with my father, when he informed me that he owed a man, whose name was Abraham Wilson, the sum of thirty-six dollars, and that if I would set in and work out the note, so as to lift it for him, he would discharge me from his service, and I might go free. I agreed to do this, and went immediately to the man who held my father's note, and contracted with him to work six months for it. I set in, and worked with all my might, not losing a single day in the six months. When my time was out, I got my father's note, and then declined working with the man any longer, though he wanted to hire me mighty bad. The reason was, it was a place where a heap of bad company met to drink and gamble, and I wanted to get away from them, for I know'd very well if I staid there, I should get a bad name, as nobody could be respectable that would live there. I therefore returned to my father, and gave him up his paper, which seemed to please him mightily, for though he was poor, he was an honest man, and always tried mighty hard to pay off his debts.

I next went to the house of an honest old Quaker, by the name of John Kennedy, who had removed from North Carolina, and proposed to hire myself to him, at two shillings a day. He agreed to take me a week on trial; at the end of which he appeared pleased with my work, and informed me that he held a note on my father for forty dollars, and that he would give me that note if I would work for him six months. I was certain enough that I should never get any part of the note; but then I remembered it was my father that owed it, and I concluded it was my duty as a child to help him along, and ease his lot as much as I could. I told the Quaker I would take him up at his offer, and immediately went to work. I never visited my father's house during the whole time of this engagement, though he lived only fifteen miles off. But when it was finished, and I had got the note, I borrowed one of my employer's horses, and, on a Sunday evening, went to pay my parents a visit. Some time after I got there, I pulled out the note and handed it to my father, who supposed Mr. Kennedy had sent it for collection. The old man looked mighty sorry, and said to me he had not the money to pay it, and didn't know what he should do. I then told him I had paid it for him, and it was then his own; that it was not presented for collection, but as a present from me. At this, he shed a heap of tears; and as soon as he got a little over it, he said he was sorry he couldn't give me any thing, but he was not able, he was too poor.

The next day, I went back to my old friend, the Quaker, and set in to work for him for some clothes; for I had now worked a year without getting any money at all, and my clothes were nearly all worn out, and what few I had left were mighty indifferent. I worked in this way for about two months; and in that time a young woman from North Carolina, who was the Quaker's niece, came on a visit to his house. And now I am just getting on a part of my history that I know I never can forget. For though I have heard people talk about hard loving, yet I reckon no poor devil in this world was ever cursed with such hard love as mine has always been, when it came on me. I soon found myself head over heels in love with this girl, whose name the public could make no use of; and I thought that if all the hills about there were pure chink, and all belonged to me, I would give them if I could just talk to her as I wanted to; but I was afraid to begin, for when I would think of saying any thing to her, my heart would begin to flutter like a duck in a puddle; and if I tried to outdo it and speak, it would get right smack up in my throat, and choak me like a cold potato. It bore on my mind in this way, till at last I concluded I must die if I didn't broach the subject; and so I determined to begin and hang on a trying to speak, till my heart would get out of my throat one way or t'other. And so one day at it I went, and after several trials I could say a little. I told her how well I loved her; that she was the darling object of my soul and body; and I must have her, or else I should pine down to nothing and just die away with the consumption.

I found my talk was not disagreeable to her; but she was an honest girl, and didn't want to deceive nobody. She told me she was engaged to her cousin, a son of the old Quaker. This news was worse to me than war, pestilence, or famine; but still I knowed I could not help myself. I saw quick enough my cake was dough, and I tried to cool off as fast as possible; but I had hardly safety pipes enough, as my love was so hot as mighty nigh to burst my boilers. But I didn't press my claims any more, seeing there was no chance to do any thing.

I began now to think, that all my misfortunes growed out of my want of learning. I had never been to school but four days, as the reader has already seen, and did not yet know a letter.

I thought I would try to go to school some; and as the Quaker had a married son, who was living about a mile and a half from him, and keeping a school, I proposed to him that I would go to school four days in the week, and work for him the other two, to pay my board and schooling. He agreed I might come on those terms; and so at it I went, learning and working back and forwards, until I had been with him nigh on to six months. In this time I learned to read a little in my primer, to write my own name, and to cypher some in the three first rules in figures. And this was all the schooling I ever had in my life, up to this day. I should have continued longer, if it hadn't been that I concluded I couldn't do any longer without a wife; and so I cut out to hunt me one.

**[He fell in love with two women. The first one disappointed him by marrying someone else; the second married him.]**

I found a family of very pretty little girls that I had known when very young. They had lived in the same neighborhood with me, and I had thought very well of them. I made an offer to one of them, whose name is nobody's business, no more than the Quaker girl's was, and I found she took it very well. I still continued paying my respects to her, until I got to love her as bad as I had the Quaker's niece; and I would have agreed to fight a whole regiment of wild cats if she would only have said she would have me. Several months passed in this way, during all of which time she continued very kind and friendly. At last, the son of the old Quaker and my first girl had concluded to bring their matter to a close, and my little queen and myself were called on to wait on them. We went on the day, and performed our duty as attendants. This made me worse than ever; and after it was over, I pressed my claim very hard on her, but she would still give me a sort of an evasive answer. However, I gave her mighty little peace, till she told me at last she would have me. I thought this was glorification enough, even without spectacles. I was then about eighteen years old. We fixed the time to be married. . . .

I remained a few days at my father's, and then went back to my new father-in-law's; where, to my surprise, I found my old Irish mother in the finest humour in the world.

She gave us two likely cows and calves, which, though it was a small marriage-portion, was still better than I had expected, and, indeed, it was about all I ever got. I rented a small farm and cabin, and went to work; but I had much trouble to find out a plan to get any thing to put in my house. At this time, my good old friend the Quaker came forward to my assistance, and gave me an order to a store for fifteen dollars' worth of such things as my little wife might choose. With this, we fixed up pretty grand, as we thought, and allowed to get on very well. My wife had a good wheel, and knowed exactly how to use it. She was also a good weaver, as most of the Irish are, whether men or women; and being very industrious with her wheel, she had, in little or no time, a fine web of cloth ready to make up; and she was good at that too, and at almost any thing else that a woman could do.

We worked on for some years, renting ground, and paying high rent, until I found it wasn't the thing it was cracked up to be; and that I couldn't make a fortune at it just at all. So I concluded to quit it, and cut out for some new country. In this time we had two sons, and I found I was better at increasing my family than my fortune. It was therefore the more necessary that I should hunt some better place to get along; and as I knowed I would have to move at some time, I thought it was better to do it before my family got too large, that I might have less to carry.

The Duck and Elk river country was just beginning to settle, and I determined to try that. I had now one old horse, and a couple of two year old colts. They were both broke to the halter, and my father-in-law proposed, that if I went, he would go with me, and take one horse to help me move. So we all fixed up, and I packed my two colts with as many of my things as they could bear; and away we went across the mountains. We got on well enough, and arrived safely in Lincoln county, on the head of the Mulberry fork of Elk river. I found this a very rich country, and so new, that game, of different sorts, was very plenty. It was here that I began to distinguish myself as a hunter, and to lay the foundation for all my future greatness; but mighty little did I know of what sort it was going to be. Of deer and smaller game I killed abundance; but the bear had been much hunted in those parts before, and were not so plenty as I could have wished. . . .

I was living ten miles below Winchester when the Creek war commenced; and as military men are making so much fuss in the world at this time, I must give an account of the part I took in the defence of the country. If it should make me president, why I can't help it; such things will sometimes happen; and my pluck is, never "to seek, nor decline office."

It is true, I had a little rather not; but yet, if the government can't get on without taking another president from Tennessee, to finish the work of "retrenchment and reform," why then, I reckon I must go in for it. But I must begin about the war, and leave the other matter for the people to begin on.

The Creek Indians had commenced their open hostilities by a most bloody butchery at Fort Mimms. There had been no war among us for so long, that but few, who were not too old to bear arms, knew any thing about the business. I, for one, had often thought about war, and had often heard it described; and I did verily believe in my own mind, that I couldn't fight in that way at all; but my after experience convinced me that this was all a notion. For when I heard of the mischief which was done at the fort, I instantly felt like going, and I had none of the dread of dying that I expected to feel. In a few days a general meeting of the militia was called for the purpose of raising volunteers; and when the day arrived for that meeting, my wife, who had heard me say I meant to go to the war, began to beg me not to turn out. She said she was a stranger in the parts where we lived, had no connexions living near her, and that she and our little children would be left in a lonesome and unhappy situation if I went away. It was mighty hard to go against such arguments as these; but my countrymen had been murdered, and I knew that the next thing would be, that the Indians would be scalping the women and children all about there, if we didn't put a stop to it. I reasoned the case with her as well as I could, and told her, that if every man would wait till his wife got willing for him to go to war, there would be no fighting done, until we would all be killed in our own houses; that I was as able to go as any man in the world; and that I believed it was a duty I owed to my country. Whether she was satisfied with this reasoning or not, she did not tell me; but seeing I was bent on it, all she did was to cry a little, and turn about to her work. The truth is, my dander was up, and nothing but war could bring it right again. . . .

About eight hundred of the volunteers, and of that number I was one, were now sent back, crossing the Tennessee river, and on through Huntsville, so as to cross the river again at another place, and to get on the Indians in another direction. After we passed Huntsville, we struck on the river at the Muscle Shoals, and at a place on them called Melton's Bluff. The river is here about two miles wide, and a rough bottom; so much so, indeed, in many places, as to be dangerous; and in fording it this time, we left several of the horses belonging to our men, with their feet fast in the crevices of the rocks. The men, whose horses were thus left, went ahead on foot. We pushed on till we got to what was called the Black Warrior's town, which stood near the very spot where Tuscaloosa now stands, which is the seat of government for the state of Alabama.

This Indian town was a large one; but when we arrived we found the Indians had all left it. There was a large field of corn standing out, and a pretty good supply in some cribs. There was also a fine quality of dried beans, which were very acceptable to us; and without delay we secured them as well as the corn, and then burned the town to ashes; after which we left the place.

In the field where we gathered the corn we saw plenty of fresh Indian tracks, and we had no doubt they had been scared off by our arrival. . . .

We then marched to a place, which we called Camp Wills; and here it was that Captain Cannon was promoted to a colonel, and Colonel Coffee to a general. We then marched to the Ten Islands, on the Coosa river, where we established a fort; and our spy companies were sent out. They soon made prisoners of Bob Catala and his warriors, and, in a few days afterwards, we heard of some Indians in a town about eight miles off. So we mounted our horses, and put out for that town, under the direction of two friendly Creeks we had taken for pilots. We had also a Cherokee colonel, Dick Brown, and some of his men with us. When we got near the town we divided; one of our pilots going with each division. And so we passed on each side of the town, keeping near to it, until our lines met on the far side. We then closed up at both ends, so as to surround it completely; and then we sent Captain Hammond's company of rangers to bring on the affray. He had advanced near the town, when the Indians saw him, and they raised the yell, and came running at him like so many red devils. The main army was now formed in a hollow square around the town, and they pursued Hammond till they came in reach of us. We then gave them a fire, and they returned it, and then ran back into their town. We began to close on the town by making our files closer and closer, and the Indians soon saw they were our property. So most of them wanted us to take them prisoners; and their squaws and all would run and take hold of any of us they could, and give themselves up. I saw seven squaws have hold of one man, which made me think of the Scriptures. So I hollered out the Scriptures was fulfilling; that there was seven women holding to one man's coat tail. But I believe it was a hunting-shirt all the time. We took them all prisoners that came out to us in this way; but I saw some warriors run into a house, until I counted forty-six of them. We pursued them until we got near the house, when we saw a squaw sitting in the door, and she placed her feet against the bow she had in her hand, and then took an arrow, and, raising her feet, she drew with all her might, and let fly at us, and she killed a man, whose name, I believe, was Moore. He was a lieutenant, and his death so enraged us all, that she was fired on, and had at least twenty balls blown through her. This was the first man I ever saw killed with a bow and arrow. We now shot them like dogs; and then set the house on fire, and burned it up with the forty-six warriors in it. I recollect seeing a boy who was shot down near the house. His arm and thigh was broken, and he was so near the burning house that the grease was stewing out of him. In this situation he was still trying to crawl along; but not a murmur escaped him, though he was only about twelve years old. So sullen is the Indian, when his dander is up, that he had sooner die than make a noise, or ask for quarters.

The number that we took prisoners, being added to the number we killed, amounted to one hundred and eighty-six; though I don't remember the exact number of either. We had five of our men killed. We then returned to our camp, at which our fort was erected, and known by the name of Fort Strother. No provisions had yet reached us, and we had now been for several days on half rations. However we went back to our Indian town on the next day, when many of the carcasses of the Indians were still to be seen. They looked very awful, for the burning had not entirely consumed them, but given them a very terrible appearance, at least what remained of them. It was, somehow or other, found out that the house had a potato cellar under it, and an immediate examination was made, for we were all as hungry as wolves. We found a fine chance of potatoes in it, and hunger compelled us to eat them, though I had a little rather not, if I could have helped it, for the oil of the Indians we had burned up on the day before had run down on them, and they looked like they had been stewed with fat meat. We then again returned to the army, and remained there for several days almost starving, as all our beef was gone. We commenced eating the beef-hides, and continued to eat every scrap we could lay our hands on. At length an Indian came to our guard one night, and hollered, and said he wanted to see "Captain Jackson." He was conducted to the general's markee, into which he entered, and in a few minutes we received orders to prepare for marching.

In an hour we were all ready, and took up the line of march. We crossed the Coosa river, and went on in the direction to Fort Taladega. When we arrived near the place, we met eleven hundred painted warriors, the very choice of the Creek nation. They had encamped near the fort, and had informed the friendly Indians who were in it, that if they didn't come out, and fight with them against the whites, they would take their fort and all their ammunition and provision. The friendly party asked three days to consider of it, and agreed that if on the third day they didn't come out ready to fight with them, they might take their fort. Thus they put them off. They then immediately started their runner to General Jackson, and he and the army pushed over, as I have just before stated.

The camp of warriors had their spies out, and discovered us coming, some time before we got to the fort. They then went to the friendly Indians, and told them Captain Jackson was coming, and had a great many fine horses, and blankets, and guns, and every thing else; and if they would come out and help to whip him, and to take his plunder, it should all be divided with those in the fort. They promised that when Jackson came, they would then come out and help to whip him. It was about an hour by sun in the morning, when we got near the fort. We were piloted by friendly Indians, and divided as we had done on a former occasion, so as to go to the right and left of the fort, and, consequently, of the warriors, who were camped near it. Our lines marched on, as before, till they met in front, and then closed in the rear, forming again into a hollow square. We then sent on old Major Russell, with his spy company, to bring on the battle; Capt. Evans' company went also. When they got near the fort, the top of it was lined with the friendly Indians, crying out as loud as they could roar, "How-dy-do, brother, how-dy-do?" They kept this up till Major Russell had passed by the fort, and was moving on towards the warriors. They were all painted as red as scarlet, and were just as naked as they were born. They had concealed themselves under the bank of a branch, that ran partly around the fort, in the manner of a half moon. Russell was going right into their circle, for he couldn't see them, while the Indians on the top of the fort were trying every plan to show him his danger. But he couldn't understand them. At last, two of them jumped from it, and ran, and took his horse by the bridle, and pointing to where they were, told him there were thousands of them lying under the bank. This brought them to a halt, and about this moment the Indians fired on them, and came rushing forth like a cloud of Egyptian locusts, and screaming like all the young devils had been turned loose, with the old devil of all at their head. Russell's company quit their horses, and took into the fort, and their horses ran up to our line, which was then in full view. The warriors then came yelling on, meeting us, and continued till they were within shot of us, when we fired and killed a considerable number of them. They then broke like a gang of steers, and ran across to our other line, where they were again fired on; and so we kept them running from one line to the other, constantly under a heavy fire, until we had killed upwards of four hundred of them. They fought with guns, and also with their bows and arrows; but at length they made their escape through a part of our line, which was made up of drafted militia, which broke ranks, and they passed. We lost fifteen of our men, as brave fellows as ever lived or died. We buried them all in one grave, and started back to our fort; but before we got there, two more of our men died of wounds they had received; making our total loss seventeen good fellows in that battle. . . .

**[In the War of 1812 he went to Florida to fight with a group of Americans and their Choctaw and Chickasaw allies against the Creek and British.]**

Nothing more, worthy of the reader's attention, transpired till I was safely landed at home once more with my wife and children. I found them all well and doing well; and though I was only a rough sort of a backwoodsman, they seemed mighty glad to see me, however little the quality folks might suppose it. For I do reckon we love as hard in the backwood country, as any people in the whole creation.

But I had been home only a few days, when we received orders to start again, and go on to the Black Warrior and Cahawba rivers, to see if there was no Indians there. I know'd well enough there was none, and I wasn't willing to trust my craw any more where there was neither any fighting to do, nor any thing to go on; and so I agreed to give a young man, who wanted to go, the balance of my wages if he would serve out my time, which was about a month. He did so, and when they returned, sure enough they hadn't seen an Indian any more than if they had been all the time chopping wood in my clearing. This closed my career as a warrior, and I am glad of it, for I like life now a heap better than I did then; and I am glad all over that I lived to see these times, which I should not have done if I had kept fooling along in war, and got used up at it. When I say I am glad, I just mean I am glad I am alive, for there is a confounded heap of things I an't glad of at all. I an't glad, for example, that the "government" moved the deposites, and if my military glory should take such a turn as to make me president after the general's time, I'll move them back; yes, I, the "government," will "take the responsibility," and move them back again. If I don't, I wish I may be shot.

But I am glad that I am now through war matters, and I reckon the reader is too, for they have no fun in them at all; and less if he had had to pass through them first, and then to write them afterwards. But for the dullness of their narrative, I must try to make amends by relating some of the curious things that happened to me in private life, and when *forced* to become a public man, as I shall have to be again, if ever I consent to take the presidential chair.

I continued at home now, working my farm for two years, as the war finally closed soon after I quit the service. The battle at New Orleans had already been fought, and treaties were made with the Indians which put a stop to their hostilities.

But in this time, I met with the hardest trial which ever falls to the lot of man. Death, that cruel leveller of all distinctions,—to whom the prayers and tears of husbands, and of even helpless infancy, are addressed in vain,—entered my humble cottage, and tore from my children an affectionate good mother, and from me a tender and loving wife.

It is a scene long gone by, and one which it would be supposed I had almost forgotten; yet when I turn my memory back on it, it seems as but the work of yesterday. It was the doing of the Almighty, whose ways are always right, though we sometimes think they fall heavily on us; and as painful as is even yet the remembrance of her sufferings, and the loss sustained by my little children and myself, yet I have no wish to lift up the voice of complaint. I was left with three children; the two oldest were sons, the youngest a daughter, and, at that time, a mere infant. It appeared to me, at that moment, that my situation was the worst in the world. I couldn't bear the thought of scattering my children, and so I got my youngest brother, who was also married, and his family to live with me. They took as good care of my children as they well could, but yet it wasn't all like the care of a mother. And though their company was to me in every respect like that of a brother and sister, yet it fell far short of being like that of a wife. So I came to the conclusion it wouldn't do, but that I must have another wife.

There lived in the neighbourhood, a widow lady whose husband had been killed in the war. She had two children, a son and daughter, and both quite small, like my own. I began to think, that as we were both in the same situation, it might be that we could do something for each other; and I therefore began to hint a little around the matter, as we were once and a while together. She was a good industrious woman, and owned a snug little farm, and lived quite comfortable. I soon began to pay my respects to her in real good earnest; but I was as sly about it as a fox when he is going to rob a hen-roost. I found that my company wasn't at all disagreeable to her; and I thought I could treat her children with so much friendship as to make her a good stepmother to mine, and in this I won't mistaken, as we soon bargained, and got married. . . .

The place on which I lived was sickly, and I was determined to leave it. I therefore set out the next fall to look at the country which had been purchased of the Chickasaw tribe of Indians. I went on to a place called Shoal Creek, about eighty miles from where I lived, and here again I got sick. I took the ague and fever, which I supposed was brought on me by camping out. I remained here for some time, as I was unable to go farther; and in that time, I became so well pleased with the country about there, that I resolved to settle in it. It was just only a little distance in the purchase, and no order had been established there; but I thought I could get along without order as well as any body else. And so I moved and settled myself down on the head of Shoal Creek. We remained here some two or three years, without any law at all; and so many bad characters began to flock in upon us, that we found it necessary to set up a sort of temporary government of our own. I don't mean that we made any president, and called him the "government," but we met and made what we called a corporation; and I reckon we called *it* wrong, for it wa'n't a bank, and hadn't any deposites; and now they call the bank a corporation. But be this as it may, we lived in the back-woods, and didn't profess to know much, and no doubt used many wrong words. But we met, and appointed magistrates and constables to keep order. We didn't fix any laws for them, tho'; for we supposed they would know law enough, whoever they might be; and so we left it to themselves to fix the laws.

I was appointed one of the magistrates; and when a man owed a debt, and wouldn't pay it, I and my constable ordered our warrant, and then he would take the man, and bring him before me for trial. I would give judgment against him, and then an order of an execution would easily scare the debt out of him. If any one was charged with marking his neighbour's hogs, or with stealing any thing, which happened pretty often in those days,—I would have him taken, and if there was tolerable grounds for the charge, I would have him well whip'd and cleared. We kept this up till our Legislature added us to the white settlements in Giles county, and appointed magistrates by law, to organize matters in the parts where I lived. They appointed nearly every man a magistrate who had belonged to our corporation. I was then, of course, made a squire according to law; though now the honour rested more heavily on me than before. For, at first, whenever I told my constable, says I—"Catch that fellow, and bring him up for trial"—away he went, and the fellow must come, dead or alive; for we considered this a good warrant, though it was only in verbal writings. But after I was appointed by the assembly, they told me, my warrants must be in real writing, and signed; and that I must keep a book, and write my proceedings in it. This was a hard business on me, for I could just barely write my own name; but to do this, and write the warrants too, was at least a huckleberry over my persimmon. I had a pretty well informed constable, however; and he aided me very much in this business. Indeed I had so much confidence in him, that I told him, when we should happen to be out anywhere, and see that a warrant was necessary, and would have a good effect, he need'nt take the trouble to come all the way to me to get one, but he could just fill out one; and then on the trial I could correct the whole business if he had committed any error. In this way I got on pretty well, till by care and attention I improved my handwriting in such manner as to be able to prepare my warrants, and keep my record book, without much difficulty. My judgments were never appealed from, and if they had been they would have stuck like wax, and I gave my decisions on the principles of common justice and honesty between man and man, and relied on natural born sense, and not on law, learning to guide me; for I had never read a page in a law book in all my life. . . .

The company had every thing to eat and drink that could be furnished in so new a country, and much fun and good humour prevailed. But before the regular frolic commenced, I mean the dancing, I was called on to make a speech as a candidate; which was a business I was as ignorant of as an outlandish negro.

A public document I had never seen, nor did I know there were such things; and how to begin I couldn't tell. I made many apologies, and tried to get off, for I know'd I had a man to run against who could speak prime, and I know'd, too, that I wa'n't able to shuffle and cut with him. He was there, and knowing my ignorance as well as I did myself, he also urged me to make a speech. The truth is, he thought my being a candidate was a mere matter of sport; and didn't think, for a moment, that he was in any danger from an ignorant back-woods bear hunter. But I found I couldn't get off, and so I determined just to go ahead, and leave it to chance what I should say. I got up and told the people, I reckoned they know'd what I come for, but if not, I could tell them. I had come for their votes, and if they didn't watch mighty close, I'd get them too. But the worst of all was, that I couldn't tell them any thing about government. I tried to speak about something, and I cared very little what, until I choked up as bad as if my mouth had been jam'd and cram'd chock full of dry mush. There the people stood, listening all the while, with their eyes, mouths and ears all open, to catch every word I would speak.

At last I told them I was like a fellow I had heard of not long before. He was beating on the head of an empty barrel near the road-side, when a traveler, who was passing along, asked him what he was doing that for? The fellow replied, that there was some cider in that barrel a few days before, and he was trying to see if there was any then, but if there was he couldn't get at it. I told them that there had been a little bit of a speech in me a while ago, but I believed I couldn't get it out. They all roared out in a mighty laugh, and I told some other anecdotes, equally amusing to them, and believing I had them in a first-rate way, I quit and got down, thanking the people for their attention. But I took care to remark that I was as dry as a powder horn, and that I thought it was time for us all to wet our whistles a little; and so I put off to the liquor stand, and was followed by the greater part of the crowd.

I felt certain this was necessary, for I knowed my competitor could open government matters to them as easy as he pleased. He had, however, mighty few left to hear him, as I continued with the crowd, now and then taking a horn, and telling good humoured stories, till he was done speaking. I found I was good for the votes at the hunt, and when we broke up, I went on to the town of Vernon, which was the same they wanted me to move. Here they pressed me again on the subject, and I found I could get either party by agreeing with them. But I told them I didn't know whether it would be right or not, and so couldn't promise either way.

Their court commenced on the next Monday, as the barbecue was on a Saturday, and the candidates for governor and for Congress, as well as my competitor and myself, all attended.

The thought of having to make a speech made my knees feel mighty weak, and set my heart to fluttering almost as bad as my first love scrape with the Quaker's niece. But as good luck would have it, these big candidates spoke nearly all day, and when they quit, the people were worn out with fatigue, which afforded me a good apology for not discussing the government. But I listened mighty close to them, and was learning pretty fast about political matters. When they were all done, I got up and told some laughable story, and quit. I found I was safe in those parts, and so I went home, and didn't go back again till after the election was over. But to cut this matter short, I was elected, doubling my competitor, and nine votes over.

A short time after this, I was in Pulaski, where I met with Colonel Polk, now a member of Congress from Tennessee. He was at that time a member elected to the Legislature, as well as myself; and in a large company he said to me, "Well, colonel, I suppose we shall have a radical change of the judiciary at the next session of the Legislature." "Very likely, sir," says I, and I put out quicker, for I was afraid some one would ask me what the judiciary was; and if I knowed I wish I may be shot. I don't indeed believe I had ever before heard that there was any such thing in all nature; but still I was not willing that the people there should know how ignorant I was about it.

When the time for meeting of the Legislature arrived, I went on; and before I had been there long, I could have told what the judiciary was, and what the government was too; and many other things that I had known nothing about before.

About this time I met with a very severe misfortune, which I may be pardoned for naming, as it made a great change in my circumstances, and kept me back very much in the world. I had built an extensive grist mill, and powder mill, all connected together, and also a large distillery. They had cost me upwards of three thousand dollars, more than I was worth in the world. The first news that I heard after I got to the Legislature, was, that my mills were—not blown up sky high, as you would guess, by my powder establishment,—but swept away all to smash by a large fresh, that came soon after I left home. I had, of course, to stop my distillery, as my grinding was broken up; and, indeed, I may say, that the misfortune just made a complete mash of me. I had some likely negroes, and a good stock of almost every thing about me, and, best of all, I had an honest wife. She didn't advise me, as is too fashionable, to smuggle up this, and that, and t'other, to go on at home; but she told me, says she, "Just pay up, as long as you have a bit's worth in the world; and then every body will be satisfied, and we will scuffle for more." This was just such talk as I wanted to hear, for a man's wife can hold him devlish uneasy, if she begins to scold, and fret, and perplex him, at a time when he has a full load for a rail-road car on his mind already. . . .

We turned in and cleared a field, and planted our corn; but it was so late in the spring, we had no time to make rails, and therefore we put no fence around our field. There was no stock, however, nor any thing else to disturb our corn, except the wild *varments;* and the old serpent himself, with a fence to help him, couldn't keep them out. I made corn enough to do me, and during that spring I killed ten bears, and a great abundance of deer. But in all this time, we saw the face of no white person in that country, except Mr. Owens' family, and a very few passengers, who went out there, looking at the country. Indians, though, were still plenty enough. Having laid by my crap, I went home, which was a distance of about a hundred and fifty miles; and when I got there, I was met by an order to attend a call-session of our Legislature. I attended it, and served out my time, and then returned, and took my family and what little plunder I had, and moved to where I had built my cabin, and made my crap.

I gathered my corn, and then set out for my Fall's hunt. This was in the last of October, 1822. I found bear very plenty, and, indeed, all sorts of game and wild varments, except buffalo. . . .

**[He hunted and killed "the [second] biggest bear that ever was seen in America." In 1823, he won election to the state legislature.]**

Col. Alexander was the representative in Congress of the district I lived in, and his vote on the tariff law of 1824 gave a mighty heap of dissatisfaction to his people. They therefore began to talk pretty strong of running me for Congress against him. At last I was called on by a good many to be a candidate. I told the people that I couldn't stand that; it was a step above my knowledge, and I know'd nothing about Congress matters.

However, I was obliged to agree to run, and myself and two other gentlemen came out. But Providence was a little against two of us this hunt, for it was the year that cotton brought twenty-five dollars a hundred; and so Colonel Alexander would get up and tell the people, it was all the good effect of this tariff law; that it had raised the price of their cotton, and that it would raise the price of every thing else they made to sell. I might as well have sung *psalms* over a dead horse, as to try to make the people believe otherwise; for they knowed their cotton had raised, sure enough, and if the colonel hadn't done it, they didn't know what had. So he rather made a mash of me this time, as he beat me exactly *two* votes, as they counted the polls, though I have always believed that many other things had been as fairly done as that same count.

He went on, and served out his term, and at the end of it cotton was down to *six* or *eight* dollars a hundred again; and I concluded I would try him once more, and see how it would go with cotton at the common price, and so I became a candidate.

But the reader, I expect, would have no objection to know a little about my employment during the two years while my competitor was in Congress. In this space I had some pretty tuff times, and will relate some few things that happened to me. So here goes, as the boy said when he run by himself.

In the fall of 1825, I concluded I would build two large boats, and load them with pipe staves for market. So I went down to the lake, which was about twenty-five miles from where I lived, and hired some hands to assist me, and went to work; some at boat building, and others to getting staves. I worked on with my hands till the bears got fat, and then I turned out to hunting, to lay in a supply of meat. I soon killed and salted down as many as were necessary for my family; but about this time one of my old neighbours, who had settled down on the lake about twenty-five miles from me, came to my house and told me he wanted me to go down and kill some bears about in his parts. He said they were extremely fat, and very plenty. I know'd that when they were fat, they were easily taken, for a fat bear can't run fast or long. But I asked a bear no favours, no way, further than civility, for I now had *eight* large dogs, and as fierce as painters; so that a bear stood no chance at all to get away from them. So I went home with him, and then went on down towards the Mississippi, and commenced hunting.

We were out two weeks, and in that time killed fifteen bears. Having now supplied my friend with plenty of meat, I engaged occasionally again with my hands in our boat building, and getting staves. But I at length couldn't stand it any longer without another hunt. So I concluded to take my little son, and cross over the lake, and take a hunt there. We got over, and that evening turned out and killed three bears, in little or no time. The next morning we drove up four forks, and made a sort of scaffold, on which we salted up our meat, so as to have it out of the reach of the wolves, for as soon as we would leave our camp, they would take possession. We had just eat our breakfast, when a company of hunters came to our camp, who had fourteen dogs, but all so poor, that when they would bark they would almost have to lean up against a tree and take a rest. I told them their dogs couldn't run in smell of a bear, and they had better stay at my camp, and feed them on the bones I had cut out of my meat. I left them there, and cut out; but I hadn't gone far, when my dogs took a first-rate start after a very large fat old *he-bear,* which run right plump towards my camp. I pursued on, but my other hunters had heard my dogs coming, and met them, and killed the bear before I got up with him. I gave him to them, and cut out again for a creek called Big Clover, which wa'n't very far off. Just as I got there, and was entering a cane brake, my dogs all broke and went ahead, and, in a little time, they raised a fuss in the cane, and seemed to be going every way. I listened a while, and found my dogs was in two companies, and that both was in a snorting fight. I sent my little son to one, and I broke for t'other. I got to mine first, and found my dogs had a two-year-old bear down, a-wooling away on him; so I just took out my big butcher, and went up and slap'd it into him, and killed him without shooting. There was five of the dogs in my company. In a short time, I heard my little son fire at his bear; when I went to him he had killed it too. He had two dogs in his team. Just at this moment we heard my other dog barking a short distance off, and all the rest immediately broke to him. We pushed on too; and when we got there, we found he had still a larger bear than either of them we had killed, treed by himself. We killed that one also, which made three we had killed in less than half an hour. We turned in and butchered them, and then started to hunt for water, and a good place to camp. But we had no sooner started, than our dogs took a start after another one, and away they went like a thunder-gust, and was out of hearing in a minute. We followed the way they had gone for some time, but at length we gave up the hope of finding them, and turned back. As we were going back, I came to where a poor fellow was grubbing, and he looked like the very picture of hard times. I asked him what he was doing away there in the woods by himself? He said he was grubbing for a man who intended to settle there; and the reason why he did it was, that he had no meat for his family, and he was working for a little.

I was mighty sorry for the poor fellow, for it was not only a hard, but a very slow way to get meat for a hungry family; so I told him if he would go with me, I would give him more meat than he could get by grubbing in a month. I intended to supply him with meat, and also to get him to assist my little boy in packing in and salting up my bears. He had never seen a bear killed in his life. I told him I had six killed then, and my dogs were hard after another. He went off to his little cabin, which was a short distance in the brush, and his wife was very anxious he should go with me. So we started and went to where I had left my three bears, and made a camp. We then gathered my meat and salted, and scaffled it, as I had done the other. Night now came on, but no word from my dogs yet. I afterwards found they had treed the bear about five miles off, near to a man's house, and had barked at it the whole enduring night. Poor fellows! many a time they looked for me, and wondered why I didn't come, for they knowed there was no mistake in me, and I know'd they were as good as ever fluttered. In the morning, as soon as it was light enough to see, the man took his gun and went to them, and shot the bear, and killed it. My dogs, however, wouldn't have any thing to say to this stranger; so they left him, and came early in the morning back to me.

We got our breakfast, and cut out again; and we killed four large and very fat bears that day. We hunted out the week, and in that time we killed seventeen, all of them first-rate. When we closed our hunt, I gave the man over a thousand weight of fine fat bear-meat, which pleased him mightily, and made him feel as rich as a Jew. I saw him the next fall, and he told me he had plenty of meat to do him the whole year from his week's hunt. My son and me now went home. This was the week between Christmas and New-year that we made this hunt. . . .

**[Crockett told tall tales about bear hunts and claimed to have killed 105 bears in one year's time.]**

I have, heretofore, informed the reader that I had determined to run this race to see what effect *the price of cotton* could have again on it. I now had Col. Alexander to run against once more, and also General William Arnold.

I had difficulties enough to fight against this time, as every one will suppose; for I had no money, and a very bad prospect, so far as I know'd, of getting any to help me along. I had, however, a good friend, who sent for me to come and see him. I went, and he was good enough to offer me some money to help me out. I borrowed as much as I thought I needed at the start, and went ahead. My friend also had a good deal of business about over the district at the different courts; and if he now and then slip'd in a good word for me, it is nobody's business. We frequently met at different places, and, as he thought I needed, he would occasionally hand me a little more cash; so I was able to buy a little of "the *creature,*" to put my friends in a good humour, as well as the other gentlemen, for they all treat in that country; not to get elected, of course—for that would be against the law; but just, as I before said, to make themselves and their friends feel their keeping a little.

Nobody ever did know how I got money to get along on, till after the election was over, and I had beat my competitors twenty-seven hundred and forty-eight votes. Even the price of cotton couldn't save my friend Aleck this time. My rich friend, who had been so good to me in the way of money, now sent for me, and loaned me a hundred dollars, and told me to go ahead; that that amount would bear my expenses to Congress, and I must then shift for myself. I came on to Washington, and draw'd two hundred and fifty dollars, and purchased with it a check on the bank at Nashville, and enclosed it to my friend; and I may say, in truth, I sent this money with a mighty good will, for I reckon nobody in this world loves a friend better than me, or remembers a kindness longer.

I have now given the close of the election, but I have skip'd entirely over the canvass, of which I will say a very few things in this place; as I know very well how to tell the truth, but not much about placing them in book order, so as to please critics.

Col. Alexander was a very clever fellow, and principal surveyor at that time; so much for one of the men I had to run against. My other competitor was a major-general in the militia, and an attorney-general at the law, and quite a smart, clever man also; and so it will be seen I had war work as well as law trick, to stand up under. Taking both together, they make a pretty considerable of a load for any one man to carry. But for war claims, I consider myself behind no man except "the government," and mighty little, if any, behind him; but this the people will have to determine hereafter, as I reckon it won't do to quit the work of "reform and retrenchment" yet for a spell.

But my two competitors seemed some little afraid of the influence of each other, but not to think me in their way at all. They, therefore, were generally working against each other, while I was going ahead for myself, and mixing among the people in the best way I could. I was as cunning as a little red fox, and wouldn't risk my tail in a "committal" trap.

I found the sign was good, almost everywhere I went. On one occasion, while we were in the eastern counties of the district, it happened that we all had to make a speech, and it fell on me to make the first one. I did so after my manner, and it turned pretty much on the old saying, "A short horse is soon curried," as I spoke not very long. Colonel Alexander followed me, and then General Arnold come on.

The general took much pains to reply to Alexander, but didn't so much as let on that there was any such candidate as myself at all. He had been speaking for a considerable time, when a large flock of guinea-fowls came very near to where he was, and set up the most unmerciful chattering that ever was heard, for they are a noisy little brute any way. They so confused the general, that he made a stop, and requested that they might be driven away. I let him finish his speech, and then walking up to him, said aloud, "Well, colonel, you are the first man I ever saw that understood the language of fowls." I told him that he had not had the politeness to name me in his speech, and that when my little friends, the guinea-fowls, had come up and began to holler "Crockett, Crockett, Crockett," he had been ungenerous enough to stop, and drive *them* away. This raised a universal shout among the people for me, and the general seemed mighty bad plagued. But he got more plagued than this at the polls in August, as I have stated before.

The election was in 1827, and I can say, on my conscience, that I was, without disguise, the friend and supporter of General Jackson, upon his principles as he laid them down, and as *"I understood them,"* before his election as president. During my two first sessions in Congress Mr. Adams was president, and I worked well with what was called the Jackson party pretty well. I was re-elected to Congress, in 1829, by an overwhelming majority; and soon after the commencement of this second term, I saw, or thought I did, that it was expected of me that I was to bow to the name of Andrew Jackson, and follow him in all his motions, and mindings, and turnings, even at the expense of my conscience and judgment. Such a thing was new to me, and a total stranger to my principles. I know'd well enough, though, that if I didn't "hurra" for his name, the hue and cry was to be raised against me, and I was to be sacrificed, if possible. His famous, or rather I should say his in-*famous*, Indian bill was brought forward, and I opposed it from the purest motives in the world. Several of my colleagues got around me, and told me how well they loved me, and that I was ruining myself. They said this was a favourite measure of the president, and I ought to go for it. I told them I believed it was a wicked, unjust measure, and that I should go against it, let the cost to myself be what it might; that I was willing to go with General Jackson in every thing that I believed was honest and right; but, further than this, I wouldn't go for him, or any other man in the whole creation; that I would sooner be honestly and politically d-nd, than hypocritically immortalized. I had been elected by a majority of three thousand five hundred and eighty-five votes, and I believed they were honest men, and wouldn't want me to vote for any unjust notion, to please Jackson or any one else; at any rate, I was of age, and was determined to trust them. I voted against this Indian bill and my conscience yet tells me that I gave a good honest vote, and one that I believe will not make me ashamed in the day of judgment. I served out my term, and though many amusing things happened, I am not disposed to swell my narrative by inserting them.

When it closed, and I returned home, I found the storm had raised against me sure enough; and it was echoed from side to side, and from end to end of my district, that I had turned against Jackson. This was considered the unpardonable sin. I was hunted down like a wild varment, and in this hunt every little newspaper in the district, and every little pin-hook lawyer was engaged. Indeed, they were ready to print any and every thing that the ingenuity of man could invent against me. Each editor was furnished with the journals of Congress from head-quarters; and hunted out every vote I had missed in four sessions, whether from sickness or not, no matter; and each one was charged against me at *eight* dollars. In all I had missed about *seventy* votes, which they made amount to five hundred and sixty dollars; and they contended I had swindled the government out of this sum, as I had received my pay, as other members do. I was now again a candidate in 1830, while all the attempts were making against me; and every one of these little papers kept up a constant war on me, fighting with every scurrilous report they could catch.

Over all I should have been elected, if it hadn't been, that but a few weeks before the election, the little four-pence-ha'penny limbs of the law fell on a plan to defeat me, which had the desired effect. They agreed to spread out over the district, and make appointments for me to speak, almost everywhere, to clear up the Jackson question. They would give me no notice of these appointments, and the people would meet in great crowds to hear what excuse Crockett had to make for quitting Jackson.

But instead of Crockett's being there, this small-fry of lawyers would be there, with their saddle-bags full of the little newspapers and their journals of Congress; and would get up and speak, and read their scurrilous attacks on me, and would tell the people that I was afraid to attend; and in this way would turn many against me. All this intrigue was kept a profound secret from me, till it was too late to counteract it; and when the election came, I had a majority in seventeen counties, putting all their votes together, but the eighteenth beat me; and so I was left out of Congress during those two years. The people of my district were induced, by these tricks, to take a stay on me for that time; but they have since found out that they were imposed on, and on re-considering my case, have reversed that decision; which, as the Dutchman said, "is as fair a ding as eber was."

When I last declared myself a candidate, I knew that the district would be divided by the Legislature before the election would come on; and I moreover knew, that from the geographical situation of the country, the county of Madison, which was very strong, and which was the country that had given the majority that had beat me in the former race, should be left off from my district.

But when the Legislature met, as I have been informed, and I have no doubt of the fact, Mr. Fitzgerald, my competitor, went up, and informed his friends in that body, that if Madison county was left off, he wouldn't run; for "that Crockett could beat Jackson himself in those parts, in any way they could fix it."

The liberal Legislature you know, of course, gave him that county; and it is too clear to admit of dispute, that it was done to make a mash of me. In order to make my district in this way, they had to form the southern district of a string of counties around three sides of mine, or very nearly so. Had my old district been properly divided, it would have made two nice ones, in convenient nice form. But as it is, they are certainly the most unreasonably laid off of any in the state, or perhaps in the nation, or even in the te-total creation.

However, when the election came on, the people of the district, and of

Madison county among the rest, seemed disposed to prove to Mr. Fitzgerald and the Jackson Legislature, that they were not to be transferred like hogs, and horses, and cattle in the market; and they determined that I shouldn't be broke down, though I had to carry Jackson, and the enemies of the bank, and the legislative works all at once. I had Mr. Fitzgerald, it is true, for my open competitor, but he was helped along by all his little lawyers again, headed by old Black Hawk, as he is sometimes called, (alias) Adam Huntsman, with all his talents for writing "*Chronicles,*" and such like foolish stuff.

But one good thing was, and I must record it, the papers in the district were now beginning to say "fair play a little," and they would publish on both sides of the question. The contest was a warm one, and the battle well-fought; but I gained the day, and the Jackson horse was left a little behind. When the polls were compared, it turned out I had beat Fitz just two hundred and two votes, having made a mash of all their intrigues. After all this, the reader will perceive that I am now here in Congress, this 28th day of January, in the year of our Lord one thousand eight hundred and thirty-four; and that, what is more agreeable to my feelings as a freeman, I am at liberty to vote as my conscience and judgment dictates to be right, without the yoke of any party on me, or the driver at my heels, with his whip in hand, commanding me to ge-wo-haw, just at his pleasure. Look at my arms, you will find no party hand-cuff on them! Look at my neck, you will not find there any collar, with the engraving

> MY DOG.
>
> ANDREW JACKSON.

But you will find me standing up to my rack, as the people's faithful representative, and the public's most obedient, very humble servant.

DAVID CROCKETT.

# BLACK HAWK
## 1767–1838

*Ma-Ka-Tai-Me-She-Kia-Kiak, better known as Black Hawk, was a Suak Indian who told his story to an interpreter, Antoine LeClair. LeClair in turn gave it to John Patterson, who put it into publication form. Black Hawk's life story became the first native American autobiography in the "as told to" tradition. It serves as antidote and reminder that white American success stories, like Franklin's and Crockett's, were predicated on the removal, death, and failure of red Americans.*

*Black Hawk became a chief by establishing himself as a warrior. He refused to allow encroachments and expansion onto hunting and farming lands claimed by his tribe. For years, he killed Cherokee, Creek, Osage, and Sioux enemies who interloped on that land. But those wars he understood as part of the natural life of competition and revenge under an honorable system that had been worked out over generations. He could not understand the ways of white America.*

*In 1804, in a dubious transaction, white officials got four members of his tribe to sign away all Sauk land east of the Mississippi River. Infuriated, Black Hawk refused to accept the treaty. In the War of 1812, he fought on the British side. Another Sauk named Keokuk gained power in his absence and counseled neutrality and compromise. Keokuk hoped to benefit the tribe by accommodation and surrender of lands. Black Hawk represented resistance. Tribal members had to pick sides.*

*When the Americans won the war, Black Hawk returned to his land. Years passed and white immigrants increasingly settled in Illinois. Finally, Black Hawk agreed to sell his land if given a fair price; but the government cited the 1804 Treaty and sent in the army to force compliance. The 100-day "Black Hawk War" that followed was really a four-month effort by the military to capture the non-treaty Sauks. In 1832, Abraham Lincoln, Zachary Taylor and Jefferson Davis were among the soldiers trying to subdue the Sauk resistance in the area around Galena, Illinois.*

*Seventy whites died. In the end, at the Battle of Bad Axe on the banks of the Mississippi, the army indiscriminately killed Indian men, women, and children and captured Black Hawk. The government had already recognized Keokuk as chief, and he began to cede tribal lands in Illinois, then Kansas, then Iowa, as resettlement followed each surrender of property. Black Hawk was taken as a hostage to Washington, D.C., to meet Andrew Jackson. After a prison sentence, he was showcased on a paid-for-by-the-government tour of Philadelphia, Boston and New York before being carried back to his tribe. Ambivalent whites flocked to see him and to salute him for his bravery as a "Noble Savage" even while they congratulated themselves on gaining his land. Someone probably told him to write about the war.*

*Convinced to tell his own story, Black Hawk produced a spiritual and secular autobiography that tells us much about Indian life. It is also the incredulous and angry voice of a man who lived under Sauk, French, Spanish, British, and American governments all struggling with each other over land.*

Life of Ma-Ka-Tai-Me-She-Kia-Kiak or Black Hawk: Embracing the Tradition of His Nation—Indian Wars in Which He Has Been Engaged—Cause of Joining the British in Their Late War with America, and Its History—Description of the Rock-River Village—Manners and Customs—Encroachments by the Whites, Contrary to Treaty—Removal from His Village in 1831, with an Account of the Cause and General History of the Late War, His Surrender and Confinement at Jefferson Barracks, and Travels Through the United States, Dictated by Himself Cincinnati, 1833; reprint, Urbana: University of Illinois, 1964.

I was born at the Sac Village, on Rock river, in the year 1767, and am now in my 67th year. My great grand father, Na-nà-ma-kee, or Thunder, (according to the tradition given me by my father, Py-e-sa,) was born in the vicinity of Montreal, where the Great Spirit first placed the Sac Nation, and inspired him with a belief that, at the end of four years, he should see a *white man,* who would be to him a father. Consequently he blacked his face, and eat but once a day, (just as the sun was going down,) for three years, and continued dreaming throughout all this time whenever he slept—when the Great Spirit again appeared to him, and told him, that, at the end of one year more, he should meet his father,—and directed him to start seven days before its expiration, and take with him his two brothers *Na-mah,* or Sturgeon, and *Pau-ka-hum-ma-wa* or Sun Fish, and travel in a direction to the left of sun-rising. After pursuing this course five days, he sent out his two brothers to listen if they could hear a noise, and if so, to fasten some grass to the end of a pole, erect it, pointing in the direction of the sound, and then return to him.

Early next morning they returned, and reported that they had heard sounds which appeared near at hand, and that they had fulfilled his order. They all then started for the place where the pole had been erected; when, on reaching it, Na-nà-ma-kee left his party, and went alone to the place from whence the sounds proceeded, and found that the white man had arrived and pitched his tent. When he came in sight, his father came out to meet him. He took him by the hand, and welcomed him into his tent. He told him that he was the son of the King of France—that he had been dreaming for four years—that the Great Spirit had directed him to come here, where he should meet a nation of people who had never yet seen a white man—that they should be his children, and he should be their father—that he had communicated these things to the King, his father, who laughed at him, and called him a Ma-she-na—but he insisted on coming here to meet his children, where the Great Spirit had directed him. The King told him

**BLACK HAWK**

that he would neither find land nor people—that this was an uninhabited region of lakes and mountains; but, finding that he would have no peace without it, fitted out a nà-pe-quâ, manned it, and gave it to him in charge, when he immediately loaded it, set sail, and had now landed on the very day that the Great Spirit had told him, in his dreams, he should meet his children. He had now met the man who should, in future, have charge of all the nation. . . .

His father remained four days—during which time he gave him guns, powder and lead, spears and lances, and showed him their use—so that in war he could chastise his enemies,—and in peace they could kill buffalo, deer and other game, necessary for the comforts and luxuries of life. He then presented the others with various kinds of cooking utensils, and learned them their uses,—and having given them a large quantity of goods, as presents, and every other thing necessary for their comfort, he set sail for France, after promising to meet them again, at the same place after the twelfth moon. . . .

The next spring, according to promise, their French father returned, with his nà-pe-quâ richly laden with goods, which were distributed among them. He continued for a long time to keep up a regular trade with them—they giving him in exchange for his goods, furs and peltries.

After a long time the British overpowered the French, (the two nations being at war,) drove them away from Quebec, and took possession of it themselves. The different tribes of Indians around our nation, envying our people, united their forces against them, and succeeded, by their great strength, to drive them to Montreal, and from thence to Mackinac.

Here our people first met our British father, who furnished them with goods. Their enemies still pursued them, and drove them to different places on the lake, until they made a village near Green Bay, on what is now called *Sac* river, having derived its name from this circumstance. Here they held a council with the Foxes, and a national treaty of friendship and alliance was concluded upon. The Foxes abandoned their village, and joined the Sacs. This arrangement being mutually obligatory upon both parties, as neither were sufficiently strong to meet their enemies with any hope of success, they soon became as one band or nation of people. They were driven, however, by the combined forces of their enemies, to the Wisconsin. They remained here some time, until a party of their young men, (who had descended Rock river to its mouth,) returned, and made a favorable report of the country. They all descended Rock river—drove the Kas-kas-kias from the country, and commenced the erection of their village, determined never to leave it.

At this village I was born, being a regular descendant of the first chief, Na-nà-ma-kee, or Thunder. Few, if any, events of note, transpired within my recollection, until about my fifteenth year. I was not allowed to paint, or wear feathers; but distinguished myself, at that early age, by wounding an enemy; consequently, I was placed in the ranks of the Braves!

Soon after this, a leading chief of the Muscow nation, came to our village for recruits to go to war against the Osages, our common enemy. I volunteered my services to go, as my father had joined him; and was proud to have an opportunity to prove to him that I was not an unworthy son, and that I had courage and bravery. It was not long before we met the enemy, when a battle immediately ensued. Standing by my father's side, I saw him kill his antagonist, and tear the scalp from his head. Fired with valor and ambition, I rushed furiously upon another, smote him to the earth with my tomahawk—run my lance through his body—took off his scalp, and returned in triumph to my father! He said nothing, but looked pleased. This was the first man I killed! The enemy's loss in this engagement having been great, they immediately retreated, which put an end to the war for the present. Our party then returned to our village, and danced over the scalps we had taken. This was the first time that I was permitted to join in a scalp-dance.

After a few moons had passed, (having acquired considerable fame as a *brave,*) I led a party of seven, and attacked *one hundred Osages*! I killed one man, and left him for my comrades to scalp, whilst I was taking an observation of the strength and preparations of the enemy; and finding that they were all equally well armed with ourselves, I ordered a retreat, and came off without losing a man! This excursion gained for me great applause, and enabled me, before a great while, to raise a party of one hundred and eighty, to go against the Osages. We left our village in high spirits, and marched over a rugged country, until we reached that of the Osages, on the Missouri. We followed their trail until we arrived at their village, which we approached with great caution, expecting that they were all there; but found, to our sorrow, that they had deserted it! The party became dissatisfied, in consequence of this disappointment,—and all, with the exception of *five,* dispersed and returned home. I then placed myself at the head of this brave little band, and thanked the Great Spirit that *so many* remained,— and took up the trail of our enemies, with a full determination never to return without some trophy of victory! We followed on for several days—killed one man and a boy, and then returned with their scalps.

In consequence of this mutiny in my camp, I was not again enabled to raise a sufficient party to go against the Osages, until about my nineteenth year. During this interim, they committed many outrages on our nation and people. I succeeded at length, in recruiting two hundred efficient warriors, and took up the line of march early in the morning. In a few days we were in the enemy's country, and had not travelled far before we met an equal force to contend with. A general battle immediately commenced, although my braves were considerably fatigued by forced marches. Each party fought desperately. The enemy seemed unwilling to yield the ground, and we were determined to conquer or die! A large number of the Osages were killed, and many wounded, before they commenced re-treating. A band of warriors more brave, skilful, and efficient than mine, could not be found. In this engagement I killed five men and one squaw, and had the good fortune to take the scalps of all I struck, except one. The enemy's loss in this engagement was about one hundred men. Ours nineteen. We now returned to our village, well pleased with our success, and danced over the scalps we had taken.

The Osages, in consequence of their great loss in this battle, became satisfied to remain on their own lands; and ceased, for awhile, their depredations on our nation. Our attention, therefore, was directed towards an ancient enemy, who had decoyed and murdered some of our helpless women and children. I started, with my father, who took command of a small party, and proceeded against the enemy. We met near Merimack, and an action ensued; the Cherokees having greatly the advantage in numbers. Early in this engagement my father was wounded in the thigh—but had the pleasure of killing his antagonist before he fell. Seeing that he had fallen, I assumed command, and fought desperately, until the enemy commenced retreating before us. I returned to my father to administer to his necessities, but nothing could be done for him. The *medicine man* said the wound was *mortal*! from which he soon after *died*! In this battle I killed three men, and wounded several. The enemy's loss being twenty-eight, and ours seven.

I now fell heir to the great *medicine bag* of my forefathers, which had belonged to my father. I took it, buried our dead, and returned with my party, all sad and sorrowful, to our village, in consequence of the loss of my father. Owing to this misfortune, I blacked my face, fasted, and prayed to the Great Spirit for five years—during which time I remained in a civil capacity, hunting and fishing.

The Osages having commenced aggressions on our people, and the Great Spirit having taken pity on me, I took a small party and went against the enemy, but could only find *six* men! Their forces being so weak, I thought it cowardly to kill them,—but took them prisoners, and carried them to our Spanish father at St. Louis, and gave them up to him; and then returned to our village. Determined on the final extermination of the Osages, for the injuries our nation and people had received from them, I commenced recruiting a strong force, immediately on my return, and started, in the third moon, with five hundred Sacs and Foxes, and one hundred Ioways, and marched against the enemy. We continued our march for several days before we came upon their trail, which was discovered late in the day. We encamped for the night; made an early start next morning, and before sun down, fell upon *forty lodges,* and killed all their inhabitants, except *two squaws*! whom I captured and made prisoners. During this attack I killed seven men and two boys, with my own hand.

In this engagement many of the bravest warriors among the Osages were killed, which caused the balance of their nation to remain on their own lands, and cease their aggressions upon our hunting grounds.

The loss of my father, by the Cherokees, made me anxious to avenge his death, by the annihilation, if possible, of all their race. I accordingly commenced recruiting another party to go against them. Having succeeded in this, I started, with my party, and went into their country, but only found five of their people, whom I took prisoners. I afterwards released four men—the other, a young *squaw,* we brought home. Great as was my hatred for this people, I could not kill so small a party.

During the close of the ninth moon, I led a large party against the Chippewas, Kaskaskias and Osages. This was the commencement of a long and arduous campaign, which terminated in my thirty-fifth year: Having had seven regular engagements, and a number of small skirmishes. During this campaign, several hundred of the enemy were slain. I killed *thirteen* of their bravest warriors, with my own hand.

Our enemies having now been driven from our hunting grounds, with so great a loss as they sustained, we returned, in peace, to our villages; and after the seasons of mourning and burying our dead relations, and of feast-dancing had passed, we commenced preparations for our winter's hunt, in which we were very successful.

We generally paid a visit to St. Louis every summer; but, in consequence of the protracted war in which we had been engaged, I had not been there for some years. Our difficulties having all been settled, I concluded to take a small party, that summer, and go down to see our Spanish father. We went—and on our arrival, put up our lodges where the market-house now stands. After painting and dressing, we called to see our Spanish father, and were well received. He gave us a variety of presents, and plenty of provisions. We danced through the town as usual, and its inhabitants all seemed to be well pleased. They appeared to us like brothers—and always gave us good advice.

On my next, and *last,* visit to my Spanish father, I discovered, on landing, that all was not right: every countenance seemed sad and gloomy! I inquired the cause, and was informed that the Americans were coming to take possession of the town and country!—and that we should then lose our Spanish father! This news made myself and band sad—because we had always heard bad accounts of the Americans from Indians who had lived near them!—and we were sorry to lose our Spanish father, who had always treated us with great friendship.

A few days afterwards, the Americans arrived. I took my band, and went to take leave, for the last time, of our father. The Americans came to see him also. Seeing them approach, we passed out at one door, as they entered another—and immediately started, in canoes, for our village on Rock river—not liking the change any more than our friends appeared to, at St. Louis.

On arriving at our village, we gave the news, that strange people had taken St. Louis—and that we should never see our Spanish father again! This information made all our people sorry!

Some time afterwards, a boat came up the river, with a young American chief, [Lieutenant (afterwards General) Pike,] and a small party of soldiers. We heard of him, (by runners,) soon after he had passed Salt river. Some of our young braves watched him every day, to see what sort of people he had on board! The boat, at length, arrived at Rock river, and the young chief came on shore with his interpreter—made a speech, and gave us some presents! We, in return, presented him with meat, and such provisions as we could spare. . . .

Some moons after this young chief descended the Mississippi, one of our people killed an American—and was confined, in the prison at St. Louis, for the offence. We held a council at our village to see what could be done for him,— which determined that Quàsh-quà-me, Pà-she-pa-ho, Oú-che-quà-ka, and Hà-she-quar-hi-qua, should go down to St. Louis, see our American father, and do all they could to have our friend released: by paying for the person killed—thus covering the blood, and satisfying the relations of the man murdered! This being the only means with us of saving a person who had killed another—and we *then* thought it was the same way with the whites!

The party started with the good wishes of the whole nation—hoping they would accomplish the object of their mission. The relatives of the prisoner blacked their faces, and fasted—hoping the Great Spirit would take pity on them, and return the husband and father to his wife and children.

Quàsh-quà-me and party remained a long time absent. They at length returned, and encamped a short distance below the village—but did not come up that day—nor did any person approach their camp! They appeared to be dressed in *fine coats,* and had *medals*! From these circumstances, we were in hopes that they had brought good news. Early the next morning, the Council Lodge was crowded—Quàsh-quà-me and party came up, and gave us the following account of their mission:

"On their arrival at St. Louis, they met their American father, and explained to him their business, and urged the release of their friend. The American chief told them he wanted land—and they had agreed to give him some on the west side of the Mississippi, and some on the Illinois side opposite the Jeffreon. When the business was all arranged, they expected to have their friend released to come home with them. But about the time they were ready to start, their friend was let out of prison, who ran a short distance, and was *shot dead*! This is all they could recollect of what was said and done. They had been drunk the greater part of the time they were in St. Louis."

This is all myself or nation knew of the treaty of 1804. It has been explained to me since. I find, by that treaty, all our country, east of the Mississippi, and south of the Jeffreon, was ceded to the United States for *one thousand dollars* a year! I will leave it to the people of the United States to say, whether our nation was properly represented in this treaty? or whether we received a fair compensation for the extent of country ceded by those *four* individuals? I could say much about this treaty, but I will not, at this time. It has been the origin of all our difficulties.

Some time after this treaty was made, a war chief, with a party of soldiers, came up in keel boats, and encamped a short distance above the head of the Des Moines rapids, and commenced cutting timber and building houses. The news of their arrival was soon carried to all the villages—when council after council was held. We could not understand the intention, or reason, why the Americans wanted to build houses at that place—but were told that they were a party of soldiers, who had brought *great guns* with them—and looked like a *war party* of whites!

A number of our people immediately went down to see what was doing—myself among them. On our arrival, we found they were building a *fort*! The soldiers were busily engaged in cutting timber; and I observed that they took their arms with them, when they went to the woods—and the whole party acted as they would do in an enemy's country! . . .

Soon after our return home, news reached us that a war was going to take place between the British and the Americans. Runners continued to arrive from different tribes, all confirming the report of the expected war. The British agent, Col. Dixon, was holding *talks* with, and making presents to, the different tribes. I had not made up my mind whether to join the British, or remain neutral. *I had not discovered one good trait in the character of the Americans that had come to the country!* They made *fair promises* but *never fulfilled them*! Whilst the *British* made but few—but we could always *rely upon their word*! . . .

The great chief at St. Louis having sent word for us to go down and confirm the treaty of peace, we did not hesitate, but started immediately, that we might smoke the *peace-pipe* with him. On our arrival, we met the great chiefs in council. They explained to us the words of our Great Father at Washington, accusing us of heinous crimes and divers misdemeanors, particularly in not coming down when first invited. We knew very well that *our Great Father had deceived us,* and thereby *forced* us to join the British, and could not believe that he had put this speech into the mouths of these chiefs to deliver to us. I was not a civil chief, and consequently made no reply: but our chiefs told the commissioners that "what they had said was a *lie*!—that our Great Father had sent no such speech, he knowing the situation in which we had been placed had been *caused by him*!" The white chiefs appeared very angry at this reply, and said they "would break off the treaty with us, and *go to war,* as they would not be insulted."

Our chiefs had no intention of insulting them, and told them so—"that they merely wished to explain to them that *they had told a lie,* without making them angry; in the same manner that the whites do, when they do not believe what is told them!" The council then proceeded, and the pipe of peace was smoked.

Here, for the first time, I touched the goose quill to the treaty—not knowing, however, that, by that act, I consented to give away my village. Had that been explained to me, I should have opposed it, and never would have signed their treaty, as my recent conduct will clearly prove.

What do we know of the manner of the laws and customs of the white people? They might buy our bodies for dissection, and we would touch the goose quill to confirm it, without knowing what we are doing. This was the case with myself and people in touching the goose quill the first time.

We can only judge of what is proper and right by our standard of right and wrong, which differs widely from the whites, if I have been correctly informed. The whites *may do bad* all their lives, and then, if they are *sorry for it* when about to die, *all is well*! But with us it is different: we must continue throughout our lives to do what we conceive to be good. If we have corn and meat, and know of a family that have none, we divide with them. If we have more blankets than sufficient, and others have not enough, we must give to them that want. But I will presently explain our customs, and the manner we live.

We were friendly treated by the white chiefs, and started back to our village on Rock river. Here we found that troops had arrived to build a fort at Rock Island. This, in our opinion, was a contradiction to what we had done—"to prepare for war in time of peace." We did not, however, object to their building the fort on the island, but we were very sorry, as this was the best island on the Mississippi, and had long been the resort of our young people during the summer. It was our garden (like the white people have near to their big villages) which supplied us with strawberries, blackberries, gooseberries, plums, apples, nuts of different kinds; and its waters supplied us with fine fish, being situated in the rapids of the river. In my early life, I spent many happy days on this island. A good spirit had care of it, who lived in a cave in the rocks immediately under the place where the fort now stands, and has often been seen by our people. He was white, with large wings like a *swan's,* but ten times larger. We were particular not to make much noise in that part of the island which he inhabited, for fear of disturbing him. But the noise of the fort has since driven him away, and no doubt a *bad spirit* has taken his place!

Our village was situate on the north side of Rock river, at the foot of its rapids, and on the point of land between Rock river and the Mississippi. In its front, a prairie extended to the bank of the Mississippi; and in our rear, a continued bluff, gently ascending from the prairie. On the side of this bluff we had our corn-fields, extending about two miles up, running parallel with the Mississippi; where we joined those of the Foxes whose village was on the bank of the Mississippi, opposite the lower end of Rock island, and three miles distant from ours. We had about eight hundred acres in cultivation, including what we had on the islands of Rock river. The land around our village, uncultivated, was covered with blue-grass, which made excellent pasture for our horses. Several fine springs broke out of the bluff, near by, from which we were supplied with good water. The rapids of Rock river furnished us with an abundance of excellent fish, and the land, being good, never failed to produce good crops of corn, beans, pumpkins, and squashes. We always had plenty—our children never cried with hunger, nor our people were never in want. Here our village had stood for more than a hundred years, during all which time we were the undisputed possessors of the valley of the Mississippi, from the Ouisconsin to the Portage des Sioux, near the mouth of the Missouri, being about seven hundred miles in length.

At this time we had very little intercourse with the whites, except our traders. Our village was healthy, and there was no place in the country possessing such advantages, nor no hunting grounds better than those we had in possession. If another prophet had come to our village in those days, and told us what has since taken place, none of our people would have believed him. What! to be driven from our village and hunting grounds, and not even permitted to visit the graves of our forefathers, our relations, and friends?

This hardship is not known to the whites. With us it is a custom to visit the graves of our friends, and keep them in repair for many years. The mother will go alone to weep over the grave of her child! The brave, with pleasure, visits the grave of his father, after he has been successful in war, and re-paints the post that shows where he lies! There is no place like that where the bones of our forefathers lie, to go to when in grief. Here the Great Spirit will take pity on us!

But, how different is our situation now, from what it was in those days! Then we were as happy as the buffalo on the plains—but now, we are as miserable as the hungry, howling wolf in the prairie! But I am digressing from my story. Bitter reflection crowds upon my mind, and must find utterance.

When we returned to our village in the spring, from our wintering grounds, we would finish trading with our traders, who always followed us to our village. We purposely kept some of our fine furs for this trade; and, as there was great opposition among them, who should get these skins, we always got our goods cheap. After this trade was over, the traders would give us a few kegs of rum, which was generally promised in the fall, to encourage us to make a good hunt, and not go to war. They would then start with their furs and peltries for their homes. Our old men would take a frolic, (at this time our young men never drank.) When this was ended, the next thing to be done was to bury our dead, (such as had died during the year.) This is a great *medicine feast*. The relations of those who have died, give all the goods they have purchased, as presents to their friends—thereby reducing themselves to poverty, to show the Great Spirit that they are humble, so that he will take pity on them. We would next open the cashes, and take out corn and other provisions, which had been put up in the fall,—and then commence repairing our lodges. As soon as this is accomplished, we repair the fences around our fields, and clean them off, ready for planting corn. This work is done by our women. The men, during this time, are feasting on dried venison, bear's meat, wild fowl, and corn, prepared in different ways; and recounting to each other what took place during the winter.

Our women plant the corn, and as soon as they get done, we make a feast, and dance the *crane* dance, in which they join us, dressed in their best, and decorated with feathers. At this feast our young braves select the young woman they wish to have for a wife. He then informs his mother, who calls on the mother of the girl, when the arrangement is made, and the time appointed for him to come. He goes to the lodge when all are asleep, (or pretend to be,) lights his matches, which have been provided for the purpose, and soon finds where his intended sleeps. He then awakens her, and holds the light to his face that she may know him—after which he places the light close to her. If she blows it out, the ceremony is ended, and he appears in the lodge the next morning, as one of the family. If she does not blow out the light, but leaves it to burn out, he retires from the lodge. The next day he places himself in full view of it, and plays his flute. The young women go out, one by one, to see who he is playing for. The tune changes, to let them know that he is not playing for them. When his intended makes her appearance at the door, he continues his *courting* tune, until she returns to the lodge. He then gives over playing, and makes another trial at night, which generally turns out favorable.

During the first year they ascertain whether they can agree with each other, and can be happy—if not, they part, and each looks out again. If we were to live together and disagree, we should be as foolish as the whites. No indiscretion can banish a woman from her parental lodge—no difference how many children she may bring home, she is always welcome—the kettle is over the fire to feed them.

The crane dance often lasts two or three days. When this is over, we feast again, and have our *national* dance. The large square in the village is swept and prepared for the purpose. The chiefs and old warriors, take seats on mats which have been spread at the upper end of the square—the drummers and singers come next, and the braves and women form the sides, leaving a large space in the middle. The drums beat, and the singers commence. A warrior enters the square, keeping time with the music. He shows the manner he started on a war party—how he approached the enemy—he strikes, and describes the way he killed him. All join in applause. He then leaves the square, and another enters and takes his place. Such of our young men as have not been out in war parties, and killed an enemy, stand back ashamed—not being able to enter the square. I remember that I was ashamed to look where our young women stood, before I could take my stand in the square as a warrior.

What pleasure it is to an old warrior, to see his son come forward and relate his exploits—it makes him feel young, and induces him to enter the square, and "fight his battles o'er again."

This national dance makes our warriors. When I was travelling last summer, on a steam boat, on a large river, going from New York to Albany, I was shown the place where the Americans dance their national dance [West Point]; where the old warriors recount to their young men, what they have done, to stimulate them to go and do likewise. This surprised me, as I did not think the whites understood our way of making braves.

When our national dance is over—our corn-fields hoed, and every weed dug up, and our corn about knee-high, all our young men would start in a direction towards sun-down, to hunt deer and buffalo—being prepared, also, to kill Sioux, if any are found on our hunting grounds—a part of our old men and women to the lead mines to make lead—and the remainder of our people start to fish, and get mat stuff. Every one leaves the village, and remains about forty days. They then return: the hunting party bringing in dried buffalo and deer meat, and sometimes *Sioux scalps,* when they are found trespassing on our hunting grounds. At other times they are met by a party of Sioux too strong for them, and are driven in. If the Sioux have killed the Sacs last, they expect to be retaliated upon, and will fly before them, and vice versa. Each party knows that the other has a right to retaliate, which induces those who have killed last, to give way before their enemy—as neither wish to strike, except to avenge the death of their relatives. All our wars are predicated by the relatives of those killed; or by aggressions upon our hunting grounds.

The party from the lead mines bring lead, and the others dried fish, and mats for our winter lodges. Presents are now made by each party; the first, giving to the others dried buffalo and deer, and they, in exchange, presenting them with lead, dried fish and mats.

This is a happy season of the year—having plenty of provisions, such as beans, squashes, and other produce, with our dried meat and fish, we continue to make feasts and visit each other, until our corn is ripe. Some lodge in the village makes a feast daily, to the Great Spirit. I cannot explain this so that the white people would comprehend me, as we have no regular standard among us. Every one makes his feast as he thinks best, to please the Great Spirit, who has the care of all beings created. Others believe in two Spirits: one good and one bad, and make feasts for the Bad Spirit, *to keep him quiet*! If they can make peace with him, the Good Spirit will not hurt them! For my part, I am of opinion, that so far as we have *reason,* we have a right to use it, in determining what is right or wrong; and should pursue that path which we believe to be right—believing, that "whatever is, is right." If the Great and Good Spirit wished us to believe and do as the whites, he could easily change our opinions, so that we would see, and think, and act as they do. We are *nothing* compared to His power, and we feel and know it. We have men among us, like the whites, who pretend to know the right path, but will not consent to show it without *pay*! I have no faith in their paths—but believe that every man must make his own path!

When our corn is getting ripe, our young people watch with anxiety for the signal to pull roasting-ears—as none dare touch them until the proper time. When the corn is fit to use, another great ceremony takes place, with feasting, and returning thanks to the Great Spirit for giving us corn.

I will here relate the manner in which corn first came. According to tradition, handed down to our people, a beautiful woman was seen to descend from the clouds, and alight upon the earth, by two of our ancestors, who had killed a deer, and were sitting by a fire, roasting a part of it to eat. They were astonished at seeing her, and concluded that she must be hungry, and had smelt the meat—and immediately went to her, taking with them a piece of the roasted venison. They presented it to her, and she eat—and told them to return to the spot where she was sitting, at the end of one year, and they would find a reward for their kindness and generosity. She then ascended to the clouds, and disappeared. The two men returned to their village, and explained to the nation what they had seen, done, and heard—but were laughed at by their people. When the period arrived, for them to visit this consecrated ground, where they were to find a reward for their attention to the beautiful woman of the clouds, they went with a large party, and found, where her right hand had rested on the ground, *corn* growing—and where the left hand had rested, *beans*—and immediately where she had been seated, *tobacco*.

The two first have, ever since, been cultivated by our people, as our principal provisions—and the last used for smoking. The white people have since found out the latter, and seem to relish it as much as we do—as they use it in different ways, viz. smoking, snuffing and eating!

We thank the Great Spirit for all the benefits he has conferred upon us. For myself, I never take a drink of water from a spring, without being mindful of his goodness.

We next have our great ball play—from three to five hundred on a side, play this game. We play for horses, guns, blankets, or any other kind of property we have. The successful party take the stakes, and all retire to our lodges in peace and friendship.

We next commence horse-racing, and continue our sport and feasting, until the corn is all secured. We then prepare to leave our village for our hunting grounds. The traders arrive, and give us credit for such articles as we want to clothe our families, and enable us to hunt. We first, however, hold a council with them, to ascertain the price they will give us for our skins, and what they will charge us for goods. We inform them where we intend hunting—and tell them where to build their houses. At this place, we deposit part of our corn, and leave our old people. The traders have always been kind to them, and relieved them when in want. They were always much respected by our people—and never since we have been a nation, has one of them been killed by any of our people.

We disperse, in small parties, to make our hunt, and as soon as it is over, we return to our traders' establishment, with our skins, and remain feasting, playing cards and other pastimes, until near the close of the winter. Our young men then start on the beaver hunt; others to hunt raccoons and muskrats—and the remainder of our people go to the sugar camps to make sugar. All leave our encampment, and appoint a place to meet on the Mississippi, so that we may return to our village together, in the spring. We always spent our time pleasantly at the sugar camp. It being the season for wild fowl, we lived well, and always had plenty, when the hunters came in, that we might make a feast for them. After this is over, we return to our village, accompanied, sometimes, by our traders. In this way, the year rolled round happily. But these are times that were!

On returning, in the spring, from our hunting ground, I had the pleasure of meeting our old friend, the trader of Peoria, at Rock Island. He came up in a boat from St. Louis, not as a trader, as in times past, but as our *agent*. We were all pleased to see him. He told us, that he narrowly escaped falling into the hands of Dixon. He remained with us a short time, gave us good advice, and then returned to St. Louis.

The Sioux having committed depredations on our people, we sent our war parties that summer, who succeeded in killing *fourteen*. I paid several visits to fort Armstrong during the summer, and was always well treated. We were not as happy then in our village as formerly. Our people got more liquor than customary. I used all my influence to prevent drunkenness, but without effect. As the settlements progressed towards us, we became worse off, and more unhappy. Many of our people, instead of going to their old hunting grounds, where game was plenty, would go near to the settlements to hunt—and, instead of saving their skins to pay the trader for goods furnished them in the fall, would sell them to the settlers for whisky! and return in the spring with their families, almost naked, and without the means of getting any thing for them.

About this time my eldest son was taken sick and died. He had always been a dutiful child, and had just grown to manhood. Soon after, my youngest daughter, an interesting and affectionate child, died also. This was a hard stroke, because I loved my children. In my distress, I left the noise of the village, and built my lodge on a mound in my corn-field, and enclosed it with a fence, around which I planted corn and beans. Here I was with my family alone. I gave every thing I had away, and reduced myself to poverty. The only covering I retained, was a piece of buffalo robe. I resolved on blacking my face and fasting, for two years, for the loss of my two children—drinking only of water in the middle of the day, and eating sparingly of boiled corn at sunset. I fulfilled my promise, hoping that the Great Spirit would take pity on me.

My nation had now some difficulty with the Ioways, with whom we wished to be at peace. Our young men had repeatedly killed some of the Ioways; and these breaches had always been made up by giving presents to the relations of those killed. But the last council we had with them, we promised that, in case any more of their people were killed by ours, instead of presents, we would give up the person, or persons, that had done the injury. We made this determination known to our people; but, notwithstanding, one of our young men killed an Ioway the following winter.

A party of our people were about starting for the Ioway village to give the young man up. I agreed to accompany them. When we were ready to start, I called at the lodge for the young man to go with us. He was sick, but willing to go. His brother, however, prevented him, and insisted on going to die in his place, as he was unable to travel. We started, and on the seventh day arrived in sight of the Ioway village, and when within a short distance of it, halted and dismounted. We all bid farewell to our young brave, who entered the village alone, singing his *death-song,* and sat down in the square in the middle of the village. One of the Ioway chiefs came out to us. We told him that we had fulfilled our promise—that we had brought the brother of the young man who had killed one of their people—that he had volunteered to come in his place, in consequence of his brother being unable to travel from sickness. We had no further conversation, but mounted our horses and rode off. As we started, I cast my eye towards the village, and observed the Ioways coming out of their lodges with spears and war clubs. We took our trail back, and travelled until dark—then encamped and made a fire. We had not been here long, before we heard the sound of horses coming towards us. We seized our arms; but instead of an enemy, it was our young brave with two horses. He told me that after we had left him, they menaced him with death for some time—then gave him something to eat—smoked the pipe with him—and made him a present of the two horses and some goods, and started him after us. When we arrived at our village, our people were much pleased; and for the noble and generous conduct of the Ioways, on this occasion, not one of their people has been killed since by any of our nation.

That fall I visited Malden with several of my band, and were well treated by our British father, who gave us a variety of presents. He also gave me a medal, and told me there never would be war between England and America again; but, for my fidelity to the British during the war that had terminated sometime before, requested me to come with my band every year and get presents, as Col. Dixon had promised me.

I returned, and hunted that winter on the Two-Rivers. The whites were now settling the country fast. I was out one day hunting in a bottom, and met three white men. They accused me of killing their hogs; I denied it; but they would not listen to me. One of them took my gun out of my hand and fired it off—then took out the flint, gave back my gun, and commenced beating me with sticks, and ordered me off. I was so much bruised that I could not sleep for several nights.

Some time after this occurrence, one of my camp cut a bee-tree, and carried the honey to his lodge. A party of white men soon followed, and told him that the bee-tree was theirs, and that he had no right to cut it. He pointed to the honey, and told them to take it; they were not satisfied with this, but took all the packs of skins that he had collected during the winter, to pay his trader and clothe his family with in the spring, and carried them off!

How could we like such people, who treated us so unjustly? We determined to break up our camp, for fear that they would do worse—and when we joined our people in the spring, a great many of them complained of similar treatment.

This summer our agent came to live at Rock Island. He treated us well, and gave us good advice. I visited him and the trader very often during the summer, and, for the first time, heard talk of our having to leave my village. The trader explained to me the terms of the treaty that had been made, and said we would be obliged to leave the Illinois side of the Mississippi, and advised us to select a good place for our village, and remove to it in the spring. He pointed out the difficulties we would have to encounter, if we remained at our village on Rock river. He had great influence with the principal Fox chief, (his adopted brother,) and persuaded him to leave his village, and go to the west side of the Mississippi river, and build another—which he did the spring following.

Nothing was now talked of but leaving our village. Ke-o-kuck had been persuaded to consent to go; and was using all his influence, backed by the war chief at fort Armstrong, and our agent and trader at Rock Island, to induce others to go with him. He sent the crier through the village to inform our people that it was the wish of our Great Father that we should remove to the west side of the Mississippi—and recommended the Ioway river as a good place for the new village—and wished his party to make such arrangements, before they started out on their winter's hunt, as to preclude the necessity of their returning to the village in the spring.

The party opposed to removing, called upon me for my opinion. I gave it freely—and after questioning Quàsh-quà-me about the sale of the lands, he assured me that he "never had consented to the sale of our village." I now promised this party to be their leader, and raised the standard of opposition to Ke-o-kuck, with a full determination not to leave my village. I had an interview with Ke-o-kuck, to see if this difficulty could not be settled with our Great Father—and told him to propose to give other land, (any that our Great Father might choose, even our *lead mines,*) to be peaceably permitted to keep the small point of land on which our village and fields were situate. I was of opinion that the white people had plenty of land, and would never take our village from us. Ke-o-kuck promised to make an exchange if possible; and applied to our agent, and the great chief at St. Louis, (who has charge of all the agents,) for permission to go to Washington to see our Great Father for that purpose. This satisfied us for some time. We started to our hunting grounds, in good hopes that something would be done for us. During the winter, I received information that three families of whites had arrived at our village, and destroyed some of our lodges, and were making fences and dividing our corn-fields for their own use—*and were quarreling among themselves about their lines, in the division!* I immediately started for Rock river, a distance of ten day's travel, and on my arrival, found the report to be true. I went to my lodge, and saw a family occupying it. I wished to talk with them, but they could not understand me. I then went to Rock Island, and (the agent being absent,) told the interpreter what I wanted to say to those people, viz: "Not to settle on our lands—nor trouble our lodges or fences—that there was plenty of land in the country for them to settle upon—and they must leave our village, as we were coming back to it in the spring." The interpreter wrote me a paper, and I went back to the village, and showed it to the intruders, but could not understand their reply. I expected, however, that they would remove, as I requested them. I returned to Rock Island, passed the night there, and had a long conversation with the trader. He again advised me to give up, and make my village with Ke-o-kuck, on the Ioway river. I told him that I would not. The next morning I crossed the Mississippi, on very bad ice—but the Great Spirit made it strong, that I might pass over safe. I travelled three days farther to see the Winnebago sub-agent, and converse with him on the subject of our difficulties. He gave me no better news than the trader had done. I started then, by way of Rock river, to see the prophet, believing that he was a man of great knowledge. When we met, I explained to him every thing as it was. He at once agreed that I was right, and advised me never to give up our village, for the whites to plough up the bones of our people. He said, that if we remained at our village, the whites would not trouble us—and advised me to get Ke-o-kuck, and the party that had consented to go with him to the Ioway in the spring, to return, and remain at our village.

I returned to my hunting ground, after an absence of one moon, and related what I had done. In a short time we came up to our village, and found that the whites had not left it—but that others had come, and that the greater part of our corn-fields had been enclosed. When we landed, the whites appeared displeased because we had come back. We repaired the lodges that had been left standing, and built others. Ke-o-kuck came to the village; but his object was to persuade others to follow him to the Ioway. He had accomplished nothing towards making arrangements for us to remain, or to exchange other lands for our village. There was no more friendship existing between us. I looked upon him as a coward, and no brave, to abandon his village to be occupied by strangers. What *right* had these people to our village, and our fields, which the Great Spirit had given us to live upon?

My reason teaches me that *land cannot be sold*. The Great Spirit gave it to his children to live upon, and cultivate, as far as is necessary for their subsistence; and so long as they occupy and cultivate it, they have the right to the soil—but if they voluntarily leave it, then any other people have a right to settle upon it. Nothing can be sold, but such things as can be carried away.

In consequence of the improvements of the intruders on our fields, we found considerable difficulty to get ground to plant a little corn. Some of the whites permitted us to plant small patches in the fields they had fenced, keeping all the best ground for themselves. Our women had great difficulty in climbing their fences, (being unaccustomed to the kind,) and were ill-treated if they left a rail down.

One of my old friends thought he was safe. His corn-field was on a small island of Rock river. He planted his corn; it came up well—but the white man saw it!— he wanted the island, and took his team over, ploughed up the corn, and re-planted it for himself! The old man shed tears; not for himself, but the distress his family would be in if they raised no corn.

The white people brought whisky into our village, made our people drunk, and cheated them out of their horses, guns, and traps! This fraudulent system was carried to such an extent that I apprehended serious difficulties might take place, unless a stop was put to it. Consequently, I visited all the whites and begged them not to sell whisky to my people. One of them continued the practice openly. I took a party of my young men, went to his house, and took out his barrel and broke in the head and turned out the whisky. I did this for fear some of the whites might be killed by my people when drunk.

Our people were treated badly by the whites on many occasions. At one time, a white man beat one of our women cruelly, for pulling a few suckers of corn out of his field, to suck, when hungry! At another time, one of our young men was beat with clubs by two white men for opening a fence which crossed our road, to take his horse through. His shoulder blade was broken, and his body badly bruised, from which he soon after *died*!

Bad, and cruel, as our people were treated by the whites, not one of them was hurt or molested by any of my band. I hope this will prove that we are a peaceable people—having permitted ten men to take possession of our corn-fields; prevent us from planting corn; burn and destroy our lodges; ill-treat our women; and *beat to death* our men, without offering resistance to their barbarous cruelties. This is a lesson worthy for the white man to learn: to use forbearance when injured.

We acquainted our agent daily with our situation, and through him, the great chief at St. Louis—and hoped that something would be done for us. The whites were *complaining* at the same time that *we* were *intruding* upon *their rights!* THEY made themselves out the *injured* party, and *we* the *intruders!* and called loudly to the great war chief to protect *their* property!

How smooth must be the language of the whites, when they can make right look like wrong, and wrong like right. . . .

We now resumed some of our games and pastimes—having been assured by the prophet that we would not be removed. But in a little while it was ascertained, that a great war chief, with a large number of soldiers, was on his way to Rock river. I again called upon the prophet, who requested a little time to see into the matter. Early next morning he came to me, and said he had been *dreaming!* "That he saw nothing bad in this great war chief, [Gen. Gaines,] who was now near Rock river. That the *object* of his mission was to *frighten* us from our village, that the white people might get our land for *nothing!*" He assured us that this "great war chief dare not, and would not, hurt any of us. That the Americans were at peace with the British, and when they made peace, the British required, (which the Americans agreed to,) that they should never interrupt any nation of Indians that was at peace—and that all we had to do to retain our village, was to *refuse* any, and every offer that might be made by this war chief.". . .

Early in the morning a party of whites, being in advance of the army, came upon our people, who were attempting to cross the Mississippi. They tried to give themselves up—the whites paid no attention to their entreaties—but commenced *slaughtering* them! In a little while the whole army arrived. Our braves, but few in number, finding that the enemy paid no regard to age or sex, and seeing that they were murdering helpless women and little children, determined to *fight until they were killed!* As many women as could, commenced swimming the Mississippi, with their children on their backs. A number of them were drowned, and some shot, before they could reach the opposite shore.

One of my braves, who gave me this information, piled up some saddles before him, (when the fight commenced,) to shield himself from the enemy's fire, and killed three white men! But seeing that the whites were coming too close to him, he crawled to the bank of the river, without being perceived, and hid himself under it, until the enemy retired. He then came to me and told me what had been done. After hearing this sorrowful news, I started, with my little party, to the Winnebago village at Prairie La Cross. On my arrival there, I entered the lodge of one of the chiefs, and told him that I wished him to go with me to his father—that I intended to give myself up to the American war chief, and *die,* if the Great Spirit saw proper! He said he would go with me. I then took my *medicine bag,* and addressed the chief. I told him that it was "the soul of the Sac nation—that it never had been dishonored in any battle—take it, it is my life—dearer than life— and give it to the American chief!" He said he would keep it, and take care of it, and if I was suffered to live, he would send it to me.

During my stay at the village, the squaws made me a white dress of deer skin. I then started, with several Winnebagoes, and went to their agent, at Prairie du Chien, and gave myself up.

On my arrival there, I found to my sorrow, that a large body of Sioux had pursued, and killed, a number of our women and children, who had got safely across the Mississippi. The whites ought not to have permitted such conduct— and none but *cowards* would ever have been guilty of such cruelty—which has always been practised on our nation by the Sioux.

The massacre, which terminated the war, lasted about two hours. Our loss in killed, was about sixty, besides a number that were drowned. The loss of the enemy could not be ascertained by my braves, exactly; but they think that they killed about *sixteen,* during the action.

I was now given up by the agent to the commanding officer at fort Crawford, (the White Beaver having gone down the river.) We remained here a short time, and then started to Jefferson Barracks, in a steam boat, under the charge of a young war chief, who treated us all with much kindness. He is a good and brave young chief, with whose conduct I was much pleased. On our way down, we called at Galena, and remained a short time. The people crowded to the boat to see us; but the war chief would not permit them to enter the apartment where we were—knowing, from what his own feelings would have been, if he had been placed in a similar situation, that we did not wish to have a gaping crowd around us.

We passed Rock Island, without stopping. The great war chief, who was then at fort Armstrong, came out in a small boat to see us; but the captain of the steam boat would not allow any body from the fort to come on board of his boat, in consequence of the cholera raging among the soldiers. I did think that the captain ought to have permitted the war chief to come on board to see me, because I could see no danger to be apprehended by it. The war chief looked well, and, I have since heard, was constantly among his soldiers, who were sick and dying, administering to their wants, and had not caught the disease from them—and I thought it absurd to think that any of the people on the steam boat, could be afraid of catching the disease from a *well* man. But these people have not got bravery like war chiefs, who never *fear* any thing!

On our way down, I surveyed the country that had cost us so much trouble, anxiety, and blood, and that now caused me to be a prisoner of war. I reflected upon the ingratitude of the whites, when I saw their fine houses, rich harvests, and every thing desirable around them; and recollected that all this land had been ours, for which me and my people had never received a dollar, and that the whites were not satisfied until they took our village and our grave-yards from us, and removed us across the Mississippi.

On our arrival at Jefferson barracks, we met the great war chief, who had commanded the American army against my little band. I felt the humiliation of my situation: a little while before, I had been the leader of my braves, now I was a prisoner of war! but had surrendered myself. He received us kindly, and treated us well.

We were now confined to the barracks, and forced to wear the *ball and chain*! This was extremely mortifying, and altogether useless. Was the White Beaver afraid that I would break out of his barracks, and run away? Or was he ordered to inflict this punishment upon me? If I had taken him prisoner on the field of battle, I would not have wounded his feelings so much, by such treatment—knowing that a brave war chief would prefer *death* to *dishonor*! But I do not blame the White Beaver for the course he pursued—it is the custom among white soldiers, and, I suppose, was a part of his duty.

The time dragged heavily and gloomy along throughout the winter, although the White Beaver done every thing in his power to render us comfortable. Having been accustomed, throughout a long life, to roam the forests o'er—to go and come at liberty—confinement, and under such circumstances, could not be less than torture!

We passed away the time making pipes, until spring, when we were visited by the agent, trader, and interpreter, from Rock Island, Ke-o-kuck, and several chiefs and braves of our nation, and my wife and daughter. I was rejoiced to see the two latter, and spent my time very agreeably with them and my people, as long as they remained.

The trader presented me with some dried venison, which had been killed and cured by some of my friends. This was a valuable present; and although he had given me many before, none ever pleased me so much. This was the first meat I had eaten for a long time, that reminded me of the former pleasures of my own wigwam, which had always been stored with plenty.

Ke-o-kuck and his chiefs, during their stay at the barracks, petitioned our Great Father, the President, to release us; and pledged themselves for our good conduct. I now began to hope that I would soon be restored to liberty, and the enjoyment of my family and friends; having heard that Ke-o-kuck stood high in the estimation of our Great Father, because he did not join me in the war. But I was soon disappointed in my hopes. An order came from our Great Father to the White Beaver, to send us on to Washington. . . .

On our arrival at Washington, we called to see our Great Father, the President. He looks as if he had seen as many winters as I have, and seems to be a *great brave*! I had very little talk with him, as he appeared to be busy, and did not seem much disposed to talk. I think he is a good man; and although he talked but little, he treated us very well. His wigwam is well furnished with every thing good and pretty, and is very strongly built.

He said he wished to know the *cause* of my going to war against his white children. I thought he ought to have known this before; and, consequently, said but little to him about it—as I expected he knew as well as I could tell him.

He said he wanted us to go to fortress Monroe, and stay awhile with the war chief who commanded it. But, having been so long from my people, I told him that I would rather return to my nation—that Ke-o-kuck had come here once on a visit to see him, as we had done, and he let him return again, as soon as he wished; and that I expected to be treated in the same way. He insisted, however, on our going to fortress Monroe; and as our interpreter could not understand enough of our language to interpret a speech, I concluded it was best to obey our Great Father, and say nothing contrary to his wishes.

During our stay at the city, we were called upon by many of the people, who treated us well, particularly the squaws! We visited the great *council house* of the Americans—the place where they keep their *big guns*—and all the public buildings, and then started to fortress Monroe. The war chief met us, on our arrival, and shook hands, and appeared glad to see me. He treated us with great friendship, and talked to me frequently. Previous to our leaving this fort, he gave us a feast, and made us some presents, which I intend to keep for his sake. He is a very good man, and a great *brave*! I was sorry to leave him, although I was going to return to my people, because he had treated me like a brother, during all the time I remained with him.

Having got a new guide, a war chief, we started for our own country, taking a circuitous route. Our Great Father being about to pay a visit to his children in the *big towns* towards sunrising, and being desirous that we should have an opportunity of seeing them, directed our guide to take us through.

On our arrival at Baltimore, we were much astonished to see so large a village; but the war chief told us that we would soon see a *larger one.* This surprised us more. During our stay here, we visited all the public buildings and places of amusement—saw much to admire, and were well entertained by the people, who crowded to see us. Our Great Father was there at the same time, and seemed to be much liked by his white children, who flocked around him, (as they had done us,) to shake him by the hand. He did not remain long—having left the city before us.

We left Baltimore in a steam boat, and travelled in this way to the big village, where they make *medals* and *money,* [Philadelphia.] We again expressed surprise at finding this village so much larger than the one we had left; but the war chief again told us, that we would soon see another much larger than this. I had no idea that the white people had such large villages, and so many people. They were very kind to us—showed us all their great public works, their ships and steam boats. We visited the place where they make money, and saw the men engaged at it. They presented each of us with a number of pieces of the *coin* as they fell from the mint, which are very handsome.

I witnessed a militia training in this city, in which were performed a number of singular military feats. The chiefs and men were well dressed, and exhibited quite a warlike appearance. I think our system of military parade far better than that of the whites—but, as I am now done going to war, I will not describe it, or say any thing more about war, or the preparations necessary for it.

We next started to New York, and on our arrival near the wharf, saw a large collection of people gathered at Castle-Garden. We had seen many wonderful sights in our way—large villages, the great *national road* over the mountains, the *rail-roads,* steam carriages, ships, steam boats, and many other things; but we were now about to witness a sight more surprising than any of these. We were told that a man was going up into the air in a balloon! We watched with anxiety to see if it could be true; and to our utter astonishment, saw him ascend in the air until the eye could no longer perceive him. Our people were all surprised, and one of our young men asked the *prophet,* if he was going up to see the Great Spirit?

After the ascension of the balloon, we landed, and got into a carriage, to go to the house that had been provided for our reception. We had proceeded but a short distance, before the street was so crowded that it was impossible for the carriage to pass. The war chief then directed the coachman to take another street, and stop at a different house from the one he had intended. On our arrival here, we were waited upon by a number of gentlemen, who seemed much pleased to see us. We were furnished with good rooms, good provisions, and every thing necessary for our comfort.

The chiefs of this *big village,* being desirous that all their people should have an opportunity to see us, fitted up their great *council-house* for this purpose, where we saw an immense number of people; all of whom treated us with friendship, and many with great generosity.

The chiefs were particular in showing us every thing that they thought would be pleasing or gratifying to us. We went with them to Castle-Garden to see the fireworks, which was quite an agreeable entertainment—but to the *whites* who witnessed it, less *magnificent* than the sight of one of our large *prairies* would be when on fire.

We visited all the public buildings and places of amusement, which to us were truly astonishing, yet very gratifying.

Every body treated us with friendship, and many with great liberality. The squaws presented us many handsome little presents, that are said to be valuable. They were very kind, very good, and very pretty—for *pale faces!* . . .

Passing down the Mississippi, I discovered a large collection of people in the mining country, on the west side of the river, *and on the ground that we had given to our relation,* DUBUQUE, *a long time ago.* I was surprised at this, as I had understood from our Great Father, that the Mississippi was to be the dividing line between his red and white children, and that he did not wish *either* to *cross it.* I was much pleased with this talk, as I knew that it would be much better for both parties. I have since found the country much settled by the white further down, and near to our people, on the west side of the river. I am very much afraid, that in a few years, they will begin to drive and abuse our people, as they have formerly done. I may not live to *see* it, but I feel certain that the day is not distant.

# HARRIET H. ROBINSON
## 1825–1911

*Harriet Robinson's story celebrates the new economic opportunities for women created by early industrialization. At the same time, however, her autobiography dramatizes the contrast between women's chances in life and those of Benjamin Franklin, Davy Crockett, and Ulysses S. Grant.*

Harriet Hanson's father, a carpenter, died in 1831. Her mother, facing certain poverty for herself and her four small children, left Boston for Lowell, where the first significant American factories, textile mills, had recently opened. Thousands of workers, male and especially female, had transformed Lowell into a bustling city. Harriet's mother supported her brood by managing a boardinghouse for forty young men, her small children helping with the domestic tasks. At age ten Harriet entered the mills herself, where she worked intermittently until she was twenty-three.

Her career in the mills coincided with their owners' early benevolent administration. Although African-American and working-class women had always worked outside the home—Elizabeth Ashbridge as an indentured servant, for example—it was rare for a native-born, white middle-class woman to join the paid work force. New England mill-owners realized that they must accommodate these cultural constraints if they were to recruit an able but cheap work force of Yankee women. The genteel boarding houses for these young women were one inducement. So were the opportunities for self-improvement including the millgirls' magazine, The Lowell Offering, for which several talented women, including Robinson herself, wrote. Even in this paternalistic work setting, however, the female workers occasionally became discontented. Young Harriet told of her participation in a strike in 1836, although she did not write of the more sustained union unrest led by the Female Reform League at Lowell in 1845–1846.

In 1848 Robinson left the mills to become, in her phrase, "a good poor man's wife," but her life did not get much easier. Her husband, journalist William Stevens Robinson, held unpopular anti-slavery opinions which made it difficult for him to earn a steady living. His clerkship in the Massachusetts House of Representatives from 1862 to 1873 eased their financial difficulties. The Robinsons had two daughters and two sons, one of whom died in infancy. Her husband died in 1876. Robinson then began her own career as a writer of plays and non-fiction, which showed the influence of sentimental literature then very popular.

By 1898 when Robinson published Loom and Spindle, *both she and the mills had changed. Rapid industrialization now forced the New*

*England mills to compete for national and international markets. The new workforce of Irish women worked longer hours in more burdensome conditions than had Anglo-American women. Robinson wrote her story of the early mills with this bleak present in mind. Although not an early advocate of women's rights, like Elizabeth Cady Stanton, Robinson had become an ardent suffragist. Her desire to prove that women deserved the vote also shaped this autobiography.*

Loom and Spindle, or Life Among the Early Mill Girls, *Boston: T. Y. Crowell, 1898. Reprint, Kailua, Hawaii: Press Pacifica, 1976.*

In 1831, under the shadow of a great sorrow, which had made her four children fatherless,—the oldest but seven years of age,—my mother was left to struggle alone; and, although she tried hard to earn bread enough to fill our hungry mouths, she could not do it, even with the help of kind friends. And so it happened that one of her more wealthy neighbors, who had looked with longing eyes on the one little daughter of the family, offered to adopt me. But my mother, who had had a hard experience in her youth in living amongst strangers, said, "No; while I have one meal of victuals a day, I will not part with my children." I always remembered this speech because of the word "victuals," and I wondered for a long time what this good old Bible word meant.

My father was a carpenter, and some of his fellow-workmen helped my mother to open a little shop, where she sold stores, candy, kindling-wood, and so on, but there was no great income from this, and we soon became poorer than ever. Dear me! I can see the small shop now, with its jars of striped candy, its loaves of bread, the room at the back where we all lived, and my oldest brother sawing the kindling-wood which we sold to the neighbors.

That was a hard, cold winter; and for warmth's sake my mother and her four children all slept in one bed, two at the foot and three at the head,—but her richer neighbor could not get the little daughter; and, contrary to all the modern notions about hygiene, we were a healthful and a robust brood. We all, except the baby, went to school every day, and Saturday afternoons I went to a charity school to learn to sew. My mother had never complained of her poverty in our hearing, and I had accepted the conditions of my life with a child's trust, knowing nothing of the relative difference between poverty and riches. And so I went to the sewing-school, like any other little girl who was taking lessons in sewing and not as a "charity child;" until a certain day when something was said by one of the teachers, about me, as a "poor little girl,"—a thoughtless remark, no doubt, such as may be said to-day in "charity schools." When I went home I told my mother that the teacher said I was *poor,* and she replied in her sententious manner, "You need not go there again."

Shortly after this my mother's widowed sister, Mrs. Angeline Cudworth, who kept a factory boarding-house in Lowell, advised her to come to that city. She secured a house for her, and my mother, with her little brood and her few household belongings, started for the new factory town.

We went by the canal-boat, The Governor Sullivan, and a long and tiresome day it was to the weary mother and her four active children, though the children often varied the scene by walking on the tow-path under the Lombardy poplars, riding on the gates when the locks were swung open, or buying glasses of water at the stopping-places along the route.

When we reached Lowell, we were carried at once to my aunt's house, whose generous spirit had well provided for her hungry relations; and we children were led into her kitchen, where, on the longest and whitest of tables, lay, oh, so many loaves of bread!

After our feast of loaves we walked with our mother to the Tremont Corporation, where we were to live, and at the old No. 5 (which imprint is still legible over the door), in the first block of tenements then built, I began my life among factory people. My mother kept forty boarders, most of them men, mill-hands, and she did all her housework with what help her children could give her between schools; for we all, even the baby three years old, were kept at school. My part in the housework was to wash the dishes, and I was obliged to stand on a cricket in order to reach the sink!

My mother's boarders were many of them young men, and usually farmers' sons. They were almost invariably of good character and behavior, and it was a continual pleasure for me and my brothers to associate with them. I was treated like a little sister, never hearing a word or seeing a look to remind me that I was not of the same sex as my brothers. I played checkers with them, sometimes "beating," and took part in their conversation, and it never came into my mind that they were not the same as so many "girls." A good object-lesson for one who was in the future to maintain, by voice and pen, her belief in the equality of the sexes!

I had been to school constantly until I was about 10 years of age, when my mother, feeling obliged to have help in her work besides what I could give, and also needing the money which I could earn, allowed me, at my urgent request (for I wanted to earn *money* like the other little girls), to go to work in the mill. I worked first in the spinning-room as a "doffer." The doffers were the very youngest girls, whose work was to doff, or take off, the full bobbins, and replace them with the empty ones.

I can see myself now, racing down the alley, between the spinning-frames, carrying in front of me a bobbin-box bigger than I was. These mites had to be very swift in their movements, so as not to keep the spinning-frames stopped long, and they worked only about fifteen minutes in every hour. The rest of the time was their own, and when the overseer was kind they were allowed to read, knit, or even to go outside the mill-yard to play.

Some of us learned to embroider in crewels, and I still have a lamb worked on cloth, a relic of those early days, when I was first taught to improve my time in the good old New England fashion. When not doffing, we were often allowed to go home, for a time, and thus we were able to help our mothers in their housework. We were paid two dollars a week; and how proud I was when my turn came to stand up on the bobbin-box, and write my name in the paymaster's book, and how indignant I was when he asked me if I could "write." "Of course I can," said I, and he smiled as he looked down on me.

The working-hours of all the girls extended from five o'clock in the morning until seven in the evening, with one-half hour for breakfast and dinner. Even the doffers were forced to be on duty nearly fourteen hours a day, and this was the greatest hardship in the lives of these children. For it was not until 1842 that the hours of labor for children under twelve years of age were limited to ten per day; but the "ten-hour law" itself was not passed until long after some of these little doffers were old enough to appear before the legislative committee on the subject, and plead, by their presence, for a reduction of the hours of labor.

I do not recall any particular hardship connected with this life, except getting up so early in the morning, and to this habit, I never was, and never shall be, reconciled, for it has taken nearly a lifetime for me to make up the sleep lost at that early age. But in every other respect it was a pleasant life. We were not hurried any more than was for our good, and no more work was required of us than we were able easily to do.

Most of us children lived at home, and we were well fed, drinking both tea and coffee, and eating substantial meals (besides luncheons) three times a day. We had very happy hours with the older girls, many of whom treated us like babies, or talked in a motherly way, and so had a good influence over us. And in the long winter evenings, when we could not run home between the doffings, we gathered in groups and told each other stories , and sung the old-time songs our mothers had sung, such as "Barbara Allen," "Lord Lovell," "Captain Kid," "Hull's Victory," and sometimes a hymn.

Among the ghost stories I remember some that would delight the hearts of the "Society for Psychical Research." The more imaginative ones told of what they had read in fairy books, or related tales of old castles and distressed maidens; and the scene of their adventures was sometimes laid among the foundation stones of the new mill, just building.

And we told each other of our little hopes and desires, and what we meant to do when we grew up. For we had our aspirations; and one of us, who danced the "shawl dance," as she called it, in the spinning-room alley, for the amusement of her admiring companions, discussed seriously with another little girl the scheme of their running away together, and joining the circus. Fortunately, there was a grain of good sense lurking in the mind of this gay little lassie, with the thought of the mother at home, and the scheme was not carried out.

There was another little girl, whose mother was suffering with consumption, and who went out of the mill almost every forenoon, to buy and cook oysters, which she brought in hot, for her mother's luncheon. The mother soon went to her rest, and the little daughter, after tasting the first bitter experience of life, followed her. Dear Lizzie Osborne! little sister of my child-soul, such friendship as ours is not often repeated in after life! Many pathetic stories might be told of these little fatherless mill-children, who worked near their mothers, and who went hand in hand with them to and from the mill.

I cannot tell how it happened that some of us knew about the English factory children, who, it was said, were treated so badly, and were even whipped by their cruel overseers. But we did know of it, and used to sing, to a doleful little tune, some verses called, "The Factory Girl's Last Day." I do not remember it well enough to quote it as written, but have refreshed my memory by reading it lately in Robert Dale Owen's writings:—

## "THE FACTORY GIRL'S LAST DAY.

"'Twas on a winter morning,
The weather wet and wild,
Two hours before the dawning
The father roused his child,

Her daily morsel bringing,
The darksome room he paced,
And cried, The bell is ringing—
My hapless darling, haste!'

The overlooker met her,
As to her frame she crept;
And with his thong he beat her,
And cursed her when she wept.
It seemed as she grew weaker,
The threads the oftener broke,
The rapid wheels ran quicker,
And heavier fell the stroke."

The song goes on to tell the sad story of her death while her "pitying comrades" were carrying her home to die, and ends:—

"That night a chariot passed her,
While on the ground she lay;
The daughters of her master,
An evening visit pay.
Their tender hearts were sighing,
As negroes' wrongs were told,
While the white slave was dying
Who gained her father's gold."

In contrast with this sad picture, we thought of ourselves as well off, in our cosey corner of the mill, enjoying ourselves in our own way, with our good mothers and our warm suppers awaiting us when the going-out bell should ring.

Holidays came when repairs to the great mill-wheel were going on or some late spring freshet caused the shutting down of the mill; these were well improved. With what freedom we enjoyed those happy times! My summer playhouse was the woodshed, which my mother always had well filled; how orderly and with what precision the logs were sawed and piled with the smooth ends outwards! The catacombs of Paris reminded me of my old playhouse. And here, in my castle of sawed wood, was my vacation retreat, where, with my only and beloved wooden doll, I lunched on slices of apple cut in shape so as to represent what I called "German half-moon cakes." I piled up my bits of crockery with sticks of cinnamon to represent candy, and many other semblances of things drawn from my mother's housekeeping stores.

The yard which led to the shed was always green, and here many half-holiday duties were performed. We children were expected to scour all the knives and forks used by the forty men-boarders, and my brothers often bought themselves off by giving me some trifle, and I was left alone to do the whole. And what a pile of knives and forks it was! But it was no task, for did I not have the open yard to work in, with the sky over me, and the green grass to stand on, as I scrubbed away at my "stent"? I don't know why I did not think such long tasks a burden, nor of my work in the mill as drudgery. Perhaps it was because I *expected* to do my part towards helping my mother to get our living, and had never heard her complain of the hardships of her life.

On other afternoons I went to walk with a playmate, who, like myself, was full of romantic dreams, along the banks of the Merrimack River, where the Indians had still their tents, or on Sundays, to see the "new converts" baptized. These baptizings in the river were very common, as the tanks in the churches were not considered *apostolic* by the early Baptists of Lowell.

Sometimes we rambled by the "race-way" or mill-race, which carried the water into the flume of the mill, along whose inclining sides grew wild roses, and the "rock-loving columbine;" and we used to listen to see if we could hear the blue-bells ring,—this was long before either of us had read a line of poetry.

The North Grammar school building stood at the base of a hilly ridge of rocks, down which we coasted in winter, and where in summer, after school-hours, we had a little cave, where we sometimes hid, and played that we were robbers; and together we rehearsed the dramatic scenes in "Alonzo and Melissa," "The Children of the Abbey," or the "Three Spaniards;" we were turned out of doors with Amanda, we exclaimed "Heavens!" with Melissa, and when night came on we fled from our playhouse pursued by the dreadful apparition of old Don Padilla through the dark windings of those old rocks, towards our commonplace home. "Ah!" as some writer has said, "if one could only add the fine imagination of those early days to the knowledge and experience of later years, what books might not be written!"

Our home amusements were very original. We had no toys, except a few homemade articles or devices of our own. I had but a single doll, a wooden-jointed thing, with red cheeks and staring black eyes. Playing-cards were tabooed, but my elder brother, who had somehow learned the game of high-low-jack, set about making a pack. The cards were cut out of thick yellow pasteboard, the spots and figures were made in ink, and, to disguise their real character, the names of the suits were changed. Instead of hearts, diamonds, spades and clubs, they were called charity, love, benevolence, and faith. The pasteboard was so thick that all together the cards made a pile at least two or three feet high, and they had to be shuffled in sections! He taught my second brother and me the game of high-low-jack; and, with delightful secrecy, as often as we could steal away, we played in the attic, keeping the cards hidden, between whiles, in an old hair trunk. In playing the game we got along very well with the names of the face-cards,—the "queen of charity," the "king of love," and so on; but the "ten-spot of faith," and particularly the "two-spot of benevolence" (we had never heard of the "deuce") was too much for our sense of humor, and almost spoiled the "rigor of the game."

I was a "little doffer" until I became old enough to earn more money; then I tended a spinning-frame for a little while; and after that I learned, on the Merrimack corporation, to be a drawing-in girl, which was considered one of the most desirable employments, as about only a dozen girls were needed in each mill. We drew in, one by one, the threads of the warp, through the harness and the reed, and so made the beams ready for the weaver's loom. I still have the two hooks I used so long, companions of many a dreaming hour, and preserve them as the "badge of all my tribe" of drawing-in girls.

It may be well to add that, although so many changes have been made in mill-work, during the last fifty years, by the introduction of machinery, this part of it still continues to be done by hand, and the drawing-in girl—I saw her last winter, as in my time—still sits on her high stool, and with her little hook patiently draws in the thousands of threads, one by one.

The education of a child is an all-around process, and he or she owes only a part of it to school or college training. The child to whom neither college nor school is open must find his whole education in his surroundings, and in the life he is forced to lead. As the cotton-factory was the means of the early schooling of so large a number of men and women, who, without the opportunity thus afforded, could not have been mentally so well developed, I love to call it their *Alma Mater*. For, without this incentive to labor, this chance to earn extra money and to use it in their own way, their influence on the times, and also, to a certain extent, on modern civilization, would certainly have been lost.

I had been to school quite constantly until I was nearly eleven years of age, and then, after going into the mill, I went to some of the evening schools that had been established, and which were always well filled with those who desired to improve their scant education, or to supplement what they had learned in the village school or academy. Here might often be seen a little girl puzzling over her sums in Colburn's Arithmetic, and at her side another "girl" of fifty poring over her lessons in Pierpont's National Reader.

Some of these schools were devoted to special studies. I went to a geography school, where the lessons were repeated in unison in a monotonous sing-song tone, like this: "Lake Winni*peg*! Lake Winni*peg*! Lake Titi*caca*! Lake Titi*caca*! *Mem*phre*magog*!" and also to a school where those who fancied they had thoughts were taught by Newman's Rhetoric to express them in writing. In this school, the relative position of the subject and the predicate was not always well taught by the master; but never to mix a metaphor or to confuse a simile was a lesson he firmly fixed in the minds of his pupils.

As a result of this particular training, I may say here, that, while I do not often mix metaphors I am to this day almost as ignorant of what is called "grammar" as Dean Swift, who, when he went up to answer for his degree, said he "could not tell a subject from a predicate;" or even James Whitcomb Riley, who said he "would not know a nominative if I should meet it on the street."

The best practical lesson in the proper use of at least one grammatical sentence was given to me by my elder brother (not two years older than I) one day, when I said, "I done it." "You done it!" said he, taking me by the shoulder and looking me severely in the face, "Don't you ever let me hear you say *I done it* again, unless you can use *have* or *had* before it." I also went to singing-school, and became a member of the church choir, and in this way learned many beautiful hymns that made a lasting impression on the serious part of my nature.

The discipline our work brought us was of great value. We were obliged to be in the mill at just such a minute, in every hour, in order to doff our full bobbins and replace them with empty ones. We went to our meals and returned at the same hour every day. We worked and played at regular intervals, and thus our hands became deft, our fingers nimble, our feet swift, and we were taught daily habits of regularity and of industry; it was, in fact, a sort of manual training or industrial school.

Some of us were fond of reading, and we read all the books we could borrow. One of my mother's boarders, a farmer's daughter from "the State of Maine," had come to Lowell to work, for the express purpose of getting books, usually novels, to read, that she could not find in her native place. She read from two to four volumes a week; and we children used to get them from the circulating library, and return them, for her. In exchange for this, she allowed us to read her books, while she was at work in the mill; and what a scurrying there used to be home from school, to get the first chance at the new book.

It was as good as a fortune to us, and all for six and a quarter cents a week! In this way I read the novels of Richardson, Madame D'Arblay, Fielding, Smollett, Cooper, Scott, Captain Marryatt, and many another old book not included in Mr. Ruskin's list of "one hundred good books." Passing through the alembic of a child's pure mind, I am not now conscious that the reading of the doubtful ones did me any lasting harm. But I should add that I do not advise such indiscriminate reading among young people, and there is no need of it, since now there are so many good books, easy of access, which have not the faults of those I was obliged to read. Then, there was no choice. Today, the best of reading, for children and young people, can be found everywhere.

"Lalla Rookh" was the first poem I ever read, and it awoke in me, not only a love of poetry, but also a desire to try my own hand at verse-making.

And so the process of education went on, and I, with many another "little doffer," had more than one chance to nibble at the root of knowledge. I had been to school for three months in each year, until I was about thirteen years old, when my mother, who was now a little better able to do without my earnings, sent me to the Lowell High School regularly for two years, adding her constant injunction, "Improve your mind, try and be somebody." There I was taught a little of everything, including French and Latin; and I may say here that my "little learning," in French at least, proved "a dangerous thing," as I had reason to know some years later, when I tried to speak my book-French in Paris, for it might as well have been Choctaw, when used as a means of oral communication with the natives of that fascinating city.

The Lowell high school, in about 1840, was kept in a wooden building over a butcher's shop, but soon afterwards the new high school, still in use, was provided, and it was co-educational. How well I remember some of the boys and girls, and I recall them with pleasure if not with affection. I could name them now, and have noted with pride their success in life. A few are so high above the rest that one would be surprised to know that they received the principal part of their school education in that little high school room over the butcher's shop.

I left the high school when fifteen years of age, my school education completed; though after that I took private lessons in German, drawing, and dancing! About this time my elder brother and I made up our minds that our mother had worked hard long enough, and we prevailed on her to give up keeping boarders. This she did, and while she remained in Lowell we supported the home by our earnings. I was obliged to have my breakfast before daylight in the winter. My mother prepared it over night, and while I was cooking and eating it I read such books as Steven's "Travels" in Yucatan and in Mexico, Tasso's "Jerusalem Delivered," and "Lights and Shadows of Scottish Life." My elder brother was the clerk in the counting-room of the Tremont Corporation, and the agent, Mr. Charles L. Tilden,—whom I thank, wherever he may be,—allowed him to carry home at night, or over Sunday, any book that might be left on his (the agent's) desk; by this means I read many a beloved volume of poetry, late into the night and on Sunday. Longfellow, in particular, I learned almost by heart, and so retentive is the young memory that I can repeat, even now, whole poems.

I read and studied also at my work; and as this was done by the job, or beam, if I chose to have a book in my lap, and glance at it at intervals, or even write a bit, nothing was lost to the "corporation."

Lucy Larcom, in her "New England Girlhood," speaks of the windows in the mill on whose sides were pasted newspaper clippings, which she calls "window gems." It was very common for the spinners and weavers to do this, as they were not allowed to read books openly in the mill; but they brought their favorite "pieces" of poetry, hymns, and extracts, and pasted them up over their looms or frames, so that they could glance at them, and commit them to memory. We little girls were fond of reading these clippings, and no doubt they were an incentive to our thoughts as well as to those of the older girls, who went to "The Improvement Circle," and wrote compositions.

A year or two after this I attempted poetry, and my verses began to appear in the newspapers, in one or two Annuals, and later in *The Lowell Offering.*

In 1846 I wrote some verses which were published in the *Lowell Journal,* and these caused me to make the acquaintance of the sub-editor of that paper, who afterwards became my life companion. I speak of this here because, in my early married life, I found the exact help that I needed for continued education,—the leisure to read good books, sent to my husband for review, in the quiet of my secluded home. For I had neither the gowns to wear nor the disposition to go into society, and as my companion was not willing to go without me, in the long evenings, when the children were in bed and I was busy making "auld claes look amaist as good as new," (old clothes look almost as good as new) he read aloud to me countless books on abstruse political and general subjects, which I never should have thought of reading for myself.

These are the "books that have helped me." In fact, of all the books I have read, I remember but very few that have not helped me. Thus I had the companionship of a mind more mature, wiser, and less prone to unrealities than my own; and if it seems to the reader that my story is that of one of the more fortunate ones among the working-girls of my time, it is because of this needed help, which I received almost at the beginning of my womanhood. And for this, as well as for those early days of poverty and toil, I am devoutly and reverently thankful....

When I look back into the factory life of fifty or sixty years ago, I do not see what is called "a class" of young men and women going to and from their daily work, like so many ants that cannot be distinguished one from another. I see them as individuals, with personalities of their own. This one has about her the atmosphere of her early home. That one is impelled by a strong and noble purpose. The other,—what she is, has been an influence for good to me and to all womankind.

Yet they were a class of factory operatives, and were spoken of (as the same class is spoken of now) as a set of persons who earned their daily bread, whose condition was fixed, and who must continue to spin and to weave to the end of their natural existence. Nothing but this was expected of them, and they were not supposed to be capable of social or mental improvement. That they could be educated and developed into something more than mere work-people, was an idea that had not yet entered the public mind. So little does one class of persons really know about the thoughts and aspirations of another! It was the good fortune of these early mill-girls to teach the people of that time that this sort of labor is not degrading; that the operative is not only "capable of virtue," but also capable of self-cultivation.

At the time the Lowell cotton-mills were started, the factory girl was the lowest among women. In England, and in France particularly, great injustice had been done to her real character; she was represented as subjected to influences that could not fail to destroy her purity and self-respect. In the eyes of her overseer she was but a brute, a slave, to be beaten, pinched, and pushed about. It was to overcome this prejudice that such high wages had been offered to women that they might be induced to become mill girls, in spite of the opprobrium that still clung to this "degrading occupation." At first only a few came; for, though tempted by the high wages to be regularly paid in "cash," there were many who still preferred to go on working at some more *genteel* employment at seventy-five cents a week and their board.

But in a short time the prejudice against factory labor wore away, and the Lowell mills became filled with blooming and energetic New England women. They were naturally intelligent, had mother-wit, and fell easily into the ways of their new life. They soon began to associate with those who formed the community in which they had come to live, and were invited to their houses. They went to the same church, and sometimes married into some of the best families. Or if they returned to their secluded homes again, instead of being looked down upon as "factory girls" by the squire's or the lawyer's family, they were more often welcomed as coming from the metropolis, bringing new fashions, new books, and new ideas with them.

In 1831 Lowell was little more than a factory village. Several corporations were started, and the cotton-mills belonging to them were building. Help was in great demand; and stories were told all over the country of the new factory town, and the high wages that were offered to all classes of work-people,—stories that reached the ears of mechanics' and farmers' sons, and gave new life to lonely and dependent women in distant towns and farmhouses. Into this Yankee El Dorado, these needy people began to pour by the various modes of travel known to those slow old days. The stage-coach and the canal-boat came every day, always filled with new recruits for this army of useful people. The mechanic and machinist came, each with his home-made chest of tools, and often-times his wife and little ones. The widow came with her little flock and her scanty housekeeping goods to open a boarding-house or variety store, and so provide a home for her fatherless children. Many farmers' daughters came to earn money to complete their wedding outfit, or buy the bride's share of housekeeping articles.

Women with past histories came, to hide their griefs and their identity, and to earn an honest living in the "sweat of their brow." Single young men came, full of hope and life, to get money for an education, or to lift the mortgage from the home-farm. Troops of young girls came by stages and baggage-wagons, men often being employed to go to other States and to Canada, to collect them at so much a head, and deliver them at the factories.

A very curious sight these country girls presented to young eyes accustomed to a more modern style of things. When the large covered baggage-wagon arrived in front of a block on the corporation, they would descend from it, dressed in various and outlandish fashions, and with their arms brimful of bandboxes containing all their worldly goods. On each of these was sewed a card, on which one could read the old-fashioned New England name of the owner. And sorrowful enough they looked, even to the fun-loving child who has lived to tell the story; for they had all left their pleasant country homes to try their fortunes in a great manufacturing town, and they were homesick even before they landed at the doors of their boarding-houses. Years after, this scene dwelt in my memory; and whenever anyone said anything about being homesick, there rose before me the picture of a young girl with a sorrowful face and a big tear in each eye, clambering down the steps at the rear of a great covered wagon, holding fast to a cloth-covered bandbox, drawn up at the top with a string, on which was sewed a paper bearing the name of Plumy Clay!

Some of these girls brought diminutive hair trunks covered with the skin of calves, spotted in dun and white, even as when they did skip and play in daisy-blooming meads. And when several of them were set together in front of one of the blocks, they looked like their living counterparts, reposing at noontide in the adjacent field. One of this kind of trunks has been handed down to me as an heirloom. The hair is worn off in patches; it cannot be invigorated, and it is now become a hairless heirloom. Within its hide-bound sides are safely stowed away the love-letters of a past generation,—love-letters that agitated the hearts of the grandparents of to-day; and I wonder that their resistless ardor has not long ago burst its wrinkled sides. It is relegated to distant attics, with its ancient crony, "ye bandbox," to enjoy an honored and well-earned repose.

Ah me! when some of us, its contemporaries, are also past our usefulness, gone clean out of fashion, may we also be as resigned, yea, as willing, to be laid quietly on some attic shelf!

These country girls had queer names, which added to the singularity of their appearance. Samantha, Triphena, Plumy, Kezia, Aseneth, Elgardy, Leafy, Ruhamah, Lovey, Almaretta, Sarepta, and Florilla were among them.

Their dialect was also very peculiar. On the broken English and Scotch of their ancestors was ingrafted the nasal Yankee twang; so that many of them, when they had just come *daown,* spoke a language almost unintelligible. But the severe discipline and ridicule which met them was as good as a school education, and they were soon taught the "city way of speaking."

Their dress was also peculiar, and was of the plainest of homespun, cut in such an old-fashioned style that each young girl looked as if she had borrowed her grandmother's gown. Their only head-covering was a shawl, which was pinned under the chin; but after the first payday, a "shaker" (or "scooter") sunbonnet usually replaced this primitive head-gear of their rural life.

But the early factory girls were not all country girls. There was others also, who had been taught that "work is no disgrace." There were some who came to Lowell solely on account of the social or literary advantages to be found there. They lived in secluded parts of New England, where books were scarce, and there was no cultivated society. They had comfortable homes, and did not perhaps need the *money* they would earn; but they longed to see this new "City of Spindles," of which they had heard so much from their neighbors and friends, who had gone there to work.

And the fame of the circulating libraries, that were soon opened, drew them there, when no other inducement would have been sufficient.

The laws relating to women were such, that a husband could claim his wife wherever he found her, and also the children she was trying to shield from his influence; and I have seen more than one poor woman skulk behind her loom or her frame when visitors were approaching the end of the aisle where she worked. Some of these were known under assumed names, to prevent their husbands from trusteeing their wages. It was a very common thing for a male person of a certain kind to do this, thus depriving his wife of *all* her wages, perhaps, month after month. The wages of minor children could be trusteed, unless the children (being fourteen years of age) were given their time. Women's wages were also trusteed for the debts of their husbands, and children's for the debts of their parents.

As an instance, my mother had some financial difficulties when I was fifteen years old, and to save herself and me from annoyance, she gave me my time. The document reads as follows:—

"Be it known that I, Harriet Hanson, of Lowell, in consideration that my minor daughter Harriet J. has taken upon herself the whole burden of her own support, and has undertaken and agreed to maintain herself henceforward without expense to me, do hereby release and quitclaim unto her all profits and wages which she may hereafter earn or acquire by her skill or labor in any occupation,—and do hereby disclaim all right to collect or interfere with the same. And I do give and release unto her the absolute control and disposal of her own time according to her own discretion, without interference from me. It being understood that I am not to be chargeable hereafter with any expense on her account.

(Signed) Harriet Hanson.

*July* 2, 1840."

It must be remembered that at this date woman had no property rights. A widow could be left without her share of her husband's (or the family) property, a legal "incumbrance" to his estate. A father could make his will without reference to his daughter's share of the inheritance. He usually left her a home on the farm as long as she remained single. A woman was not supposed to be capable of spending her own or of using other people's money. In Massachusetts, before 1840, a woman could not legally be treasurer of her own sewing society, unless some man were responsible for her.

The law took no cognizance of woman as a money-spender. She was a ward, an appendage, a relict. Thus it happened, that if a woman did not choose to marry, or, when left a widow, to re-marry, she had no choice but to enter one of the few employments open to her, or to become a burden on the charity of some relative.

In almost every New England home could be found one or more of these women, sometimes welcome, more often unwelcome, and leading joyless, and in many instances unsatisfactory, lives. The cotton-factory was a great opening to these lonely and dependent women. From a condition aproaching pauperism they were at once placed above want, they could earn money, and spend it as they pleased; and could gratify their tastes and desires without restraint, and without rendering an account to anybody. At last they had found a place in the universe; they were no longer obliged to finish out their faded lives mere burdens to male relatives. Even the *time* of these women was their own, on Sundays and in the evening after the day's work was done. For the first time in this country woman's labor had a money value. She had become not only an earner and a producer, but also a spender of money, a recognized factor in the political economy of her time. And thus a long upward step in our material civilization was taken; woman had begun to earn and hold her own money, and through its aid had learned to think and to act for herself.

Among the older women who sought this new employment were very many lonely and dependent ones, such as used to be mentioned in old wills as "incumbrances" and "relicts," and to whom a chance of earning money was indeed a new revelation. How well I remember some of these solitary ones! As a child of eleven years, I often made fun of them—for children do not see the pathetic side of human life—and imitated their limp carriage and inelastic gait. I can see them now, even after sixty years, just as they looked,—depressed, modest, mincing, hardly daring to look one in the face, so shy and sylvan had been their lives. But after the first pay-day came, and they felt the jingle of silver in their pockets, and had begun to feel its mercurial influence, their bowed heads were lifted, their necks seemed braced with steel, they looked you in the face, sang blithely among their looms or frames, and walked with elastic step to and from their work. And when Sunday came, homespun was no longer their only wear; and how sedately gay in their new attire they walked to church, and how proudly they dropped their silver four-pences into the contribution-box! It seemed as if a great hope impelled them,—the harbinger of the new era that was about to dawn for them and for all woman-kind.

In passing, let me not forget to pay a tribute, also to those noble single and widowed women, who are "set solitary in families," but whose presence cements the domestic fabric, and whose influence is unseen and oftentimes unappreciated, until they are taken away and the integral part of the old home-life begins to crumble.

Except in rare instances, the rights of the early mill-girls were secure. They were subject to no extortion, if they did extra work they were always paid in full, and their own account of labor done by the piece was always accepted. They kept the figures, and were paid accordingly. This was notably the case with the weavers and drawing-in girls. Though the hours of labor were long, they were not over-worked; they were obliged to tend no more looms and frames than they could easily take care of, and they had plenty of time to sit and rest. I have known a girl to sit idle twenty or thirty minutes at a time. They were not driven, and their work-a-day life was made easy. They were treated with consideration by their employers, and there was a feeling of respectful equality between them. The most favored of the girls were sometimes invited to the houses of the dignitaries of the mills, showing that the line of social division was not rigidly maintained.

Their life in the factory was made pleasant to them. In those days there was no need of advocating the doctrine of the proper relation between employer and employed. *Help was too valuable to be ill-treated.* If these early agents, or over-seers, had been disposed to exercise undue authority, or to establish unjust or arbitrary laws, the high character of the operatives, and the fact that women employees were scarce would have prevented it. A certain agent of one of the first corporations in Lowell (an old sea-captain) said to one of his boarding-house keepers, "I should like to rule my help as I used to rule my sailors, but so many of them are women I do not dare to do it."

The knowledge of the antecedents of these operatives was the safeguard of their liberties. The majority of them were as well born as their "overlookers," if not better; and they were also far better educated.

The agents and overseers were usually married men, with families of growing sons and daughters. They were members, and sometimes deacons, of the church, and teachers in the same Sunday-school with the girls employed under them. They were generally of good morals and temperate habits, and often exercised a good influence over their help. The feeling that the agents and overseers were inter-ested in their welfare caused the girls, in turn, to feel an interest in the work for which their employers were responsible. The conscientious among them took as much pride in spinning a smooth thread, drawing in a perfect web, or in making good cloth, as they would have done if the material had been for their own wearing. And thus was practised, long before it was preached, that principle of true political economy,—the just relation, the mutual interest, that ought to exist between employers and employed.

Those of the mill-girls who had homes generally worked from eight to ten months in the year; the rest of the time was spent with parents or friends. A few taught school during the summer months.

When we left the mill, or changed our place of work from one corporation to another, we were given an "honorable discharge." Mine, of which I am still quite proud, is dated the year of my marriage, and is as follows:—

"Harriet J. Hanson has been employed in the Boott Cotton Mills, in a dressing-room, twenty-five months, and is honorable discharged."

(Signed) J. F. Trott.

It may be added here, that the majority of the mill-girls made just as good use of their money, so newly earned, and of whose value they had hitherto known so little. They were necessarily industrious. They were also frugal and saving. It was their custom on the first day of every month, after paying their board-bill ($1.25 a week), to put their wages in the savings-bank. There the money stayed, on interest, until they withdrew it, to carry home or to use for a special purpose. It is easy to see how much good this sum would do in a rural community where money, as a means of exchange, had been scarce. Into the barren homes many of them had left it went like a quiet stream, carrying with it beauty and refreshment. The mortgage was lifted from the homestead; the farmhouse was painted; the barn rebuilt; modern improvements (including Mrs. Child's "Frugal Housewife"—the first American cook-book) were introduced into the mother's kitchen, and books and newspapers began to ornament the sitting-room table.

Some of the mill-girls helped maintain widowed mothers, or drunken, incompetent, or invalid fathers. Many of them educated the younger children of the family, and young men were sent to college with the money furnished by the untiring industry of their women relatives.

Indeed, the most prevailing incentive to our labor was to secure the means of education for some *male* member of the family. To make a *gentleman* of a brother or a son, to give him a college education, was the dominant thought in the minds of a great many of these provident mill-girls. I have known more than one to give every cent of her wages, month after month, to her brother, that he might get the education necessary to enter some profession. I have known a mother to work years in this way for her boy. I have known women to educate by their earnings young men who were not sons or relatives. There are men now living who were helped to an education by the wages of the early mill-girls.

In speaking of this subject, Mr. Thomas Wentworth Higginson says,—

"I think it was the late President Walker who told me that in his judgment one-quarter of the men in Harvard College were being carried through by the special self-denial and sacrifices of women. I cannot answer for the ratio; but I can testify to having been an instance of this myself, and to having known a never-ending series of such cases of self-devotion."

Lowell, in this respect, was indeed a remarkable town, and it might be said of it, as of Thrums in "Auld Licht Idyls," "There are scores and scores of houses in it that have sent their sons to college (by what a struggle), some to make their way to the front in their professions, and others, perhaps, despite their broadcloth, never to be a patch upon their parents."

The early mill-girls were religious by nature and by Puritan inheritance, true daughters of those men and women who, as some one has said, "were as devoted to education as they were to religion;" for they planted the church and the school-house side by side. On entering the mill, each one was obliged to sign a "regulation paper" which required her to attend regularly some place of public worship. They were of many denominations. In one boarding-house that I knew, there were girls belonging to eight different religious sects.

In 1843, there were in Lowell fourteen regularly organized religious societies. Ten of these constituted a "Sabbath School Union," which consisted of over five thousand scholars and teachers; three-fourths of the scholars, and a large proportion of the teachers, were mill-girls. Once a year, every Fourth of July, this "Sabbath School Union," each section, or division, under its own sectarian banner, marched in procession to the grove on Chapel Hill, where a picnic was held, with lemonade, and long speeches by the ministers of the different churches—speeches which the little boys and girls did not seem to think were made to be listened to.

The mill-girls went regularly to meeting and "Sabbath-school;" and every Sunday the streets of Lowell were alive with neatly dressed young women, going or returning there from. Their fine appearance on "the Sabbath" was often spoken of by strangers visiting Lowell.

Dr. Scoresby, in his "American Factories and their Operatives," (with selections from *The Lowell Offering*,) holds up the Lowell mill-girls to their sister operatives of Bradford, England, as an example of neatness and good behavior. Indeed, it was a pretty sight to see so many wide-awake young girls in the bloom of life, clad in their holiday dresses,—

> "Whose delicate feet to the Temple of God,
> Seemed to move as if wings had carried them there."

The morals of these girls were uniformly good. The regulation paper, before spoken of, required each one to be of good moral character; and if any one proved to be disreputable, she was very soon turned out of the mill. Their standard of behavior was high, and the majority kept aloof from those who were suspected of wrong-doing. They had, perhaps, less temptation than the working-girls of to-day, since they were not required to dress beyond their means, and comfortable homes were provided by their employers, where they could board cheaply. Their surroundings were pure, and the whole atmosphere of their boarding-houses was as refined as that of their own homes. They expected men to treat them with courtesy; they looked forward to becoming the wives of good men. Their attitude was that of the German *Fraulein,* who said, "Treat every maiden with respect, for you do not know whose *wife* she will be."

But there were exceptions to the general rule, just enough to prove the doctrine of averages; there were girls who came to the mill to work whom no one knew anything about, but they did not stay long, the life there being "too clean for them."

The health of the girls was good. The regularity and simplicity of their lives, and the plain and substantial food provided for them, kept them free from illness. From their Puritan ancestry they had inherited sound bodies and a fair share of endurance. Fevers and similar diseases were rare among them; they had no time to pet small ailments; the boarding-house mother was often both nurse and doctor, and so the physician's fee was saved. It may be said that, at that time, there was but one *pathy* and no "faith cures" nor any "science" to be supported by the many diseases "that flesh is heir to."

By reading the weekly newspapers the girls became interested in public events; they knew all about the Mexican war, and the anti-slavery cause had its adherents among them. Lectures on the doctrine of Fourier were read, or listened to, but none of them were "carried away" with the idea of spending their lives in large "phalansteries," as they seemed too much like cotton-factories to be models for their own future housekeeping.

The Brook Farm experiment was familiar to some of them; but the fault of this scheme was apparent to the practical ones who foresaw that a few would have to do all the manual labor and that an undue share would naturally fall to those who had already contracted the working-habit.

Mrs. Amelia Bloomer, one of the early pioneers of the dress-reform movement, found followers in Lowell; and parlor meetings were held at some of the boarding-houses to discuss the feasibility of this great revolution in the style of woman's dress. *The Lowell Journal* of 1850 states that on the Fourth of July a party of "Bloomerites" walked in the procession through the public streets, and *The London Punch* embellished its pages with a neat cartoon, a fashion-plate showing the different styles of the Bloomer costume. This first attempt at a reform in woman's dress was ridiculed out of existence by "public opinion;" but from it has been evolved the modern bicycle costume, now worn by women cyclers.

It seems to have been the fashion of the mill-girls to appear in procession on all public occasions. Mr. Cowley, in his "History of Lowell," speaks of President Jackson's visit to that city in 1833. He says: "On the day the President came, all the lady operatives turned out to meet him. They walked in procession, like troops of liveried angels clothed in white [with green-fringed parasols], with cannons booming, drums beating, banners flying, handkerchiefs waving, etc. The old hero was not more moved by the bullets that whistled round him in the battle of New Orleans than by the exhilarating spectacle here presented, and remarked, 'They are very pretty women, by the Eternal!' "

One of the first strikes of cotton-factory operatives that ever took place in this country was that in Lowell, in October, 1836. When it was announced that the wages were to be cut down, great indignation was felt, and it was decided to strike, *en masse.* This was done. The mills were shut down, and the girls went in procession from their several corporations to the "grove" on Chapel Hill, and listened to "incendiary" speeches from early labor reformers.

One of the girls stood on a pump, and gave vent to the feelings of her companions in a neat speech, declaring that it was their duty to resist all attempts at cutting down the wages. This was the first time a woman had spoken in public in Lowell, and the event caused surprise and consternation among her audience.

Cutting down the wages was not their only grievance, nor the only cause of this strike. Hitherto the corporations had paid twenty-five cents a week towards the board of each operative, and now it was their purpose to have the girls pay the sum; and this, in addition to the cut in wages, would make a difference of at least one dollar a week. It was estimated that as many as twelve or fifteen hundred girls turned out, and walked in procession through the streets. They had neither flags nor music, but sang songs, a favorite (but rather inappropriate) one being a parody on "I won't be a nun."

> "Oh! isn't it a pity, such a pretty girl as I—
> Should be sent to the factory to pine away and die?
> Oh! I cannot be a slave,
> I will not be a slave,
> For I'm so fond of liberty
> That I cannot be a slave."

My own recollection of this first strike (or "turn out" as it was called) is very vivid. I worked in a lower room, where I had heard the proposed strike fully, if not vehemently, discussed; I had been an ardent listener to what was said against this attempt at "oppression" on the part of the corporation, and naturally I took sides with the strikers. When the day came on which the girls were to turn out, those in the upper rooms started first, and so many of them left that our mill was at once shut down. Then, when the girls in my room stood irresolute, uncertain what to do, asking each other, "Would you?" or "Shall we turn out?" and not one of them having the courage to lead off, I, who began to think they would not go out, after all their talk, became impatient, and started on ahead, saying, with childish bravado, "I don't care what you do, *I* am going to turn out, whether any one else does or not;" and I marched out, and was followed by the others.

As I looked back at the long line that followed me, I was more proud than I have ever been since at any success I may have achieved, and more proud than I shall ever be again until my own beloved State gives to its women citizens the right of suffrage.

The agent of the corporation where I then worked took some small revenges on the supposed ringleaders; on the principle of sending the weaker to the wall, my mother was turned away from her boarding-house, that functionary saying, "Mrs. Hanson, you could not prevent the older girls from turning out, but your daughter is a child, and *her* you could control."

It is hardly necessary to say that so far as results were concerned this strike did no good. The dissatisfaction of the operatives subsided, or burned itself out, and though the authorities did not accede to their demands, the majority returned to their work, and the corporation went on cutting down the wages.

And after a time, as the wages became more and more reduced, the best portion of the girls left and went to their homes, or to the other employments that were fast opening to women, until there were very few of the old guard left; and thus the *status* of the factory population of New England gradually became what we know it to be to day.

Some of us took part in a political campaign, for the first time, in 1840, when William H. Harrison, the first Whig President, was elected; we went to the political meetings, sat in the gallery, heard speeches against Van Buren and the Democratic paty, and helped sing the great campaign song beginning:—

> "Oh have you heard the news of late?"

the refrain of which was:

> "Tippecanoe and Tyler too,
> Oh with them we'll beat little Van, Van,
> Van is a used-up man."

And we named our sunbonnets "log-cabins," and set our teacups (we drank from saucers then) in little glass teaplates, with log-cabins impressed on the bottom. The part the Lowell mill-girls took in these and similar events serves to show how wide-awake and up to date many of these middle-century working-women were.

Among the *fads* of those days may be mentioned those of the "water-cure" and the "Grahamite." The former was a theory of doctoring by means of cold water, used as packs, daily baths, and immoderate drinks. Quite a number of us adopted this practice, and one at least has not even yet wholly abandoned it.

Several members of my mother's family adopted "Professor" Graham's regimen, and for a few months we ate no meat, nor, as he said, "anything that had life in it." It was claimed that this would regenerate the race; that by following a certain line of diet, a person would live longer, do better work, and be able to endure any hardship, in fact, that not what we were, but what we ate, would be the making of us. Two young men, whom I knew, made their boasts that they had "walked from Boston to Lowell on an apple."

We ate fruit, vegetables, and unleavened or whole-wheat bread, baked in little round pats ("bullets," my mother called them), and without butter; there were no *relishes*. I soon got tired of the feeling of "goneness" this diet gave me; I found that although I might eat a pint of mashed potato, and the same quantity of squash, it was if I had not dined, and I gave up the experiment. But my elder brother, who had carried to the extremest extreme this "potato gospel," as Carlyle called it, induced my mother to make his Thanksgiving squash-pie after a receipt of his own. The crust was made of Indian meal and water, and the filling was of squash, water, and sugar! And he ate it, and called it good. But I thought then, and still think, that his enjoyment of the eating was in the principle rather than in the pie.

A few of the girls were interested in phrenology; and we had our heads examined by Professor Fowler, who, if not the first, was the chief exponent of this theory in Lowell. He went about into all the schools, examining children's heads. Mine, he said, "lacked veneration;" and this I supposed was an awful thing, because my teacher looked so reproachfully at me when the professor said it.

A few were interested in Mesmerism; and those of us who had the power to make ourselves *en rapport* with others tried experiments on "subjects," and sometimes held meetings in the evening for that purpose.

The life in the boarding houses was very agreeable. These houses belonged to the corporation, and were usually kept by widows (mothers of mill-girls), who were often the friends and advisers of their boards.

Among these may be mentioned the mothers of Lucy Larcom; the Hon. Gustavus Vasa Fox, once Assistant Secretary of the Navy; John W. Hanson, D.D.; the Rev. W.H. Cudworth; Major General B.F. Butler; and several others.

Each house was a village or community of itself. There fifty or sixty young women from different parts of New England met and lived together. When not at their work, by natural selection they sat in groups in their chambers, or in a corner of the large dining-room, busy at some agreeable employment; or they wrote letters, read, studied, or sewed, for, as a rule, they were their own seamstresses and dressmakers.

It is refreshing to remember their simplicity of dress; they wore no ruffles and very few ornaments. It is true that some of them had gold watches and gold pencils, but they were worn only on grand occasions; as a rule, the early mill-girls were not of that class that is said to be "always suffering for a breast-pin." Though their dress was so simple and so plain, yet it was so tasteful that they were often accused of looking like ladies; the complaint was sometimes made that no one could tell the difference in *church* between the factory-girls and the daughters of some of the first families in the city.

Mrs. Sarah J. Hale, in *The Lady's Book,* in 1842, speaking of the impossibility of considering dress a mark of distinction, says: "Many of the factory-girls wear gold watches and an imitation at least of all the ornaments which grace the daughters of our most opulent citizens."

The boarding-houses were considered so attractive that strangers, by invitation, often came to look in upon them, and see for themselves how the mill-girls lived. Dickens, in his "American Notes," speaks with surprise of their home life. He says, "There is a piano in a great many of the boarding-houses, and nearly all the young ladies subscribe to circulating libraries." There was a feeling of *esprit de corps* among these households; any advantage secured to one of the number was usually shared by others belonging to her set or group. Books were exchanged, letters from home were read, and "pieces," intended for the Improvement Circle, were presented for friendly criticism.

There was always a best room in the boarding-house, to entertain callers in; but if any of the girls had a regular gentleman caller, a special evening was set apart each week to receive him. This room was furnished with a carpet, sometimes with a piano, as Dickens says, and with the best furniture, including oftentimes the relics of household treasures left of the old-time gentility of the house-mother.

This mutual acquaintanceship was of great advantage. They discussed the books they read, debated religious and social questions, compared their thoughts and experiences, and advised and helped one another. And so their mental growth went on, and they soon became educated far beyond what their mothers or their grandmothers could have been. The girls also stood by one another in the mills; when one wanted to be absent half a day, two or three others would tend an extra loom or frame apiece, so that the absent one might not lose her pay. At this time the mule and spinning-jenny had not been introduced; two or three looms, or spinning-frames, were as much as one girl was required to tend, more than that being considered "double work."

The inmates of what may be called these literary households were omniverous readers of books, and were also subscribers to the few magazines and literary newspapers; and it was their habit, after reading their copies, to send them by mail or stage-coach to their widely scattered homes, where they were read all over a village or a neighborhood; and thus was current literature introduced into by and lonely places.

From an article in *The Lowell Offering,* ("Our Household," signed H.T.,) I am able to quote a sketch of one factory boarding-house interior. The author said, "In our house there are eleven boarders, and in all thirteen members of the family. I will class them according to their religious tenets as follows: Calvinist Baptist, Unitarian, Congregational, Catholic, Episcopalian, and Mormonite, one each; Universalist and Methodist, two each; Christian Baptist, three. Their reading is from the following sources: They receive regularly fifteen newspapers and periodicals; these are, the *Boston Daily Times,* the *Herald of Freedom,* the *Signs of the Times,* and the *Christian Herald,* two copies each; the *Christian Register, Vox Populi Literary Souvenir, Boston Pilot, Young Catholic's Friend, Star of Bethlehem,* and *The Lowell Offering,* three copies each. A magazine, one copy. We also borrow regularly the *Non-Resistant,* the *Liberator,* the *Lady's Book,* the *Ladies' Pearl,* and the *Ladies' Companion.* We have also in the house what perhaps cannot be found anywhere else in the city of Lowell,—a Mormon Bible.

The "magazine" mentioned may have been *The Dial,* that exponent of New England Transcendentalism, of which *The Offering* was the humble contemporary. The writer adds to her article: "Notwithstanding the divers faiths embraced among us, we live in much harmony, and seldom is difference of opinion the cause of dissensions among us."

Novels were not very popular with us, as we inclined more to historical writings and to poetry. But such books as "Charlotte Temple," "Eliza Wharton," "Maria Monk," "The Arabian Nights," "The Mysteries of Udolpho," "Abellino, the Bravo of Venice," or "The Castle of Otranto," were sometimes taken from the circulating library, read with delight, and secretly lent from one young girl to another.

Our religious reading was confined to the Bible, Baxter's "Saints' Rest," "The Pilgrim's Progress," "The Religious Courtship," "The Widow Directed," and Sunday-school books.

It was fortunate for us that we were obliged to read good books, such as histories, the English classics, and the very few American novels that were then in existence. Cheap editions of Scott were but just publishing; "Pickwick," in serial numbers, soon followed; Frederika Bremer was hardly translated; Lydia Maria Child was beginning to write; Harriet Beecher Stowe was busy in her nursery, and the great American novel was not written,—nor yet the small one, which was indeed a blessing!

There were many representative women among us who did not voice their thoughts in writing, and whose names are not on the list of the contributers to *The Offering.* This was but one phase of their development, as many of them have exerted a widespread influence in other directions. They graduated from the cotton-factory, carrying with them the results of their manual training; and they have done their little part towards performing the useful labor of life. Into whatever vocation they entered they made practical use of the habits of industry and perseverance learned during those early years, and they have exemplified them in their stirring and fruitful lives.

In order to show how far the influence of individual effort may extend, it will be well to mention the after-fate of some of them. One became an artist of note, another a poet of more than local fame, a third an inventor, and several were among the pioneers in Florida, in Kansas, and in other Western States. A limited number married those who were afterwards doctors of divinity, major-generals, and members of Congress, and these, in more than one instance, had been their work-mate in the factory.

And in late years, when, through the death of the bread-winner, the pecuniary support of those dependent on him fell to their lot, some of these factory-girls carried on business, entered the trades, or went to college and thereby were enabled to practise in some of the professions. They thus resumed their old-time habit of supporting the helpless ones, and educating the children of the family.

These women were all self-made in the truest sense; and it is well to mention their success in life, that others, who now earn their living at what is called "ungenteel" employment, may see that what one does is not of so much importance as what one is. I do not know why it should not be just as commendable for a woman who has risen to have been once a factory-girl, as it is for an ex-governor or a major-general to have been a "bobbin-boy." A woman ought to be as proud of being self-made as a man; not proud in a boasting way, but proud enough to assert the fact in her life and in her works.

All these of whom I speak are widely scattered. I hear of them in the far West, in the South, and in foreign countries, even so far away as the Himalaya Mountains. But wherever they may be, I know that they will join with me in saying that the discipline of their youth helped to make them what they are; and that the cotton-factory was to them the means of education, their preparatory school, in which they learned the alphabet of their life-work.

Such is the brief story of the life of every-day working-girls; such as it was then, so it might be to-day. Undoubtedly there might have been another side to this picture, but I give the side I knew best,—the bright side!

# FREDERICK DOUGLASS
## 1817–1895

*While Black Hawk and Crockett struggled over lands of the western frontier, a young Frederick Augustus Washington Bailey fought against the bonds of slavery along the eastern shore of Maryland. Born of a slave mother and a white master, but raised by a black grandmother, Bailey changed his name to Douglass and rose to be the most eloquent spokesperson for abolition and most famous black man in nineteenth-century America.*

*When he was eight, Douglass was sent to be a house servant for Hugh Auld in Baltimore. Even though it was unlawful to teach a slave to read, Auld's wife did just that until Auld made her stop. Douglass pursued his education as he could, teaching himself or getting help from the boys in the streets. At sixteen, his master died and Douglass became a field hand on a plantation before being sent back to Baltimore where he was hired out for wages.*

*In 1838, Douglass escaped to New York City and sent for Anna Murray, a free black woman, whom he married three days after she joined him. They quickly moved to New Bedford, Massachusetts, and Douglass got a job at the wharves. At an 1841 Antislavery Convention in Nantucket, Douglass charmed the audience with his logic, physical stature, good looks and speaking ability. Soon, he was involved full time in northern cities and in Britain talking and writing for the abolition of slavery.*

*British supporters gave him money by which he purchased his freedom from his Southern master and invested in a printing press. From 1847–1860, Douglass published a newspaper in Rochester, N.Y. He argued for political action to overturn slavery and advised Lincoln to use black soldiers to help win the Civil War. He recruited for Union armies and fought for equal rights for blacks and women. Late in life, he served as U.S. minister to Haiti.*

*Douglass wrote an autobiography, which he revised four times:* Narrative of the Life of Frederick Douglass *(1845),* My Bondage and My Freedom *(1855), and* Life and Times of Frederick Douglass *(1881 and 1892). The editors have chosen his first autobiography because Douglass was nearer to slavery and still in transition to freedom.*

*Like Franklin and Crockett, Douglass framed his* Narrative *as an American success story. He beat all the odds to learn to read and to free himself from slavery. His autobiography is the best example of the fifty or so slave narratives that were published in antebellum America and Britain.*

*It is scripture and verse for revising society while it celebrates the triumph of the human will. And for Douglass, to write about his life was the supreme expression of self-liberation and freedom.*

Narrative of the Life of Frederick Douglass, An American Slave: Written by Himself. *Reprint, New York: Penguin, 1968.*

I was born in Tuckahoe, near Hillsborough, and about twelve miles from Easton, in Talbot county, Maryland. I have no accurate knowledge of my age, never having seen any authentic record containing it. By far the larger part of the slaves know as little of their ages as horses know of theirs, and it is the wish of most masters within my knowledge to keep their slaves thus ignorant. I do not remember to have ever met a slave who could tell of his birthday. They seldom come nearer to it than planting-time, harvest-time, cherry-time, spring-time, or fall-time. A want of information concerning my own was a source of unhappiness to me even during childhood. The white children could tell their ages. I could not tell why I ought to be deprived of the same privilege. I was not allowed to make any inquiries of my master concerning it. He deemed all such inquiries on the part of a slave improper and impertinent, and evidence of a restless spirit. The nearest estimate I can give makes me now between twenty-seven and twenty-eight years of age. I come to this, from hearing my master say, some time during 1835, I was about seventeen years old.

My mother was named Harriet Bailey. She was the daughter of Isaac and Betsey Bailey, both colored, and quite dark. My mother was of a darker complexion than either my grandmother or grandfather.

My father was a white man. He was admitted to be such by all I ever heard speak of my parentage. The opinion was also whispered that my master was my father; but of the correctness of this opinion, I know nothing; the means of knowing was withheld from me. My mother and I were separated when I was but an infant—before I knew her as my mother. It is a common custom, in the part of Maryland from which I ran away, to part children from their mothers at a very early age. Frequently, before the child has reached its twelfth month, its mother is taken from it, and hired out on some farm a considerable distance off, and the child is placed under the care of an old woman, too old for field labor. For what this separation is done, I do not know, unless it be to hinder the development of the child's affection toward its mother, and to blunt and destroy the natural affection of the mother for the child. This is the inevitable result.

I never saw my mother, to know her as such, more than four or five times in my life; and each of these times was very short in duration, and at night. She was hired by a Mr. Stewart, who lived about twelve miles from my home. She made her journeys to see me in the night, travelling the whole distance on foot, after the performance of her day's work. She was a field hand, and a whipping is the penalty of not being in the field at sunrise, unless a slave has special permission from his or her master to the contrary—a permission which they seldom get, and one that gives to him that gives it the proud name of being a kind master. I do not recollect of ever seeing my mother by the light of day. She was with me in the night. She would lie down with me, and get me to sleep, but long before I waked she was gone. Very little communication ever took place between us. Death soon ended what little we could have while she lived, and with it her hardships and

**FREDERICK DOUGLASS**

suffering. She died when I was about seven years old, on one of my master's farms, near Lee's Mill. I was not allowed to be present during her illness, at her death, or burial. She was gone long before I knew any thing about it. Never having enjoyed, to any considerable extent, her soothing presence, her tender and watchful care, I received the tidings of her death with much the same emotions I should have probably felt at the death of a stranger.

Called thus suddenly away, she left me without the slightest intimation of who my father was. The whisper that may master was my father, may or may not be true; and, true or false, it is of but little consequence to my purpose whilst the fact remains, in all its glaring odiousness, that slaveholders have ordained, and by law established, that the children of slave women shall in all cases follow the condition of their mothers; and this is done too obviously to administer to their own lusts, and make a gratification of their wicked desires profitable as well as pleasurable; for by this cunning arrangement, the slaveholder, in cases not a few, sustains to his slaves the double relation of master and father.

I know of such cases; and it is worthy of remark that such slaves invariably suffer greater hardships, and have more to contend with, than others. They are, in the first place, a constant offence to their mistress. She is ever disposed to find fault with them; they can seldom do any thing to please her; she is never better pleased than when she sees them under the lash, especially when she suspects her husband of showing to his mulatto children favors which he withholds from his black slaves. The master is frequently compelled to sell this class of his slaves, out of deference to the feelings of his white wife; and, cruel as the deed may strike any one to be, for a man to sell his own children to human flesh-mongers, it is often the dictate of humanity for him to do so; for, unless he does this, he must not only whip them himself, but must stand by and see one white son tie up his brother, of but few shades darker complexion than himself, and ply the glory lash to his naked back; and if he lisp one word of disapproval, it is set down to his parental partiality, and only makes a bad matter worse, both for himself and the slave whom he would protect and defend.

Every year brings with it multitudes of this class of slaves. It was doubtless in consequence of a knowledge of this fact, that one great statesman of the south predicted the downfall of slavery by the inevitable laws of population. Whether this prophecy is ever fulfilled or not, it is nevertheless plain that a very different-looking class of people are springing up at the south, and are now held in slavery, from those originally brought to this country from Africa; and if their increase will do no other good, it will do away the force of the argument, that God cursed Ham, and therefore American slavery is right. If the lineal descendants of Ham are alone to be scripturally enslaved, it is certain that slavery at the south must soon become unscriptural; for thousands are ushered into the world, annually, who, like myself, owe their existence to white fathers, and those fathers most frequently their own masters.

I have had two masters. My first master's name was Anthony. I do not remember his first name. He was generally called Captain Anthony—a title which, I presume, he acquired by sailing a craft on the Chesapeake Bay. He was not considered a rich slaveholder. He owned two or three farms, and about thirty slaves. His farms and slaves were under the care of an overseer. The overseer's name was Plummer. Mr. Plummer was a miserable drunkard, a profane swearer, and a savage monster. He always went armed with a cowskin and a heavy cudgel.

I have known him to cut and slash the women's heads so horribly, that even master would be enraged at his cruelty, and would threaten to whip him if he did not mind himself. Master, however, was not a humane slaveholder. It required extraordinary barbarity on the part of an overseer to affect him. He was a cruel man, hardened by a long life of slaveholding. He would at times seem to take great pleasure in whipping a slave. I have often been awakened at the dawn of day by the most heart-rending shrieks of an own aunt of mine, whom he used to tie up to a joist, and whip upon her naked back till she was literally covered with blood. No words, no tears, no prayers, from his gory victim, seemed to move his iron heart from its bloody purpose. The louder she screamed, the harder he whipped; and where the blood ran fastest, there he whipped longest. He would whip her to make her scream, and whip her to make her hush; and not until overcome by fatigue, would he cease to swing the blood-clotted cowskin. I remember the first time I ever witnessed this horrible exhibition. I was quite a child, but I well remember it. I never shall forget it whilst I remember any thing. It was the first of a long series of such outrages, of which I was doomed to be a witness and a participant. It struck me with awful force. It was the blood-stained gate, the entrance to the hell of slavery, through which I was about to pass. It was a most terrible spectacle. I wish I could commit to paper the feelings with which I beheld it. . . .

My master's family consisted of two sons, Andrew and Richard; one daughter, Lucretia, and her husband, Captain Thomas Auld. They lived in one house, upon the home plantation of Colonel Edward Lloyd. My master was Colonel Lloyd's clerk and superintendent. He was what might be called the overseer of the overseers. I spent two years of childhood on this plantation in my old master's family. It was here that I witnessed the bloody transaction recorded in the first chapter; and as I received my first impressions of slavery on this plantation, I will give some description of it, and of slavery as it there existed. The plantation is about twelve miles north of Easton, in Talbot county, and is situated on the border of Miles River. The principal products raised upon it were tobacco, corn, and wheat. These were raised in great abundance; so that, with the products of this and the other farms belonging to him, he was able to keep in almost constant employment a large sloop, in carrying them to market at Baltimore. This sloop was named Sally Lloyd, in honor of one of the colonel's daughters. My master's son-in-law, Captain Auld, was master of the vessel; she was otherwise manned by the colonel's own slaves. Their names were Peter, Isaac, Rich, and Jake. These were esteemed very highly by the other slaves, and looked upon as the privileged ones of the plantation; for it was no small affair, in the eyes of the slaves, to be allowed to see Baltimore.

Colonel Lloyd kept from three to four hundred slaves on his home plantation, and owned a large number more on the neighboring farms belonging to him. The names of the farms nearest to the home plantation were Wye Town and New Design. "Wye Town" was under the overseership of a man named Noah Willis. New Design was under the overseership of a Mr. Townsend. The overseers of these, and all the rest of the farms, numbering over twenty, received advice and direction from the managers of the home plantation. This was the great business place. It was the seat of government for the whole twenty farms. All disputes among the overseers were settled here. If a slave was convicted of any high misdemeanor, became unmanageable, or evinced a determination to run away, he was brought immediately here, severely whipped, put on board the sloop, carried to Baltimore, and sold to Austin Woolfolk, or some other slave-trader, as a warning to the slaves remaining.

Here, too, the slaves of all the other farms received their monthly allowance of food, and their yearly clothing. The men and women slaves received, as their monthly allowance of food, eight pounds of pork, or its equivalent in fish, and one bushel of corn meal. Their yearly clothing consisted of two coarse linen shirts, one pair of linen trousers, like the shirts, one jacket, one pair of trousers for winter, made of coarse negro cloth, one pair of stockings, and one pair of shoes; the whole of which could not have cost more than seven dollars. The allowance of the slave children was given to their mothers, or the old women having the care of them. The children unable to work in the field had neither shoes, stockings, jackets, nor trousers, given to them; their clothing consisted of two coarse linen shirts per year. When these failed them, they went naked until the next allowance-day. Children from seven to ten years old, of both sexes, almost naked, might be seen at all seasons of the year.

There were no beds given the slaves, unless one coarse blanket be considered such, and none but the men and women had these. This, however, is not considered a very great privation. They find less difficulty from the want of beds, than from the want of time to sleep; for when their day's work in the field is done, the most of them having their washing, mending, and cooking to do, and having few or none of the ordinary facilities for doing either of these, very many of their sleeping hours are consumed in preparing for the field the coming day; and when this is done, old and young, male and female, married and single, drop down side by side, on one common bed,—the cold, damp floor,— each covering himself or herself with their miserable blankets; and here they sleep till they are summoned to the field by the driver's horn. At the sound of this, all must rise, and be off to the field. There must be no halting; every one must be at his or her post; and woe betides them who hear not this morning summons to the field; for if they are not awakened by the sense of hearing, they are by the sense of feeling; no age nor sex finds any favor. Mr. Severe, the overseer, used to stand by the door of the quarter, armed with a large hickory stick and heavy cowskin, ready to whip any one who was so unfortunate as not to hear, or, from any other cause, was prevented from being ready to start for the field at the sound of the horn.

Mr. Severe was rightly named: he was a cruel man. I have seen him whip a woman, causing the blood to run half an hour at the time; and this, too, in the midst of her crying children, pleading for their mother's release. He seemed to take pleasure in manifesting his fiendish barbarity. Added to his cruelty, he was a profane swearer. It was enough to chill the blood and stiffen the hair of an ordinary man to hear him talk. Scarce a sentence escaped him but that was commenced or concluded by some horrid oath. The field was the place to witness his cruelty and profanity. His presence made it both the field of blood and of blasphemy. From the rising till the going down of the sun, he was cursing, raving, cutting, and slashing among the slaves of the field, in the most frightful manner. His career was short. He died very soon after I went to Colonel Lloyd's; and he died as he lived, uttering, with his dying groans, bitter curses and horrid oaths. His death was regarded by the slaves as the result of a merciful providence.

Mr. Severe's place was filled by a Mr. Hopkins. He was a very different man. He was less cruel, less profane, and made less noise, than Mr. Severe. His course was characterized by no extraordinary demonstrations of cruelty. He whipped, but seemed to take no pleasure in it. He was called by the slaves a good overseer. . . .

[He evaluated the wealth of Colonel Lloyd as "almost equal to describing the riches of Job." He also described the "savage brutality" of the overseer Austin Gore.]

As to my own treatment while I lived on Colonel Lloyd's plantation, it was very similar to that of the other slave children. I was not old enough to work in the field, and there being little else than field work to do, I had a great deal of leisure time. The most I had to do was to drive up the cows at evening, keep the fowls out of the garden, keep the front yard clean, and run of errands for my old master's daughter, Mrs. Lucretia Auld. The most of my leisure time I spent in helping Master Daniel Lloyd in finding his birds, after he had shot them. My connection with Master Daniel was of some advantage to me. He became quite attached to me, and was a sort of protector of me. He would not allow the older boys to impose upon me, and would divide his cakes with me.

I was seldom whipped by my old master, and suffered little from any thing else than hunger and cold. I suffered much from hunger, but much more from cold. In hottest summer and coldest winter, I was kept almost naked—no shoes, no stockings, no jacket, no trousers, nothing on but a coarse tow linen shirt, reaching only to my knees. I had no bed. I must have perished with cold, but that, the coldest nights, I used to steal a bag which was used for carrying corn to the mill. I would crawl into this bag, and there sleep on the cold, damp, clay floor, with my head in and feet out. My feet have been so cracked with the frost, that the pen with which I am writing might be laid in the gashes.

We were not regularly allowanced. Our food was coarse corn meal boiled. This was called *mush*. It was put into a large wooden tray or trough, and set down upon the ground. The children were then called, like so many pigs, and like so many pigs they would come and devour the mush; some with oyster-shells, others with pieces of shingle, some with naked hands, and none with spoons. He that ate fastest got most; he that was strongest secured the best place; and few left the trough satisfied.

I was probably between seven and eight years old when I left Colonel Lloyd's plantation. I left it with joy. I shall never forget the ecstasy with which I received the intelligence that my old master (Anthony) had determined to let me go to Baltimore, to live with Mr. Hugh Auld, brother to my old master's son-in-law, Captain Thomas Auld. I received this information about three days before my departure. They were three of the happiest days I ever enjoyed. I spent the most part of all these three days in the creek, washing off the plantation scurf, and preparing myself for my departure.

The pride of appearance which this would indicate was not my own. I spent the time in washing, not so much because I wished to, but because Mrs. Lucretia had told me I must get all the dead skin off my feet and knees before I could go to Baltimore; for the people in Baltimore were very cleanly, and would laugh at me if I looked dirty. Besides, she was going to give me a pair of trousers, which I should not put on unless I got all the dirt off me. The thought of owning a pair of trousers was great indeed! It was almost a sufficient motive, not only to make me take off what would be called by pig-drovers the mange, but the skin itself. I went at it in good earnest, working for the first time with the hope of reward.

The ties that ordinarily bind children to their homes were all suspended in my case. I found no severe trial in my departure. My home was charmless; it was not home to me; on parting from it, I could not feel that I was leaving any thing which I could have enjoyed by staying. My mother was dead, my grandmother lived far off, so that I seldom saw her. I had two sisters and one brother, that lived in the same house with me; but the early separation of us from our mother had well nigh blotted the fact of our relationship from our memories. I looked for home elsewhere, and was confident of finding none which I should relish less than the one which I was leaving. If, however, I found in my new home hardship, hunger, whipping, and nakedness, I had the consolation that I should not have escaped any one of them by staying. Having already had more than a taste of them in the house of my old master, and having endured them there, I very naturally inferred my ability to endure them elsewhere, and especially at Baltimore; for I had something of the feeling about Baltimore that is expressed in the proverb, that "being hanged in England is preferable to dying a natural death in Ireland." I had the strongest desire to see Baltimore. Cousin Tom, though not fluent in speech, had inspired me with that desire by his eloquent description of the place. I could never point out any thing at the Great House, no matter how beautiful or powerful, but that he had seen something at Baltimore far exceeding, both in beauty and strength, the object which I pointed out to him. Even the Great House itself, with all its pictures, was far inferior to many buildings in Baltimore. So strong was my desire, that I thought a gratification of it would fully compensate for whatever loss of comforts I should sustain by the exchange. I left without a regret, and with the highest hopes of future happiness. . . .

My new mistress proved to be all she appeared when I first met her at the door,—a woman of the kindest heart and finest feelings. She had never had a slave under her control previously to myself, and prior to her marriage she had been dependent upon her own industry for a living. She was by trade a weaver; and by constant application to her business, she had been in a good degree preserved from the blighting and dehumanizing effects of slavery. I was utterly astonished at her goodness. I scarcely knew how to behave towards her. She was entirely unlike any other white woman I had ever seen. I could not approach her as I was accustomed to approach other white ladies. My early instruction was all out of place. The crouching servility, usually so acceptable a quality in a slave, did not answer when manifested toward her. Her favor was not gained by it; she seemed to be disturbed by it. She did not deem it impudent or unmannerly for a slave to look her in the face. The meanest slave was put fully at ease in her presence, and none left without feeling better for having seen her. Her face was made of heavenly smiles, and her voice of tranquil music.

But, alas! this kind heart had but a short time to remain such. The fatal poison of irresponsible power was already in her hands, and soon commenced its infernal work. That cheerful eye, under the influence of slavery, soon became red with rage; that voice, made all of sweet accord, changed to one of harsh and horrid discord; and that angelic face gave place to that of a demon.

Very soon after I went to live with Mr. and Mrs. Auld, she very kindly commenced to teach me the A, B, C. After I had learned this, she assisted me in learning to spell words of three or four letters. Just at this point of my progress, Mr. Auld found out what was going on, and at once forbade Mrs. Auld to instruct me further, telling her, among other things, that it was unlawful, as well as unsafe, to teach a slave to read. To use his own words, further, he said, "If you give a nigger an inch, he will take an ell. A nigger should know nothing but to obey his master—to do as he is told to do. Learning would *spoil* the best nigger in the world. Now," said he, "if you teach that nigger (speaking of myself) how to read, there would be no keeping him. It would forever unfit him to be a slave. He would at once become unmanageable, and of no value to his master. As to himself, it could do him no good, but a great deal of harm. It would make him discontented and unhappy." These words sank deep into my heart, stirred up sentiments within that lay slumbering, and called into existence an entirely new train of thought. It was a new and special revelation, explaining dark and mysterious things, with which my youthful understanding had struggled, but struggled in vain. I now understood what had been to me a most perplexing difficulty—to wit, the white man's power to enslave the black man. It was a grand achievement, and I prized it highly. From that moment, I understood the pathway from slavery to freedom. It was just what I wanted, and I got it at a time when I the least expected it. Whilst I was saddened by the thought of losing the aid of my kind mistress, I was gladdened by the invaluable instruction which, by the merest accident, I had gained from my master. Though conscious of the difficulty of learning without a teacher, I set out with high hope, and a fixed purpose, at whatever cost of trouble, to learn how to read. The very decided manner with which he spoke, and strove to impress his wife with the evil consequences of giving me instruction, served to convince me that he was deeply sensible of the truths he was uttering. It gave me the best assurance that I might rely with the utmost confidence on the results which, he said, would flow from teaching me to read. What he most dreaded, that I most desired. What he most loved, that I most hated. That which to him was a great evil, to be carefully shunned, was to me a great good, to be diligently sought; and the argument which he so warmly urged, against my learning to read, only served to inspire me with a desire and determination to learn. In learning to read, I owe almost as much to the bitter opposition of my master, as to the kindly aid of my mistress. I acknowledge the benefit of both.

I had resided but a short time in Baltimore before I observed a marked difference, in the treatment of slaves, from that which I had witnessed in the country. A city slave is almost a freeman, compared with a slave on the plantation. He is much better fed and clothed, and enjoys privileges altogether unknown to the slave on the plantation. There is a vestige of decency, a sense of shame, that does much to curb and check those outbreaks of atrocious cruelty so commonly enacted upon the plantation. He is a desperate slaveholder, who will shock the humanity of his nonslaveholding neighbors with the cries of his lacerated slave. Few are willing to incur the odium attaching to the reputation of being a cruel master; and above all things, they would not be known as not giving a slave enough to eat. Every city slaveholder is anxious to have it known of him, that he feeds his slaves well; and it is due to them to say, that most of them do give their slaves enough to eat. There are, however, some painful exceptions to this rule. Directly opposite to us, on Philpot Street, lived Mr. Thomas Hamilton. He owned two slaves. Their names were Henrietta and Mary. Henrietta was about twenty-two years of age, Mary was about fourteen; and of all the mangled and emaciated creatures I ever looked upon, these two were the most so. His heart must be harder than stone, that could look upon these unmoved. The head, neck, and shoulders of Mary were literally cut to pieces. I have frequently felt her head, and found it nearly covered with festering sores, caused by the lash of her cruel mistress. . . .

I lived in Master Hugh's family about seven years. During this time, I succeeded in learning to read and write. In accomplishing this, I was compelled to resort to various stratagems. I had no regular teacher. My mistress, who had kindly commenced to instruct me, had, in compliance with the advice and direction of her husband, not only ceased to instruct, but had set her face against my being instructed by any one else. It is due, however, to my mistress to say of her, that she did not adopt this course of treatment immediately. She at first lacked the depravity indispensable to shutting me up in mental darkness. It was at least necessary for her to have some training in the exercise of irresponsible power, to make her equal to the task of treating me as though I were a brute.

My mistress was, as I have said, a kind and tender-hearted woman; and in the simplicity of her soul she commenced, when I first went to live with her, to treat me as she supposed one human being ought to treat another. In entering upon the duties of a slaveholder, she did not seem to perceive that I sustained to her the relation of a mere chattel, and that for her to treat me as a human being was not only wrong, but dangerously so. Slavery proved as injurious to her as it did to me. When I went there, she was a pious, warm, and tender-hearted woman. There was no sorrow or suffering for which she had not a tear. She had bread for the hungry, clothes for the naked, and comfort for every mourner that came within her reach. Slavery soon proved its ability to divest her of these heavenly qualities. Under its influence, the tender heart became stone, and the lamblike disposition gave way to one of tiger-like fierceness. The first step in her downward course was in her ceasing to instruct me. She now commenced to practise her husband's precepts. She finally became even more violent in her opposition than her husband himself. She was not satisfied with simply doing as well as he had commanded; she seemed anxious to do better. Nothing seemed to make her more angry than to see me with a newspaper. She seemed to think that here lay the danger. I have had her rush at me with a face made all up of fury, and snatch from me a newspaper, in a manner that fully revealed her apprehension. She was an apt woman; and a little experience soon demonstrated, to her satisfaction, that education and slavery were incompatible with each other.

From this time I was most narrowly watched. If I was in a separate room any considerable length of time, I was sure to be suspected of having a book, and was at once called to give an account of myself. All this, however, was too late. The first step had been taken. Mistress, in teaching me the alphabet, had given me the *inch*, and no precaution could prevent me from taking the *ell*.

The plan which I adopted, and the one by which I was most successful, was that of making friends of all the little white boys whom I met in the street. As many of these as I could, I converted into teachers. With their kindly aid, obtained at different times and in different places, I finally succeeded in learning to read. When I was sent on errands, I always took my book with me, and by doing one part of my errand quickly, I found time to get a lesson before my return. . . .

I was now about twelve years old, and the thought of being *a slave for life* began to bear heavily upon my heart. Just about this time, I got hold of a book entitled "The Columbian Orator." Every opportunity I got, I used to read this book. Among much of other interesting matter, I found in it a dialogue between a master and his slave. The slave was represented as having run away from his master three times. The dialogue represented the conversation which took place between them, when the slave was retaken the third time. In this dialogue, the whole argument in behalf of slavery was brought forward by the master, all of which was disposed of by the slave. The slave was made to say some very smart as well as impressive things in reply to his master—things which had the desired though unexpected effect; for the conversation resulted in the voluntary emancipation of the slave on the part of the master.

In the same book, I met with one of Sheridan's mighty speeches on and in behalf of Catholic emancipation. These were choice documents to me. I read them over and over again with unabated interest. They gave tongue to interesting thoughts of my own soul, which had frequently flashed through my mind, and died away for want of utterance. The moral which I gained from the dialogue was the power of truth over the conscience of even a slaveholder. What I got from Sheridan was a bold denunciation of slavery, and a powerful vindication of human rights. The reading of these documents enabled me to utter my thoughts, and to meet the arguments brought forward to sustain slavery; but while they relieved me of one difficulty, they brought on another even more painful than the one of which I was relieved. The more I read, the more I was led to abhor and detest my enslavers. I could regard them in no other light than a band of successful robbers, who had left their homes, and gone to Africa, and stolen us from our homes, and in a strange land reduced us to slavery. I loathed them as being the meanest as well as the most wicked of men. As I read and contemplated the subject, behold! that very discontentment which Master Hugh had predicted would follow my learning to read had already come, to torment and sting my soul to unutterable anguish. As I writhed under it, I would at times feel that learning to read had been a curse rather than a blessing. It had given me a view of my wretched condition, without the remedy. It opened my eyes to the horrible pit, but to no ladder upon which to get out. In moments of agony, I envied my fellow-slaves for their stupidity. I have often wished myself a beast. I preferred the condition of the meanest reptile to my own. Any thing, no matter what, to get rid of thinking! It was this everlasting thinking of my condition that tormented me. There was no getting rid of it. It was pressed upon me by every object within sight or hearing, animate or inanimate. The silver trump of freedom had roused my soul to eternal wakefulness. Freedom now appeared, to disappear no more forever. It was heard in every sound, and seen in every thing. It was ever present to torment me with a sense of my wretched condition. I saw nothing without seeing it, I heard nothing without hearing it, and felt nothing without feeling it. It looked from every star, it smiled in every calm, breathed in every wind, and moved in every storm.

I often found myself regretting my own existence, and wishing myself dead; and but for the hope of being free, I have no doubt but that I should have killed myself, or done something for which I should have been killed. While in this state of mind, I was eager to hear any one speak of slavery. I was a ready listener. Every little while, I could hear something about the abolitionists. It was some time before I found what the word meant. It was always used in such connections as to make it an interesting word to me. If a slave ran away and succeeded in getting clear, or if a slave killed his master, set fire to a barn, or did any thing very wrong in the mind of a slaveholder, it was spoken of as the fruit of *abolition*.

Hearing the word in this connection very often, I set about learning what it meant. The dictionary afforded me little or no help. I found it was "the act of abolishing;" but then I did not know what was to be abolished. Here I was perplexed. I did not dare to ask any one about its meaning, for I was satisfied that it was something they wanted me to know very little about. After a patient waiting, I got one of our city papers, containing an account of the number of petitions from the north, praying for the abolition of slavery in the District of Columbia, and of the slave trade between the States. From this time I understood the words *abolition* and *abolitionist,* and always drew near when that word was spoken, expecting to hear something of importance to myself and fellow-slaves. . . .

### [He learned to write and continued living in Baltimore.]

I have now reached a period of my life when I can give dates. I left Baltimore, and went to live with Master Thomas Auld, at St. Michael's, in March, 1832. It was now more than seven years since I lived with him in the family of my old master, on Colonel Lloyd's plantation. We of course were now almost entire strangers to each other. He was to me a new master, and I to him a new slave. I was ignorant of his temper and disposition; he was equally so of mine. A very short time, however, brought us into full acquaintance with each other. I was made acquainted with his wife not less than with himself. They were well matched, being equally mean and cruel. I was now, for the first time during a space of more than seven years, made to feel the painful gnawings of hunger—a something which I had not experienced before since I left Colonel Lloyd's plantation. . . .

My master and myself had quite a number of differences. He found me unsuitable to his purpose. My city life, he said, had had a very pernicious effect upon me. It had almost ruined me for every good purpose, and fitted me for every thing which was bad. One of my greatest faults was that of letting his horse run away, and go down to his father-in-law's farm, which was about five miles from St. Michael's. I would then have to go after it. My reason for this kind of carelessness, or carefulness, was, that I could always get something to eat when I went there. Master William Hamilton, my master's father-in-law, always gave his slaves enough to eat. I never left there hungry, no matter how great the need of my speedy return. Master Thomas at length said he would stand it no longer. I had lived with him nine months, during which time he had given me a number of severe whippings, all to no good purpose. He resolved to put me out, as he said, to be broken; and, for this purpose, he let me for one year to a man named Edward Covey. Mr. Covey was a poor man, a farm-renter. He rented the place upon which he lived, as also the hands with which he tilled it. Mr. Covey had acquired a very high reputation for breaking young slaves, and this reputation was of immense value to him. It enabled him to get his farm tilled with much less expense to himself than he could have had it done without such a reputation. Some slaveholders thought it not much loss to allow Mr. Covey to have their slaves one year, for the sake of the training to which they were subjected, without any other compensation. He could hire young help with great ease, in consequence of this reputation. Added to the natural good qualities of Mr. Covey, he was a professor of religion—a pious soul—a member and a class-leader in the Methodist church. All of this added weight to his reputation as a "nigger-breaker." I was aware of all the facts, having been made acquainted with them by a young man who had lived there. I nevertheless made the change gladly; for I was sure of getting enough to eat, which is not the smallest consideration to a hungry man.

I left Master Thomas's house, and went to live with Mr. Covey, on the 1st of January, 1833. I was now, for the first time in my life, a field hand. In my new employment, I found myself even more awkward than a country boy appeared to be in a large city. I had been at my new home but one week before Mr. Covey gave me a very severe whipping, cutting my back, causing the blood to run, and raising ridges on my flesh as large as my little finger. . . .

I lived with Mr. Covey one year. During the first six months, of that year, scarce a week passed without his whipping me. I was seldom free from a sore back. My awkwardness was almost always his excuse for whipping me. We were worked fully up to the point of endurance. Long before day we were up, our horses fed, and by the first approach of day we were off to the field with our hoes and ploughing teams. Mr. Covey gave us enough to eat, but scarce time to eat it. We were often less than five minutes taking our meals. We were often in the field from the first approach of day till its last lingering ray had left us; and at saving-fodder time, midnight often caught us in the field binding blades.

Covey would be out with us. The way he used to stand it, was this. He would spend the most of his afternoons in bed. He would then come out fresh in the evening, ready to urge us on with his words, example, and frequently with the whip. Mr. Covey was one of the few slaveholders who could and did work with his hands. He was a hard-working man. He knew by himself just what a man or a boy could do. There was no deceiving him. His work went on in his absence almost as well as in his presence; and he had the faculty of making us feel that he was ever present with us. . . .

Mr. Covey was a poor man; he was just commencing in life; he was only able to buy one slave; and, shocking as is the fact, he bought her, as he said, for *a breeder*. This woman was named Caroline. Mr. Covey bought her from Mr. Thomas Lowe, about six miles from St. Michael's. She was a large, able-bodied woman, about twenty years old. She had already given birth to one child, which proved her to be just what he wanted. After buying her, he hired a married man of Mr. Samuel Harrison, to live with him one year; and him he used to fasten up with her every night! The result was, that, at the end of the year, the miserable woman gave birth to twins. At this result Mr. Covey seemed to be highly pleased, both with the man and the wretched woman. Such was his joy, and that of his wife, that nothing they could do for Caroline during her confinement was too good, or too hard, to be done. The children were regarded as being quite an addition to his wealth.

If at any one time of my life more than another, I was made to drink the bitterest dregs of slavery, that time was during the first six months of my stay with Mr. Covey. We were worked in all weathers. It was never too hot or too cold; it could never rain, blow, hail, or snow, too hard for us to work in the field. Work, work, work, was scarcely more the order of the day than of the night. The longest days were too short for him, and the shortest nights too long for him. I was somewhat unmanageable when I first went there, but a few months of this discipline tamed me. Mr. Covey succeeded in breaking me. I was broken in body, soul, and spirit. My natural elasticity was crushed, my intellect languished, the disposition to read departed, the cheerful spark that lingered about my eye died; the dark night of slavery closed in upon me; and behold a man transformed into a brute!

Sunday was my only leisure time. I spent this in a sort of beast-like stupor, between sleep and wake, under some large tree. At times I would rise up, a flash of energetic freedom would dart through my soul, accompanied with a faint beam of hope, that flickered for a moment, and then vanished. I sank down again, mourning over my wretched condition. I was sometimes prompted to take my life, and that of Covey, but was prevented by a combination of hope and fear. My sufferings on this plantation seem now like a dream rather than a stern reality.

Our house stood within a few rods of the Chesapeake Bay, whose broad bosom was ever white with sails from every quarter of the habitable globe. Those beautiful vessels, robed in purest white, so delightful to the eye of freemen, were to me so many shrouded ghosts, to terrify and torment me with thoughts of my wretched condition. I have often, in the deep stillness of a summer's Sabbath, stood all alone upon the lofty banks of that noble bay, and traced, with saddened heart and tearful eye, the countless number of sails moving off to the mighty ocean. The sight of these always affected me powerfully. My thoughts would compel utterance; and there, with no audience but the Almighty, I would pour out my soul's complaint, in my rude way, with an apostrophe to the moving multitude of ships: —

"You are loosed from your moorings, and are free; I am fast in my chains, and am a slave! You move merrily before the gentle gale, and I sadly before the bloody whip! You are freedom's swift-winged angels, that fly round the world; I am confined in bands of iron! O that I were free! O, that I were on one of your gallant decks, and under your protecting wing! Alas! betwixt me and you, the turbid waters roll. Go on, go on. O that I could also go! Could I but swim! If I could fly! O, why was I born a man, of whom to make a brute! The glad ship is gone; she hides in the dim distance. I am left in the hottest hell of unending slavery. O God, save me! God, deliver me! Let me be free! Is there any God? Why am I a slave? I will run away. I will not stand it. Get caught, or get clear, I'll try it. I had as well die with ague as the fever. I have only one life to lose. I had as well be killed running as die standing. Only think of it; one hundred miles straight north, and I am free! Try it? Yes! God helping me, I will. . . .

I have already intimated that my condition was much worse, during the first six months of my stay at Mr. Covey's, than in the last six. The circumstances leading to the change in Mr. Covey's course toward me form an epoch in my humble history. You have seen how a man was made a slave; you shall see how a slave was made a man. On one of the hottest days of the month of August, 1833, Bill Smith, William Hughes, a slave named Eli, and myself, were engaged in fanning wheat. Hughes was clearing the fanned wheat from before the fan. Eli was turning, Smith was feeding, and I was carrying wheat to the fan. The work was simple, requiring strength rather than intellect; yet, to one entirely unused to such work, it came very hard. About three o'clock of that day, I broke down; my strength failed me; I was seized with a violent aching of the head, attended with extreme dizziness; I trembled in every limb. Finding what was coming, I nerved myself up, feeling it would never do to stop work. I stood as long as I could stagger to the hopper with grain. When I could stand no longer, I fell, and felt as if held down by an immense weight. The fan of course stopped; every one had his own work to do; and no one could do the work of the other, and have his own go on at the same time.

Mr. Covey was at the house, about one hundred yards from the treading-yard where we were fanning. On hearing the fan stop, he left immediately, and came to the spot where we were. He hastily inquired what the matter was. Bill answered that I was sick, and there was no one to bring wheat to the fan. I had by this time crawled away under the side of the post and rail-fence by which the yard was enclosed, hoping to find relief by getting out of the sun. He then asked where I was. He was told by one of the hands. He came to the spot, and, after looking at me awhile, asked me what was the matter. I told him as well as I could, for I scarce had strength to speak. He then gave me a savage kick in the side, and told me to get up. I tried to do so, but fell back in the attempt. He gave me another kick, and again told me to rise. I again tried, and succeeded in gaining my feet; but, stooping to get the tub with which I was feeding the fan, I again staggered and fell. While down in this situation, Mr. Covey took up the hickory slat with which Hughes had been striking off the half-bushel measure, and with it gave me a heavy blow upon the head, making a large wound, and the blood ran freely; and with this again told me to get up. I made no effort to comply, having now made up my mind to let him do his worst. In a short time after receiving this blow, my head grew better. Mr. Covey had now left me to my fate. At this moment I resolved, for the first time, to go to my master, enter a complaint, and ask his protection. In order to do this, I must that afternoon walk seven miles; and this, under the circumstances, was truly a severe undertaking. I was exceedingly feeble; made so as much by the kicks and blows which I received, as by the severe fit of sickness to which I had been subjected. I, however, watched my chance, while Covey was looking in an opposite direction, and started for St. Michael's: I succeeded in getting a considerable distance on my way to the woods, when Covey discovered me, and called after me to come back, threatening what he would do if I did not come. I disregarded both his calls and his threats, and made my way to the woods as fast as my feeble state would allow; and thinking I might be over-hauled by him if I kept the road, I walked through the woods, keeping far enough from the road to avoid detection, and near enough to prevent losing my way. I had not gone far before my little strength again failed me. I could go no farther. I fell down, and lay for a considerable time. The blood was yet oozing from the wound on my head. For a time I thought I should bleed to death; and think now that I should have done so, but that the blood so matted my hair as to stop the wound. After lying there about three quarters of an hour, I nerved myself up again, and started on my way, through bogs and briers, barefooted and bare-headed, tearing my feet sometimes at nearly every step; and after a journey of about seven miles, occupying some five hours to perform it, I arrived at master's store. I then presented an appearance enough to affect any but a heart of iron. From the crown of my head to my feet, I was covered with blood. My hair was all clotted with dust and blood; my shirt was stiff with blood. My legs and feet were torn in sundry places with briers and thorns, and were also covered with blood. I suppose I looked like a man who had escaped a den of wild beasts, and barely escaped them. In this state I appeared before my master, humbly entreating him to interpose his authority for my protection. I told him all the circumstances as well as I could, and it seemed, as I spoke, at times to affect him. He would then walk the floor, and seek to justify Covey by saying he expected I deserved it. He asked me what I wanted. I told him, to let me get a new home; that as sure as I lived with Mr. Covey again, I should live with but to die with him; that Covey would surely kill me; he was in a fair way for it. Master Thomas ridiculed the idea that there was any danger of Mr. Covey's killing me, and said that he knew Mr. Covey, that he was a good man, and that he could not think of taking me from him; that, should he do so, he would lose the whole year's wages; that I belonged to Mr. Covey for one year, and that I must go back to him, come what might; and that I must not trouble him with any more stories, or that he would himself *get hold of me.* After threatening me thus, he gave me a very large dose of salts, telling me that I might remain in St. Michael's that night, (it being quite late,) but that I must be off back to Mr. Covey's early in the morning; and that if I did not, he would *get hold of me,* which meant that he would whip me. I remained all night, and, according to his orders, I started off to Covey's in the morning, (Saturday morning,) wearied in body and broken in spirit. I got no supper that night, or breakfast that morning. I reached Covey's about nine o'clock; and just as I was getting over the fence that divided Mrs. Kemp's fields from ours, out ran Covey with his cowskin, to give me another whipping. Before he could reach me, I succeeded in getting to the cornfield; and as the corn was very high, it afforded me the means of hiding. He seemed very angry, and searched for me a long time. My behavior was altogether unaccountable. He finally gave up the chase, thinking, I suppose, that I must come home for something to eat; he would give himself no further trouble in looking for me. I spent that day mostly in the woods, having the alternative before me,—to go home and be whipped to death, or stay in the woods and be starved to death. That night, I fell in with Sandy Jenkins, a slave with whom I was somewhat acquainted. Sandy had a free wife who lived about four miles from Mr. Covey's; and it being Saturday, he was on his way to see her. I told him my circumstances, and he very kindly invited me to go home with him. I went home with him, and talked this whole matter over, and got his advice as to what course it was best for me to pursue. I found Sandy an old adviser. He told me, with great solemnity, I must go back to Covey; but that before I went, I must go with him into another part of the woods, where there was a certain *root,* which, if I would take some of it with me, carrying it *always on my right side,* would render it impossible for Mr. Covey, or any other white man, to whip me. He said he had carried it for years; and since he had done so, he had never received a blow, and never expected to while he carried it. I at first rejected the idea, that the simple carrying of a root in my pocket would have any such effect as he had said, and was not disposed to take it; but Sandy impressed the necessity with much earnestness, telling me it could do no harm, if it did no good. To please him, I at length took the root, and, according to his direction, carried it upon my right side. This was Sunday morning. I immediately started for home; and upon entering the yard gate, out came Mr. Covey on his way to meeting. He spoke to me very kindly, bade me drive the pigs from a lot near by, and passed on towards the church. Now, this singular conduct of Mr. Covey really made me begin to think that there was something in the *root* which Sandy had given me; and had it been on any other day than Sunday, I could have attributed the conduct to no other cause than the influence of that root; and as it was, I was half inclined to think the *root* to be something more than I at first had taken it to be. All went well till Monday morning. On this morning, the virtue of the *root* was fully tested. Long before daylight, I was called to go and rub, curry, and feed, the horses. I obeyed, and was glad to obey. But whilst thus engaged, whilst in the act of throwing down some blades from the loft, Mr. Covey entered the stable with a long rope; and just as I was half out of the loft, he caught hold of my legs, and was about tying me. As soon as I found what he was up to, I gave a sudden spring, and as I did so, he holding to my legs, I was brought sprawling on the stable floor. Mr. Covey seemed now to think he had me, and could do what he pleased; but at this moment—from whence came the spirit I don't know—I resolved to fight; and, suiting my action to the resolution, I seized Covey hard by the throat; and as I did so, I rose. He held on to me, and I to him. My resistance was so entirely unexpected, that Covey seemed taken all aback. He trembled like a leaf. This gave me assurance, and I held him uneasy, causing the blood to run where I touched him with the ends of my fingers. Mr. Covey soon called out to Hughes for help. Hughes came, and, while Covey held me, attempted to tie my right hand. While he was in the act of doing so, I watched my chance, and gave him a heavy kick close under the ribs. This kick fairly sickened Hughes, so that he left me in the hands of Mr. Covey. This kick had the effect of not only weakening Hughes, but Covey also. When he saw Hughes bending over with pain, his courage quailed. He asked me if I meant to persist in my resistance. I told him I did, come what might; that he had used me like a brute for six months, and that I was determined to be used so no longer. With that, he strove to drag me to a stick that was lying just out of the stable door. He meant to knock me down. But just as he was leaning over to get the stick, I seized him with both hands by his collar, and brought him by a sudden snatch to the ground. By this time, Bill came. Covey called upon him for assistance. Bill wanted to know what he could do. Covey said, "Take hold of him, take hold of him!" Bill said his master hired him out to work, and not to help to whip me; so he left Covey and myself to fight our own battle out. We were at it for nearly two hours. Covey at length let me go, puffing and blowing at a great rate, saying that if I had not resisted, he would not have whipped me half so much. The truth was, that he had not whipped me at all. I considered him as getting entirely the worst end of the bargain; for he had drawn no blood from me, but I had from him. The whole six months afterwards, that I spent with Mr. Covey, he never laid the weight of his finger upon me in anger. He would occasionally say, he didn't want to get hold of me again, "No," thought I, "you need not; for you will come off worse than you did before."

This battle with Mr. Covey was the turning-point in my career as a slave. It rekindled the few expiring embers of freedom, and revived within me a sense of my own manhood. It recalled the departed self-confidence, and inspired me again with a determination to be free. The gratification afforded by the triumph was a full compensation for whatever else might follow, even death itself. He only can understand the deep satisfaction which I experienced, who has himself repelled by force the bloody arm of slavery. I felt as I never felt before. It was a glorious resurrection, from the tomb of slavery, to the heaven of freedom. My long-crushed spirit rose, cowardice departed, bold defiance took its place; and I now resolved that, however long I might remain a slave in form, the day had passed forever when I could be a slave in fact. I did not hesitate to let it be known of me, that the white man who expected to succeed in whipping, must also succeed in killing me.

From this time I was never again what might be called fairly whipped, though I remained a slave four years afterwards. I had several fights, but was never whipped.

It was for a long time a matter of surprise to me why Mr. Covey did not immediately have me taken by the constable to the whipping-post, and there regularly whipped for the crime of raising my hand against a white man in defence of myself. And the only explanation I can now think of does not entirely satisfy me; but such as it is, I will give it. Mr. Covey enjoyed the most unbounded reputation for being a first-rate overseer and negro-breaker. It was of considerable importance to him. That reputation was at stake; and had he sent me—a boy about sixteen years old—to the public whipping-post, his reputation would have been lost; so, to save his reputation, he suffered me to go unpunished.

My term of actual service to Mr. Edward Covey ended on Christmas day, 1833. . . .

On the first of January, 1834, I left Mr. Covey, and went to live with Mr. William Freeland, who lived about three miles from St. Michael's. I soon found Mr. Freeland a very different man from Mr. Covey. Though not rich, he was what would be called an educated southern gentleman. Mr. Covey, as I have shown, was a well-trained negro-breaker and slave-driver. The former (slaveholder though he was) seemed to possess some regard for honor, some reverence for justice, and some respect for humanity. The latter seemed totally insensible to all such sentiments. Mr. Freeland had many of the faults peculiar to slaveholders, such as being very passionate and fretful; but I must do him the justice to say, that he was exceedingly free from those degrading vices to which Mr. Covey was constantly addicted. The one was open and frank, and we always knew where to find him. The other was a most artful deceiver, and could be understood only by such as were skillful enough to detect his cunningly-devised frauds. Another advantage I gained in my new master was, he made no pretensions to, or profession of, religion; and this, in my opinion, was truly a great advantage. I assert most unhesitatingly, that the religion of the south is a mere covering for the most horrid crimes,—a justifier of the most appalling barbarity,—a sanctifier of the most hateful frauds,—and a dark shelter under which the darkest, foulest, grossest, and most infernal deeds of slaveholders find the strongest protection. Were I to be again reduced to the chains of slavery, next to that enslavement, I should regard being the slave of a religious master the greatest calamity that could befall me. For of all slaveholders with whom I have ever met, religious slaveholders are the worst. I have ever found them the meanest and basest, the most cruel and cowardly, of all others. It was my unhappy lot not only to belong to a religious shareholder, but to live in a community of such religionists. . . .

**[He continued as a hired slave to William Freeland, but his discontent grew and he and others planned an escape. When the plot was discovered, Douglass spent time in jail before Captain Auld sent him back to Baltimore. He worked in a shipyard and looked for a chance to escape.]**

In the early part of the year 1838, I became quite restless. I could see no reason why I should, at the end of each week, pour the reward of my toil into the purse of my master. When I carried to him my weekly wages, he would, after counting the money, look me in the face with a robber-like fierceness, and ask, "Is this all?" He was satisfied with nothing less than the last cent. He would, however, when I made him six dollars, sometimes give me six cents, to encourage me. It had the opposite effect. I regarded it as a sort of admission of my right to the whole. The fact that he gave me any part of my wages was proof, to my mind, that he believed me entitled to the whole of them. I always felt worse for having received any thing; for I feared that the giving me a few cents would ease his conscience, and make him feel himself to be a pretty honorable sort of robber. My discontent grew upon me. I was ever on the look-out for means of escape; and, finding no direct means, I determined to try to hire my time, with a view of getting money with which to make my escape. In the spring of 1838, when Master Thomas came to Baltimore to purchase his spring goods, I got an opportunity, and applied to him to allow me to hire my time. He unhesitatingly refused my request, and told me this was another stratagem by which to escape. He told me I could go nowhere but that he could get me; and that, in the event of my running away, he should spare no pains in his efforts to catch me. He exhorted me to content myself, and be obedient. He told me, if I would be happy, I must lay out no plans for the future. He said, if I behaved myself properly, he would take care of me. Indeed, he advised me to complete thoughtlessness of the future, and taught me to depend solely upon him for happiness. He seemed to see fully the pressing necessity of setting aside my intellectual nature, in order to contentment in slavery. But in spite of him, and even in spite of myself, I continued to think, and to think about the injustice of my enslavement, and the means of escape.

About two months after this, I applied to Master Hugh for the privilege of hiring my time. He was not acquainted with the fact that I had applied to Master Thomas, and had been refused. He too, at first, seemed disposed to refuse; but, after some reflection, he granted me the privilege, and proposed the following terms: I was to be allowed all my time, make all contracts with those for whom I worked, and find my own employment; and, in return for this liberty, I was to pay him three dollars at the end of each week; find myself in calking tools, and in board and clothing. My board was two dollars and a half per week. This, with the wear and tear of clothing and calking tools, made my regular expenses about six dollars per week. This amount I was compelled to make up, or relinquish the privilege of hiring my time. Rain or shine, work or no work, at the end of each week the money must be forthcoming, or I must give up my privilege. This arrangement, it will be perceived, was decidedly in my master's favor. It relieved him of all need of looking after me. His money was sure. He received all the benefits of slaveholding without its evils; while I endured all the evils of a slave, and suffered all the care and anxiety of a freeman. I found it a hard bargain. But, hard as it was, I thought it better than the old mode of getting along. It was a step towards freedom to be allowed to bear the responsibilities of a freeman, and I was determined to hold on upon it. I bent myself to the work of making money. I was ready to work at night as well as day, and by the most untiring perseverance and industry, I made enough to meet my expenses, and lay up a little money every week. I went on thus from May till August. Master Hugh then refused to allow me to hire my time longer. The ground for his refusal was a failure on my part, one Saturday night, to pay him for my week's time. This failure was occasioned by my attending a camp meeting about ten miles from Baltimore. During the week, I had entered into an engagement with a number of young friends to start from Baltimore to the camp ground early Saturday evening; and being detained by my employer, I was unable to get down to Master Hugh's without disappointing the company. I knew that Master Hugh was in no special need of the money that night. I therefore decided to go to camp meeting, and upon my return pay him the three dollars. I stayed at the camp meeting one day longer than I intended when I left. But as soon as I returned, I called upon him to pay him what he considered his due. I found him very angry; he could scarce restrain his wrath. He said he had a great mind to give me a severe whipping. He wished to know how I dared go out of the city without asking his permission. I told him I hired my time, and while I paid him the price which he asked for it, I did not know that I was bound to ask him when and where I should go. This reply troubled him; and, after reflecting a few moments, he turned to me, and said I should hire my time no longer; that the next thing he should know of, I would be running away. Upon the same plea, he told me to bring my tools and clothing home forthwith. I did so; but instead of seeking work, as I had been accustomed to do previously to hiring my time, I spent the whole week without the performance of a single stroke of work. I did this in retaliation. Saturday night, he called upon me as usual for my week's wages. I told him I had no wages; I had done no work that week. Here we were upon the point of coming to blows. He raved, and swore his determination to get hold of me. I did not allow myself a single word; but was resolved, if he laid the weight of his hand upon me, it should be blow for blow. He did not strike me, but told me that he would find me in constant employment in future. I thought the matter over during the next day, Sunday, and finally resolved upon the third day of September, as the day upon which I would make a second attempt to secure my freedom. I now had three weeks during which to prepare for my journey. Early on Monday morning, before Master Hugh had time to make any engagement for me, I went out and got employment of Mr. Butler, at his ship-yard near the draw-bridge, upon what is called the City Block, thus making it unnecessary for him to seek employment for me. At the end of the week, I brought him between eight and nine dollars. He seemed very well pleased, and asked why I did not do the same the week before. He little knew what my plans were. My object in working steadily was to remove any suspicion he might entertain of my intent to run away; and in this I succeeded admirably. I suppose he thought I was never better satisfied with my condition than at the very time during which I was planning my escape. The second week passed, and again I carried him my full wages; and so well pleased was he, that he gave me twenty-five cents, (quite a large sum for a slaveholder to give a slave,) and bade me to make a good use of it. I told him I would.

Things went on without very smoothly indeed, but within there was trouble. It is impossible for me to describe my feelings as the time of my contemplated start drew near. I had a number of warm-hearted friends in Baltimore,—friends that I loved almost as I did my life,—and the thought of being separated from them forever was painful beyond expression. It is my opinion that thousands would escape from slavery, who now remain, but for the strong cords of affection that bind them to their friends. The thought of leaving my friends was decidedly the most painful thought with which I had to contend. The love of them was my tender point, and shook my decision more than all things else. Besides the pain of separation, the dread and apprehension of a failure exceeded what I had experienced at my first attempt. The appalling defeat I then sustained returned to torment me. I felt assured that, if I failed in this attempt, my case would be a hopeless one—it would seal my fate as a slave forever. I could not hope to get off with any thing less than the severest punishment, and being placed beyond the means of escape. It required no very vivid imagination to depict the most frightful scenes through which I should have to pass, in case I failed. The wretchedness of slavery, and the blessedness of freedom, were perpetually before me. It was life and death with me. But I remained firm, and, according to my resolution, on the third day of September, 1838, I left my chains, and succeeded in reaching New York without the slightest interruption of any kind. How I did so,—what means I adopted,—what direction I travelled, and by what mode of conveyance,—I must leave unexplained, for the reasons before mentioned.

I have been frequently asked how I felt when I found myself in a free State. I have never been able to answer the question with any satisfaction to myself. It was a moment of the highest excitement I ever experienced. I suppose I felt as one may imagine the unarmed mariner to feel when he is rescued by a friendly man-of-war from the pursuit of a pirate. In writing to a dear friend, immediately after my arrival at New York, I said I felt like one who had escaped a den of hungry lions. This state of mind, however, very soon subsided; and I was again seized with a feeling of great insecurity and loneliness. I was yet liable to be taken back, and subjected to all the tortures of slavery. This in itself was enough to damp the ardor of my enthusiasm. But the loneliness overcame me. There I was in the midst of thousands, and yet a perfect stranger; without home and without friends, in the midst of thousands of my own brethren—children of a common Father, and yet I dared not to unfold to any of them my sad condition. I was afraid to speak to any one for fear of speaking to the wrong one, and thereby falling into the hands of money-loving kidnappers, whose business it was to lie in wait for the panting fugitive, as the ferocious beasts of the forest lie in wait for their prey. The motto which I adopted when I started from slavery was this—"Trust no man!" I saw in every white man an enemy, and in almost every colored man cause for distrust. It was a most painful situation; and, to understand it, one must needs experience it, or imagine himself in similar circumstances. Let him be a fugitive slave in a strange land—a land given up to be the hunting-ground for slaveholders—whose inhabitants are legalized kidnappers—where he is every moment subjected to the terrible liability of being seized upon by his fellowmen, as the hideous crocodile seizes upon his prey!—I say, let him place himself in my situation—without home or friends—without money or credit—wanting shelter, and no one to give it—wanting bread, and no money to buy it,—and at the same time let him feel that he is pursued by merciless men-hunters, and in total darkness as to what to do, where to go, or where to stay,—perfectly helpless both as to the means of defence and means of escape,—in the midst of plenty, yet suffering the terrible gnawings of hunger,—in the midst of houses, yet having no home,—among fellow-men, yet feeling as if in the midst of wild beasts, whose greediness to swallow up the trembling and half-famished fugitive is only equalled by that with which the monsters of the deep swallow up the helpless fish upon which they subsist,—I say, let him be placed in this most trying situation,—the situation in which I was placed,—then, and not till then, will he fully appreciate the hardships of, and know how to sympathize with, the toil-worn and whip-scarred fugitive slave.

Thank Heaven, I remained but a short time in this distressed situation. I was relieved from it by the humane hand of Mr. David Ruggles, whose vigilance, kindness, and perseverance, I shall never forget. I am glad of an opportunity to express, as far as words can, the love and gratitude I bear him. Mr. Ruggles is now afflicted with blindness, and is himself in need of the same kind offices which he was once so forward in the performance of toward others. I had been in New York but a few days, when Mr. Ruggles sought me out, and very kindly took me to his boarding-house at the corner of Church and Lespenard Streets. Mr. Ruggles was then very deeply engaged in the memorable *Darg* case, as well as attending to a number of other fugitive slaves, devising ways and means for their successful escape; and, though watched and hemmed in on almost every side, he seemed to be more than a match for his enemies.

Very soon after I went to Mr. Ruggles, he wished to know of me where I wanted to go; as he deemed it unsafe for me to remain in New York. I told him I was a calker, and should like to go where I could get work. I thought of going to Canada; but he decided against it, and in favor of my going to New Bedford, thinking I should be able to get work there at my trade. At this time, Anna, my intended wife, came on; for I wrote to her immediately after my arrival at New York, (notwithstanding my homeless, houseless, and helpless condition,) informing her of my successful flight, and wishing her to come on forthwith. In a few days after her arrival, Mr. Ruggles called in the Rev. J. W. C. Pennington, who, in the presence of Mr. Ruggles, Mrs. Michaels, and two or three others, performed the marriage ceremony, and gave us a certificate, of which the following is an exact copy:—

> "This may certify, that I joined together in holy matrimony Frederick Johnson* and Anna Murray, as man and wife, in the presence of Mr. David Ruggles and Mrs. Michaels.
>
> "JAMES W. C. PENNINGTON
>
> "*New York, Sept. 15, 1838.*"

Upon receiving this certificate, and a five-dollar bill from Mr. Ruggles, I shouldered one part of our baggage, and Anna took up the other, and we set out forthwith to take passage on board of the steamboat John W. Richmond for Newport, on our way to New Bedford. Mr. Ruggles gave me a letter to a Mr. Shaw in Newport, and told me, in case my money did not serve me to New Bedford, to stop in Newport and obtain further assistance, but upon our arrival at Newport, we were so anxious to get to a place of safety, that, notwithstanding we lacked the necessary money to pay our fare, we decided to take seats in the stage, and promise to pay when we got to New Bedford. We were encouraged to do this by two excellent gentlemen, residents of New Bedford, whose names I afterward ascertained to be Joseph Ricketson and William C. Taber. They seemed at once to understand our circumstances, and gave us such assurance of their friendliness as put us fully at ease in their presence. It was good indeed to meet with such friends, at such a time. Upon reaching New Bedford, we were directed to the house of Mr. Nathan Johnson, by whom we were kindly received, and hospitably provided for. Both Mr. and Mrs. Johnson took a deep and lively interest in our welfare. They proved themselves quite worthy of the name of abolitionists. When the stage-driver found us unable to pay our fare, he held on upon our baggage as security for the debt. I had but to mention the fact to Mr. Johnson, and he forthwith advanced the money.

We now began to feel a degree of safety, and to prepare ourselves for the duties and responsibilities of a life of freedom. On the morning after our arrival at New Bedford, while at the breakfast-table, the question arose as to what name I should be called by. The name given me by my mother was, "Frederick Augustus Washington Bailey." I, however, had dispensed with the two middle names long

---

*I had changed my name from Frederick *Bailey* to that of *Johnson*.

before I left Maryland so that I was generally known by the name of "Frederick Bailey." I started from Baltimore bearing the name of "Stanley." When I got to New York, I again changed my name to "Frederick Johnson," and thought that would be the last change. But when I got to New Bedford, I found it necessary again to change my name. The reason of this necessity was, that there were so many Johnsons in New Bedford, it was already quite difficult to distinguish between them. I gave Mr. Johnson the privilege of choosing me a name, but told him he must not take from me the name of "Frederick." I must hold on to that, to preserve a sense of my identity. Mr. Johnson had just been reading the "Lady of the Lake," and at once suggested that my name be "Douglass." From that time until now I have been called "Frederick Douglass;" and as I am more widely known by that name than by either of the others, I shall continue to use it as my own.

I was quite disappointed at the general appearance of things in New Bedford. The impression which I had received respecting the character and condition of the people of the north, I found to be singularly erroneous. I had very strangely supposed, while in slavery, that few of the comforts, and scarcely any of the luxuries, of life were enjoyed at the north, compared with what were enjoyed by the slaveholders of the south. I probably came to this conclusion from the fact that northern people owned no slaves. I supposed that they were about upon a level with the non-slaveholding population of the south. I knew *they* were exceedingly poor, and I had been accustomed to regard their poverty as the necessary consequence of their being non-slaveholders. I had somehow imbibed the opinion that, in the absence of slaves, there could be no wealth, and very little refinement. And upon coming to the north, I expected to meet with a rough, hard-handed, and uncultivated population, living in the most Spartan-like simplicity, knowing nothing of the ease, luxury, pomp, and grandeur of southern slaveholders. Such being my conjectures, any one acquainted with the appearance of New Bedford may very readily infer how palpably I must have seen my mistake.

In the afternoon of the day when I reached New Bedford, I visited the wharves, to take a view of the shipping. Here I found myself surrounded with the strongest proofs of wealth. Lying at the wharves, and riding in the stream, I saw many ships of the finest model, in the best order, and of the largest size. Upon the right and left, I was walled in by granite warehouses of the widest dimensions, stowed to their utmost capacity with the necessaries and comforts of life. Added to this, almost every body seemed to be at work, but noiselessly so, compared with what I had been accustomed to in Baltimore. There were no loud songs heard from those engaged in loading and unloading ships. I heard no deep oaths or horrid curses on the laborer. I saw no whipping of men; but all seemed to go smoothly on. Every man appeared to understand his work, and went at it with a sober, yet cheerful earnestness, which betokened the deep interest which he felt in what he was doing, as well as a sense of his own dignity as a man. To me this looked exceedingly strange. From the wharves I strolled around and over the town, gazing with wonder and admiration at the splendid churches, beautiful dwellings, and finely-cultivated gardens; evincing an amount of wealth, comfort, taste, and refinement, such as I had never seen in any part of slaveholding Maryland.

Every thing looked clean, new, and beautiful. I saw few or no dilapidated houses, with poverty-stricken inmates; no half-naked children and bare-footed women, such as I had been accustomed to see in Hillsborough, Easton, St.

Michael's, and Baltimore. The people looked more able, stronger, healthier, and happier, than those of Maryland. I was for once made glad by a view of extreme wealth, without being saddened by seeing extreme poverty. But the most astonishing as well as the most interesting thing to me was the condition of the colored people, a great many of whom, like myself, had escaped thither as a refuge from the hunters of men. I found many, who had not been seven years out of their chains, living in finer houses, and evidently enjoying more of the comforts of life, than the average of slaveholders in Maryland. I will venture to assert, that my friend Mr. Nathan Johnson (of whom I can say with a grateful heart, "I was hungry, and he gave me meat; I was thirsty, and he gave me drink; I was a stranger, and he took me in") lived in a neater house; dined at a better table; took, paid for, and read, more newspapers; better understood the moral, religious, and political character of the nation,—than nine tenths of the slaveholders in Talbot county, Maryland. Yet Mr. Johnson was a working man. His hands were hardened by toil, and not his alone, but those also of Mrs. Johnson. I found the colored people much more spirited than I had supposed they would be. I found among them a determination to protect each other from the blood-thirsty kidnapper, at all hazards. Soon after my arrival, I was told of a circumstance which illustrated their spirit. A colored man and a fugitive slave were on unfriendly terms. The former was heard to threaten the latter with informing his master of his whereabouts. Straightway a meeting was called among the colored people, under the stereotyped notice, "Business of importance!" The betrayer was invited to attend. The people came at the appointed hour, and organized the meeting by appointing a very religious old gentleman as president, who, I believe, made a prayer, after which he addressed the meeting as follows: *"Friends, we have got him here, and I would recommend that you young men just take him outside the door, and kill him!"* With this, a number of them bolted at him; but they were intercepted by some more timid than themselves, and the betrayer escaped their vengeance, and has not been seen in New Bedford since. I believe there have been no more such threats, and should there be hereafter, I doubt not that death would be the consequence.

I found employment, the third day after my arrival, in stowing a sloop with a load of oil. It was new, dirty, and hard work for me; but I went at it with a glad heart and a willing hand. I was now my own master. It was a happy moment, the rapture of which can be understood only by those who have been slaves. It was the first work, the reward of which was to be entirely my own. There was no Master Hugh standing ready, the moment I earned the money, to rob me of it. I worked that day with a pleasure I had never before experienced. I was at work for myself and newly-married wife. It was to me the starting-point of a new existence. When I got through with that job, I went in pursuit of a job of calking; but such was the strength of prejudice against color, among the white calkers, that they refused to work with me, and of course I could get no employment. Finding my trade of no immediate benefit, I threw off my calking habiliments, and prepared myself to do any kind of work I could get to do. Mr. Johnson kindly let me have his woodhorse and saw, and I very soon found myself a plenty of work. There was no work too hard—none too dirty. I was ready to saw wood, shovel coal, carry wood, sweep the chimney, or roll oil casks,—all of which I did for nearly three years in New Bedford, before I became known to the anti-slavery world.

In about four months after I went to New Bedford, there came a young man to me, and inquired if I did not wish to take the "Liberator." I told him I did; but, just having made my escape from slavery, I remarked that I was unable to pay for it then. I, however, finally became a subscriber to it. The paper came, and I read it from week to week with such feelings as it would be quite idle for me to attempt to describe. The paper became my meat and my drink. My soul was set all on fire. Its sympathy for my brethren in bonds—its scathing denunciations of slave-holders—its faithful exposures of slavery—and its powerful attacks upon the upholders of the institution—sent a thrill of joy through my soul, such as I had never felt before!

I had not long been a reader of the "Liberator," before I got a pretty correct idea of the principles, measures and spirit of the anti-slavery reform. I took right hold of the cause. I could do but little; but what I could, I did with a joyful heart, and never felt happier than when in an anti-slavery meeting. I seldom had much to say at the meetings, because what I wanted to say was said so much better by others. But, while attending an anti-slavery convention at Nantucket, on the 11th of August, 1841, I felt strongly moved to speak, and was at the same time much urged to do so by Mr. William C. Coffin, a gentleman who had heard me speak in the colored people's meeting at New Bedford. It was a severe cross, and I took it up reluctantly. The truth was, I felt myself a slave, and the idea of speaking to white people weighed me down. I spoke but a few moments, when I felt a degree of freedom, and said what I desired with considerable ease. From that time until now, I have been engaged in pleading the cause of my brethren—with what success, and with what devotion, I leave those acquainted with my labors to decide.

# HARRIET JACOBS
## 1813?–1897

*Harriet Jacobs's autobiography corroborates Frederick Douglass's grim picture of life under slavery; both described an institution that brutalized the body and shackled the spirit.* Incidents in the Life of a Slave Girl, *however, describes the unique plight of an enslaved woman.*

*Jacobs, who disguised herself in the autobiography by using the name "Linda Brent," was born to slave parents in Edenton, North Carolina. Orphaned at a young age, she was raised by her maternal grandmother, a freed woman. Her first mistress taught Jacobs to read but at her death left the young slave to her own three-year-old niece. The child's father, the Dr. Flint of the story, began to make sexual advances to Jacobs when she was fifteen. To avoid these, Jacobs contracted a relationship with another white man, Mr. Sands, and bore him a son and a daughter, who remained the property of Flint's daughter. Hoping that Flint would sell her children to their father, Jacobs engineered a daring escape and after seven years in hiding, a successful flight north. Here she was reunited with her children and found employment with a sympathetic mistress. She was still not safe, however, for Flint and his family repeatedly pursued her, her safety further threatened by the passage of the Fugitive Slave Law in 1850. Like Douglass's, her freedom was assured only when a white person purchased her.*

*The decision to write* Incidents *after her emancipation was not easy. In 1849 Jacobs had lived in Rochester and joined the abolitionist movement, working in an anti-slavery reading room above Douglass' newspaper office. Urged to write her autobiography by the Quaker abolitionist and women's rights advocate Amy Post, Jacobs was torn between the benefit her autobiography might bring to the abolitionist movement and the damage it might do her personally. Although she had polished her reading skills during her years in hiding, she was understandably reluctant to write for the public. She began her career as an author with articles in the abolitionist press.* Incidents *was published in 1861. Jacobs received some editorial help and direction from abolitionist author Lydia Maria Child, but most historians are convinced that Jacobs's story is an authentic autobiography.*

*From 1862 to 1868, Jacobs raised funds for the freedmen as an agent for Philadelphia and New York Quakers. In 1885 she moved from Cambridge to Washington D.C., where she lived with her daughter Louisa Matilda Jacobs until her death.*

*Douglass and Jacobs wrote to further their shared cause of abolitionism, but their story tellings are different. Jacobs almost certainly intended to appeal to a female audience who could probably identify with her sexual vulnerability. Her genteel language, reminiscent of Harriet Robinson's, is in striking contrast to the powerful rhetoric of Douglass. Both struggled for freedom, but her escape from slavery was inspired by a desire to save her children from servitude, not to save herself, and when she fled north, she intended to rejoin her daughter. Her most persistent characterization of herself was as a mother. The shame of her pregnancy out-of-wedlock, however, cast a shadow on her maternal identity. It is significant that although Douglass proudly named himself as author, she never shed her disguise as Linda Brent.*

Incidents in the Life of a Slave Girl, Written By Herself. *Boston. Published for the Author, 1861. Reprint, Cambridge: Harvard University Press, 1987, edited by Jean Fagan Yellin.*

I was born a slave; but I never knew it till six years of happy childhood had passed away. My father was a carpenter, and considered so intelligent and skilful in his trade, that, when buildings out of the common line were to be erected, he was sent for from long distances, to be head workman. On condition of paying his mistress two hundred dollars a year, and supporting himself, he was allowed to work at his trade, and manage his own affairs. His strongest wish was to purchase his children; but, though he several times offered his hard earnings for that purpose, he never succeeded. In complexion my parents were a light shade of brownish yellow, and were termed mulattoes. They lived together in a comfortable home; and, though we were all slaves, I was so fondly shielded that I never dreamed I was a piece of merchandise, trusted to them for safe keeping, and liable to be demanded of them at any moment. I had one brother, William, who was two years younger than myself—a bright, affectionate child. I had also a great treasure in my maternal grandmother, who was a remarkable woman in many respects. She was the daughter of a planter in South Carolina, who, at his death, left her mother and his three children free, with money to go to St. Augustine, where they had relatives. It was during the Revolutionary War; and they were captured on their passage, carried back, and sold to different purchasers. Such was the story my grandmother used to tell me; but I do not remember all the particulars. She was a little girl when she was captured and sold to the keeper of a large hotel. I have often heard her tell how hard she fared during childhood. But as she grew older she evinced so much intelligence, and was so faithful, that her master and mistress could not help seeing it was for their interest to take care of such a valuable piece of property. She became an indispensable personage in the household, officiating in all capacities, from cook and wet nurse to seamstress. She was much praised for her cooking; and her nice crackers became so famous in the neighborhood that many people were desirous of obtaining them. In consequence of numerous requests of this kind, she asked permission of her mistress to bake crackers at night, after all the household work was done; and she obtained leave to do it, provided she would clothe herself and her children from the profits. Upon these terms, after working hard all day for her mistress, she began her midnight bakings, assisted by her two oldest children. The business proved profitable; and each year she laid by a little, which was saved for a fund to purchase her children. Her master died, and the property was divided among his heirs. The widow had her dower in the hotel, which she continued to keep open. My grandmother remained in her service as a slave; but her children were divided among her master's children. As she had five, Benjamin, the youngest one, was sold, in order that each heir might have an equal portion of dollars and cents. There was so little difference in our ages that he seemed more like my brother than my uncle. He was a bright, handsome lad, nearly white; for he inherited the complexion my grandmother had derived from Anglo-Saxon ancestors. Though only ten years old, seven hundred and twenty dollars were paid for him. His sale was a terrible blow to my grandmother; but she was naturally hopeful, and she went to work with renewed energy, trusting in time to be able to purchase some of her children. She had laid up three hundred dollars, which her mistress one day begged as a loan, promising to pay her soon. The reader probably knows that no promise or writing given to a slave is legally binding; for, according to Southern laws, a slave, *being* property, can *hold* no property. When my grandmother lent her hard earnings to her mistress, she trusted solely to her honor. The honor of a slaveholder to a slave!

To this good grandmother I was indebted for many comforts. My brother Willie and I often received portions of the crackers, cakes, and preserves, she made to sell; and after we ceased to be children we were indebted to her for many more important services.

Such were the unusually fortunate circumstances of my early childhood. When I was six years old, my mother died; and then, for the first time, I learned, by the talk around me, that I was a slave. My mother's mistress was the daughter of my grandmother's mistress. She was the foster sister of my mother; they were both nourished at my grandmother's breast. In fact, my mother had been weaned at three months old, that the babe of the mistress might obtain sufficient food. They played together as children; and, when they became women, my mother was a most faithful servant to her whiter foster sister. On her death-bed her mistress promised that her children should never suffer for any thing; and during her life-time she kept her word. They all spoke kindly of my dead mother, who had been a slave merely in name, but in nature was noble and womanly. I grieved for her, and my young mind was troubled with the thought who would now take care of me and my little brother. I was told that my home was now to be with her mistress; and I found it a happy one. No toilsome or disagreeable duties were imposed upon me. My mistress was so kind to me that I was always glad to do her bidding, and proud to labor for her as much as my young years would permit. I would sit by her side for hours, sewing diligently, with a heart as free from care as that of any free-born white child. When she thought I was tired, she would send me out to run and jump; and away I bounded, to gather berries or flowers to decorate her room. Those were happy days—too happy to last. The slave child had no thought for the morrow; but there came that blight, which too surely waits on every human being born to be a chattel.

When I was nearly twelve years old, my kind mistress sickened and died. As I saw the cheek grow paler, and the eye more glassy, how earnestly I prayed in my heart that she might live! I loved her; for she had been almost like a mother to me. My prayers were not answered. She died, and they buried her in the little church-yard, where, day after day, my tears fell upon her grave.

I was sent to spend a week with my grandmother. I was now old enough to begin to think of the future; and again and again I asked myself what they would

**HARRIET JACOBS**

do with me. I felt sure I should never find another mistress so kind as the one who was gone. She had promised my dying mother that her children should never suffer for any thing; and when I remembered that, and recalled her many proofs of attachment to me, I could not help having some hopes that she had left me free. My friends were almost certain it would be so. They thought she would be sure to do it, on account of my mother's love and faithful service. But, alas! we all know that the memory of a faithful slave does not avail much to save her children from the auction block.

After a brief period of suspense, the will of my mistress was read, and we learned that she had bequeathed me to her sister's daughter, a child of five years old. So vanished our hopes. My mistress had taught me the precepts of God's Word: "Thou shalt love thy neighbor as thyself." "Whatsoever ye would that men should do unto you, do ye even so unto them." But I was her slave, and I suppose she did not recognize me as her neighbor. I would give much to blot out from my memory that one great wrong. As a child, I loved my mistress; and, looking back on the happy days I spent with her, I try to think with less bitterness of this act of injustice. While I was with her, she taught me to read and spell; and for this privilege, which so rarely falls to the lot of a slave, I bless her memory.

She possessed but few slaves; and at her death those were all distributed among her relatives. Five of them were my grandmother's children, and had shared the same milk that nourished her mother's children. Notwithstanding my grandmother's long and faithful service to her owners, not one of her children escaped the auction block. These God-breathing machines are no more, in the sight of their masters, than the cotton they plant, or the horses they tend.

Dr. Flint, a physician in the neighborhood, had married the sister of my mistress, and I was now the property of their little daughter. It was not without murmuring that I prepared for my new home; and what added to my unhappiness, was the fact that my brother William was purchased by the same family. My father, by his nature, as well as by habit of transacting business as a skilful mechanic, had more of the feelings of a freeman than is common among slaves. My brother was a spirited boy; and being brought up under such influences, he early detested the name of master and mistress. One day, when his father and his mistress had happened to call him at the same time, he hesitated between the two; being perplexed to know which had the strongest claim upon his obedience. He finally concluded to go to his mistress. When my father reproved him for it, he said, "You both called me, and I didn't know which I ought to go to first."

"You are *my* child," replied our father, "and when I call you, you should come immediately, if you have to pass through fire and water."

Poor Willie! He was now to learn his first lesson of obedience to a master. Grandmother tried to cheer us with hopeful words, and they found an echo in the credulous hearts of youth.

When we entered our new home we encountered cold looks, cold words, and cold treatment. We were glad when the night came. On my narrow bed I moaned and wept, I felt so desolate and alone.

I had been there nearly a year, when a dear little friend of mine was buried. I heard her mother sob, as the clods fell on the coffin of her only child, and I turned away from the grave, feeling thankful that I still had something left to love. I met my grandmother, who said, "Come with me, Linda;" and from her tone I knew that something sad had happened. She led me apart from the people, and then said, "My child, your father is dead." Dead! How could I believe it? He had died so suddenly I had not even heard that he was sick. I went home with my grandmother. My heart rebelled against God, who had taken from me mother, father, mistress, and friend. The good grandmother tried to comfort me. "Who knows the ways of God?" said she. "Perhaps they have been kindly taken from the evil days to come." Years afterward I often thought of this. She promised to be a mother to her grandchildren, so far as she might be permitted to do so; and strengthened by her love, I returned to my master's. I thought I should be allowed to go to my father's house the next morning; but I was ordered to go for flowers, that my mistress's house might be decorated for an evening party. I spent the day gathering flowers and weaving them into festoons, while the dead body of my father was lying within a mile of me. What cared my owners for that? he was merely a piece of property. Moreover, they thought he had spoiled his children, by teaching them to feel that they were human beings. This was blasphemous doctrine for a slave to teach; presumptuous in him, and dangerous to the masters.

The next day I followed his remains to a humble grave beside that of my dear mother. There were those who knew my father's worth, and respected his memory.

My home now seemed more dreary than ever. The laugh of the little slave-children sounded harsh and cruel. It was selfish to feel so about the joy of others. My brother moved about with a very grave face. I tried to comfort him, by saying, "Take courage, Willie; brighter days will come by and by."

"You don't know any thing about it, Linda," he replied. "We shall have to stay here all our days; we shall never be free."

I argued that we were growing older and stronger, and that perhaps we might, before long, be allowed to hire our own time, and then we could earn money to buy our freedom. William declared this was much easier to say than to do; moreover, he did not intend to *buy* his freedom. We held daily controversies upon this subject.

Little attention was paid to the slaves' meals in Dr. Flint's house. If they could catch a bit of food while it was going, well and good. I gave myself no trouble on that score, for on my various errands I passed my grandmother's house, where there was always something to spare for me. I was frequently threatened with punishment if I stopped there; and my grandmother, to avoid detaining me, often stood at the gate with something for my breakfast or dinner. I was indebted to *her* for all my comforts, spiritual or temporal. It was *her* labor that supplied my scanty wardrobe. I have a vivid recollection of the linsey-woolsey dress given me every winter by Mrs. Flint. How I hated it! It was one of the badges of slavery.

While my grandmother was thus helping to support me from her hard earnings, the three hundred dollars she had lent her mistress were never repaid. When her mistress died, her son-in-law, Dr. Flint, was appointed executor. When grandmother applied to him for payment, he said the estate was insolvent, and the law prohibited payment. It did not, however, prohibit him from retaining the silver candelabra, which had been purchased with that money. I presume they will be handed down in the family, from generation to generation.

My grandmother's mistress had always promised her that, at her death, she should be free; and it was said that in her will she made good the promise. But when the estate was settled, Dr. Flint told the faithful old servant that, under existing circumstances, it was necessary she should be sold.

On the appointed day, the customary advertisement was posted up, proclaiming that there would be a "public sale of negroes, horses, &c." Dr. Flint called to tell my grandmother that he was unwilling to wound her feelings by putting her up at auction, and that he would prefer to dispose of her at private sale. My grandmother saw through his hypocrisy; she understood very well that he was ashamed of the job. She was a very spirited woman, and if he was base enough to sell her, when her mistress intended she should be free, she was determined the public should know it. She had for a long time supplied many families with crackers and preserves; consequently, "Aunt Marthy," as she was called, was generally known, and every body who knew her respected her intelligence and good character. Her long and faithful service in the family was also well known, and the intention of her mistress to leave her free. When the day of sale came, she took her place among the chattels, and at the first call she sprang upon the auction-block. Many voices called out, "Shame! Shame! Who is going to sell *you*, Aunt Marthy? Don't stand there! That is no place for *you*." Without saying a word, she quietly awaited her fate. No one bid for her. At last, a feeble voice said, "Fifty dollars." It came from a maiden lady, seventy years old, the sister of my grandmother's deceased mistress. She had lived forty years under the same roof with my grandmother, she knew how faithfully she had served her owners, and how cruelly she had been defrauded of her rights; and she resolved to protect her. The auctioneer waited for a higher bid; but her wishes were respected; no one bid above her. She could neither read nor write; and when the bill of sale was made out, she signed it with a cross. But what consequence was that, when she had a big heart overflowing with human kindness? She gave the old servant her freedom.

At that time, my grandmother was just fifty years old. Laborious years had passed since then; and now my brother and I were slaves to the man who had defrauded her of her money, and tried to defraud her of her freedom. One of my mother's sisters, called Aunt Nancy, was also a slave in his family. She was a kind, good aunt to me; and supplied the place of both housekeeper and waiting maid to her mistress. She was, in fact, at the beginning and end of every thing.

Mrs. Flint, like many southern women, was totally deficient in energy. She had not strength to superintend her household affairs; but her nerves were so strong, that she could sit in her easy chair and see a woman whipped, till the blood trickled from every stroke of the lash. She was a member of the church; but partaking of the Lord's supper did not seem to put her in a Christian frame of mind. If dinner was not served at the exact time on that particular Sunday, she would station herself in the kitchen, and wait till it was dished, and then spit in all the kettles and pans that had been used for cooking. She did this to prevent the cook and her children from eking out their meagre fare with the remains of the gravy and other scrapings. The slaves could get nothing to eat except what she chose to give them. Provisions were weighed out by the pound and ounce, three times a day. I can assure you she gave them no chance to eat wheat bread from her flour barrel. She knew how many biscuits a quart of flour would make, and exactly what size they ought to be.

Dr. Flint was an epicure. The cook never sent a dinner to his table without fear and trembling; for if there happened to be a dish not to his liking, he would either order her to be whipped, or compel her to eat every mouthful of it in his presence. The poor, hungry creature might not have objected to eating it; but she did object to having her master cram it down her throat till she choked.

They had a pet dog, that was a nuisance in the house. The cook was ordered to make some Indian mush for him. He refused to eat, and when his head was held over it, the froth flowed from his mouth into the basin. He died a few minutes after. When Dr. Flint came in, he said the mush had not been well cooked, and that was the reason the animal would not eat it. He sent for the cook, and compelled her to eat it. He thought that the woman's stomach was stronger than the dog's; but her sufferings afterwards proved that he was mistaken. This poor woman endured many cruelties from her master and mistress; sometimes she was locked up, away from her nursing baby, for a whole day and night.

When I had been in the family a few weeks, one of the plantation slaves was brought to town, by order of his master. It was near night when he arrived, and Dr. Flint ordered him to be taken to the work house, and tied up to the joist, so that his feet would just escape the ground. In that situation he was to wait till the doctor had taken his tea. I shall never forget that night. Never before, in my life, had I heard hundreds of blows fall, in succession, on a human being. His piteous groans, and his "O, pray don't, massa," rang in my ear for months afterwards. There were many conjectures as to the cause of this terrible punishment. Some said master accused him of stealing corn; others said the slave had quarrelled with his wife, in presence of the overseer, and had accused his master of being the father of her child. They were both black, and the child was very fair.

I went into the work house next morning, and saw the cowhide still wet with blood, and the boards all covered with gore. The poor man lived, and continued to quarrel with his wife. A few months afterwards Dr. Flint handed them both over to a slavetrader. The guilty man put their value into his pocket, and had the satisfaction of knowing that they were out of sight and hearing. When the mother was delivered into the trader's hands, she said, "You *promised* to treat me well." To which he replied, "You have let your tongue run too far; damn you!" She had forgotten that it was a crime for a slave to tell who was the father of her child.

From others than the master persecution also comes in such cases. I once saw a young slave girl dying soon after the birth of a child nearly white. In her agony she cried out, "O Lord, come and take me!" Her mistress stood by, and mocked at her like an incarnate fiend. "You suffer, do you!" she exclaimed. "I am glad of it. You deserve it all, and more too."

The girl's mother said, "The baby is dead, thank God; and I hope my poor child will soon be in heaven, too."

"Heaven!" retorted the mistress. "There is no such place for the like of her and her bastard."

The poor mother turned away, sobbing. Her dying daughter called her, feebly, and as she bent over her, I heard her say, "Don't grieve so, mother; God knows all about it; and He will have mercy upon me."

Her sufferings, afterwards, became so intense, that her mistress felt unable to stay; but when she left the room, the scornful smile was still on her lips. Seven children called her mother. The poor black woman had but the one child, whose eyes she saw closing in death, while she thanked God for taking her away from the greater bitterness of life....

**[Brent was raised by her grandmother, a free woman. Her uncle Benjamin escaped to freedom.]**

During the first years of my service in Dr. Flint's family, I was accustomed to share some indulgences with the children of my mistress. Though this seemed to me no more than right, I was grateful for it, and tried to merit the kindness by the faithful discharge of my duties. But I now entered on my fifteenth year—a sad epoch in the life of a slave girl. My master began to whisper foul words in my ear. Young as I was, I could not remain ignorant of their import. I tried to treat them with indifference or contempt. The master's age, my extreme youth, and the fear that his conduct would be reported to my grandmother, made him bear this treatment for many months. He was a crafty man, and resorted to many means to accomplish his purposes. Sometimes he had stormy, terrific ways, that made his victims tremble; sometimes he assumed a gentleness that he thought must surely subdue. Of the two, I preferred his stormy moods, although they left me trembling. He tried his utmost to corrupt the pure principles my grandmother had instilled. He peopled my young mind with unclean images, such as only a vile monster could think of. I turned from him with disgust and hatred. But he was my master. I was compelled to live under the same roof with him—where I saw a man forty years my senior daily violating the most sacred commandments of nature. He told me I was his property; that I must be subject to his will in all things. My soul revolted against the mean tyranny. But where could I turn for protection? No matter whether the slave girl be as black as ebony or as fair as her mistress. In either case, there is no shadow of law to protect her from insult, from violence, or even from death; all these all inflicted by fiends who bear the shape of men. The mistress, who ought to protect the helpless victim, has no other feelings towards her but those of jealousy and rage. The degradation, the wrongs, the vices, that grow out of slavery, are more than I can describe. They are greater than you would willingly believe. Surely, if you credited one half the truths that are told you concerning the helpless millions suffering in this cruel bondage, you at the north would not help to tighten the yoke. You surely would refuse to do for the master on your own soil, the mean and cruel work which trained bloodhounds and the lowest class of whites do for him at the south. . . .

I longed for some one to confide in. I would have given the world to have laid my head on my grandmother's faithful bosom, and told her all my troubles. But Dr. Flint swore he would kill me, if I was not as silent as the grave. Then, although my grandmother was all in all to me, I feared her as well as loved her. I had been accustomed to look up to her with a respect bordering upon awe. I was very young, and felt shamefaced about telling her such impure things, especially as I knew her to be very strict on such subjects. Moreover, she was a woman of a high spirit. She was usually very quiet in her demeanor; but if her indignation was once roused, it was not very easily quelled. I had been told that she once chased a white gentleman with a loaded pistol, because he insulted one of her daughters. I dreaded the consequences of a violent outbreak; and both pride and fear kept me silent. But though I did not confide in my grandmother, and even evaded her vigilant watchfulness and inquiry, her presence in the neighborhood was some protection to me. Though she had been a slave, Dr. Flint was afraid of her. He dreaded her scorching rebukes. Moreover, she was known and patronized by many people; and he did not wish to have his villainy made public. It was lucky for me that I did not live on a distant plantation, but in a town not so large that the inhabitants were ignorant of each other's affairs. Bad as are the laws and customs in a slaveholding community, the doctor, as a professional man, deemed it prudent to keep up some outward show of decency. . . .

Mrs. Flint possessed the key to her husband's character before I was born. She might have used this knowledge to counsel and to screen the young and the innocent among her slaves; but for them she had no sympathy. They were the objects of her constant suspicion and malevolence. She watched her husband with unceasing vigilance; but he was well practised in means to evade it. What he could not find opportunity to say in words he manifested in signs. He invented more than were ever thought of in a deaf and dumb asylum. I let them pass, as if I did not understand what he meant; and many were the curses and threats bestowed on me for my stupidity. One day he caught me teaching myself to write. He frowned, as if he was not well pleased; but I suppose he came to the conclusion that such an accomplishment might help to advance his favorite scheme. Before long, notes were often slipped into my hand. I would return them, saying, "I can't read them, sir." "Can't you?" he replied; "then I must read them to you." He always finished the reading by asking, "Do you understand?" Sometimes he would complain of the heat of the tea room, and order his supper to be placed on a small table in the piazza. He would seat himself there with a well-satisfied smile, and tell me to stand by and brush away the flies. He would eat very slowly, pausing between the mouthfuls. These intervals were employed in describing the happiness I was so foolishly throwing away, and in threatening me with the penalty that finally awaited my stubborn disobedience. He boasted much of the forbearance he had exercised towards me, and reminded me that there was a limit to his patience. When I succeeded in avoiding opportunities for him to talk to me at home, I was ordered to come to his office, to do some errand. When there, I was obliged to stand and listen to such language as he saw fit to address to me. Sometimes I so openly expressed my contempt for him that he would become violently enraged, and I wondered why he did not strike me. Circumstanced as he was, he probably thought it was better policy to be forbearing. But the state of things grew worse and worse daily. In desperation I told him that I must and would apply to my grandmother for protection. He threatened me with death, and worse than death, if I made any complaint to her. Strange to say, I did not despair. I was naturally of a buoyant disposition, and always I had a hope of somehow getting out of his clutches. Like many a poor, simple slave before me, I trusted that some threads of joy would yet be woven into my dark destiny....

There was in the neighborhood a young colored carpenter; a free born man. We had been well acquainted in childhood, and frequently met together afterwards. We became mutually attached, and he proposed to marry me. I loved him with all the ardor of a young girl's first love. But when I reflected that I was a slave, and that the laws gave no sanction to the marriage of such, my heart sank within me. My lover wanted to buy me; but I knew that Dr. Flint was too wilful and arbitrary a man to consent to that arrangement. From him, I was sure of experiencing all sorts of opposition, and I had nothing to hope from my mistress. She would have been delighted to have got rid of me, but not in that way. It would have relieved her mind of a burden if she could have seen me sold to some distant state, but if I was married near home I should be just as much in her husband's power as I had previously been, for the husband of a slave has no power to protect her. Moreover, my mistress, like many others, seemed to think that slaves had no right to any family ties of their own; that they were created merely to wait upon the family of the mistress. I once heard her abuse a young slave girl, who told her that a colored man wanted to make her his wife. "I will have you peeled and pickled, my lady," said she, "if I ever hear you mention that subject again. Do you suppose that I will have you tending *my* children with the children of that nigger?" The girl to whom she said this had a mulatto child, of course not acknowledged by its father. The poor black man who loved her would have been proud to acknowledge his helpless offspring. . . .

Again and again I revolved in my mind how all this would end. There was no hope that the doctor would consent to sell me on any terms. He had an iron will, and was determined to keep me, and to conquer me. My lover was an intelligent and religious man. Even if he could have obtained permission to marry me while I was a slave, the marriage would give him no power to protect me from my master. It would have made him miserable to witness the insults I should have been subjected to. And then, if we had children, I knew they must "follow the condition of the mother." What a terrible blight that would be on the heart of a free, intelligent father! For *his* sake, I felt that I ought not to link his fate with my own unhappy destiny. He was going to Savannah to see about a little property left him by an uncle; and hard as it was to bring my feelings to it, I earnestly entreated him not to come back. I advised him to go to the Free States, where his tongue would not be tied, and where his intelligence would be of more avail to him. He left me, still hoping the day would come when I could be bought. With me the lamp of hope had gone out. The dream of my girlhood was over. I felt lonely and desolate. . . .

No pen can give an adequate description of the all-pervading corruption produced by slavery. The slave girl is reared in an atmosphere of licentiousness and fear. The lash and the foul talk of her master and his sons are her teachers. When she is fourteen or fifteen, her owner, or his sons, or the overseer, or perhaps all of them, begin to bribe her with presents. If these fail to accomplish their purpose, she is whipped or starved into submission to their will. She may have had religious principles inculcated by some pious mother or grandmother, or some good mistress; she may have a lover, whose good opinion and peace of mind are dear to her heart; or the profligate men who have power over her may be exceedingly odious to her. But resistance is hopeless.

> "The poor worm
> Shall prove her contest vain. Life's little day
> Shall pass, and she is gone!"

The slaveholder's sons are, of course, vitiated, even while boys, by the unclean influences every where around them. Nor do the master's daughters always escape. Severe retributions sometimes come upon him for the wrongs he does to the daughters of the slaves. The white daughters early hear their parents quarreling about some female slave. Their curiosity is excited, and they soon learn the cause. They are attended by the young slave girls whom their father has corrupted; and they hear such talk as should never meet youthful ears, or any other ears. They know that the women slaves are subject to their father's authority in all things; and in some cases they exercise the same authority over the men slaves. I have myself seen the master of such a household whose head was bowed down in shame; for it was known in the neighborhood that his daughter had selected one of the meanest slaves on his plantation to be the father of his first grandchild. She did not make her advances to her equals, nor even to her father's more intelligent servants. She selected the most brutalized, over whom her authority could be exercised with less fear of exposure. Her father, half frantic with rage, sought to revenge himself on the offending black man; but his daughter, foreseeing the storm that would arise, had given him free papers, and sent him out of the state.

In such cases the infant is smothered, or sent where it is never seen by any who know its history. But if the white parent is the *father,* instead of the mother, the offspring are unblushingly reared for the market. If they are girls, I have indicated plainly enough what will be their inevitable destiny....

After my lover went away, Dr. Flint contrived a new plan. He seemed to have an idea that my fear of my mistress was his greatest obstacle. In the blandest tones, he told me that he was going to build a small house for me, in a secluded place, four miles away from the town. I shuddered; but I was constrained to listen, while he talked of his intention to give me a home of my own, and to make a lady of me. Hitherto, I had escaped my dreaded fate, by being in the midst of people. My grandmother had already had high words with my master about me. She had told him pretty plainly what she thought of his character, and there was considerable gossip in the neighborhood about our affairs, to which the open-mouthed jealousy of Mrs. Flint contributed not a little. When my master said he was going to build a house for me, and that he could do it with little trouble and expense, I was in hopes something would happen to frustrate his scheme; but I soon heard that the house was actually begun. I vowed before my Maker that I would never enter it. I had rather toil on the plantation from dawn till dark; I had rather live and die in jail, than drag on, from day to day, through such a living death. I was determined that the master, whom I so hated and loathed, who had blighted the prospects of my youth, and made my life a desert, should not, after my long struggle with him, succeed at last in trampling his victim under his feet. I would do any thing, every thing, for the sake of defeating him. What *could* I do? I thought and thought, till I became desperate, and made a plunge into the abyss.

And now, reader, I come to a period in my unhappy life, which I would gladly forget if I could. The remembrance fills me with sorrow and shame. It pains me to tell you of it; but I have promised to tell you the truth, and I will do it honestly, let it cost me what it may. I will not try to screen myself behind the plea of compulsion from a master; for it was not so. Neither can I plead ignorance or thoughtlessness. For years, my master had done his utmost to pollute my mind with foul images, and to destroy the pure principles inculcated by my grand-mother, and the good mistress of my childhood. The influences of slavery had had the same effect on me that they had on other young girls; they had made me prematurely knowing, concerning the evil ways of the world. I knew what I did, and I did it with deliberate calculation.

But, O, ye happy women, whose purity has been sheltered from childhood, who have been free to choose the objects of your affection, whose homes are protected by law, do not judge the poor desolate slave girl too severely! If slavery had been abolished, I, also, could have married the man of my choice; I could have had a home shielded by the laws; and I should have been spared the painful task of confessing what I am now about to relate; but all my prospects had been blighted by slavery. I wanted to keep myself pure; and, under the most adverse circumstances, I tried hard to preserve my self-respect; but I was struggling alone in the powerful grasp of the demon Slavery; and the monster proved too strong for me. I felt as if I was forsaken by God and man; as if all my efforts must be frus-trated; and I became reckless in my despair.

I have told you that Dr. Flint's persecutions and his wife's jealousy had given rise to some gossip in the neighborhood. Among others, it chanced that a white unmarried gentleman had obtained some knowledge of the circumstances in which I was placed. He knew my grandmother, and often spoke to me in the street. He became interested for me, and asked questions about my master, which I answered in part. He expressed a great deal of sympathy, and a wish to aid me. He constantly sought opportunities to see me, and wrote to me frequently. I was a poor slave girl, only fifteen years old.

So much attention from a superior person was, of course, flattering; for human nature is the same in all. I also felt grateful for his sympathy, and encouraged by his kind words. It seemed to me a great thing to have such a friend. By degrees, a more tender feeling crept into my heart. He was an educated and eloquent gentleman; too eloquent, alas, for the poor slave girl who trusted in him. Of course I saw whither all this was tending. I knew the impassable gulf between us; but to be an object of interest to a man who is not married, and who is not her master, is agreeable to the pride and feelings of a slave, if her miserable situation has left her any pride or sentiment. It seems less degrading to give one's self, than to submit to compulsion. There is something akin to freedom in having a lover who has no control over you, except that which he gains by kindness and attachment. A master may treat you as rudely as he pleases, and you dare not speak; moreover, the wrong does not seem so great with an unmarried man, as with one who has a wife to be made unhappy. There may be sophistry in all this; but the condition of a slave confuses all principles of morality, and, in fact, renders the practice of them impossible.

When I found that my master had actually begun to build the lonely cottage, other feelings mixed with those I have described. Revenge, and calculations of interest, were added to flattered vanity and sincere gratitude for kindness. I knew nothing would enrage Dr. Flint so much as to know that I favored another; and it was something to triumph over my tyrant even in that small way. I thought he would revenge himself by selling me, and I was sure my friend, Mr. Sands, would buy me. He was a man of more generosity and feeling than my master, and I thought my freedom could be easily obtained from him. The crisis of my fate now came so near that I was desperate. I shuddered to think of being the mother of children that should be owned by my old tyrant. I knew that as soon as a new fancy took him, his victims were sold far off to get rid of them; especially if they had children. I had seen several women sold, with his babies at the breast. He never allowed his offspring by slaves to remain long in sight of himself and his wife. Of a man who was not my master I could ask to have my children well supported; and in this case, I felt confident I should obtain the boon. I also felt quite sure that they would be made free. With all these thoughts revolving in my mind, and seeing no other way of escaping the doom I so much dreaded, I made a headlong plunge. Pity me, and pardon me, O virtuous reader! You never knew what it is to be a slave; to be entirely unprotected by law or custom; to have the laws reduce you to the condition of a chattel, entirely subject to the will of another. You never exhausted your ingenuity in avoiding the snares, and eluding the power of a hated tyrant; you never shuddered at the sound of his footsteps, and trembled within hearing of his voice. I know I did wrong. No one can feel it more sensibly than I do. The painful and humiliating memory will haunt me to my dying day. Still, in looking back, calmly, on the events of my life, I feel that the slave woman ought not to be judged by the same standard as others.

The months passed on. I had many unhappy hours. I secretly mourned over the sorrow I was bringing on my grandmother, who had so tried to shield me from harm. I knew that I was the greatest comfort of her old age, and that it was a source of pride to her that I had not degraded myself, like most of the slave. I wanted to confess to her that I was no longer worthy of her love; but I could not utter the dreaded words.

As for Dr. Flint, I had a feeling of satisfaction and triumph in the thought of telling *him*. From time to time he told me of his intended arrangements, and I was silent. At last, he came and told me the cottage was completed, and ordered me to go to it. I told him I would never enter it. He said, "I have heard enough of such talk as that. You shall go, if you are carried by force; and you shall remain there."

I replied, "I will never go there. In a few months I shall be a mother."

He stood and looked at me in dumb amazement, and left the house without a word. I thought I should be happy in my triumph over him. But now that the truth was out, and my relatives would hear of it, I felt wretched. Humble as were their circumstances, they had pride in my good character. Now, how could I look them in the face? My self-respect was gone! I had resolved that I would be virtuous, though I was a slave. I had said, "Let the storm beat! I will brave it till I die." And now, how humiliated I felt!

I went to my grandmother. My lips moved to make confession, but the words stuck in my throat. I sat down in the shade of a tree at her door and began to sew. I think she saw something unusual was the matter with me. The mother of slaves is very watchful. She knows there is no security for her children. After they have entered their teens she lives in daily expectation of trouble. This leads to many questions. If the girl is of a sensitive nature, timidity keeps her from answering truthfully, and this well-meant course has a tendency to drive her from maternal counsels. Presently, in came my mistress, like a mad woman, and accused me concerning her husband. My grandmother, whose suspicions had been previously awakened, believed what she said. She exclaimed, "O Linda! has it come to this? I had rather see you dead than to see you as you now are. You are a disgrace to your dead mother." She tore from my fingers my mother's wedding ring and her silver thimble. "Go away!" she exclaimed, "and never come to my house, again." Her reproaches fell so hot and heavy, that they left me no chance to answer. Bitter tears, such as the eyes never shed but once, were my only answer. I rose from my seat, but fell back again, sobbing. She did not speak to me; but the tears were running down her furrowed cheeks, and they scorched me like fire. She had always been so kind to me! *So* kind! How I longed to throw myself at her feet, and tell her all the truth! But she had ordered me to go, and never to come there again. After a few minutes, I mustered strength, and started to obey her. With what feelings did I now close that little gate, which I used to open with such an eager hand in my childhood! It closed upon me with a sound I never heard before.

Where could I go? I was afraid to return to my master's. I walked on recklessly, not caring where I went, or what would become of me. When I had gone four or five miles, fatigue compelled me to stop. I sat down on the stump of an old tree. The stars were shining through the boughs above me. How they mocked me, with their bright, calm light! The hours passed by, and as I sat there alone a chilliness and deadly sickness came over me. I sank on the ground. My mind was full of horrid thoughts. I prayed to die; but the prayer was not answered. At last, with great effort I roused myself, and walked some distance further, to the house of a woman who had been a friend of my mother. When I told her why I was there, she spoke soothingly to me; but I could not be comforted. I thought I could bear my shame if I could only be reconciled to my grandmother. I longed to open my heart to her. I thought if she could know the real state of the case, and all I had been bearing for years, she would perhaps judge me less harshly. My friend advised me to send for her. I did so; but days of agonizing suspense passed before she came. Had she utterly forsaken me? No. She came at last. I knelt before her, and told her the things that had poisoned my life; how long I had been persecuted; that I saw no way of escape; and in an hour of extremity I had become desperate. She listened in silence. I told her I would bear any thing and do any thing, if in time I had hopes of obtaining her forgiveness. I begged of her to pity me, for my dead mother's sake. And she did pity me. She did not say, "I forgive you;" but she looked at me lovingly, with her eyes full of tears. She laid her old hand gently on my head, and murmured, "Poor child! Poor child!"

I returned to my grandmother's house. She had an interview with Mr. Sands. When she asked him why he could not have left her one ewe lamb,—whether there were not plenty of slaves who did not care about character,—he made no answer; but he spoke kind and encouraging words. He promised to care for my child, and to buy me, be the conditions they might.

I had not seen Dr. Flint for five days. I had never seen him since I made the avowal to him. He talked of the disgrace I had brought on myself; how I had sinned against my master, and mortified my old grandmother. He intimated that if I had accepted his proposals, he, as a physician, could have saved me from exposure. He even condescended to pity me. Could he have offered wormwood more bitter? He, whose persecutions had been the cause of my sin!

"Linda," said he, "though you have been criminal towards me, I feel for you, and I can pardon you if you obey my wishes. Tell me whether the fellow you wanted to marry is the father of your child. If you deceive me, you shall feel the fires of hell."

I did not feel as proud as I had done. My strongest weapon with him was gone. I was lowered in my own estimation, and had resolved to bear his abuse in silence. But when he spoke contemptuously of the lover who had always treated me honorably; when I remembered that but for *him* I might have been a virtuous, free, and happy wife, I lost my patience. "I have sinned against God and myself," I replied; "but not against you."

He clinched his teeth, and muttered, "Curse you!" He came towards me, with ill-suppressed rage, and exclaimed, "You obstinate girl! I could grind your bones to powder! You have thrown yourself away on some worthless rascal. You are weak-minded, and have been easily persuaded by those who don't care a straw for you. The future will settle accounts between us. You are blinded now; but hereafter you will be convinced that your master was your best friend. My lenity towards you is a proof of it. I might have punished you in many ways. I might have had you whipped till you fell dead under the lash. But I wanted you to live; I would have bettered your condition. Others cannot do it. You are my slave. Your mistress, disgusted by your conduct, forbids you to return to the house; therefore I leave you here for the present; but I shall see you often. I will call tomorrow."

He came with frowning brows, that showed a dissatisfied state of mind. After asking about my health, he inquired whether my board was paid, and who visited me. He then went on to say that he had neglected his duty; that as a physician there were certain things that he ought to have explained to me. Then followed talk such as would have made the most shameless blush. He ordered me to stand up before him. I obeyed. "I command you," said he, "to tell me whether the father of your child is white or black." I hesitated. "Answer me this instant!" he exclaimed. I did answer. He sprang upon me like a wolf, and grabbed my arm as if he would have broken it. "Do you love him?" said he, in a hissing tone.

"I am thankful that I do not despise him," I replied.

He raised his hand to strike me; but it fell again. I don't know what arrested the blow. He sat down, with lips tightly compressed. At last he spoke. "I came here," said he, "to make you a friendly proposition; but your ingratitude chafes me beyond endurance. You turn aside all my good intentions towards you. I don't know what it is that keeps me from killing you." Again he rose, as if he had a mind to strike me.

But he resumed. "On one condition I will forgive your insolence and crime. You must henceforth have no communication of any kind with the father of your child. You must not ask any thing from him, or receive any thing from him. I will take care of you and your child. You had better promise this at once, and not wait till you are deserted by him. This is the last act of mercy I shall show towards you."

I said something about being unwilling to have my child supported by a man who had cursed it and me also. He rejoined, that a woman who had sunk to my level had no right to expect any thing else. He asked, for the last time, would I accept his kindness? I answered that I would not.

"Very well," said he; "then take the consequences of your wayward course. Never look to me for help. You are my slave, and shall always be my slave. I will never sell you, that you may depend upon."

Hope died away in my heart as he closed the door after him. I had calculated that in his rage he would sell me to a slave-trader; and I knew the father of my child was on the watch to buy me.

About this time my uncle Phillip was expected to return from a voyage. The day before his departure I had officiated as bridesmaid to a young friend. My heart was then ill at ease, but my smiling countenance did not betray it. Only a year had passed; but what fearful changes it had wrought! My heart had grown gray in misery. Lives that flash in sunshine, and lives that are born in tears, receive their hue from circumstances. None of us know what a year may bring forth.

I felt no joy when they told me my uncle had come. He wanted to see me, though he knew what had happened. I shrank from him at first; but at last consented that he should come to my room. He received me as he always had done. O, how my heart smote me when I felt his tears on my burning cheeks! The words of my grandmother came to my mind,—"Perhaps your mother and father are taken from the evil days to come." My disappointed heart could now praise God that it was so. But why, thought I, did my relatives ever cherish hopes for me? What was there to save me from the usual fate of slave girls? Many more beautiful and more intelligent than I had experienced a similar fate, or a far worse one. How could they hope that I should escape?

My uncle's stay was short, and I was not sorry for it. I was too ill in mind and body to enjoy my friends as I had done. For some weeks I was unable to leave my bed. I could not have any doctor but my master, and I would not have him sent for. At last, alarmed by my increasing illness, they sent for him. I was very weak and nervous; and as soon as he entered the room, I began to scream. They told him my state was very critical. He had no wish to hasten me out of the world, and he withdrew.

When my babe was born, they said it was premature. It weighed only four pounds; but God let it live. I heard the doctor say I could not survive till morning. I had often prayed for death; but now I did not want to die, unless my child could die too. Many weeks passed before I was able to leave my bed. I was a mere wreck of my former self. For a year there was scarcely a day when I was free from chills and fever. My babe also was sickly. His little limbs were often racked with pain. Dr. Flint continued his visits, to look after my health; and he did not fail to remind me that my child was an addition to his stock of slaves....

When Dr. Flint learned that I was again to be a mother, he was exasperated beyond measure. He rushed from the house, and returned with a pair of shears. I had a fine head of hair; and he often railed about my pride of arranging it nicely. He cut every hair close to my head, storming and swearing all the time. I replied to some of his abuse, and he struck me. Some months before, he had pitched me down stairs in a fit of passion; and the injury I received was so serious that I was unable to turn myself in bed for many days. He then said, "Linda, I swear by God I will never raise my hand against you again;" but I knew that he would forget his promise.

After he discovered my situation, he was like a restless spirit from the pit. He came every day; and I was subjected to such insults as no pen can describe. I would not describe them if I could; they were too low, too revolting. I tried to keep them from my grandmother's knowledge as much as I could. I knew she had enough to sadden her life, without having my troubles to bear. When she saw the doctor treat me with violence, and heard him utter oaths terrible enough to palsy a man's tongue, she could not always hold her peace. It was natural and mother-like that she should try to defend me; but it ony made matters worse.

When they told me my new-born babe was a girl, my heart was heavier than it had ever been before. Slavery is terrible for men; but it is far more terrible for women. Superadded to the burden common to all, *they* have wrongs, and suffer-ings, and mortifications peculiarly their own.

Dr. Flint had sworn that he would make me suffer, to my last day, for this new crime against *him,* as he called it; and as long as he had me in his power he kept his word. On the fourth day after the birth of my babe, he entered my room suddenly, and commanded me to rise and bring my baby to him. The nurse who took care of me had gone out of the room to prepare some nourishment, and I was alone. There was no alternative. I rose, took up my babe, and crossed the room to where he sat. "Now stand there," said he, "till I tell you to go back!" My child bore a strong resemblance to her father, and to the deceased Mrs. Sands, her grandmother. He noticed this; and while I stood before him, trembling with weak-ness, he heaped upon me and my little one every vile epithet he could think of. Even the grandmother in her grave did not escape his curses. In the midst of his vituperations I fainted at his feet. This recalled him to his senses. He took the baby from my arms, laid it on the bed, dashed cold water in my face, took me up, and shook me violently, to restore my consciousness before any one entered the room. Just then my grandmother came in, and he hurried out of the house. I suffered in consequence of this treatment; but I begged my friends to let me die, rather than send for the doctor. There was nothing I dreaded so much as his pres-ence. My life was spared; and I was glad for the sake of my little ones. Had it not been for these ties to life, I should have been glad to be released by death, though I had lived only nineteen years.

Always it gave me a pang that my children had no lawful claim to a name.

Their father offered his; but, if I had wished to accept the offer, I dared not while my master lived. Moreover, I knew it would not be accepted at their baptism. A Christian name they were at least entitled to; and we resolved to call my boy for our dear good Benjamin, who had gone far away from us. . . .

> [Realizing his duplicity, Brent refused Flint's offer to free her and her children. Flint then sent Brent to work on his son's plantation. She decided to flee, hoping that Flint would tire of pursuing her and sell her and her children to their father.]

I went forth into the darkness and rain. I ran on till I came to the house of the friend who was to conceal me.

Early the next morning Mr. Flint [the doctor's son] was at my grandmother's inquiring for me. She told him she had not seen me, and supposed I was at the plantation. He watched her face narrowly, and said, "Don't you know any thing about her running off?" She assured him that she did not. He went on to say, "Last night she ran off without the least provocation. We had treated her very kindly. My wife liked her. She will soon be found and brought back. Are her children with you?" When told that they were, he said, "I am very glad to hear that. If they are here, she cannot be far off. If I find out that any of my niggers have had any thing to do with this damned business, I'll give 'em five hundred lashes." As he started to go to his father's, he turned round and added, persuasively, "Let her be brought back, and she shall have her children to live with her."

The tidings made the old doctor rave and storm at a furious rate. It was a busy day for them. My grandmother's house was searched from top to bottom. As my trunk was empty, they concluded I had taken my clothes with me. Before ten o'clock every vessel northward bound was thoroughly examined, and the law against harboring fugitives was read to all on board. At night a watch was set over the town. Knowing how distressed my grandmother would be, I wanted to send her a message; but it could not be done. Every one who went in or out of her house was closely watched. The doctor said he would take my children, unless she became responsible for them; which of course she willingly did. The next day was spent in searching. Before night, the following advertisement was posted at every corner, and in every public place for miles round:—

> "$300 Reward! Ran away from the subscriber, an intelligent, bright, mulatto girl, named Linda, 21 years of age. Five feet four inches high. Dark eyes, and black hair inclined to curl; but it can be made straight. Has a decayed spot on a front tooth. She can read and write, and in all probability will try to get to the Free States. All persons are forbidden, under penalty of the law, to harbor or employ said slave. $150 will be given to whoever takes her in the state, and $300 if taken out of the state and delivered to me, or lodged in jail.
> Dr. Flint."

The search for me was kept up with more perseverance than I had anticipated. I began to think that escape was impossible. I was in great anxiety lest I should implicate the friend who harbored me. I knew the consequences would be frightful; and much as I dreaded being caught, even that seemed better than causing an innocent person to suffer for kindness to me. A week had passed in terrible suspense, when my pursuers came into such close vicinity that I concluded they had tracked me to my hiding-place. I flew out of the house, and concealed myself in a thicket of bushes. There I remained in an agony of fear for two hours. Suddenly, a reptile of some kind seized my leg. In my fright, I struck a blow which loosened its hold, but I could not tell whether I had killed it; it was so dark, I could not see what it was; I only knew it was something cold and slimy. The pain I felt soon indicated that the bite was poisonous. I was compelled to leave my place of concealment, and I groped my way back into the house. The pain had become intense, and my friend was startled by my look of anguish. I asked her to prepare a poultice of warm ashes and vinegar, and I applied it to my leg, which was already much swollen. The application gave me some relief, but the swelling did not abate. The dread of being disabled was greater than the physical pain I endured. My friend asked an old woman, who doctored among the slaves, what was good for the bite of a snake or a lizard. She told her to steep a dozen coppers in vinegar, over night, and apply the cankered vinegar to the inflamed part.

I had succeeded in cautiously conveying some messages to my relatives. They were harshly threatened, and despairing of my having a chance to escape, they advised me to return to my master, ask his forgiveness, and let him make an example of me. But such counsel had no influence with me. When I started upon this hazardous undertaking, I had resolved that, come what would, there should be no turning back. "Give me liberty, or give me death," was my motto. When my friend contrived to make known to my relatives the painful situation I had been in for twenty-four hours, they said no more about my going back to my master. Something must be done, and that speedily; but where to turn for help, they knew not. God in his mercy raised up "a friend in need."

Among the ladies who were acquainted with my grandmother, was one who had known her from childhood, and always been very friendly to her. She had also known my mother and her children, and felt interested for them. At this crisis of affairs she called to see my grandmother, as she not unfrequently did. She observed the sad and troubled expression of her face, and asked if she knew where Linda was, and whether she was safe. My grandmother shook her head, without answering. "Come, Aunt Martha," said the kind lady, "tell me all about it. Perhaps I can do something to help you." The husband of this lady held many slaves, and bought and sold slaves. She also held a number in her own name; but she treated them kindly, and would never allow any of them to be sold. She was unlike the majority of slaveholders' wives. My grandmother looked earnestly at her. Something in the expression of her face said "Trust me!" and she did trust her. She listened attentively to the details of my story, and sat thinking for a while. At last she said, "Aunt Martha, I pity you both. If you think there is any chance of Linda's getting to the Free States, I will conceal her for a time. But first you must solemnly promise that my name shall never be mentioned. If such a thing should become known, it would ruin me and my family. No one in my house must know of it, except the cook. She is so faithful that I would trust my own life with her; and I know she likes Linda. It is a great risk; but I trust no harm will come of it. Get word to Linda to be ready as soon as it is dark, before the patrols are out. I will send the housemaids on errands, and Betty shall go to meet Linda." The place where we were to meet was designated and agreed upon. My grandmother was unable to thank the lady for this noble deed; overcome by her emotions, she sank on her knees and sobbed like a child.

I received a message to leave my friend's house at such an hour, and go to a certain place where a friend would be waiting for me. As a matter of prudence no names were mentioned. I had no means of conjecturing who I was to meet, or where I was going. I did not like to move thus blindfolded, but I had no choice. It would not do for me to remain where I was. I disguised myself, summoned up courage to meet the worst, and went to the appointed place. My friend Betty was there; she was the last person I expected to see. We hurried along in silence. The pain in my leg was so intense that it seemed as if I should drop; but fear gave me strength. We reached the house and entered unobserved. Her first words were: "Honey, now you is safe. Dem devils ain't coming to search *dis* house. When I get you into missis' safe place, I will bring some nice hot supper. I specs you need it after all dis skeering." Betty's vocation led her to think eating the most important thing in life. She did not realize that my heart was too full for me to care much about supper.

The mistress came to meet us, and led me up stairs to a small room over her own sleeping apartment. "You will be safe here, Linda," said she; "I keep this room to store away things that are out of use. The girls are not accustomed to be sent to it, and they will not suspect any thing unless they hear some noise. I always keep it locked, and Betty shall take care of the key. But you must be very careful, for my sake as well as your own; and you must never tell my secret; for it would ruin me and my family. I will keep the girls busy in the morning, that Betty may have a chance to bring your breakfast; but it will not do for her to come to you again till night. I will come to see you sometimes. Keep up your courage. I hope this state of things will not last long." Betty came with the "nice hot supper," and the mistress hastened down stairs to keep things straight till she returned. How my heart overflowed with gratitude! Words choked in my throat; but I could have kissed the feet of my benefactress. For that deed of Christian womanhood, may God forever bless her!

I went to sleep that night with the feeling that I was for the present the most fortunate slave in town. Morning came and filled my little cell with light. I thanked the heavenly Father for this safe retreat. Opposite my window was a pile of feather beds. On the top of these I could lie perfectly concealed, and command a view of the street through which Dr. Flint passed to his office. Anxious as I was, I felt a gleam of satisfaction when I saw him. Thus far I had outwitted him, and I triumphed over it. Who can blame slaves for being cunning? They are constantly compelled to resort to it. It is the only weapon of the weak and oppressed against the strength of their tyrants....

**[Flint did sell her two children, Benjamin and Ellen, to their father, Mr. Sands, and they were returned to her grandmother's home. In disguise, Brent left her first hiding place and went to another in her grandmother's home.]**

A small shed had been added to my grandmother's house years ago. Some boards were laid across the joists at the top, and between these boards and the roof was a very small garret, never occupied by any thing but rats and mice. It was a pent roof, covered with nothing but shingles, according to the southern custom for such buildings. The garret was only nine feet long and seven wide. The highest part was three feet high, and sloped down abruptly to the loose board floor. There was no admission for either light or air. My uncle Phillip, who was a carpenter, had very skilfully made a concealed trap-door, which communicated with the storeroom. He had been doing this while I was waiting in the swamp. The storeroom opened upon a piazza. To this hole I was conveyed as soon as I entered the house. The air was stifling; the darkness total. A bed had been spread on the floor. I could sleep quite comfortably on one side; but the slope was so sudden that I could not turn on the other without hitting the roof. The rats and mice ran over my bed; but I was weary, and I slept such sleep as the wretched may, when a tempest has passed over them. Morning came. I knew it only by the noises I heard; for in my small den day and night were all the same. I suffered for air even more than for light. But I was not comfortless. I heard the voices of my children. There was joy and there was sadness in the sound. It made my tears flow. How I longed to speak to them! I was eager to look on their faces; but there was no hole, no crack, through which I could peep. This continued darkness was oppressive. It seemed horrible to sit or lie in a cramped position day after day, without one gleam of light. Yet I would have chosen this, rather than my lot as a slave, though white people considered it an easy one; and it was so compared with the fate of others. I was never cruelly over-worked; I was never lacerated with the whip from head to foot; I was never so beaten and bruised that I could not turn from one side to the other; I never had my heel-strings cut to prevent my running away; I was never chained to a log and forced to drag it about, while I toiled in the fields from morning till night; I was never branded with hot iron, or torn by bloodhounds. On the contrary, I had always been kindly treated, and tenderly cared for, until I came into the hands of Dr. Flint. I had never wished for freedom till then. But though my life in slavery was comparatively devoid of hardships, God pity the woman who is compelled to lead such a life!

My food was passed up to me through the trap-door my uncle had contrived; and my grandmother, my uncle Phillip, and aunt Nancy would seize such opportunities as they could, to mount up there and chat with me at the opening. But of course this was not safe in the daytime. It must all be done in darkness. It was impossible for me to move in an erect position, but I crawled about my den for exercise. One day I hit my head against something, and found it was a gimlet. My uncle had left it sticking there when he made the trap-door. I was as rejoiced as Robinson Crusoe could have been at finding such a treasure. It put a lucky thought into my head. I said to myself, "Now I will have some light. Now I will see my children." I did not dare to begin my work during the daytime, for fear of attracting attention. But I groped round; and having found the side next the street, where I could frequently see my children, I stuck the gimlet in and waited for evening. I bored three rows of holes, one above another; then I bored out the interstices between. I thus succeeded in making one hole about an inch long and an inch broad. I sat by it till late into the night, to enjoy the little whiff of air that floated in. In the morning I watched for my children. The first person I saw in the street was Dr. Flint. I had a shuddering, superstitious feeling that it was a bad omen. Several familiar faces passed by. At last I heard the merry laugh of children, and presently two sweet little faces were looking up at me, as though they knew I was there, and were conscious of the joy they imparted. How I longed to *tell* them I was there!

My condition was now a little improved. But for weeks I was tormented by hundreds of little red insects, fine as a needle's point, that pierced through my skin, and produced an intolerable burning. The good grandmother gave me herb teas and cooling medicines, and finally I got rid of them. The heat of my den was intense, for nothing but thin shingles protected me from the scorching summer's sun. But I had my consolations. Through my peeping-hole I could watch the children, and when they were near enough, I could hear their talk. Aunt Nancy brought me all the news she could hear at Dr. Flint's. From her I learned that the doctor had written to New York to a colored woman, who had been born and raised in our neighborhood, and had breathed his contaminating atmosphere. He offered her a reward if she could find out any thing about me. I know not what was the nature of her reply; but he soon after started for New York in haste, saying to his family that he had business of importance to transact. I peeped at him as he passed on his way to the steamboat. It was a satisfaction to have miles of land and water between us, even for a little while; and it was a still greater satisfaction to know that he believed me to be in the Free States. My little den seemed less dreary than it had done. He returned, as he did from his former journey to New York, without obtaining any satisfactory information. When he passed our house next morning, Benny was standing at the gate. He had heard them say that he had gone to find me, and he called out, "Dr. Flint, did you bring my mother home? I want to see her." The doctor stamped his foot at him in a rage, and exclaimed, "Get out of the way, you little damned rascal! If you don't, I'll cut off your head."

Benny ran terrified into the house saying, "You can't put me in jail again. I don't belong to you now." It was well that the wind carried the words away from the doctor's ear. I told my grandmother of it, when we had our next conference at the trap-door; and begged of her not to allow the children to be impertinent to the irascible old man.

Autumn came, with a pleasant abatement of heat. My eyes had become accustomed to the dim light, and by holding my book or work in a certain position near the aperture I contrived to read and sew. That was a great relief to the tedious monotony of my life. But when winter came, the cold penetrated through the thin shingle roof, and I was dreadfully chilled. The winters there are not so long, or so severe, as in northern latitudes; but the houses are not built to shelter from cold, and my little den was peculiarly comfortless. The kind grandmother brought me bed-clothes and warm drinks. Often I was obliged to lie in bed all day to keep comfortable; but with all my precautions, my shoulders and feet were frostbitten. O, those long, gloomy days, with no object for my eye to rest upon, and no thoughts to occupy my mind, except the dreary past and the uncertain future! I was thankful when there came a day sufficiently mild for me to wrap myself up and sit at the loophole to watch the passers by. Southerners have the habit of stopping and talking in the streets, and I heard many conversations not intended to meet my ears. I heard slave-hunters planning how to catch some poor fugitive. Several times I heard allusions to Dr. Flint, myself, and the history of my children, who, perhaps, were playing near the gate. One would say, "I wouldn't move my little finger to catch her, as old Flint's property." Another would say, "I'll catch *any* nigger for the reward. A man ought to have what belongs to him, if he *is* a damned brute." The opinion was often expressed that I was in the Free States. Very rarely did any one suggest that I might be in the vicinity. Had the least suspicion rested on my grandmother's house, it would have been burned to the ground. But it was the last place they thought of. Yet there was no place, where slavery existed, that could have afforded me so good a place of concealment.

Dr. Flint and his family repeatedly tried to coax and bribe my children to tell something they had heard said about me. One day the doctor took them into a shop, and offered them some bright little silver pieces and gay handkerchiefs if they would tell where their mother was. Ellen shrank away from him, and would not speak; but Benny spoke up, and said, "Dr. Flint, I don't know where my mother is. I guess she's in New York; and when you go there again, I wish you'd ask her to come home, for I want to see her; but if you put her in jail, or tell her you'll cut her head off, I'll tell her to go right back."

Christmas was approaching. Grandmother brought me materials, and I busied myself making some new garments and little playthings for my children. Were it not that hiring day is near at hand, and many families are fearfully looking forward to the probability of separation in a few days, Christmas might be a happy season for the poor slaves. Even slave mothers try to gladden the hearts of their little ones on that occasion. Benny and Ellen had their Christmas stockings filled. Their imprisoned mother could not have the privilege of witnessing their surprise and joy. But I had the pleasure of peeping at them as they went into the street with their new suits on. I heard Benny ask a little playmate whether Santa Claus brought him any thing. "Yes," replied the boy; "but Santa Claus ain't a real man. It's the children's mothers that put things into the stockings." "No, that can't be," replied Benny, "for Santa Claus brought Ellen and me these new clothes, and my mother has been gone this long time."

How I longed to tell him that his mother made those garments, and that many a tear fell on them while she worked!...

**[She begged her children's father, newly elected to Congress, to free his children. He promised that he would. Still in hiding, Brent managed to smuggle letters north, which were mailed back to her grandmother so that Dr. Flint would think that she had fled. Mr. Sands married and sent his daughter to live in Brooklyn.]**

I hardly expect that the reader will credit me, when I affirm that I lived in that little dismal hole, almost deprived of light and air, and with no space to move my limbs, for nearly seven years. But it is a fact; and to me a sad one, even now; for my body still suffers from the effects of that long imprisonment, to say nothing of my soul. Members of my family, now living in New York and Boston, can testify to the truth of what I say.

Countless were the nights that I sat late at the little loophole scarcely large enough to give me a glimpse of one twinkling star. There, I heard the patrols and slave-hunters conferring together about the capture of runaways, well knowing how rejoiced they would be to catch me.

Season after season, year after year, I peeped at my children's faces, and heard their sweet voices, with a heart yearning all the while to say, "Your mother is here." Sometimes it appeared to me as if ages had rolled away since I entered upon that gloomy, monotonous existence. At times, I was stupefied and listless; at other times I became very impatient to know when these dark years would end, and I should again be allowed to feel the sunshine, and breathe the pure air.

After Ellen left us, this feeling increased. Mr. Sands had agreed that Benny might go to the north whenever his uncle Phillip could go with him; and I was anxious to be there also, to watch over my children, and protect them so far as I was able. Moreover, I was likely to be drowned out of my den, if I remained much longer; for the slight roof was getting badly out of repair, and uncle Phillip was afraid to remove the shingles, lest some one should get a glimpse of me. When storms occurred in the night, they spread mats and bits of carpet, which in the morning appeared to have been laid out to dry; but to cover the roof in the daytime might have attracted attention. Consequently, my clothes and bedding were often drenched; a process by which the pains and aches in my cramped and stiffened limbs were greatly increased. I revolved various plans of escape in my mind, which I sometimes imparted to my grandmother, when she came to whisper with me at the trap-door. The kind-hearted old woman had an intense sympathy for runaways. She had known too much of the cruelties inflicted on those who were captured. Her memory always flew back at once to the sufferings of her bright and handsome son, Benjamin, the youngest and dearest of her flock. So, whenever I alluded to the subject, she would groan out, "O, don't think of it, child. You'll break my heart." I had no good old aunt Nancy now to encourage me; but my brother William and my children were continually beckoning me to the north.

And now I must go back a few months in my story. I have stated that the first of January was the time for selling slaves, or leasing them out to new masters. If time were counted by heart-throbs, the poor slaves might reckon years of suffering during that festival so joyous to the free. On the New Year's day preceding my aunt's death, one of my friends, named Fanny, was to be sold at auction, to pay her master's debts. My thoughts were with her during all the day, and at night I anxiously inquired what had been her fate. I was told that she had been sold to one master, and her four little girls to another master, far distant; that she had escaped from her purchaser, and was not to be found. Her mother was the old Aggie I have spoken of. She lived in a small tenement belonging to my grandmother, and built on the same lot with her own house. Her dwelling was searched and watched, and that brought the patrols so near me that I was obliged to keep very close in my den. The hunters were somehow eluded; and not long afterwards Benny accidentally caught sight of Fanny in her mother's hut. He told his grandmother, who charged him never to speak of it, explaining to him the frightful consequences; and he never betrayed the trust. Aggie little dreamed that my grandmother knew where her daughter was concealed, and that the stooping form of her old neighbor was bending under a similar burden of anxiety and fear; but these dangerous secrets deepened the sympathy between the two old persecuted mothers.

My friend Fanny and I remained many weeks hidden within call of each other; but she was unconscious of the fact. I longed to have her share my den, which seemed a more secure retreat than her own; but I had brought so much trouble on my grandmother, that it seemed wrong to ask her to incur greater risks. My restlessness increased. I had lived too long in bodily pain and anguish of spirit. Always I was in dread that by some accident, or some contrivance, slavery would succeed in snatching my children from me. This thought drove me nearly frantic, and I determined to steer for the North Star at all hazards. At this crisis, Providence opened an unexpected way for me to escape. My friend Peter came one evening, and asked to speak with me. "Your day has come, Linda," said he. "I have found a chance for you to go to the Free States. You have a fortnight to decide." The news seemed too good to be true; but Peter explained his arrangements, and told me all that was necessary was for me to say I would go. I was going to answer him with a joyful yes, when the thought of Benny came to my mind. I told him the temptation was exceedingly strong, but I was terribly afraid of Dr. Flint's alleged power over my child, and that I could not go and leave him behind. Peter remonstrated earnestly. He said such a good chance might never occur again; that Benny was free, and could be sent to me; and that for the sake of my children's welfare I ought not to hesitate a moment. I told him I would consult with uncle Phillip. My uncle rejoiced in the plan, and bade me go by all means. He promised, if his life was spared, that he would either bring or send my son to me as soon as I reached a place of safety. I resolved to go, but thought nothing had better be said to my grandmother till very near the time of departure. But my uncle thought she would feel it more keenly if I left her so suddenly. "I will reason with her," said he, "and convince her how necessary it is, not only for your sake, but for hers also. You cannot be blind to the fact that she is sinking under her burdens." I was not blind to it. I knew that my concealment was an ever-present source of anxiety, and that the older she grew the more nervously fearful she was of discovery. My uncle talked with her, and finally succeeded in persuading her that it was absolutely necessary for me to seize the chance so unexpectedly offered.

The anticipation of being a free woman proved almost too much for my weak frame. The excitement stimulated me, and at the same time bewildered me. I made busy preparations for my journey, and for my son to follow me. I resolved to have an interview with him before I went, that I might give him cautions and advice, and tell him how anxiously I should be waiting for him at the north. Grandmother stole up to me as often as possible to whisper words of counsel. She insisted upon my writing to Dr. Flint, as soon as I arrived in the Free States, and asking him to sell me to her. She said she would sacrifice her house, and all she had in the world, for the sake of having me safe with my children in any part of the world. If she could only live to know *that* she could die in peace. I promised the dear old faithful friend that I would write to her as soon as I arrived, and put the letter in a safe way to reach her; but in my own mind I resolved that not another cent of her hard earnings should be spent to pay rapacious slaveholders for what they called their property. And even if I had not been unwilling to buy what I had already a right to possess, common humanity would have prevented me from accepting the generous offer, at the expense of turning my aged relative out of house and home, when she was trembling on the brink of the grave.

I was to escape in a vessel; but I forbear to mention any further particulars. I was in readiness, but the vessel was unexpectedly detained several days. Meantime, news came to town of a most horrible murder committed on a fugitive slave, named James. Charity, the mother of this unfortunate young man, had been an old acquaintance of ours. I have told the shocking particulars of his death, in my description of some of the neighboring slaveholders. My grandmother, always nervously sensitive about runaways, was terribly frightened. She felt sure that a similar fate awaited me, if I did not desist from my enterprise. She sobbed, and groaned, and entreated me not to go. Her excessive fear was somewhat contagious, and my heart was not proof against her extreme agony. I was grievously disappointed, but I promised to relinquish my project.

When my friend Peter was apprised of this, he was both disappointed and vexed. He said, that judging from our past experience, it would be a long time before I had such another chance to throw away. I told him it need not be thrown away; that I had a friend concealed near by, who would be glad enough to take the place that had been provided for me. I told him about poor Fanny, and the kind-hearted, noble fellow, who never turned his back upon any body in distress, white or black, expressed his readiness to help her. Aggie was much surprised when she found that we knew her secret. She was rejoiced to hear of such a chance for Fanny, and arrangements were made for her to go on board the vessel the next night. They both supposed that I had long been at the north, therefore my name was not mentioned in the transaction. Fanny was carried on board at the appointed time, and stowed away in a very small cabin. This accommodation had been purchased at a price that would pay for a voyage to England. But when one proposes to go to fine old England, they stop to calculate whether they can afford the cost of the pleasure; while in making a bargain to escape from slavery, the trembling victim is ready to say, "Take all I have, only don't betray me!"

The next morning I peeped through my loophole, and saw that it was dark and cloudy. At night I received news that the wind was ahead, and the vessel had not sailed. I was exceedingly anxious about Fanny, and Peter too, who was running a tremendous risk at my instigation. Next day the wind and weather remained the same. Poor Fanny had been half dead with fright when they carried her on board, and I could readily imagine how she must be suffering now. Grandmother came often to my den, to say how thankful she was I did not go. On the third morning she rapped for me to come down to the storeroom. The poor old sufferer was breaking down under her weight of trouble. She was easily flurried now. I found her in a nervous, excited state, but I was not aware that she had forgotten to lock the door behind her, as usual. She was exceedingly worried about the detention of the vessel. She was afraid all would be discovered, and then Fanny, and Peter, and I, would all be tortured to death, and Phillip would be utterly ruined, and her house would be torn down. Poor Peter! If he should die such a horrible death as the poor slave James had lately done, and all for his kindness in trying to help me, how dreadful it would be for us all! Alas, the thought was familiar to me, and had sent many a sharp pang through my heart. I tried to suppress my own anxiety, and speak soothingly to her. She brought in some allusion to aunt Nancy, the dear daughter she had recently buried, and then she lost all control of herself. As she stood there, trembling and sobbing, a voice from the piazza called out, "Whar is you, aunt Marthy?" Grandmother was startled, and in her agitation opened the door, without thinking of me. In stepped Jenny, the mischievous housemaid, who had tried to enter my room, when I was concealed in the house of my white bene-factress. "I's bin huntin ebery whar for you, aunt Marthy," said she. "My missis wants you to send her some crackers." I had slunk down behind a barrel, which entirely screened me, but I imagined that Jenny was looking directly at the spot, and my heart beat violently. My grandmother immediately thought what she had done, and went out quickly with Jenny to count the crackers locking the door after her. She returned to me, in a few minutes, the perfect picture of despair. "Poor child!" she exclaimed, "my carelessness has ruined you. The boat ain't gone yet. Get ready immediately, and go with Fanny. I ain't got another word to say against it now; for there's no telling what may happen this day."

Uncle Phillip was sent for, and he agreed with his mother in thinking that Jenny would inform Dr. Flint in less than twenty-four hours. He advised getting me on board the boat, if possible; if not, I had better keep very still in my den, where they could not find me without tearing the house down. He said it would not do for him to move in the matter, because suspicion would be immediately excited; but he promised to communicate with Peter. I felt reluctant to apply to him again, having implicated him too much already; but there seemed to be no alternative. Vexed as Peter had been by my indecision, he was true to his generous nature, and said at once that he would do his best to help me, trusting I should show myself a stronger woman this time.

He immediately proceeded to the wharf, and found that the wind had shifted, and the vessel was slowly beating down stream. On some pretext of urgent necessity, he offered two boatmen a dollar apiece to catch up with her. He was of lighter complexion than the boatmen he hired, and when the captain saw them coming so rapidly, he thought officers were pursuing his vessel in search of the runaway slave he had on board. They hoisted sails, but the boat gained upon them, and the indefatigable Peter sprang on board.

The captain at once recognized him. Peter asked him to go below, to speak about a bad bill he had given him. When he told his errand, the captain replied, "Why, the woman's here already; and I've put her where you or the devil would have a tough job to find her."

"But it is another woman I want to bring," said Peter. "*She* is in great distress, too, and you shall be paid any thing within reason, if you'll stop and take her."

"What's her name?" inquired the captain.

"Linda," he replied.

"That's the name of the woman already here," rejoined the captain. "By George! I believe you mean to betray me."

"O!" exclaimed Peter, "God knows I wouldn't harm a hair of your head. I am too grateful to you. But there really *is* another woman in great danger. Do have the humanity to stop and take her!"

After a while they came to an understanding. Fanny, not dreaming I was any where about in that region, had assumed my name, though she had called herself Johnson. "Linda is a common name," said Peter, "and the woman I want to bring is Linda Brent."

The captain agreed to wait at a certain place till evening, being handsomely paid for his detention.

Of course, the day was an anxious one for us all. But we concluded that if Jenny had seen me, she would be too wise to let her mistress know of it; and that she probably would not get a chance to see Dr. Flint's family till evening, for I knew very well what were the rules in that household. I afterwards believed that she did not see me; for nothing ever came of it, and she was one of those base characters that would have jumped to betray a suffering fellow being for the sake of thirty pieces of silver.

I made all my arrangements to go on board as soon as it was dusk. The intervening time I resolved to spend with my son. I had not spoken to him for seven years, though I had been under the same roof, and seen him every day, when I was well enough to sit at the loophole. I did not dare to venture beyond the storeroom; so they brought him there, and locked us up together, in a place concealed from the piazza door. It was an agitating interview for both of us. After we had talked and wept together for a little while, he said, "Mother, I'm glad you're going away. I wish I could go with you. I knew you was here; and I have been *so* afraid they would come and catch you!"

I was greatly surprised, and asked him how he had found it out.

He replied, "I was standing under the eaves, one day, before Ellen went away, and I heard somebody cough up over the wood shed. I don't know what made me think it was you, but I did think so. I missed Ellen, the night before she went away; and grandmother brought her back into the room in the night; and I thought maybe she'd been to see *you,* before she went, for I heard grandmother whisper to her, 'Now go to sleep; and remember never to tell.' "

I asked him if he ever mentioned his suspicions to his sister. He said he never did; but after he heard the cough, if he saw her playing with other children on that side of the house, he always tried to coax her round to the other side, for fear they would hear me cough, too. He said he had kept a close lookout for Dr. Flint, and if he saw him speak to a constable, or a patrol, he always told grandmother. I now recollected that I had seen him manifest uneasiness, when people were on that side of the house, and I had at the time been puzzled to conjecture a motive for his actions. Such prudence may seem extraordinary in a boy of twelve years, but slaves, being surrounded by mysteries, deceptions, and dangers, early learn to be suspicious and watchful, and prematurely cautious and cunning. He had never asked a question of grandmother, or uncle Phillip, and I had often heard him chime in with other children, when they spoke of my being at the north.

I told him I was now really going to the Free States, and if he was a good, honest boy, and a loving child to his dear old grandmother, the Lord would bless him, and bring him to me, and we and Ellen would live together. He began to tell me that grandmother had not eaten any thing all day. While he was speaking, the door was unlocked, and she came in with a small bag of money, which she wanted me to take. I begged her to keep a part of it, at least, to pay for Benny's being sent to the north; but she insisted, while her tears were falling fast, that I should take the whole. "You may be sick among strangers," she said, "and they would send you to the poorhouse to die." Ah, that good grandmother!

For the last time I went up to my nook. Its desolate appearance no longer chilled me, for the light of hope had risen in my soul. Yet, even with the blessed prospect of freedom before me, I felt very sad at leaving forever that old homestead, where I had been sheltered so long by the dear old grandmother; where I had dreamed my first young dream of love; and where, after that had faded away, my children came to twine themselves so closely round my desolate heart. As the hour approached for me to leave, I again descended to the storeroom. My grandmother and Benny were there. She took me by the hand, and said, "Linda, let us pray." We knelt down together, with my child pressed to my heart, and my other arm round the faithful, loving old friend I was about to leave forever. On no other occasion has it ever been my lot to listen to so fervent a supplication for mercy and protection. It thrilled through my heart, and inspired me with trust in God.

Peter was waiting for me in the street. I was soon by his side, faint in body, but strong of purpose. I did not look back upon the old place, though I felt that I should never see it again....

**[In 1842 she arrived safely in Philadelphia, where she met abolitionists who helped her get to New York City. Here she was reunited with her daughter, who had not been emancipated by her father. Brent got a job as a nursemaid with the sympathetic Bruce family and was reunited with her children. The Flints made several trips to New York to re-capture her, their efforts facilitated by the Fugitive Slave Law of 1850.]**

Without my knowledge, Mrs. Bruce employed a gentleman in New York to enter into negotiations with Mr. Dodge [Dr. Flint's son-in-law]. He proposed to pay three hundred dollars down, if Mr. Dodge would sell me, and enter into obligations to relinquish all claim to me or my children forever after. He who called himself my master said he scorned so small an offer for such a valuable servant. The gentleman replied, "You can do as you choose, sir. If you reject this offer you will never get any thing; for the woman has friends who will convey her and her children out of the country."

Mr. Dodge concluded that "half a loaf was better than no bread," and he agreed to the proffered terms. By the next mail I received this brief letter from Mrs. Bruce: "I am rejoiced to tell you that the money for your freedom has been paid to Mr. Dodge. Come home to-morrow. I long to see you and my sweet babe."

My brain reeled as I read these lines. A gentleman near me said, "It's true; I have seen the bill of sale." "The bill of sale!" Those words struck me like a blow. So I was *sold* at last! A human being *sold* in the free city of New York! The bill of sale is on record, and future generations will learn from it that women were articles of traffic in New York, late in the nineteenth century of the Christian religion. It may hereafter prove a useful document to antiquaries, who are seeking to measure the progress of civilization in the United States. I well know the value of that bit of paper; but much as I love freedom, I do not like to look upon it. I am deeply grateful to the generous friend who procured it, but I despise the miscreant who demanded payment for what never rightfully belonged to him or his.

I had objected to having my freedom bought, yet I must confess that when it was done I felt as if a heavy load had been lifted from my weary shoulders. When I rode home in the cars I was no longer afraid to unveil my face and look at people as they passed. I should have been glad to have met Daniel Dodge himself; to have had him seen me and known me, that he might have mourned over the untoward circumstances which compelled him to sell me for three hundred dollars.

When I reached home, the arms of my benefactress were thrown round me, and our tears mingled. As soon as she could speak, she said, "O Linda, I'm *so* glad it's all over! You wrote to me as if you thought you were going to be transferred from one owner to another. But I did not buy you for your services. I should have done just the same, if you had been going to sail for California tomorrow. I should, at least, have the satisfaction of knowing that you left me a free woman."

My heart was exceedingly full. I remembered how my poor father had tried to buy me, when I was a small child, and how he had been disappointed. I hoped his spirit was rejoicing over me now. I remembered how my good old grandmother had laid up her earnings to purchase me in later years, and how often her plans had been frustrated. How that faithful, loving old heart would leap for joy, if she could look on me and my children now that we were free! My relatives had been foiled in all their efforts, but God had raised me up a friend among strangers, who had bestowed on me the precious, long-desired boon. Friend! It is a common word, often lightly used. Like other good and beautiful things, it may be tarnished by careless handling; but when I speak of Mrs. Bruce as my friend, the word is sacred.

My grandmother lived to rejoice in my freedom; but not long after, a letter came with a black seal. She had gone "where the wicked cease from troubling, and the weary are at rest."

Time passed on, and a paper came to me from the south, containing an obituary notice of my uncle Phillip. It was the only case I ever knew of such an honor conferred upon a colored person. It was written by one of his friends, and contained these words: "Now that death has laid him low, they call him a good man and a useful citizen; but what are eulogies to the black man, when the world has faded from his vision? It does not require man's praise to obtain rest in God's kingdom." So they called a colored man a *citizen*! Strange words to be uttered in that region!

Reader, my story ends with freedom; not in the usual way, with marriage. I and my children are now free! We are as free from the power of slaveholders as are the white people of the north; and though that, according to my ideas, is not saying a great deal, it is a vast improvement in *my* condition. The dream of my life is not yet realized. I do not sit with my children in a home of my own. I still long for a hearthstone of my own, however humble. I wish it for my children's sake far more than for my own. But God so orders circumstances as to keep me with my friend Mrs. Bruce. Love, duty, gratitude, also bind me to her side. It is a privilege to serve her who pities my oppressed people, and who has bestowed the inestimable boon of freedom on me and my children.

It has been painful to me, in many ways, to recall the dreary years I passed in bondage. I would gladly forget them if I could. Yet the retrospection is not altogether without solace; for with those gloomy recollections come tender memories of my good old grandmother, like light, fleecy clouds floating over a dark and troubled sea.

# ELIZABETH CADY STANTON
## 1815–1902

*At another time and in another place, Elizabeth Cady Stanton, born into middle-class comfort, well educated, contentedly married, the enthusiastic mother of seven, might have lived a conventional life. Instead, she grew up in the optimistic, utopian decades before the Civil War when Americans believed they could reform—perhaps even perfect—themselves and their society. Stanton embraced many reforms, especially the cause of woman's rights, for which she became the century's most outspoken advocate.*

*She accepted nothing as she found it. As a child she chafed at the discipline of her family, rejected the gloomy teachings of conventional Protestantism, and rebelled against the constraints of gender. She married the abolitionist Henry B. Stanton, and joining him in the cause of freedom for the slave, came to see that even white middle-class women like herself were not free. When she and other women called the first woman's rights convention in the United States in 1848, attended by Frederick Douglass, Stanton discovered that she could write and speak eloquently. She began a career as a philosopher and propagandist which would last a half a century.*

*In 1851, she and Susan B. Anthony formed the political, intellectual, and emotional partnership that sustained them over the next difficult decades as they struggled on many fronts to win legal, political, and economic equality for women. In 1866, the two women founded the Equal Rights Association, hoping to tie the politically expedient enfranchisement of black freedmen to the politically impossible enfranchisement of women. In 1868, they collaborated on a short-lived newspaper, The Revolution ("Women their rights and nothing less; men their rights and nothing more" was its motto), and in 1869 they formed the radical National Woman Suffrage Association. Stanton and Anthony lectured from coast to coast on women's rights, disrupted the smug self-congratulations of the national Centennial celebration in 1876, and co-edited the invaluable, multi-volume* History of Woman Suffrage.

*Stanton did not mellow with age. She attacked conventional marriage, advocated more equitable divorce laws, and launched her final battle against Christian orthodoxy by writing* The Woman's Bible. *She became the first president of the National American Woman Suffrage Association in 1890 when the National Woman Suffrage Association merged with the moderate American Woman Suffrage Association, but she served only two years because her wide-ranging radicalism was increasingly at odds with the suffrage movement's own narrowing focus.*

*Stanton's forceful prose, developed during decades of platform speaking, asserted her self-confidence and self-esteem. She admitted no contradictions between her childhood wish to have been born a boy and her later lectures on responsible motherhood. Hers is not a journey with an uncertain outcome. Born in an age of reform which believed that even an American woman could shape her own destiny, Stanton claimed to know from the beginning her life-time vocation: to rebel.*

Eighty Years and More: Reminiscences, 1815–1897, *1898. Reprint, New York: Schocken Books, 1971.*

The psychical growth of a child is not influenced by days and years, but by the impressions passing events make on its mind. What may prove a sudden awakening to one, giving an impulse in a certain direction that may last for years, may make no impression on another. People wonder why the children of the same family differ so widely, though they have had the same domestic discipline, the same school and church teaching, and have grown up under the same influences and with the same environments. As well wonder why lilies and lilacs in the same latitude are not all alike in color and equally fragrant. Children differ as widely as these in the primal elements of their physical and psychical life.

Who can estimate the power of antenatal influences, or the child's surroundings in its earliest years, the effect of some passing word or sight on one, that makes no impression on another? The unhappiness of one child under a certain home discipline is not inconsistent with the content of another under this same discipline. One, yearning for broader freedom, is in a chronic condition of rebellion; the other, more easily satisfied, quietly accepts the situation. Everything is seen from a different standpoint; everything takes its color from the mind of the beholder.

I am moved to recall what I can of my early days, what I thought and felt, that grown people may have a better understanding of children and do more for their happiness and development. I see so much tyranny exercised over children, even by well-disposed parents, and in so many varied forms,—a tyranny to which these parents are themselves insensible,—that I desire to paint my joys and sorrows in as vivid colors as possible, in the hope that I may do something to defend the weak from the strong. People never dream of all that is going on in the little heads of the young, for few adults are given to introspection, and those who are incapable of recalling their own feelings under restraint and disappointment can have no appreciation of the sufferings of children who can neither describe nor analyze what they feel. In defending themselves against injustice they are as helpless as dumb animals. What is insignificant to their elders is often to them a source of great joy or sorrow.

With several generations of vigorous, enterprising ancestors behind me, I commenced the struggle of life under favorable circumstances on the 12th day of November, 1815, the same year that my father, Daniel Cady, a distinguished lawyer and judge in the State of New York, was elected to Congress. Perhaps the excitement of a political campaign, in which my mother took the deepest interest, may have had an influence on my prenatal life and given me the strong desire that I have always felt to participate in the rights and duties of government.

My father was a man of firm character and unimpeachable integrity, and yet sensitive and modest to a painful degree. There were but two places in which he felt at ease—in the courthouse and at his own fireside. Though gentle and tender, he had such a dignified repose and reserve of manner that, as children, we regarded him with fear rather than affection.

My mother, Margaret Livingston, a tall, queenly looking woman, was courageous, self-reliant, and at her ease under all circumstances and in all places. She was the daughter of Colonel James Livingston, who took an active part in the War of the Revolution....

Our parents were as kind, indulgent, and considerate as the Puritan ideas of those days permitted, but fear, rather than love, of God and parents alike, predominated. Add to this our timidity in our intercourse with servants and teachers, our dread of the ever present devil, and the reader will see that, under such conditions, nothing but strong self-will and a good share of hope and mirthfulness could have saved an ordinary child from becoming a mere nullity.

The first event engraved on my memory was the birth of a sister when I was four years old. It was a cold morning in January when the brawny Scotch nurse carried me to see the little stranger, whose advent was a matter of intense interest to me for many weeks after. The large, pleasant room with the white curtains and bright wood fire on the hearth, where panada, catnip, and all kinds of little messes which we were allowed to taste were kept warm, was the center of attraction for the older children. I heard so many friends remark, "What a pity it is she's a girl!" that I felt a kind of compassion for the little baby. True, our family consisted of five girls and only one boy, but I did not understand at that time that girls were considered an inferior order of beings....

I am told that I was pensively looking out of the nursery window one day, when Mary Dunn, the Scotch nurse, who was something of a philosopher, and a stern Presbytrian, said: "Child, what are you thinking about; are you planning some new form of mischief?" "No, Mary," I replied, "I was wondering why it was that everything we like to do is a sin, and that everything we dislike is commanded by God or someone on earth. I am so tired of that everlasting no! no! no! At school, at home, everywhere it is *no*! Even at church all the commandments begin 'Thou shalt not.' I suppose God will say 'no' to all we like in the next world, just as you do here." Mary was dreadfully shocked at my dissatisfaction with the things of time and prospective eternity, and exhorted me to cultivate the virtues of obedience and humility.

I well remember the despair I felt in those years, as I took in the whole situation, over the constant cribbing and crippling of a child's life. I suppose I found fit language in which to express my thoughts, for Mary Dunn told me, years after, how our discussion roused my sister Margaret, who was an attentive listener. I must have set forth our wrongs in clear, unmistakable terms; for Margaret exclaimed one day, "I tell you what to do. Hereafter let us act as we choose, without asking." "Then," said I, "we shall be punished." "Suppose we are," said she, "we shall have had our fun at any rate, and that is better than to mind the everlasting 'no' and not have any fun at all." Her logic seemed unanswerable, so together we gradually acted on her suggestions. Having less imagination than I, she took a common-sense view of life and suffered nothing from anticipation of troubles, while my sorrows were intensified fourfold by innumerable apprehensions of possible exigencies.

**ELIZABETH CADY STANTON**

Our nursery, a large room over a back building, had three barred windows reaching nearly to the floor. Two of these opened on a gently slanting roof over a veranda. In our night robes, on warm summer evenings we could, by dint of skillful twisting and compressing, get out between the bars, and there, snugly braced against the house, we would sit and enjoy the moon and stars and what sounds might reach us from the streets, while the nurse, gossiping at the back door, imagined we were safely asleep.

I have a confused memory of being often under punishment for what, in those days, were called "tantrums." I suppose they were really justifiable acts of rebellion against the tyranny of those in authority. I have often listened since, with real satisfaction, to what some of our friends had to say of the high-handed manner in which sister Margaret and I defied all the transient orders and strict rules laid down for our guidance. If we had observed them we might as well have been embalmed as mummies, for all the pleasure and freedom we should have had in our childhood. As very little was then done for the amusement of children, happy were those who *conscientiously* took the liberty of amusing themselves....

When I was eleven years old, two events occurred which changed considerably the current of my life. My only brother, who had just graduated from Union College, came home to die. A young man of great talent and promise, he was the pride of my father's heart. We early felt that this son filled a larger place in our father's affections and future plans than the five daughters together. Well do I remember how tenderly he watched my brother in his last illness, the sighs and tears he gave vent to as he slowly walked up and down the hall, and, when the last sad moment came, and we were all assembled to say farewell in the silent chamber of death, how broken were his utterances as he knelt and prayed for comfort and support. I still recall, too, going into the large darkened parlor to see my brother, and finding the casket, mirrors, and pictures all draped in white, and my father seated by his side, pale and immovable. As he took no notice of me, after standing a long while, I climbed upon his knee, when he mechanically put his arm about me and, with my head resting against his beating heart, we both sat in silence, he thinking of the wreck of all his hopes in the loss of a dear son, and I wondering what could be said or done to fill the void in his breast. At length he heaved a deep sigh and said: "Oh, my daughter, I wish you were a boy!" Throwing my arms about his neck, I replied: "I will try to be all my brother was."

Then and there I resolved that I would not give so much time as heretofore to play, but would study and strive to be at the head of all my classes and thus delight my father's heart. All that day and far into the night I pondered the problem of boyhood. I thought that the chief thing to be done in order to equal boys was to be learned and courageous. So I decided to study Greek and learn to manage a horse. Having formed this conclusion I fell asleep. My resolutions, unlike many such made at night, did not vanish with the coming light. I arose early and hastened to put them into execution. They were resolutions never to be forgotten—destined to mold my character anew. As soon as I was dressed I hastened to our good pastor, Rev. Simon Hosack, who was always early at work in his garden.

"Doctor," said I, "which do you like best, boys or girls?"

"Why, girls, to be sure; I would not give you for all the boys in Christendom."

"My father," I replied, "prefers boys; he wishes I was one, and I intend to be as near like one as possible. I am going to ride on horseback and study Greek. Will you give me a Greek lesson now, doctor? I want to begin at once."

"Yes, child," said he, throwing down his hoe, "come into my library and we will begin without delay."

He entered fully into the feeling of suffering and sorrow which took possession of me when I discovered that a girl weighed less in the scale of being than a boy, and he praised my determination to prove the contrary. The old grammar which he had studied in the University of Glasgow was soon in my hands, and the Greek article was learned before breakfast.

Then came the sad pageantry of death, the weeping of friends, the dark rooms, the ghostly stillness, the exhortation to the living to prepare for death, the solemn prayer, the mournful chant, the funeral cortège, the solemn, tolling bell, the burial. How I suffered during those sad days! What strange undefined fears of the unknown took possession of me! For months afterward, at the twilight hour, I went with my father to the new-made grave. Near it stood two tall poplar trees, against one of which I leaned, while my father threw himself on the grave, with outstretched arms, as if to embrace his child. At last the frosts and storms of November came and threw a chilling barrier between the living and the dead, and we went there no more.

During all this time I kept up my lessons at the parsonage and made rapid progress. I surprised even my teacher, who thought me capable of doing anything. I learned to drive, and to leap a fence and ditch on horseback. I taxed every power, hoping some day to hear my father say: "Well, a girl is as good as a boy, after all." But he never said it. When the doctor came over to spend the evening with us, I would whisper in his ear: "Tell my father how fast I get on," and he would tell him, and was lavish in his praises. But my father only paced the room, sighed, and showed that he wished I were a boy; and I, not knowing why he felt thus, would hide my tears of vexation on the doctor's shoulder.

Soon after this I began to study Latin, Greek, and mathematics with a class of boys in the Academy, many of whom were much older than I. For three years one boy kept his place at the head of the class, and I always stood next. Two prizes were offered in Greek. I strove for one and took the second. How well I remember my joy in receiving that prize. There was no sentiment of ambition, rivalry, or triumph over my companions, nor feeling of satisfaction in receiving this honor in the presence of those assembled on the day of the exhibition. One thought alone filled my mind. "Now," said I, "my father will be satisfied with me." So, as soon as we were dismissed, I ran down the hill, rushed breathless into his office, laid the new Greek Testament, which was my prize, on his table and exclaimed: "There, I got it!" He took up the book, asked me some questions about the class, the teachers, the spectators, and, evidently pleased, handed it back to me. Then, while I stood looking and waiting for him to say something which would show that he recognized the equality of the daughter with the son, he kissed me on the forehead and exclaimed, with a sigh, "Ah, you should have been a boy!"....

As my father's office joined the house, I spent there much of my time, when out of school, listening to the clients stating their cases, talking with the students, and reading the laws in regard to woman. In our Scotch neighborhood many men still retained the old feudal ideas of women and property. Fathers, at their death, would will the bulk of their property to the eldest son, with the proviso that the mother was to have a home with him. Hence it was not unusual for the mother, who had brought all the property into the family, to be made an unhappy dependent on the bounty of an uncongenial daughter-in-law and a dissipated son. The tears and complaints of the women who came to my father for legal advice touched my heart and early drew my attention to the injustice and cruelty of the laws. As the practice of the law was my father's business, I could not exactly understand why he could not alleviate the sufferings of these women. So, in order to enlighten me, he would take down his books and show me the inexorable statutes. The students, observing my interest, would amuse themselves by reading to me all the worst laws they could find, over which I would laugh and cry by turns. One Christmas morning I went into the office to show them, among other of my presents, a new coral necklace and bracelets. They all admired the jewelry and then began to tease me with hypothetical cases of future ownership. "Now," said Henry Bayard, "if in due time you should be my wife, those ornaments would be mine; I could take them and lock them up, and you could never wear them except with my permission. I could even exchange them for a box of cigars, and you could watch them evaporate in smoke."

With this constant bantering from students and the sad complaints of the women, my mind was sorely perplexed. So when, from time to time, my attention was called to these odious laws, I would mark them with a pencil, and becoming more and more convinced of the necessity of taking some active measures against these unjust provisions, I resolved to seize the first opportunity, when alone in the office, to cut every one of them out of the books; supposing my father and his library were the beginning and the end of the law. However, this mutilation of his volumes was never accomplished, for dear old Flora Campbell, to whom I confided my plan for the amelioration of the wrongs of my unhappy sex, warned my father of what I proposed to do. Without letting me know that he had discovered my secret, he explained to me one evening how laws were made, the large number of lawyers and libraries there were all over the State, and that if his library should burn up it would make no difference in woman's condition. "When you are grown up, and able to prepare a speech," said he, "you must go down to Albany and talk to the legislators; tell them all you have seen in this office—the sufferings of these Scotchwomen, robbed of their inheritance and left dependent on their unworthy sons, and, if you can persuade them to pass new laws, the old ones will be a dead letter." Thus was the future object of my life foreshadowed and my duty plainly outlined by him who was most opposed to my public career when, in due time, I entered upon it....

It was in Peterboro [New York] that I first met one who was then considered the most eloquent and impassioned orator on the anti-slavery platform, Henry B. Stanton. He had come over from Utica with Alvin Stewart's beautiful daughter, to whom report said he was engaged; but, as she soon after married Luther R. Marsh, there was a mistake somewhere. However, the rumor had its advantages. Regarding him as not in the matrimonial market, we were all much more free and easy in our manners with him than we would otherwise have been. A series of anti-slavery conventions was being held in Madison County, and there I had the pleasure of hearing him for the first time. As I had a passion for oratory, I was deeply impressed with his power. He was not so smooth and eloquent as Phillips, but he could make his audience both laugh and cry; the latter, Phillips himself said he never could do. Mr. Stanton was then in his prime, a fine-looking, affable young man, with remarkable conversational talent, and was ten years my senior, with the advantage that that number of years necessarily gives....

My engagement was a season of doubt and conflict—doubt as to the wisdom of changing a girlhood of freedom and enjoyment for I knew not what, and conflict because the step I proposed was in opposition to the wishes of all my family. Whereas, heretofore, friends were continually suggesting suitable matches for me and painting the marriage relation in the most dazzling colors, now that state was represented as beset with dangers and disappointments, and men, of all God's creatures as the most depraved and unreliable. Hard pressed, I broke my engagement, after months of anxiety and bewilderment; suddenly I decided to renew it, as Mr. Stanton was going to Europe as a delegate to the World's Anti-slavery Convention, and we did not wish the ocean to roll between us.

Thursday, May 10, 1840, I determined to take the fateful step, without the slightest preparation for a wedding or a voyage; but Mr. Stanton, coming up the North River, was detained on "Marcy's Overslaugh," a bar in the river where boats were frequently stranded for hours. This delay compelled us to be married on Friday, which is commonly supposed to be a most unlucky day. But as we lived together, without more than the usual matrimonial friction, for nearly a half a century, had seven children, all but one of whom are still living, and have been well sheltered, clothed, and fed, enjoying sound minds in sound bodies, no one need be afraid of going through the marriage ceremony on Friday for fear of bad luck. The Scotch clergyman who married us, being somewhat superstitious, begged us to postpone it until Saturday; but, as we were to sail early in the coming week, that was impossible. That point settled, the next difficulty was to persuade him to leave out the word "obey" in the marriage ceremony. As I obstinately refused to obey one with whom I supposed I was entering into an equal relation, that point, too, was conceded. A few friends were invited to be present and, in a simple white evening dress, I was married....

**[The couple set out on a ten-month long honeymoon in Europe. A significant stop was at a World Anti-Slavery Convention, to which Henry B. Stanton was a delegate.]**

Our chief object in visiting England at this time was to attend the World's Anti-slavery Convention, to meet June 12, 1840, in Freemasons' Hall, London. Delegates from all the anti-slavery societies of civilized nations were invited, yet, when they arrived, those representing associations of women were rejected. Though women were members of the National Anti-slavery Society, accustomed to speak and vote in all its conventions, and to take an equally active part with men in the whole anti-slavery struggle, and were there as delegates from associations of men and women, as well as those distinctively of their own sex, yet all alike were rejected because they were women. Women, according to English prejudices at that time, were excluded by Scriptural texts from sharing equal dignity and authority with men in all reform associations; hence it was to English minds pre-eminently unfitting that women should be admitted as equal members to a World's Convention. The question was hotly debated through an entire day. My husband made a very eloquent speech in favor of admitting the women delegates.

When we consider that Lady Byron, Anna Jameson, Mary Howitt, Mrs. Hugo Reid, Elizabeth Fry, Amelia Opie, Ann Green Phillips, Lucretia Mott, and many remarkable women, speakers and leaders in the Society of Friends, were all compelled to listen in silence to the masculine platitudes on woman's sphere, one may form some idea of the indignation of unprejudiced friends, and especially that of such women as Lydia Maria Child, Maria Chapman, Deborah Weston,

Angelina and Sarah Grimké, and Abby Kelly, who were impatiently waiting and watching on this side, in painful suspense, to hear how their delegates were received. Judging from my own feelings, the women on both sides of the Atlantic must have been humiliated and chagrined, except as these feelings were outweighed by contempt for the shallow reasoning of their opponents and their comical pose and gestures in some of the intensely earnest flights of their imagination.

The clerical portion of the convention was most violent in its opposition. The clergymen seemed to have God and his angels especially in their care and keeping, and were in agony lest the women should do or say something to shock the heavenly hosts. Their all-sustaining conceit gave them abundant assurance that their movements must necessarily be all-pleasing to the celestials whose ears were open to the proceedings of the World's Convention. Deborah, Huldah, Vashti, and Esther might have questioned the propriety of calling it a World's Convention, when only half of humanity was represented there; but what were their opinions worth compared with those of the Rev. A. Harvey, the Rev. C. Stout, or the Rev. J. Burnet, who, Bible in hand, argued woman's subjection, divinely decreed when Eve was created.

One of our champions in the convention, George Bradburn, a tall thick-set man with a voice like thunder, standing head and shoulders above the clerical representatives, swept all their arguments aside by declaring with tremendous emphasis that, if they could prove to him that the Bible taught the entire subjection of one-half of the race to the other, he should consider that the best thing he could do for humanity would be to bring together every Bible in the universe and make a grand bonfire of them.

It was really pitiful to hear narrow-minded bigots, pretending to be teachers and leaders of men, so cruelly remanding their own mothers, with the rest of woman-kind, to absolute subjection to the ordinary masculine type of humanity. I always regretted that the women themselves had not taken part in the debate before the convention was fully organized and the question of delegates settled. It seemed to me then, and does now, that all delegates with credentials from recognized societies should have had a voice in the organization of the convention, though subject to exclusion afterward. However, the women sat in a low curtained seat like a church choir, and modestly listened to the French, British, and American Solons for twelve of the longest days in June, as did, also, our grand Garrison and Rogers in the gallery. They scorned a convention that ignored the rights of the very women who had fought, side by side, with them in the anti-slavery conflict. "After battling so many long years," said Garrison, "for the liberties of African slaves, I can take no part in a convention that strikes down the most sacred rights of all women." After coming three thousand miles to speak on the subject nearest his heart, he nobly shared the enforced silence of the rejected delegates. It was a great act of self-sacrifice that should never be forgotten by women.

Thomas Clarkson was chosen president of the convention and made a few remarks in opening, but he soon retired, as his age and many infirmities made all public occasions too burdensome, and Joseph Sturge, a Quaker, was made chairman. Sitting next to Mrs. Mott, I said:

"As there is a Quaker in the chair now, what could he do if the spirit should move you to speak?"

"Ah," she replied, evidently not believing such a contingency possible, "where the spirit of the Lord is, there is liberty."

She had not much faith in the sincerity of abolitionists who, while eloquently defending the natural rights of slaves, denied freedom of speech to one-half the people of their own race. Such was the consistency of an assemblage of philanthropists! They would have been horrified at the idea of burning the flesh of the distinguished women present with red-hot irons, but the crucifixion of their pride and self-respect, the humiliation of the spirit, seemed to them a most trifling matter. The action of this convention was the topic of discussion, in public and private, for a long time, and stung many women into new thought and action and gave rise to the movement for women's political equality both in England and the United States.

As the convention adjourned, the remark was heard on all sides, "It is about time some demand was made for new liberties for women." As Mrs. Mott and I walked home, arm in arm, commenting on the incidents of the day, we resolved to hold a convention as soon as we returned home, and form a society to advocate the rights of women. At the lodging house on Queen Street, where a large number of delegates had apartments, the discussions were heated at every meal, and at times so bitter that, at last, Mr. Birney packed his valise and sought more peaceful quarters. Having strongly opposed the admission of women as delegates to the convention it was rather embarrassing to meet them, during the intervals between the various sessions, at the table and in the drawing room.

These were the first women I had ever met who believed in the equality of the sexes and who did not believe in the popular orthodox religion. The acquaintance of Lucretia Mott, who was a broad, liberal thinker on politics, religion, and all questions of reform, opened to me a new world of thought. As we walked about to see the sights of London, I embraced every opportunity to talk with her. It was intensely gratifying to hear all that, through years of doubt, I had dimly thought, so freely discussed by other women, some of them no older than myself—women, too, of rare intelligence, cultivation, and refinement. After six weeks' sojourn under the same roof with Lucretia Mott, whose conversation was uniformly on a high plane, I felt that I knew her too well to sympathize with the orthodox Friends, who denounced her as a dangerous woman because she doubted certain dogmas they fully believed. . . .

**[The Stantons returned to Johnstown, where Stanton's husband entered her father's law practice, and the first of her seven children was born.]**

The puzzling questions of theology and poverty that had occupied so much of my thoughts, now gave place to the practical one, "what to do with a baby." Though motherhood is the most important of all the professions,—requiring more knowledge than any other department in human affairs,—yet there is not sufficient attention given to the preparation for this office. If we buy a plant of a horticulturist we ask him many questions as to its needs, whether it thrives best in sunshine or in shade, whether it needs much or little water, what degrees of heat or cold; but when we hold in our arms for the first time, a being of infinite possibilities, in whose wisdom may rest the destiny of a nation, we take it for granted that the laws governing its life, health, and happiness are intuitively understood, that there is nothing new to be learned in regard to it. Yet here is a science to which philosophers have, as yet, given but little attention. An important fact has only been discovered and acted upon within the last ten years, that children come into the world tired, and not hungry, exhausted with the perilous journey. Instead of being thoroughly bathed and dressed, and kept on the rack while the nurse makes a prolonged toilet and feeds it some nostrum supposed to have much needed medicinal influence, the child's face, eyes, and mouth should be hastily washed with warm water, and the rest of its body thoroughly oiled, and then it should be slipped into a soft pillow case, wrapped in a blanket, and laid to sleep. Ordinarily, in the proper conditions, with its face uncovered in a cool, pure atmosphere, it will sleep twelve hours. Then it should be bathed, fed, and clothed in a high-necked, long-sleeved silk shirt and a blanket, all of which could be done in five minutes. As babies lie still most of the time the first six weeks, they need no dressing. I think the nurse was a full hour bathing and dressing my firstborn, who protested with a melancholy wail every blessed minute.

Ignorant myself of the initiative steps on the threshold of time, I supposed this proceeding was approved by the best authorities. However, I had been thinking, reading, observing, and had as little faith in the popular theories in regard to babies as on any other subject. I saw them, on all sides, ill half the time, pale and peevish, dying early, having no joy in life. I heard parents complaining of weary days and sleepless nights, while each child, in turn, ran the gauntlet of red gum, jaundice, whooping cough, chicken-pox, mumps, measles, scarlet fever, and fits. They all seemed to think these inflictions were a part of the eternal plan—that Providence had a kind of Pandora's box, from which he scattered these venerable diseases most liberally among those whom he especially loved. Having gone through the ordeal of bearing a child, I was determined, if possible, to keep him, so I read everything I could find on the subject. But the literature on this subject was as confusing and unsatisfactory as the longer and shorter catechisms and the Thirty-nine Articles of our faith. I had recently visited our dear friends, Theodore and Angelina Grimke-Weld, and they warned me against books on this subject. They had been so misled by one author, who assured them that the stomach of a child could only hold one tablespoonful, that they nearly starved their firstborn to death. Though the child dwindled, day by day, and, at the end of a month, looked like a little old man, yet they still stood by the distinguished author. Fortunately, they both went off, one day, and left the child with Sister "Sarah," who thought she would make an experiment and see what a child's stomach could hold, as she had grave doubts about the tablespoonful theory. To her surprise the baby took a pint bottle full of milk, and had the sweetest sleep thereon he had known in his earthly career. After that he was permitted to take what he wanted, and "the author" was informed of his libel on the infantile stomach.

So here, again, I was entirely afloat, launched on the seas of doubt without chart or compass. The life and well-being of the race seemed to hang on the slender thread of such traditions as we were handed down by ignorant mothers and nurses. One powerful ray of light illuminated the darkness; it was the work of Andrew Combe on "Infancy." He had evidently watched some of the manifestations of man in the first stages of his development, and could tell, at least, as much of babies as naturalists could of beetles and bees. He did give young mothers some hints of what to do, the whys and wherefores of certain lines of procedure during antenatal life, as well as the proper care thereafter. I read several chapters to the nurse. Although, out of her ten children, she had buried five, she still had too much confidence in her own wisdom and experience to pay much attention to any new idea that might be suggested to her. Among other things, Combe said that a child's bath should be regulated by the thermometer, in order to be always of the same temperature. She ridiculed the idea, and said her elbow was better than any thermometer, and, when I insisted on its use, she would invariably, with a smile of derision, put her elbow in first, to show how exactly it tallied with the thermometer. When I insisted that the child should not be bandaged, she rebelled outright, and said she would not take the responsibility of nursing a child without a bandage. I said, "Pray, sit down, dear nurse, and let us reason together. Do not think I am setting up my judgment against yours, with all your experience. I am simply trying to act on the opinions of a distinguished physician, who says there should be no pressure on a child anywhere; that the limbs and body should be free; that it is cruel to bandage an infant from hip to armpit, as is usually done in America; or both body and legs, as is done in Europe; or strap them to boards, as is done by savages on both continents. Can you give me one good reason, nurse, why a child should be bandaged?"

"Yes," she said emphatically, "I can give you a dozen."

"I only asked for one," I replied.

"Well," said she, after much hesitation, "the bones of a newborn infant are soft, like cartilage, and, unless you pin them up snugly, there is danger of their falling apart."

"It seems to me," I replied, "you have given the strongest reason why they should be carefully guarded against the slightest pressure. It is very remarkable that kittens and puppies should be so well put together that they need no artificial bracing, and the human family be left wholly to the mercy of a bandage. Suppose a child was born where you could not get a bandage, what then? Now I think this child will remain intact without a bandage, and, if I am willing to take the risk, why should you complain?"

"Because," said she, "if the child should die, it would injure my name as a nurse. I therefore wash my hands of all these new-fangled notions."

So she bandaged the child every morning, and I as regularly took it off. It has been fully proved since to be as useless an appendage as the vermiform. She had several cups with various concoctions of herbs standing on the chimney-corner, ready for insomnia, colic, indigestion, etc., etc., all of which were spirited away when she was at her dinner. In vain I told her we were homeopathists, and afraid of everything in the animal, vegetable, or mineral kingdoms lower than the two-hundredth dilution. I tried to explain the Hahnemann system of therapeutics, the philosophy of the principle *similia similibus curantur,* but she had no capacity for first principles, and did not understand my discourse. I told her that, if she would wash the baby's mouth with pure cold water morning and night and give it a teaspoonful to drink occasionally during the day, there would be no danger of red gum; that if she would keep the blinds open and let in the air and sunshine, keep the temperature of the room at sixty-five degrees, leave the child's head uncovered so that it could breathe freely, stop rocking and trotting it and singing such melancholy hymns as "Hark, from the tombs a doleful sound!" the baby and I would both be able to weather the cape without a bandage. I told her I should nurse the child once in two hours, and that she must not feed it any of her nostrums in the meantime; that a child's stomach, being made on the same general plan as our own, needed intervals of rest as well as ours. She said it would be racked with colic if the stomach was empty any length of time, and that it would surely have rickets if it were kept too still. I told her if the child had no anodynes, nature would regulate its sleep and motions. She said she could not stay in a room with the thermometer at sixty-five degrees, so I told her to sit in the next room and regulate the heat to suit herself; that I would ring a bell when her services were needed. . . .

In the autumn of 1843 my husband was admitted to the bar and commenced the practice of law in Boston with Mr. Bowles, brother-in-law of the late General John A. Dix. This gave me the opportunity to make many pleasant acquaintances among the lawyers in Boston, and to meet, intimately, many of the noble men and women among reformers, whom I had long worshiped at a distance. Here, for the first time, I met Lydia Maria Child, Abby Kelly, Paulina Wright, Elizabeth Peabody, Maria Chapman and her beautiful sisters, the Misses Weston, Oliver and Marianna Johnson, Joseph and Thankful Southwick and their three bright daughters. The home of the Southwicks was always a harbor of rest for the weary, where the anti-slavery hosts were wont to congregate, and where one was always sure to meet someone worth knowing. Their hospitality was generous to an extreme, and so boundless that they were, at last, fairly eaten out of house and home. Here, too, for the first time, I met Theodore Parker, John Pierpont, John G. Whittier, Emerson, Alcott, Lowell, Hawthorne, Mr. and Mrs. Samuel E. Sewall, Sidney Howard Gay, Pillsbury, Foster, Frederick Douglass, and last though not least, those noble men, Charles Hovey and Francis Jackson, the only men who ever left any money to the cause of woman suffrage. . . .

During the winter in Boston I attended all the lectures, churches, theaters, concerts, and temperance, peace, and prison-reform conventions within my reach. I had never lived in such an enthusiastically literary and reform latitude before, and my mental powers were kept at the highest tension. . . .

Mr. Stanton announced to me, in starting, that his business would occupy all his time, and that I must take entire charge of the housekeeping. So, with two good servants and two babies under my sole supervision, my time was pleasantly occupied.

When first installed as mistress over an establishment, one has the same feeling of pride and satisfaction that a young minister must have in taking charge of his first congregation. It is a proud moment in a woman's life to reign supreme within four walls, to be the one to whom all questions of domestic pleasure and economy are referred, and to hold in her hand that little family book in which the daily expenses, the outgoings and incomings, are duly registered. I studied up everything pertaining to housekeeping, and enjoyed it all. Even washing day— that day so many people dread—had its charms for me. The clean clothes on the lines and on the grass looked so white, and smelled so sweet, that it was to me a pretty sight to contemplate. I inspired my laundress with an ambition to have her clothes look white and to get them out earlier than our neighbors, and to have them ironed and put away sooner.

As Mr. Stanton did not come home to dinner, we made a picnic of our noon meal on Mondays, and all thoughts and energies were turned to speed the washing. No unnecessary sweeping or dusting, no visiting nor entertaining angels unawares on that day—it was held sacred to soap suds, blue-bags, and clothes-lines. The children, only, had no deviation in the regularity of their lives. They had their drives and walks, their naps and rations, in quantity and time, as usual. I had all the most approved cook books, and spent half my time preserving, pickling, and experimenting in new dishes. I felt the same ambition to excel in all departments of the culinary art that I did at school in the different branches of learning. My love of order and cleanliness was carried throughout, from parlor to kitchen, from the front door to the back. I gave a man an extra shilling to pile the logs of firewood with their smooth ends outward, though I did not have them scoured white, as did our Dutch grandmothers. I tried, too, to give an artistic touch to everything—the dress of my children and servants included. My dining table was round, always covered with a clean cloth of a pretty pattern and a centerpiece of flowers in their season, pretty dishes, clean silver, and set with neatness and care. I put my soul into everything, and hence enjoyed it. I never could understand how housekeepers could rest with rubbish all round their back doors; eggshells, broken dishes, tin cans, and old shoes scattered round their premises; servants ragged and dirty, with their hair in papers, and with the kitchen and dining room full of flies. I have known even artists to be indifferent to their personal appearance and their surroundings. Surely a mother and child, tastefully dressed, and a pretty home for a framework, is, as a picture, even more attractive than a domestic scene hung on the wall. The love of the beautiful can be illustrated as well in life as on canvas. There is such a struggle among women to become artists that I really wish some of their gifts could be illustrated in clean, orderly, beautiful homes....

### [The Stantons moved from Boston to Seneca Falls, New York, in 1847.]

In Seneca Falls my life was comparatively solitary, and the change from Boston was somewhat depressing. There, all my immediate friends were reformers, I had near neighbors, a new home with all the modern conveniences, and well-trained servants. Here our residence was on the outskirts of the town, roads very often muddy and no sidewalks most of the way, Mr. Stanton was frequently from home, I had poor servants, and an increasing number of children. To keep a house and grounds in good order, purchase every article for daily use, keep the wardrobes of half a dozen human beings in proper trim, take the children to dentists, shoe-makers, and different schools, or find teachers at home, altogether made suffi-cient work to keep one brain busy, as well as all the hands I could impress into the service. Then, too, the novelty of housekeeping had passed away, and much that was once attractive in domestic life was now irksome. I had so many cares that the company I needed for intellectual stimulus was a trial rather than a pleasure....

I now fully understood the practical difficulties most women had to contend with in the isolated household, and the impossibility of woman's best develop-ment if in contact, the chief part of her life, with servants and children. Fourier's phalansterie community life and co-operative households had a new significance for me. Emerson says, "A healthy discontent is the first step to progress." The general discontent I felt with woman's portion as wife, mother, housekeeper, physician, and spiritual guide, the chaotic conditions into which everything fell without her constant supervision, and the wearied, anxious look of the majority of women impressed me with a strong feeling that some active measures should be taken to remedy the wrongs of society in general, and of women in particular. My experience at the World's Anti-slavery Convention, all I had read of the legal status of women, and the oppression I saw everywhere, together swept across my soul, intensified now by many personal experiences. It seemed as if all the elements had conspired to impel me to some onward step. I could not see what to do or where to begin—my only thought was a public meeting for protest and discussion.

In this tempest-tossed condition of mind I received an invitation to spend the day with Lucretia Mott, at Richard Hunt's, in Waterloo. There I met several members of different families of Friends, earnest, thoughtful women. I poured out, that day, the torrent of my long-accumulating discontent, with such vehemence and indignation that I stirred myself, as well as the rest of the party, to do and dare anything. My discontent, according to Emerson, must have been healthy, for it moved us all to prompt action, and we decided, then and there, to call a "Woman's Rights Convention." We wrote the call that evening and published it in the *Seneca County Courier* the next day, the 14th of July, 1848, giving only five days' notice, as the convention was to be held on the 19th and 20th. The call was inserted without signatures,—in fact it was a mere announcement of a meeting,—but the chief movers and managers were Lucretia Mott, Mary Ann McClintock, Jane Hunt, Martha C. Wright, and myself. The convention, which was held two days in the Methodist Church, was in every way a grand success. The house was crowded at every session, the speaking good, and a religious earnestness dignified all the proceedings.

These were the hasty initiative steps of "the most momentous reform that had yet been launched on the world—the first organized protest against the injustice which had brooded for ages over the character and destiny of one-half the race." No words could express our astonishment on finding, a few days afterward, that what seemed to us so timely, so rational, and so sacred, should be a subject for sarcasm and ridicule to the entire press of the nation. With our Declaration of Rights and Resolutions for a text, it seemed as if every man who could wield a pen prepared a homily on "woman's sphere." All the journals from Maine to Texas seemed to strive with each other to see which could make our movement appear the most ridiculous. The anti-slavery papers stood by us manfully and so did Frederick Douglass, both in the convention and in his paper, *The North Star,* but so pronounced was the popular voice against us, in the parlor, press, and pulpit, that most of the ladies who had attended the convention and signed the declaration, one by one, withdrew their names and influence and joined our persecutors. Our friends gave us the cold shoulder and felt themselves disgraced by the whole proceeding.

If I had had the slightest premonition of all that was to follow that convention, I fear I should not have had the courage to risk it, and I must confess that it was with fear and trembling that I consented to attend another, one month afterward, in Rochester. Fortunately, the first one seemed to have drawn all the fire, and of the second but little was said. But we had set the ball in motion, and now, in quick succession, conventions were held in Ohio, Indiana, Massachusetts, Pennsylvania, and in the City of New York, and have been kept up nearly every year since.

The most noteworthy of the early conventions were those held in Massachusetts, in which such men as Garrison, Phillips, Channing, Parker, and Emerson took part. It was one of these that first attracted the attention of Mrs. John Stuart Mill, and drew from her pen that able article on "The Enfranchisement of Woman," in the *Westminster Review* of October, 1852.

The same year of the convention, the Married Woman's Property Bill, which had given rise to some discussion on woman's rights in New York, had passed the legislature. This encouraged action on the part of women, as the reflection naturally arose that, if the men who make the laws were ready for some onward step, surely the women themselves should express some interest in the legislation. Ernestine L. Rose, Paulina Wright (Davis), and I had spoken before committees of the legislature years before, demanding equal property rights for women. We had circulated petitions for the Married Woman's Property Bill for many years, and so also had the leaders of the Dutch aristocracy, who desired to see their life-long accumulations descend to their daughters and grandchildren rather than pass into the hands of dissipated, thriftless sons-in-law. Judge Hertell, Judge Fine, and Mr. Geddes of Syracuse prepared and championed the several bills, at different times, before the legislature. Hence the demands made in the convention were not entirely new to the reading and thinking public of New York—the first State to take any action on the question. As New York was the first State to put the word "male" in her constitution in 1778, it was fitting that she should be first in more liberal legislation. The effect of the convention on my own mind was most salutary. The discussions had cleared my ideas as to the primal steps to be taken for woman's enfranchisement, and the opportunity of expressing myself fully and freely on a subject I felt so deeply about was a great relief. I think all women who attended the convention felt better for the statement of their wrongs, believing that the first step had been taken to right them.

Soon after this I was invited to speak at several points in the neighborhood. One night, in the Quaker Meeting House at Farmington, I invited, as usual, discussion and questions when I had finished. We all waited in silence for a long time; at length a middle-aged man, with a broad-brimmed hat, arose and responded in a sing-song tone: "All I have to say is, if a hen can crow, let her crow," emphasizing "crow" with an upward inflection on several notes of the gamut. The meeting adjourned with mingled feelings of surprise and merriment. I confess that I felt somewhat chagrined in having what I considered my unanswerable arguments so summarily disposed of, and the serious impression I had made on the audience so speedily dissipated. The good man intended no disrespect, as he told me afterward. He simply put the whole argument in a nutshell: "Let a woman do whatever she can."

With these new duties and interests, and a broader outlook on human life, my petty domestic annoyances gradually took a subordinate place. Now I began to write articles for the press, letters to conventions held in other States, and private letters to friends, to arouse them to thought on this question....

The reports of the conventions held in Seneca Falls and Rochester, N.Y., in 1848, attracted the attention of one destined to take a most important part in the new movement—Susan B. Anthony, who, for her courage and executive ability, was facetiously called by William Henry Channing, the Napoleon of our struggle. At this time she was teaching in the academy at Canajoharie, a little village in the beautiful valley of the Mohawk.

"The Woman's Declaration of Independence" issued from those conventions startled and amused her, and she laughed heartily at the novelty and presumption of the demand. But, on returning home to spend her vacation, she was surprised to find that her sober Quaker parents and sister, having attended the Rochester meetings, regarded them as very profitable and interesting, and the demands made as proper and reasonable. She was already interested in the anti-slavery and temperance reforms, was an active member of an organization called "The Daughters of Temperance," and had spoken a few times in their public meetings. But the new gospel of "Woman's Rights," found a ready response in her mind, and, from that time, her best efforts have been given to the enfranchisement of women....

Miss Anthony and I wrote addresses for temperance, anti-slavery, educational, and woman's rights conventions. Here we forged resolutions, protests, appeals, petitions, agricultural reports, and constitutional arguments; for we made it a matter of conscience to accept every invitation to speak on every question, in order to maintain woman's right to do so. To this end we took turns on the domestic watchtowers, directing amusements, settling disputes, protecting the weak against the strong, and trying to secure equal rights to all in the home as well as the nation. I can recall many a stern encounter between my friend and the young experimenter. It is pleasant to remember that he never seriously injured any of his victims, and only once came near fatally shooting himself with a pistol. The ball went through his hand; happily a brass button prevented it from penetrating his heart.

It is often said, by those who know Miss Anthony best, that she has been my good angel, always pushing and goading me to work, and that but for her pertinacity I should never have accomplished the little I have. On the other hand it has been said that I forged the thunderbolts and she fired them. Perhaps all this is, in a measure, true. With the cares of a large family I might, in time, like too many women, have become wholly absorbed in a narrow family selfishness, had not my friend been continually exploring new fields for missionary labors. Her description of a body of men on any platform, complacently deciding questions in which woman had an equal interest, without an equal voice, readily roused me to a determination to throw a firebrand into the midst of their assembly.

Thus, whenever I saw that stately Quaker girl coming across my lawn, I knew that some happy convocation of the sons of Adam was to be set by the ears, by one of our appeals or resolutions. The little portmanteau, stuffed with facts, was opened, and there we had what the Rev. John Smith and Hon. Richard Roe had said: false interpretations of Bible texts, the statistics of women robbed of their property, shut out of some college, half paid for their work, the reports of some disgraceful trial; injustice enough to turn any woman's thoughts from stockings and puddings. Then we would get out our pens and write articles for papers, or a petition to the legislature; indite letters to the faithful, here and there; stir up the women in Ohio, Pennsylvania, or Massachusetts; call on *The Lily, The Una, The Liberator, The Standard* to remember our wrongs as well as those of the slave. We never met without issuing a pronunciamento on some question. In thought and sympathy we were one, and in the division of labor we exactly complemented each other. In writing we did better work than either could alone. While she is slow and analytical in composition, I am rapid and synthetic. I am the better writer, she the better critic. She supplied the facts and statistics, I the philosophy and rhetoric, and, together, we have made arguments that have stood unshaken through the storms of long years; arguments that no one has answered. Our speeches may be considered the united product of our two brains....

Many of those enjoying all these blessings now complacently say, "If these pioneers in reform had only pressed their measures more judiciously, in a more ladylike manner, in more choice language, with a more deferential attitude, the gentlemen could not have behaved so rudely." I give, in these pages, enough of the characteristics of these women, of the sentiments they expressed, of their education, ancestry, and position to show that no power could have met the prejudice and bigotry of that period more successfully than they did who so bravely and persistently fought and conquered them....

I soon convinced Miss Anthony that the ballot was the key to the situation; that when we had a voice in the laws we should be welcome to any platform. In turning the intense earnestness and religious enthusiasm of this great-souled woman into this channel, I soon felt the power of my convert in goading me forever forward to more untiring work. Soon fastened, heart to heart, with hooks of steel in a friendship that years of confidence and affection have steadily strengthened, we have labored faithfully together.

From the year 1850 conventions were held in various States, and their respective legislatures were continually besieged; New York was thoroughly canvassed by Miss Anthony and others. Appeals, calls for meetings, and petitions were circulated without number. In 1854 I prepared my first speech for the New York legislature. That was a great event in my life. I felt so nervous over it, lest it should not be worthy the occasion, that Miss Anthony suggested that I should slip up to Rochester and submit it to the Rev. William Henry Channing, who was preaching there at that time. I did so, and his opinion was so favorable as to the merits of my speech that I felt quite reassured. My father felt equally nervous when he saw, by the Albany *Evening Journal,* that I was to speak at the Capitol, and asked me to read my speech to him also. Accordingly, I stopped at Johnstown on my way to Albany, and, late one evening, when he was alone in his office, I entered and took my seat on the opposite side of his table. On no occasion, before or since, was I ever more embarrassed—an audience of one, and that the one of all others whose approbation I most desired, whose disapproval I most feared. I knew he condemned the whole movement, and was deeply grieved at the active part I had taken. Hence I was fully aware that I was about to address a wholly unsympathetic audience. However, I began, with a dogged determination to give all the power I could to my manuscript, and not to be discouraged or turned from my purpose by any tender appeals or adverse criticisms. I described the widow in the first hours of her grief, subject to the intrusions of the coarse minions of the law, taking inventory of the household goods, of the old armchair in which her loved one had breathed his last, of the old clock in the corner that told the hour he passed away. I threw all the pathos I could into my voice and language at this point, and, to my intense satisfaction, I saw tears filling my father's eyes. I cannot express the exultation I felt, thinking that now he would see, with my eyes, the injustice women suffered under the laws he understood so well.

Feeling that I had touched his heart I went on with renewed confidence, and, when I had finished, I saw he was thoroughly magnetized. With beating heart I waited for him to break the silence. He was evidently deeply pondering over all he had heard, and did not speak for a long time. I believed I had opened to him a new world of thought. He had listened long to the complaints of women, but from the lips of his own daughter they had come with a deeper pathos and power. At last, turning abruptly, he said: "Surely you have had a happy, comfortable life, with all your wants and needs supplied; and yet that speech fills me with self-reproach; for one might naturally ask, how can a young woman, tenderly brought up, who has had no bitter personal experience, feel so keenly the wrongs of her sex? Where did you learn this lesson?" "I learned it here," I replied, "in your office, when a child, listening to the complaints women made to you. They who have sympathy and imagination to make the sorrows of others their own can readily learn all the hard lessons of life from the experience of others." "Well, well!" he said, "you have made your points clear and strong; but I think I can find you even more cruel laws than those you have quoted." He suggested some improvements in my speech, looked up other laws, and it was one o'clock in the morning before we kissed each other good-night. How he felt on the question after that I do not know, as he never said anything in favor of or against it. He gladly gave me any help I needed, from time to time, in looking up the laws, and was very desirous that whatever I gave to the public should be carefully prepared.

Miss Anthony printed twenty thousand copies of this address, laid it on the desk of every member of the legislature, both in the Assembly and Senate, and, in her travels that winter, she circulated it throughout the State. I am happy to say I never felt so anxious about the fate of a speech since.

The first woman's convention in Albany was held at this time, and we had a kind of protracted meeting for two weeks after. There were several hearings before both branches of the legislature, and a succession of meetings in Association Hall, in which Phillips, Channing, Ernestine L. Rose, Antoinette L. Brown, and Susan B. Anthony took part. Being at the capital of the State, discussion was aroused at every fireside, while the comments of the press were numerous and varied. Every little country paper had something witty or silly to say about the uprising of the "strong-minded." Those editors whose heads were about the size of an apple were the most opposed to the uprising of women, illustrating what Sidney Smith said long ago: "There always was, and there always will be a class of men so small that, if women were educated, there would be nobody left below them." Poor human nature loves to have something to look down upon!

Here is a specimen of the way such editors talked at that time. The *Albany Register,* in an article on "Woman's Rights in the Legislature," dated March 7, 1854, says:

"While the feminine propagandists of women's rights confined themselves to the exhibition of short petticoats and long-legged boots, and to the holding of conventions and speech-making in concert rooms, the people were disposed to be amused by them, as they are by the wit of the clown in the circus, or the performances of Punch and Judy on fair days, or the minstrelsy of gentlemen with blackened faces, on banjos, the tambourine, and bones. But the joke is becoming stale. People are getting cloyed with these performances, and are looking for some healthier and more intellectual amusement. The ludicrous is wearing away, and disgust is taking the place of pleasurable sensations, arising from the novelty of this new phase of hypocrisy and infidel fanaticism.

"People are beginning to inquire how far public sentiment should sanction or tolerate these unsexed women, who would step out from the true sphere of the mother, the wife, and the daughter, and taking upon themselves the duties and the business of men, stalk into the public gaze, and, by engaging in the politics, the rough controversies and trafficking of the world, upheave existing institutions, and overrun all the social relations of life.

"It is a melancholy reflection that, among our American women, who have been educated to better things, there should be found any who are willing to follow the lead of such foreign propagandists as the ringleted, gloved, exotic, Ernestine L. Rose. We can understand how such a man as the Rev. Mr. May, or the sleek-headed Dr. Channing, may be deluded by her into becoming one of her disciples. They are not the first instances of infatuation that may overtake weak-minded men, if they are honest in their devotion to her and her doctrines; nor would they be the first examples of a low ambition that seeks notoriety as a substitute for true fame, if they are dishonest. Such men there are always, and, honest or dishonest, their true position is that of being tied to the apron strings of some strong-minded woman, and to be exhibited as rare specimens of human wickedness or human weakness and folly. But that one educated American should become her disciple and follow her insane teachings is a marvel."

When we see the abuse, and ridicule to which the best of men were subjected for standing on our platform in the early days, we need not wonder that so few have been brave enough to advocate our cause in later years, either in conventions or in the halls of legislation....

The frivolous objections some women made to our appeals were as exasperating as they were ridiculous. To reply to them politely, at all times, required a divine patience. On one occasion, after addressing the legislature, some of the ladies, in congratulating me, inquired, in a deprecating tone, "What do you do with your children?" "Ladies," I said, "it takes me no longer to speak, than you to listen; what have you done with your children the two hours you have been sitting here? But, to answer your question, I never leave my children to go to Saratoga, Washington, Newport, or Europe, or even to come here. They are, at this moment, with a faithful nurse at the Delevan House, and, having accomplished my mission, we shall all return home together."...

I was often told by fashionable women that they objected to the woman's rights movement because of the publicity of a convention, the immodesty of speaking from a platform, and the trial of seeing one's name in the papers. Several ladies made such remarks to me one day, as a bevy of us were sitting together in one of the fashionable hotels in Newport. We were holding a convention there at that time, and some of them had been present at one of the sessions. "Really," said I, "ladies, you surprise me; our conventions are not as public as the ballroom where I saw you all dancing last night. As to modesty, it may be a question, in many minds, whether it is less modest to speak words of soberness and truth, plainly dressed on a platform, than gorgeously arrayed, with bare arms and shoulders, to waltz in the arms of strange gentlemen. And as to the press, I noticed you all reading, in this morning's papers, with evident satisfaction, the personal compliments and full descriptions of your dresses at the last ball. I presume that any one of you would have felt slighted if your name had not been mentioned in the general description. When my name is mentioned, it is in connection with some great reform movement. Thus we all suffer or enjoy the same publicity—we are alike ridiculed. Wise men pity and ridicule you, and fools pity and ridicule me—you as the victims of folly and fashion, me as the representative of many of the disagreeable 'isms' of the age, as they choose to style liberal opinions. It is amusing, in analyzing prejudices, to see on what slender foundation they rest." And the ladies around me were so completely cornered that no one attempted an answer....

The widespread discussion we are having, just now, on the subject of marriage and divorce, reminds me of an equally exciting one in 1860. A very liberal bill, introduced into the Indiana legislature by Robert Dale Owen, and which passed by a large majority, roused much public thought on the question, and made that State free soil for unhappy wives and husbands. A similar bill was introduced into the legislature of New York by Mr. Ramsey, which was defeated by four votes, owing, mainly, to the intense opposition of Horace Greeley. He and Mr. Owen had a prolonged discussion, in the New York *Tribune*, in which Mr. Owen got decidedly the better of the argument.

There had been several aggravated cases of cruelty to wives among the Dutch aristocracy, so that strong influences in favor of the bill had been brought to bear on the legislature, but the *Tribune* thundered every morning in its editorial column its loudest peals, which reverberated through the State. So bitter was the opposition to divorce, for any cause, that but few dared to take part in the discussion. I was the only woman, for many years, who wrote and spoke on the question. Articles on divorce, by a number of women, recently published in the *North American Review,* are a sign of progress, showing that women dare speak out now more freely on the relations that most deeply concern them.

My feelings had been stirred to their depths very early in life by the sufferings of a dear friend of mine, at whose wedding I was one of the bridemaids. In listening to the facts in her case, my mind was fully made up as to the wisdom of a liberal divorce law. We read Milton's essays on divorce, together, and were thoroughly convinced as to the right and duty not only of separation, but of absolute divorce. While the New York bill was pending, I was requested, by Lewis Benedict, one of the committee who had the bill in charge, to address the legislature. I gladly accepted, feeling that here was an opportunity not only to support my friend in the step she had taken, but to make the path clear for other unhappy wives who might desire to follow her example. I had no thought of the persecution I was drawing down on myself for thus attacking so venerable an institution. I was always courageous in saying what I saw to be true, for the simple reason that I never dreamed of opposition. What seemed to me to be right I thought must be equally plain to all other rational beings. Hence I had no dread of denunciation. I was only surprised when I encountered it, and no number of experiences have, as yet, taught me to fear public opinion. What I said on divorce thirty-seven years ago seems quite in line with what many say now. The trouble was not in what I said, but that I said it too soon, and before the people were ready to hear it. It may be, however, that I helped them to get ready; who knows?...

On April 15, 1861, the President of the United States called out seventy-five thousand militia, and summoned Congress to meet July 4, when four hundred thousand men were called for, and four hundred millions of dollars were voted to suppress the Rebellion.

These startling events roused the entire people, and turned the current of their thoughts in new directions. While the nation's life hung in the balance, and the dread artillery of war drowned, alike, the voices of commerce, politics, religion, and reform, all hearts were filled with anxious forebodings, all hands were busy in solemn preparations for the awful tragedies to come.

At this eventful hour the patriotism of woman shone forth as fervently and spontaneously as did that of man; and her self-sacrifice and devotion were displayed in as many varied fields of action. While he buckled on his knapsack and marched forth to conquer the enemy, she planned the campaigns which brought the nation victory; fought in the ranks, when she could do so without detection; inspired the sanitary commission; gathered needed supplies for the grand army; provided nurses for the hospitals; comforted the sick; smoothed the pillows of the dying; inscribed the last messages of love to those far away; and marked the resting places where the brave men fell. The labor women accomplished, the hardships they endured, the time and strength they sacrificed in the War that summoned three million men to arms, can never be fully appreciated.

Indeed, we may safely say that there is scarcely a loyal woman in the North who did not do something in aid of the cause; who did not contribute time, labor, and money to the comfort of our soldiers and the success of our arms. The story of the War will never be fully written if the achievements of women are left untold. They do not figure in the official reports; they are not gazetted for gallant deeds; the names of thousands are unknown beyond the neighborhood where they lived, or the hospitals where they loved to labor; yet there is no feature in our War more creditable to us as a nation, none from its positive newness so well worthy of record.

While the mass of women never philosophize on the principles that underlie national existence, there were those in our late War who understood the political significance of the struggle; the "irrepressible conflict" between freedom and slavery, between National and State rights. They saw that to provide lint, bandages, and supplies for the army, while the War was not conducted on a wise policy, was to labor in vain; and while many organizations, active, vigilant, and self-sacrificing, were multiplied to look after the material wants of the army, these few formed themselves into a National Loyal League, to teach sound principles of government and to impress on the nation's conscience that freedom for the slaves was the only way to victory. Accustomed, as most women had been to works of charity and to the relief of outward suffering, it was difficult to rouse their enthusiasm for an idea, to persuade them to labor for a principle. They clamored for practical work, something for their hands to do; for fairs and sewing societies to raise money for soldiers' families, for tableaux, readings, theatricals—anything but conventions to discuss principles and to circulate petitions for emancipation. They could not see that the best service they could render the army was to suppress the Rebellion, and that the most effective way to accomplish that was to transform the slaves into soldiers. This Woman's Loyal League voiced the solemn lessons of the War: Liberty to all; national protection for every citizen under our flag; universal suffrage, and universal amnesty.

After consultation with Horace Greeley, William Lloyd Garrison, Governor Andrews, and Robert Dale Owen, Miss Anthony and I decided to call a meeting of women in Cooper Institute and form a Woman's Loyal League, to advocate the immediate emancipation and enfranchisement of the Southern slaves, as the most speedy way of ending the War....

It was agreed that the practical work to be done to secure freedom for the slaves was to circulate petitions through all the Northern States. For months these petitions were circulated diligently everywhere, as the signatures show—some signed on fence posts, plows, the anvil, the shoemaker's bench—by women of fashion and those in the industries, alike in the parlor and the kitchen; by statesmen, professors in colleges, editors, bishops; by sailors, and soldiers, and the hard-handed children of toil, building railroads and bridges, and digging canals, and in mines in the bowels of the earth. Petitions, signed by three hundred thousand persons, can now be seen in the national archives in the Capitol at Washington. Three of my sons spent weeks in our office in Cooper Institute, rolling up the petitions from each State separately, and inscribing on the outside the number of names of men and women contained therein. We sent appeals to the President, the House of Representatives, and the Senate, from time to time, urging emancipation and the passage of the proposed Thirteenth, Fourteenth, and Fifteenth Amendments to the National Constitution....

Liberty, victorious over slavery on the battlefield, had now more powerful enemies to encounter at Washington. The slaves set free, the master conquered, the South desolate; the two races standing face to face, sharing alike the sad results of war, turned with appealing looks to the general government, as if to say, "How stand we now?" "What next?" Questions our statesmen, beset with dangers, with fears for the nation's life, of party divisions, of personal defeat, were wholly unprepared to answer. The reconstruction of the South involved the reconsideration of the fundamental principles of our Government and the natural rights of man. The nation's heart was thrilled with prolonged debates in Congress and State legislatures, in the pulpits and public journals, and at every fireside on these vital questions, which took final shape in the three historic amendments to the Constitution.

The first point, his emancipation, settled, the political status of the negro was next in order; and to this end various propositions were submitted to Congress. But to demand his enfranchisement on the broad principle of natural rights was hedged about with difficulties, as the logical result of such action must be the enfranchisement of all ostracized classes; not only the white women of the entire country, but the slave women of the South. Though our senators and representatives had an honest aversion to any proscriptive legislation against loyal women, in view of their varied and self-sacrificing work during the War, yet the only way they could open the constitutional door just wide enough to let the black man pass in was to introduce the word "male" into the national Constitution. After the generous devotion of such women as Anna Carroll and Anna Dickinson in sustaining the policy of the Republicans, both in peace and war, they felt it would come with a bad grace from that party to place new barriers in woman's path to freedom. But how could the amendment be written without the word "male," was the question.

Robert Dale Owen being at Washington, and behind the scenes at the time, sent copies of the various bills to the officers of the Loyal League, in New York, and related to us some of the amusing discussions. One of the committee proposed "persons" instead of "males." "That will never do," said another, "it would enfranchise wenches." "Suffrage for black men will be all the strain the Republican party can stand," said another. Charles Sumner said, years afterward, that he wrote over nineteen pages of foolscap to get rid of the word "male" and yet keep "negro suffrage" as a party measure intact; but it could not be done.

Miss Anthony and I were the first to see the full significance of the word "male" in the Fourteenth Amendment, and we at once sounded the alarm, and sent out petitions for a constitutional amendment to "prohibit the States from disfranchising any of their citizens on the ground of sex."...

**[The passage of the Fourteenth Amendment re-opened the suffrage issue, and Elizabeth Cady Stanton and Susan B. Anthony spent the rest of their lifetimes in the battle to enfranchise women.]**

# ULYSSES S. GRANT
## 1822–1885

*In 1861, when he was thirty-eight years old, Ulysses Grant had little money and less fame. His family struggled to make ends meet on the few dollars he brought home from his job as a clerk in his father's Galena, Illinois, leather goods store. Seven years later he was the nation's most revered man and had been elected to the first of two terms as president of the United States.*

*His parents named him Hiram Ulysses Grant and sent him to West Point to get a good and free education. The military academy made a mistake and registered him as Ulysses S. Grant—a name which stuck then and forevermore. Grant finished in the middle of his class and was assigned to a post near St. Louis where he met and married Julia Dent in 1848. They had four children.*

*Grant fought in the Mexican War before being reassigned to posts in California and Oregon. He resigned from the army in 1854 to try his hand at farming and real estate ventures in Missouri. He failed at both, and adrift, moved to Galena to work for his father. The Civil War came and Grant found himself. Any man with his military education could start with a high-rank as the war needed men. Grant signed on as a colonel, but was made a brigadier general before he had seen any action. In 1862, he forced the capitulation of Forts Henry and Donelson—the first major Union victories of the war. He established himself at the siege of Vicksburg and soon thereafter commanded all Northern armies.*

*Grant understood that war meant killing. He knew that the North must pound away at the South to win. This earned him the reputation as a "butcher" who threw away lives. But his method worked and as the hero of the war, he twice won the presidency. He knew little about rich men and his administration was soon mired in corruption and scandal, which he managed to escape personally. Later, after a thirty-month speaking tour around the world, he put all his money into his son's investment firm. When the business collapsed in 1884, Grant was dying of throat cancer and nearly destitute.*

*To make money, he wrote a few short pieces for* Century Magazine *before his friend Samuel Clemens encouraged him to write his memoirs. Grant finished the two-volume work in 1885 just three days before cancer finished him. Grant depicted himself as a compassionate man who did his duty with what he had available. He criticized the manifest destiny of the Mexican War, regretted the lives lost in foolish charges during the Civil War, and showed a sense of humor not usually associated with him. The autobiography is a brilliant tour-de-force and may be the best personal military story ever written. Certainly, it is the finest literary work of substantial length ever penned by a president of the United States.*

The Personal Memoirs of U. S. Grant, *1885–86. Reprint, New York: Da Capo, 1982.*

"Man proposes and God disposes." There are but few important events in the affairs of men brought about by their own choice.

Although frequently urged by friends to write my memoirs I had determined never to do so, nor to write anything for publication. At the age of nearly sixty-two I received an injury from a fall, which confined me closely to the house while it did not apparently affect my general health. This made study a pleasant pastime. Shortly after, the rascality of a business partner [Ferdinand Ward] developed itself by the announcement of a failure. This was followed soon after by universal depression of all securities, which seemed to threaten the extinction of a good part of the income still retained, and for which I am indebted to the kindly act of friends. At this juncture the editor of the *Century Magazine* asked me to write a few articles for him. I consented for the money it gave me; for at that moment I was living upon borrowed money. The work I found congenial, and I determined to continue it. The event is an important one for me, for good or evil; I hope for the former.

In preparing these volumes for the public, I have entered upon the task with the sincere desire to avoid doing injustice to any one, whether on the National or Confederate side, other than the unavoidable injustice of not making mention often where special mention is due. There must be many errors of omission in this work, because the subject is too large to be treated of in two volumes in such way as to do justice to all the officers and men engaged. There were thousands of instances, during the rebellion, of individual, company, regimental and brigade deeds of heroism which deserve special mention and are not here alluded to. The troops engaged in them will have to look to the detailed reports of their individual commanders for the full history of those deeds.

The first volume, as well as a portion of the second, was written before I had reason to suppose I was in a critical condition of health. Later I was reduced almost to the point of death, and it became impossible for me to attend to anything for weeks. I have, however, somewhat regained my strength, and am able, often, to devote as many hours a day as a person should devote to such work. I would have more hope of satisfying the expectation of the public if I could have allowed myself more time. I have used my best efforts, with the aid of my eldest son, F. D. Grant, assisted by his brothers, to verify from the records every statement of fact given. The comments are my own, and show how I saw the matters treated of whether others saw them in the same light or not.

With these remarks I present these volumes to the public, asking no favor but hoping they will meet the approval of the reader.

U. S. GRANT

In June, 1821, my father, Jesse R. Grant, married Hannah Simpson. I was born on the 27th of April, 1822, at Point Pleasant, Clermont County, Ohio. In the fall

**ULYSSES S. GRANT**

of 1823 we moved to Georgetown, the county seat of Brown, the adjoining county east. This place remained my home, until at the age of seventeen, in 1839, I went to West Point.

The schools, at the time of which I write, were very indifferent. There were no free schools, and none in which the scholars were classified. They were all supported by subscription, and a single teacher—who was often a man or a woman incapable of teaching much, even if they imparted all they knew—would have thirty or forty scholars, male and female, from the infant learning the A B C's up to the young lady of eighteen and the boy of twenty, studying the highest branches taught—the three R's, "Reading, 'Riting, 'Rithmetic." I never saw an algebra, or other mathematical work higher than the arithmetic, in Georgetown, until after I was appointed to West Point. I then bought a work on algebra in Cincinnati; but having no teacher it was Greek to me.

My life in Georgetown was uneventful. From the age of five or six until seventeen, I attended the subscription schools of the village, except during the winters of 1836–7 and 1838–9. The former period was spent in Maysville, Kentucky, attending the school of Richardson and Rand; the latter in Ripley, Ohio, at a private school. I was not studious in habit, and probably did not make progress enough to compensate for the outlay for board and tuition. At all events both winters were spent in going over the same old arithmetic which I knew every word of before, and repeating: "A noun is the name of a thing," which I had also heard my Georgetown teachers repeat, until I had come to believe it—but I cast no reflections upon my old teacher, Richardson. He turned out bright scholars from his school, many of whom have filled conspicuous places in the service of their States. Two of my contemporaries there—who, I believe, never attended any other institution of learning—have held seats in Congress, and one, if not both, other high offices; these are Wadsworth and Brewster.

My father was, from my earliest recollection, in comfortable circumstances, considering the times, his place of residence, and the community in which he lived. Mindful of his own lack of facilities for acquiring an education, his greatest desire in maturer years was for the education of his children. Consequently, as stated before, I never missed a quarter from school from the time I was old enough to attend till the time of leaving home. This did not exempt me from labor. In my early days, every one labored more or less, in the region where my youth was spent, and more in proportion to their private means. It was only the very poor who were exempt. While my father carried on the manufacture of leather and worked at the trade himself, he owned and tilled considerable land. I detested the trade, preferring almost any other labor; but I was fond of agriculture, and of all employment in which horses were used. We had, among other lands, fifty acres of forest within a mile of the village. In the fall of the year choppers were employed to cut enough wood to last a twelve-month. When I was seven or eight years of age, I began hauling all the wood used in the house and shops. I could not load it on the wagons, of course, at that time, but I could drive, and the choppers would load, and some one at the house unload. When about eleven years old, I was strong enough to hold a plough. From that age until seventeen I did all the work done with horses, such as breaking up the land, furrowing, ploughing corn and potatoes, bringing in the crops when harvested, hauling all the wood, besides tending two or three horses, a cow or two, and sawing wood for stoves, etc., while still attending school. For this I was compensated by the fact that there was never any scolding or punishing by my parents; no objection to rational enjoyments, such as fishing, going to the creek a mile away to swim in summer, taking a horse and visiting my grandparents in the adjoining county, fifteen miles off, skating on the ice in winter, or taking a horse and sleigh when there was snow on the ground.

While still quite young I had visited Cincinnati, forty-five miles away, several times, alone; also Maysville, Kentucky, often, and once Louisville. The journey to Louisville was a big one for a boy of that day. I had also gone once with a two-horse carriage to Chillicothe, about seventy miles, with a neighbor's family, who were removing to Toledo, Ohio, and returned alone; and had gone once, in like manner, to Flat Rock, Kentucky, about seventy miles away. On this latter occasion I was fifteen years of age....

I have described enough of my early life to give an impression of the whole. I did not like to work; but I did as much of it, while young, as grown men can be hired to do in these days, and attended school at the same time. I had as many privileges as any boy in the village, and probably more than most of them. I have no recollection of ever having been punished at home, either by scolding or by the rod. But at school the case was different. The rod was freely used there, and I was not exempt from its influence. I can see John D. White—the school teacher—now, with his long beech switch always in his hand. It was not always the same one, either. Switches were brought in bundles, from a beech wood near the school house, by the boys for whose benefit they were intended. Often a whole bundle would be used up in a single day. I never had any hard feelings against my teacher, either while attending the school, or in later years when reflecting upon my experience. Mr. White was a kind-hearted man, and was much respected by the community in which he lived. He only followed the universal custom of the period, and that under which he had received his own education.

In the winter of 1838–9 I was attending school at Ripley, only ten miles distant from Georgetown, but spent the Christmas holidays at home. During this vacation my father received a letter from the Honorable Thomas Morris, then United States Senator from Ohio. When he read it he said to me, "Ulysses, I believe you are going to receive the appointment." "What appointment?" I inquired. "To West Point; I have applied for it." "But I won't go," I said. He said he thought I would, *and I thought so too, if he did.* I really had no objection to going to West Point, except that I had a very exalted idea of the acquirements necessary to get through. I did not believe I possessed them, and could not bear the idea of failing. There had been four boys from our village, or its immediate neighborhood, who had been graduated from West Point, and never a failure of any one appointed from Georgetown, except in the case of the one whose place I was to take. He was the son of Dr. Bailey, our nearest and most intimate neighbor. Young Bailey had been appointed in 1837. Finding before the January examination following that he could not pass, he resigned and went to a private school, and remained there until the following year when he was reappointed. Before the next examination he was dismissed. Dr. Bailey was a proud and sensitive man, and felt the failure of his son so keenly that he forbade his return home. There were no telegraphs in those days to disseminate news rapidly, no railroads west of the Alleghenies, and but few east; and above all, there were no reporters prying into other people's private affairs. Consequently it did not become generally known that there was a vacancy at West Point from our district until I was appointed. I presume Mrs. Bailey confided to my mother the fact that Bartlett had been dismissed, and that the doctor had forbidden his son's return home.

The Honorable Thomas L. Hamer, one of the ablest men Ohio ever produced, was our member of Congress at the time, and had the right of nomination. He and my father had been members of the same debating society (where they were generally pitted on opposite sides), and intimate personal friends from their early manhood up to a few years before. In politics they differed. Hamer was a life-long Democrat, while my father was a Whig. They had a warm discussion, which finally became angry—over some act of President Jackson, the removal of the deposit of public moneys, I think—after which they never spoke until after my appointment. I know both of them felt badly over this estrangement, and would have been glad at any time to come to a reconciliation; but neither would make the advance. Under these circumstances my father would not write to Hamer for the appointment, but he wrote to Thomas Morris, United States Senator from Ohio, informing him that there was a vacancy at West Point from our district, and that he would be glad if I could be appointed to fill it. This letter, I presume, was turned over to Mr. Hamer, and, as there was no other applicant, he cheerfully appointed me. This healed the breach between the two, never after reopened.

Besides the argument used by my father in favor of my going to West Point—that "he thought I would go"—there was another very strong inducement. I had always a great desire to travel. I was already the best travelled boy in Georgetown, except the sons of one man, John Walker, who had emigrated to Texas with his family, and immigrated back as soon as he could get the means to do so. In his short stay in Texas he acquired a very different opinion of the country from what one would form going there now.

I had been east to Wheeling, Virginia, and north to the Western Reserve, in Ohio, west to Louisville, and south to Bourbon County, Kentucky, besides having driven or ridden pretty much over the whole country within fifty miles of home. Going to West Point would give me the opportunity of visiting the two great cities of the continent, Philadelphia and New York. This was enough. When these places were visited I would have been glad to have had a steamboat or railroad collision, or any other accident happen, by which I might have received a temporary injury sufficient to make me ineligible, for a time, to enter the Academy. Nothing of the kind occurred, and I had to face the music.

Georgetown has a remarkable record for a western village. It is, and has been from its earliest existence, a democratic town. There was probably no time during the rebellion when, if the opportunity could have been afforded, it would not have voted for Jefferson Davis for President of the United States, over Mr. Lincoln, or any other representative of his party; unless it was immediately after some of John Morgan's men, in his celebrated raid through Ohio, spent a few hours in the village. The rebels helped themselves to whatever they could find, horses, boots and shoes, especially horses, and many ordered meals to be prepared for them by the families. This was no doubt a far pleasanter duty for some families than it would have been to render a like service for Union soldiers. The line between the Rebel and Union element in Georgetown was so marked that it led to divisions even in the churches. There were churches in that part of Ohio where treason was preached regularly, and where, to secure membership, hostility to the government, to the war and to the liberation of the slaves, was far more essential than a belief in the authenticity or credibility of the Bible. There were men in Georgetown who filled all the requirements for membership in these churches.

Yet this far-off western village, with a population, including old and young, male and female, of about one thousand—about enough for the organization of a single regiment if all had been men capable of bearing arms—furnished the Union army four general officers and one colonel, West Point graduates, and nine generals and field officers of Volunteers, that I can think of....

I took passage on a steamer at Ripley, Ohio, for Pittsburgh, about the middle of May, 1839. Western boats at that day did not make regular trips at stated times, but would stop anywhere, and for any length of time, for passengers or freight. I have myself been detained two or three days at a place after steam was up, the gang planks, all but one, drawn in, and after the time advertised for starting had expired. On this occasion we had no vexatious delays, and in about three days Pittsburgh was reached. From Pittsburgh I chose passage by the canal to Harrisburg, rather than by the more expeditious stage. This gave me a better opportunity of enjoying the fine scenery of Western Pennsylvania, and I had rather a dread of reaching my destination at all. At that time the canal was much patronized by travellers, and, with the comfortable packets of the period, no mode of conveyance could be more pleasant, when time was not an object. From Harrisburg to Philadelphia there was a railroad, the first I had ever seen, except the one on which I had just crossed the summit of the Allegheny Mountains, and over which canal boats were transported. In travelling by the road from Harrisburg, I thought the perfection of rapid transit had been reached. We travelled at least eighteen miles an hour, when at full speed, and made the whole distance averaging probably as much as twelve miles an hour. This seemed like annihilating space. I stopped five days in Philadelphia, saw about every street in the city, attended the theatre, visited Girard College (which was then in course of construction), and got reprimanded from home afterwards, for dallying by the way so long. My sojourn in New York was shorter, but long enough to enable me to see the city very well. I reported at West Point on the 30th or 31st of May, and about two weeks later passed my examination for admission, without difficulty, very much to my surprise.

A military life had no charms for me, and I had not the faintest idea of staying in the army even if I should be graduated, which I did not expect. The encampment which preceded the commencement of academic studies was very wearisome and uninteresting. When the 28th of August came—the date for breaking up camp and going into barracks—I felt as though I had been at West Point always, and that if I staid to graduation, I would have to remain always. I did not take hold of my studies with avidity, in fact I rarely ever read over a lesson the second time during my entire cadetship. I could not sit in my room doing nothing. There is a fine library connected with the Academy from which cadets can get books to read in their quarters. I devoted more time to these, than to books relating to the course of studies. Much of the time, I am sorry to say, was devoted to novels, but not those of a trashy sort. I read all of Bulwer's then published, Cooper's, Marryat's, Scott's, Washington Irving's works, Lever's, and many others that I do not now remember. Mathematics was very easy to me, so that when January came, I passed the examination, taking a good standing in that branch. In French, the only other study at that time in the first year's course, my standing was very low. In fact, if the class had been turned the other end foremost I should have been near head. I never succeeded in getting squarely at either end of my class, in any one study, during the four years. I came near it in French, artillery, infantry, and cavalry tactics, and conduct.

Early in the session of the Congress which met in December, 1839, a bill was discussed abolishing the Military Academy. I saw in this an honorable way to obtain a discharge, and read the debates with much interest, but with impatience at the delay in taking action, for I was selfish enough to favor the bill. It never passed, and a year later, although the time hung drearily with me, I would have been sorry to have seen it succeed. My idea then was to get through the course, secure a detail for a few years as assistant professor of mathematics at the Academy, and afterwards obtain a permanent position as professor in some respectable college; but circumstances always did shape my course different from my plans....

### [He graduated from West Point, chose cavalry, and was assigned to the infantry.]

On the 30th of September I reported for duty at Jefferson Barracks, St. Louis, with the 4th United States infantry. It was the largest military post in the country at that time, being garrisoned by sixteen companies of infantry, eight of the 3d regiment, the remainder of the 4th. Colonel Steven Kearney, one of the ablest officers of the day, commanded the post, and under him discipline was kept at a high standard, but without vexatious rules or regulations. Every drill and roll-call had to be attended, but in the intervals officers were permitted to enjoy themselves, leaving the garrison, and going where they pleased, without making written application to state where they were going for how long, etc., so that they were back for their next duty. It did seem to me, in my early army days, that too many of the older officers, when they came to command posts, made it a study to think what orders they could publish to annoy their subordinates and render them uncomfortable. I noticed, however, a few years later, when the Mexican war broke out, that most of this class of officers discovered they were possessed of disabilities which entirely incapacitated them for active field service. They had the moral courage to proclaim it, too. They were right; but they did not always give their disease the right name.

At West Point I had a class-mate—in the last year of our studies he was room-mate also—F. T. Dent, whose family resided some five miles west of Jefferson Barracks. Two of his unmarried brothers were living at home at that time, and as I had taken with me from Ohio, my horse, saddle and bridle, I soon found my way out to White Haven, the name of the Dent estate. As I found the family congenial my visits became frequent. There were at home, besides the young men, two daughters, one a school miss of fifteen, the other a girl of eight or nine. There was still an older daughter of seventeen, who had been spending several years at boarding-school in St. Louis, but who, though through school, had not yet returned home. She was spending the winter in the city with connections, the family of Colonel John O'Fallon, well known in St. Louis. In February she returned to her country home. After that I do not know but my visits became more frequent; they certainly did become more enjoyable. We would often take walks, or go on horseback to visit the neighbors, until I became quite well acquainted in that vicinity. Sometimes one of the brothers would accompany us, sometimes one of the younger sisters. If the 4th infantry had remained at Jefferson Barracks it is possible, even probable, that this life might have continued for some years without my finding out that there was anything serious the matter with me; but in the following May a circumstance occurred which developed my sentiment so palpably that there was no mistaking it.

The annexation of Texas was at this time the subject of violent discussion in Congress, in the press, and by individuals. The administration of President Tyler, then in power, was making the most strenuous efforts to effect the annexation, which was, indeed, the great and absorbing question of the day. During these discussions the greater part of the single rifle regiment in the army—the 2d dragoons, which had been dismounted a year or two before, and designated "Dismounted Rifles"—was stationed at Fort Jessup, Louisiana, some twenty-five miles east of the Texas line, to observe the frontier. About the 1st of May the 3d infantry was ordered from Jefferson Barracks to Louisiana, to go into camp in the neighborhood of Fort Jessup, and there await further orders. The troops were embarked on steamers and were on their way down the Mississippi within a few days after the receipt of this order. About the time they started I obtained a leave of absence for twenty days to go to Ohio to visit my parents. I was obliged to go to St. Louis to take a steamer for Louisville or Cincinnati, or the first steamer going up the Ohio River to any point. Before I left St. Louis orders were received at Jefferson Barracks for the 4th infantry to follow the 3d. A messenger was sent after me to stop my leaving; but before he could reach me I was off, totally ignorant of these events. A day or two after my arrival at Bethel I received a letter from a class-mate and fellow lieutenant in the 4th, informing me of the circumstances related above, and advising me not to open any letter postmarked St. Louis or Jefferson Barracks, until the expiration of my leave, and saying that he would pack up my things and take them along for me. His advice was not necessary, for no other letter was sent to me. I now discovered that I was exceedingly anxious to get back to Jefferson Barracks, and I understood the reason without explanation from any one. My leave of absence required me to report for duty, at Jefferson Barracks, at the end of twenty days. I knew my regiment had gone up the Red River, but I was not disposed to break the letter of my leave; besides, if I had proceeded to Louisiana direct, I could not have reached there until after the expiration of my leave. Accordingly, at the end of the twenty days, I reported for duty to Lieutenant Ewell, commanding at Jefferson Barracks, handing him at the same time my leave of absence. After noticing the phraseology of the order—leaves of absence were generally worded, "at the end of which time he will report for duty with his proper command"—he said he would give me an order to join my regiment in Louisiana. I then asked for a few days' leave before starting, which he readily granted. This was the same Ewell who acquired considerable reputation as a Confederate general during the rebellion. He was a man much esteemed, and deservedly so, in the old army, and proved himself a gallant and efficient officer in two wars—both in my estimation unholy.

I immediately procured a horse and started for the country, taking no baggage with me, of course. There is an insignificant creek—the Gravois—between Jefferson Barracks and the place to which I was going, and at that day there was not a bridge over it from its source to its mouth. There is not water enough in the creek at ordinary stages to run a coffee mill, and at low water there is none running whatever. On this occasion it had been raining heavily, and, when the creek was reached, I found the banks full to overflowing, and the current rapid. I looked at it a moment to consider what to do. One of my superstitions had always been when I started to go any where, or to do anything, not to turn back, or stop until the thing intended was accomplished. I have frequently started to go to places where I had never been and to which I did not know the way, depending upon making inquiries on the road, and if I got past the place without knowing it, instead of turning back, I would go on until a road was found turning in the right direction, take that, and come in by the other side. So I struck into the stream, and in an instant the horse was swimming and I being carried down by the current. I headed the horse towards the other bank and soon reached it, wet through and without other clothes on that side of the stream. I went on, however, to my destination and borrowed a dry suit from my—future—brother-in-law. We were not of the same size, but the clothes answered every purpose until I got more of my own.

Before I returned I mustered up courage to make known, in the most awkward manner imaginable, the discovery I had made on learning that the 4th infantry had been ordered away from Jefferson Barracks. The young lady afterwards admitted that she too, although until then she had never looked upon me other than as a visitor whose company was agreeable to her, had experienced a depression of spirits she could not account for when the regiment left. Before separating it was definitely understood that at a convenient time we would join our fortunes, and not let the removal of a regiment trouble us. This was in May, 1844. It was the 22d of August, 1848, before the fulfilment of this agreement. My duties kept me on the frontier of Louisiana with the Army of Observation during the pendency of Annexation; and afterwards I was absent through the war with Mexico, provoked by the action of the army, if not by the annexation itself. During that time there was a constant correspondence between Miss Dent and myself, but we only met once in the period of four years and three months. In May, 1845, I procured a leave for twenty days, visited St. Louis, and obtained the consent of the parents for the union, which had not been asked for before.

As already stated, it was never my intention to remain in the army long, but to prepare myself for a professorship in some college. Accordingly, soon after I was settled at Jefferson Barracks, I wrote a letter to Professor Church—Professor of Mathematics at West Point—requesting him to ask my designation as his assistant, when next a detail had to be made. Assistant professors at West Point are all officers of the army, supposed to be selected for their special fitness for the particular branch of study they are assigned to teach. The answer from Professor Church was entirely satisfactory, and no doubt I should have been detailed a year or two later but for the Mexican War coming on. Accordingly I laid out for myself a course of studies to be pursued in garrison, with regularity, if not persistency. I reviewed my West Point course of mathematics during the seven months at Jefferson Barracks, and read many valuable historical works, besides an occasional novel. To help my memory I kept a book in which I would write up, from time to time, my recollections of all I had read since last posting it. When the regiment was ordered away, I being absent at the time, my effects were packed up by Lieutenant Haslett, of the 4th infantry, and taken along. I never saw my journal after, nor did I ever keep another, except for a portion of the time while travelling abroad. Often since a fear has crossed my mind lest that book might turn up yet, and fall into the hands of some malicious person who would publish it. I know its appearance would cause me as much heart-burning as my youthful horse trade, or the later rebuke for wearing uniform clothes.

The 3d infantry had selected camping grounds on the reservation at Fort Jessup, about midway between the Red River and the Sabine. Our orders required us to go into camp in the same neighborhood, and await further instructions. Those authorized to do so selected a place in the pine woods, between the old town of Natchitoches and Grand Ecore, about three miles from each, and on high ground back from the river. The place was given the name of Camp Salubrity, and proved entitled to it. The camp was on a high, sandy, pine ridge, with spring branches in the valley, in front and rear. The springs furnished an abundance of cool, pure water, and the ridge was above the flight of mosquitoes, which abound in that region in great multitudes and of great voracity. In the valley they swarmed in myriads, but never came to the summit of the ridge. The regiment occupied this camp six months before the first death occurred, and that was caused by an accident.

There was no intimation given that the removal of the 3d and 4th regiments of infantry to the western border of Louisiana was occasioned in any way by the prospective annexation of Texas, but it was generally understood that such was the case. Ostensibly we were intended to prevent filibustering in Texas, but really as a menace to Mexico in case she appeared to contemplate war. Generally the officers of the army were indifferent whether the annexation was consummated or not; but not so all of them. For myself, I was bitterly opposed to the measure, and to this day regard the war which resulted as one of the most unjust ever waged by a stronger against a weaker nation. It was an instance of a republic following the bad example of European monarchies, in not considering justice in their desire to acquire additional territory.

Texas was originally a state belonging to the republic of Mexico. It extended from the Sabine River on the east to the Rio Grande on the west, and from the Gulf of Mexico on the south and east to the territory of the United States and New Mexico—another Mexican state at that time—on the north and west. An empire in territory, it had but a very sparse population, until settled by Americans who had received authority from Mexico to colonize. These colonists paid very little attention to the supreme government, and introduced slavery into the state almost from the start, though the constitution of Mexico did not, nor does it now, sanction that institution. Soon they set up an independent government of their own, and war existed, between Texas and Mexico, in name from that time until 1836, when active hostilities very nearly ceased upon the capture of Santa Anna, the Mexican President. Before long, however, the same people—who with permission of Mexico had colonized Texas, and afterwards set up slavery there, and then seceded as soon as they felt strong enough to do so—offered themselves and the State to the United States, and in 1845 their offer was accepted. The occupation, separation and annexation were, from the inception of the movement to its final consummation, a conspiracy to acquire territory out of which slave states might be formed for the American Union.

Even if the annexation itself could be justified, the manner in which the subsequent war was forced upon Mexico cannot. The fact is, annexationists wanted more territory than they could possibly lay any claim to, as part of the new acquisition. Texas, as an independent State, never had exercised jurisdiction over the territory between the Nueces River and the Rio Grande. Mexico had never recognized the independence of Texas, and maintained that, even if independent, the State had no claim south of the Nueces. I am aware that a treaty, made by the Texans with Santa Anna while he was under duress, ceded all the territory between the Nueces and the Rio Grande; but he was a prisoner of war when the treaty was made, and his life was in jeopardy. He knew, too, that he deserved execution at the hands of the Texans, if they should ever capture him. The

Texans, if they had taken his life, would have only followed the example set by Santa Anna himself a few years before, when he executed the entire garrison of the Alamo and the villagers of Goliad.

In taking military possession of Texas after annexation, the army of occupation, under General Taylor, was directed to occupy the disputed territory. The army did not stop at the Nueces and offer to negotiate for a settlement of the boundary question, but went beyond, apparently in order to force Mexico to initiate war. It is to the credit of the American nation, however, that after conquering Mexico, and while practically holding the country in our possession, so that we could have retained the whole of it, or made any terms we chose, we paid a round sum for the additional territory taken; more than it was worth, or was likely to be, to Mexico. To us it was an empire and of incalculable value; but it might have been obtained by other means. The Southern rebellion was largely the outgrowth of the Mexican war. Nations, like individuals, are punished for their transgressions. We got our punishment in the most sanguinary and expensive war of modern times....

**[His unit went first to New Orleans, then to Corpus Christi, Texas territory, the launching port for the invasion of Mexico.]**

General Zachary Taylor commanded the whole. There were troops enough in one body to establish a drill and discipline sufficient to fit men and officers for all they were capable of in case of battle. The rank and file were composed of men who had enlisted in time of peace, to serve for seven dollars a month, and were necessarily inferior as material to the average volunteers enlisted later in the war expressly to fight, and also to the volunteers in the war for the preservation of the Union. The men engaged in the Mexican war were brave, and the officers of the regular army, from highest to lowest, were educated in their profession. A more efficient army for its number and armament I do not believe ever fought a battle than the one commanded by General Taylor in his first two engagements on Mexican—or Texas soil.

The presence of United States troops on the edge of the disputed territory furthest from the Mexican settlements, was not sufficient to provoke hostilities. We were sent to provoke a fight, but it was essential that Mexico should commence it. It was very doubtful whether Congress would declare war; but if Mexico should attack our troops, the Executive could announce, "Whereas, war exists by the acts of, etc.," and prosecute the contest with vigor. Once initiated there were but few public men who would have the courage to oppose it. Experience proves that the man who obstructs a war in which his nation is engaged, no matter whether right or wrong, occupies no enviable place in life or history. Better for him, individually, to advocate "war, pestilence, and famine," than to act as obstructionist to a war already begun. The history of the defeated rebel will be honorable hereafter, compared with that of the Northern man who aided him by conspiring against his government while protected by it. The most favorable posthumous history the stay-at-home traitor can hope for is—oblivion.

Mexico showing no willingness to come to the Nueces to drive the invaders from her soil, it became necessary for the "invaders" to approach to within a convenient distance to be struck. Accordingly, preparations were begun for moving the army to the Rio Grande, to a point near Matamoras. It was desirable to occupy a position near the largest centre of population to reach, without absolutely invading territory to which we set up no claim whatever....

I had never been a sportsman in my life; had scarcely ever gone in search of game, and rarely seen any when looking for it. On this trip there was no minute of time while travelling between San Patricio and the settlements on the San Antonio River, from San Antonio to Austin, and again from the Colorado River back to San Patricio, when deer or antelope could not be seen in great numbers. Each officer carried a shot-gun, and every evening after going into camp, some would go out and soon return with venison and wild turkeys enough for the entire camp. I, however, never went out, and had no occasion to fire my gun; except, being detailed over a day at Goliad, Benjamin and I concluded to go down to the creek—which was fringed with timber, much of it the pecan—and bring back a few turkeys. We had scarcely reached the edge of the timber when I heard the flutter of wings overhead, and in an instant I saw two or three turkeys flying away. These were soon followed by more, then more, and more, until a flock of twenty or thirty had left from just over my head. All this time I stood watching the turkeys to see where they flew—with my gun on my shoulder, and never once thought of levelling it at the birds. When I had time to reflect upon the matter, I came to the conclusion that as a sportsman I was a failure, and went back to the house. Benjamin remained out, and got as many turkeys as he wanted to carry back.

After the second night at Goliad, Benjamin and I started to make the remainder of the journey alone. We reached Corpus Christi just in time to avoid "absence without leave." We met no one—not even an Indian—during the remainder of our journey, except at San Patricio. A new settlement had been started there in our absence of three weeks, induced possibly by the fact that there were houses already built, while the proximity of troops gave protection against the Indians. On the evening of the first day out from Goliad we heard the most unearthly howling of wolves, directly in our front. The prairie grass was tall and we could not see the beasts, but the sound indicated that they were near. To my ear it appeared that there must have been enough of them to devour our party, horses and all, at a single meal. The part of Ohio that I hailed from was not thickly settled, but wolves had been driven out long before I left. Benjamin was from Indiana, still less populated, where the wolf yet roamed over the prairies. He understood the nature of the animal and the capacity of a few to make believe there was an unlimited number of them. He kept on towards the noise, unmoved. I followed in his trail, lacking moral courage to turn back and join our sick companion. I have no doubt that if Benjamin had proposed returning to Goliad, I would not only have "seconded the motion" but have suggested that it was very hard-hearted in us to leave Augur sick there in the first place; but Benjamin did not propose turning back. When he did speak it was to ask: "Grant, how many wolves do you think there are in that pack?" Knowing where he was from, and suspecting that he thought I would overestimate the number, I determined to show my acquaintance with the animal by putting the estimate below what possibly could be correct, and answered: "Oh, about twenty," very indifferently. He smiled and rode on. In a minute we were close upon them, and before they saw us. There were just *two* of them. Seated upon their haunches, their mouths close together, they had made all the noise we had been hearing for the past ten minutes. I have often thought of this incident since when I have heard the noise of a few disappointed politicians who had deserted their associates. There are always more of them before they are counted. . . .

**[Grant fought in the Mexican War and met many of the generals he would later confront in the Civil War.]**

My experience in the Mexican war was of great advantage to me afterwards. Besides the many practical lessons it taught, the war brought nearly all the officers of the regular army together so as to make them personally acquainted. It also brought them in contact with volunteers, many of whom served in the war of the rebellion afterwards. Then, in my particular case, I had been at West Point at about the right time to meet most of the graduates who were of a suitable age at the breaking out of the rebellion to be trusted with large commands. Graduating in 1843, I was at the military academy from one to four years with all cadets who graduated between 1840 and 1846—seven classes. These classes embraced more than fifty officers who afterwards became generals on one side or the other in the rebellion, many of them holding high commands. All the older officers, who became conspicuous in the rebellion, I had also served with and known in Mexico: Lee, J. E. Johnston, A. S. Johnston, Holmes, Herbért and a number of others on the Confederate side; McCall, Mansfield, Phil. Kearney and others on the National side. The acquaintance thus formed was of immense service to me in the war of the rebellion—I mean what I learned of the characters of those to whom I was afterwards opposed. I do not pretend to say that all movements, or even many of them, were made with special reference to the characteristics of the commander against whom they were directed. But my appreciation of my enemies was certainly affected by this knowledge. The natural disposition of most people is to clothe a commander of a large army whom they do not known, with almost superhuman abilities. A large part of the National army, for instance, and most of the press of the country, clothed General Lee with just such qualities, but I had known him personally, and knew that he was mortal; and it was just as well that I felt this.

The treaty of peace was at last ratified, and the evacuation of Mexico by United States troops was ordered. Early in June the troops in the City of Mexico began to move out. Many of them, including the brigade to which I belonged, were assembled at Jalapa, above the vomito, to await the arrival of transports at Vera Cruz: but with all this precaution my regiment and others were in camp on the sand beach in a July sun, for about a week before embarking, while the fever raged with great virulence in Vera Cruz, not two miles away. I can call to mind only one person, an officer, who died of the disease. My regiment was sent to Pascagoula, Mississippi, to spend the summer. As soon as it was settled in camp I obtained a leave of absence for four months and proceeded to St. Louis. On the 22d of August, 1848, I was married to Miss Julia Dent, the lady of whom I have before spoken. We visited my parents and relations in Ohio, and, at the end of my leave, proceeded to my post at Sackett's Harbor, New York. In April following I was ordered to Detroit, Michigan, where two years were spent with but few important incidents. . . .

San Francisco at that day was a lively place. Gold, or placer digging as it was called, was at its height. Steamers plied daily between San Francisco and both

Stockton and Sacramento. Passengers and gold from the southern mines came by the Stockton boat; from the northern mines by Sacramento. In the evening when these boats arrived, Long Wharf—there was but one wharf in San Francisco in 1852—was alive with people crowding to meet the miners as they came down to sell their "dust" and to "have a time." Of these some were runners for hotels, boarding houses or restaurants; others belonged to a class of impecunious adventurers, of good manners and good presence, who were ever on the alert to make the acquaintance of people with some ready means, in the hope of being asked to take a meal at a restaurant. Many were young men of good family, good education and gentlemanly instincts. Their parents had been able to support them during their minority, and to give them good educations, but not to maintain them afterwards. From 1849 to 1853 there was a rush of people to the Pacific coast, of the class described. All thought that fortunes were to be picked up, without effort, in the gold fields on the Pacific. Some realized more than their most sanguine expectations; but for one such there were hundreds disappointed, many of whom now fill unknown graves; others died wrecks of their former selves, and many, without a vicious instinct, became criminals and outcasts. Many of the real scenes in early California life exceed in strangeness and interest any of the mere products of the brain of the novelist.

Those early days in California brought out character. It was a long way off then, and the journey was expensive. The fortunate could go by Cape Horn or by the Isthmus of Panama; but the mass of pioneers crossed the plains with their ox-teams. This took an entire summer. They were very lucky when they got through with a yoke of wornout cattle. All other means were exhausted in procuring the outfit on the Missouri River. The immigrant, on arriving, found himself a stranger, in a strange land, far from friends. Time pressed, for the little means that could be realized from the sale of what was left of the outfit would not support a man long at California prices. Many became discouraged. Others would take off their coats and look for a job, no matter what it might be. These succeeded as a rule. There were many young men who had studied professions before they went to California, and who had never done a day's manual labor in their lives, who took in the situation at once and went to work to make a start at anything they could get to do. Some supplied carpenters and masons with material—carrying plank, brick, or mortar, as the case might be; others drove stages, drays, or baggage wagons, until they could do better. More became discouraged early and spent their time looking up people who would "treat," or lounging about restaurants and gambling houses where free lunches were furnished daily. They were welcomed at these places because they often brought in miners who proved good customers.

My regiment spent a few weeks at Benicia barracks, and then was ordered to Fort Vancouver, on the Columbia River, then in Oregon Territory. During the winter of 1852–3 the territory was divided, all north of the Columbia River being taken from Oregon to make Washington Territory.

Prices for all kinds of supplies were so high on the Pacific coast from 1849 until at least 1853—that it would have been impossible for officers of the army to exist upon their pay, if it had not been that authority was given them to purchase from the commissary such supplies as he kept, at New Orleans wholesale prices. A cook could not be hired for the pay of a captain. The cook could do better. At Benicia, in 1852, flour was 25 cents per pound; potatoes were 16 cents; beets, turnips and cabbage, 6 cents; onions, 37½ cents; meat and other articles in proportion. In 1853 at Vancouver vegetables were a little lower. I with three other officers concluded that we would raise a crop for ourselves, and by selling the surplus realize something handsome. I bought a pair of horses that had crossed the plains that summer and were very poor. They recuperated rapidly, however, and proved a good team to break up the ground with. I performed all the labor of breaking up the ground while the other officers planted the potatoes. Our crop was enormous. Luckily for us the Columbia River rose to a great height from the melting of the snow in the mountains in June, and overflowed and killed most of our crop. This saved digging it up, for everybody on the Pacific coast seemed to have come to the conclusion at the same time that agriculture would be profitable. In 1853 more than three-quarters of the potatoes raised were permitted to rot in the ground, or had to be thrown away. The only potatoes we sold were to our own mess.

While I was stationed on the Pacific coast we were free from Indian wars. There were quite a number of remnants of tribes in the vicinity of Portland in Oregon, and of Fort Vancouver in Washington Territory. They had generally acquired some of the vices of civilization, but none of the virtues, except in individual cases. The Hudson's Bay Company had held the North-west with their trading posts for many years before the United States was represented on the Pacific coast. They still retained posts along the Columbia River and one at Fort Vancouver, when I was there. Their treatment of the Indians had brought out the better qualities of the savages. Farming had been undertaken by the company to supply the Indians with bread and vegetables; they raised some cattle and horses; and they had now taught the Indians to do the labor of the farm and herd. They always compensated them for their labor, and always gave them goods of uniform quality and at uniform price.

Before the advent of the American, the medium of exchange between the Indian and the white man was pelts. Afterward it was silver coin. If an Indian received in the sale of a horse a fifty dollar gold piece, not an infrequent occurrence, the first thing he did was to exchange it for American half dollars. These he could count. He would then commence his purchases, paying for each article separately, as he got it. He would not trust any one to add up the bill and pay it all at once. At that day fifty dollar gold pieces, not the issue of the government, were common on the Pacific coast. They were called slugs.

The Indians, along the lower Columbia as far as the Cascades and on the lower Williamette, died off very fast during the year I spent in that section; for besides acquiring the vices of the white people they had acquired also their diseases. The measles and the small-pox were both amazingly fatal....

My family, all this while, was at the East. It consisted now of a wife and two children. I saw no chance of supporting them on the Pacific coast out of my pay as an army officer. I concluded, therefore, to resign, and in March applied for a leave of absence until the end of July following, tendering my resignation to take effect at the end of that time. I left the Pacific coast very much attached to it, and with the full expectation of making it my future home. That expectation and that hope remained uppermost in my mind until the Lieutenant-Generalcy bill was introduced into Congress in the winter of 1863–4. The passage of that bill, and my promotion, blasted my last hope of ever becoming a citizen of the further West.

In the late summer of 1854 I rejoined my family, to find in it a son whom I had never seen, born while I was on the Isthmus of Panama. I was now to commence, at the age of thirty-two, a new struggle for our support. My wife had a farm near

St. Louis, to which we went, but I had no means to stock it. A house had to be built also. I worked very hard, never losing a day because of bad weather, and accomplished the object in a moderate way. If nothing else could be done I would load a cord of wood on a wagon and take it to the city for sale. I managed to keep along very well until 1858, when I was attacked by fever and ague. I had suffered very severely and for a long time from this disease, while a boy in Ohio. It lasted now over a year, and, while it did not keep me in the house, it did interfere greatly with the amount of work I was able to perform. In the fall of 1858 I sold out my stock, crops and farming utensils at auction, and gave up farming.

In the winter I established a partnership with Harry Boggs, a cousin of Mrs. Grant, in the real estate agency business. I spent that winter at St. Louis myself, but did not take my family into town until the spring. Our business might have become prosperous if I had been able to wait for it to grow. As it was, there was no more than one person could attend to, and not enough to support two families. While a citizen of St. Louis and engaged in the real estate agency business, I was a candidate for the office of county engineer, an office of respectability and emolument which would have been very acceptable to me at that time. The incumbent was appointed by the county court, which consisted of five members. My opponent had the advantage of birth over me (he was a citizen by adoption) and carried off the prize. I now withdrew from the copartnership with Boggs, and, in May, 1860, removed to Galena, Illinois, and took a clerkship in my father's store.

While a citizen of Missouri, my first opportunity for casting a vote at a Presidential election occurred. I had been in the army from before attaining my majority and had thought but little about politics, although I was a Whig by education and a great admirer of Mr. Clay. But the Whig party had ceased to exist before I had an opportunity of exercising the privilege of casting a ballot; the Know-Nothing party had taken its place, but was on the wane; and the Republican party was in a chaotic state and had not yet received a name. It had no existence in the Slave States except at points on the borders next to Free States. In St. Louis City and County, what afterwards became the Republican party was known as the Free-Soil Democracy, led by the Honorable Frank P. Blair. Most of my neighbors had known me as an officer of the army with Whig proclivities. They had been on the same side, and, on the death of their party, many had become Know-Nothings, or members of the American party. There was a lodge near my new home, and I was invited to join it. I accepted the invitation; was initiated; attended a meeting just one week later, and never went to another afterwards.

I have no apologies to make for having been one week a member of the American party; for I still think native-born citizens of the United States should have as much protection, as many privileges in their native country, as those who voluntarily select it for a home. But all secret, oath-bound political parties are dangerous to any nation, no matter how pure or how patriotic the motives and principles which first bring them together. No political party can or ought to exist when one of its cornerstones is opposition to freedom of thought and to the right to worship God "according to the dictate of one's own conscience," or according to the creed of any religious denomination whatever. Nevertheless, if a sect sets up its laws as binding above the State laws, wherever the two come in conflict this claim must be resisted and suppressed at whatever cost.

Up to the Mexican war there were a few out and out abolitionists, men who carried their hostility to slavery into all elections, from those for a justice of the peace up to the Presidency of the United States. They were noisy but not numerous. But the great majority of people at the North, where slavery did not exist, were opposed to the institution, and looked upon its existence in any part of the country as unfortunate. They did not hold the States where slavery existed responsible for it; and believed that protection should be given to the right of property in slaves until some satisfactory way could be reached to be rid of the institution. Opposition to slavery was not a creed of either political party. In some sections more anti-slavery men belonged to the Democratic party, and in others to the Whigs. But with the inauguration of the Mexican war, in fact with the annexation of Texas, "the inevitable conflict" commenced.

As the time for the Presidential election of 1856—the first at which I had the opportunity of voting—approached, party feeling began to run high. The Republican party was regarded in the South and the border States not only as opposed to the extension of slavery, but as favoring the compulsory abolition of the institution without compensation to the owners. The most horrible visions seemed to present themselves to the minds of people who, one would suppose, ought to have known better. Many educated and, otherwise, sensible persons appeared to believe that emancipation meant social equality. Treason to the Government was openly advocated and was not rebuked. It was evident to my mind that the election of a Republican President in 1856 meant the secession of all the Slave States, and rebellion. Under these circumstances I preferred the success of a candidate whose election would prevent or postpone secession, to seeing the country plunged into a war the end of which no man could foretell. With a Democrat elected by the unanimous vote of the Slave States, there could be no pretext for secession for four years. I very much hoped that the passions of the people would subside in that time, and the catastrophe be averted altogether; if it was not, I believed the country would be better prepared to receive the shock and to resist it. I therefore voted for James Buchanan for President. Four years later the Republican party was successful in electing its candidate to the Presidency. The civilized world has learned the consequence. Four millions of human beings held as chattels have been liberated; the ballot has been given to them; the free schools of the country have been opened to their children. The nation still lives, and the people are just as free to avoid social intimacy with the blacks as ever they were, or as they are with white people.

While living in Galena I was nominally only a clerk supporting myself and family on a stipulated salary. In reality my position was different. My father had never lived in Galena himself, but had established my two brothers there, the one next younger than myself in charge of the business, assisted by the youngest. When I went there it was my father's intention to give up all connection with the business himself, and to establish his three sons in it; but the brother who had really built up the business was sinking with consumption, and it was not thought best to make any change while he was in this condition. He lived until September, 1861, when he succumbed to that insidious disease which always flatters its victims into the belief that they are growing better up to the close of life. A more honorable man never transacted business. In September, 1861, I was engaged in an employment which required all my attention elsewhere.

During the eleven months that I lived in Galena prior to the first call for volunteers, I had been strictly attentive to my business, and had made but few acquaintances other than customers and people engaged in the same line with myself. When the election took place in November, 1860, I had not been a resident of Illinois long enough to gain citizenship and could not, therefore, vote. I was really glad of this at the time, for my pledges would have compelled me to vote for Stephen A. Douglas, who had no possible chance of election. The contest was really between Mr. Breckinridge and Mr. Lincoln; between minority rule and rule by the majority. I wanted, as between these candidates, to see Mr. Lincoln elected. Excitement ran high during the canvass, and torch-light processions enlivened the scene in the generally quiet streets of Galena many nights during the campaign. I did not parade with either party, but occasionally met with the "wide awakes"—Republicans—in their rooms, and superintended their drill. It was evident, from the time of the Chicago nomination to the close of the canvass, that the election of the Republican candidate would be the signal for some of the Southern States to secede. I still had hopes that the four years which had elapsed since the first nomination of a Presidential candidate by a party distinctly opposed to slavery extension, had given time for the extreme pro-slavery sentiment to cool down; for the Southerners to think well before they took the awful leap which they had so vehemently threatened. But I was mistaken.

The Republican candidate was elected, and solid substantial people of the North-west, and I presume the same order of people throughout the entire North, felt very serious, but determined, after this event. It was very much discussed whether the South would carry out its threat to secede and set up a separate government, the corner-stone of which should be, protection to the "Divine" institution of slavery. For there were people who believed in the "divinity" of human slavery, as there are now people who believe Mormonism and Polygamy to be ordained by the Most High. We forgive them for entertaining such notions, but forbid their practice. It was generally believed that there would be a flurry; that some of the extreme Southern States would go so far as to pass ordinances of secession. But the common impression was that this step was so plainly suicidal for the South, that the movement would not spread over much of the territory and would not last long.

Doubtless the founders of our government, the majority of them at least, regarded the confederation of the colonies as an experiment. Each colony considered itself a separate government; that the confederation was for mutual protection against a foreign foe, and the prevention of strife and war among themselves. If there had been a desire on the part of any single State to withdraw from the compact at any time while the number of States was limited to the original thirteen, I do not suppose there would have been any to contest the right, no matter how much the determination might have been regretted. The problem changed on the ratification of the Constitution by all the colonies; it changed still more when amendments were added; and if the right of any one State to withdraw continued to exist at all after the ratification of the Constitution, it certainly ceased on the formation of new States, at least so far as the new States themselves were concerned. It was never possessed at all by Florida or the States west of the Mississippi, all of which were purchased by the treasury of the entire nation. Texas and the territory brought into the Union in consequence of annexation, were purchased with both blood and treasure; and Texas, with a domain greater than that of any European state except Russia, was permitted to retain as state property all the public lands within its borders. It would have been ingratitude and injustice of the most flagrant sort for this State to withdraw from the Union after all that had been spent and done to introduce her; yet, if separation had actually occurred, Texas must necessarily have gone with the South, both on account of her institutions and her geographical position. Secession was illogical as well as impracticable; it was revolution.

Now, the right of revolution is an inherent one. When people are oppressed by their government, it is a natural right they enjoy to relieve themselves of the oppression, if they are strong enough, either by withdrawal from it, or by overthrowing it and substituting a government more acceptable. But any people or part of a people who resort to this remedy, stake their lives, their property, and every claim for protection given by citizenship—on the issue. Victory, or the conditions imposed by the conqueror—must be the result.

In the case of the war between the States it would have been the exact truth if the South had said,—"We do not want to live with you Northern people any longer; we know our institution of slavery is obnoxious to you, and, as you are growing numerically stronger than we, it may at some time in the future be endangered. So long as you permitted us to control the government, and with the aid of a few friends at the North to enact laws constituting your section a guard against the escape of our property, we were willing to live with you. You have been submissive to our rule heretofore; but it looks now as if you did not intend to continue so, and we will remain in the Union no longer." Instead of this the seceding States cried lustily,—"Let us alone; you have no constitutional power to interfere with us." Newspapers and people at the North reiterated the cry. Individuals might ignore the constitution; but the Nation itself must not only obey it, but must enforce the strictest construction of that instrument; the construction put upon it by the Southerners themselves. The fact is the constitution did not apply to any such contingency as the one existing from 1861 to 1865. Its framers never dreamed of such a contingency occurring. If they had foreseen it, the probabilities are they would have sanctioned the right of a State or States to withdraw rather than that there should be war between brothers.

The framers were wise in their generation and wanted to do the very best possible to secure their own liberty and independence, and that also of their descendants to the latest days. It is preposterous to suppose that the people of one generation can lay down the best and only rules of government for all who are to come after them, and under unforeseen contingencies. At the time of the framing of our constitution the only physical forces that had been subdued and made to serve man and do his labor, were the currents in the streams and in the air we breathe. Rude machinery, propelled by water power, had been invented; sails to propel ships upon the waters had been set to catch the passing breeze—but the application of steam to propel vessels against both wind and current, and machinery to do all manner of work had not been thought of. The instantaneous transmission of messages around the world by means of electricity would probably at that day have been attributed to witchcraft or a league with the Devil. Immaterial circumstances had changed as greatly as material ones. We could not and ought not to be rigidly bound by the rules laid down under circumstances so different for emergencies so utterly unanticipated. The fathers themselves would have been the first to declare that their prerogatives were not irrevocable. They would surely have resisted secession could they have lived to see the shape it assumed.

I travelled through the Northwest considerably during the winter of 1860–1. We had customers in all the little towns in south-west Wisconsin, south-east Minnesota and north-east Iowa. These generally knew I had been a captain in the regular army and had served through the Mexican war. Consequently wherever I stopped at night, some of the people would come to the public-house where I was, and sit till a late hour discussing the probabilities of the future....

[With the call for volunteers, he helped recruit Illinois regiments and accepted a commission as a colonel. In August, Grant was a brigadier-general. With victories at Forts Henry and Donelson, he became a major-general. He won the battle of Shiloh but was accused of poor leadership. In 1863 he led the siege against Vicksburg and cut the Confederacy in two with his victory.]

The capture of Vicksburg, with its garrison, ordnance and ordnance stores, and the successful battles fought in reaching them, gave new spirit to the loyal people of the North. New hopes for the final success of the cause of the Union were inspired. The victory gained at Gettysburg, upon the same day, added to their hopes. Now the Mississippi river was entirely in the possession of the National troops; for the fall of Vicksburg gave us Port Hudson at once. The army of northern Virginia was driven out of Pennsylvania and forced back to about the same ground it occupied in 1861. The Army of the Tennessee united with the Army of the Gulf, dividing the Confederate States completely....

At Vicksburg 31,600 prisoners were surrendered, together with 172 cannon, about 60,000 muskets and a large amount of ammunition. The small-arms of the enemy were far superior to the bulk of ours. Up to this time our troops at the West had been limited to the old United States flint-lock muskets changed into percussion, or the Belgium musket imported early in the war—almost as dangerous to the person firing it as to the one aimed at—and a few new and improved arms. These were of many different calibers, a fact that caused much trouble in distributing ammunition during an engagement. The enemy had generally new arms which had run the blockade and were of uniform caliber. After the surrender I authorized all colonels whose regiments were armed with inferior muskets, to place them in the stack of captured arms and replace them with the latter. A large number of arms turned in to the Ordnance Department as captured, were thus arms that had really been used by the Union army in the capture of Vicksburg.

In this narrative I have not made the mention I should like of officers, dead and alive, whose services entitle them to special mention. Neither have I made that mention of the navy which its services deserve. Suffice it to say, the close of the siege of Vicksburg found us with an army unsurpassed, in proportion to its numbers, taken as a whole of officers and men. A military education was acquired which no other school could have given. Men who thought a company was quite enough for them to command properly at the beginning, would have made good regimental or brigade commanders; most of the brigade commanders were equal to the command of a division, and one, Ransom, would have been equal to the command of a corps at least. Logan and Crocker ended the campaign fitted to command independent armies.

General F. P. Blair joined me at Milliken's Bend a full-fledged general, without having served in a lower grade. He commanded a division in the campaign. I had known Blair in Missouri, where I had voted against him in 1858 when he ran for Congress. I knew him as a frank, positive and generous man, true to his friends even to a fault, but always a leader. I dreaded his coming; I knew from experience that it was more difficult to command two generals desiring to be leaders than it was to command one army officered intelligently and with subordination. It affords me the greatest pleasure to record now my agreeable disappointment in respect to his character. There was no man braver than he, nor was there any who obeyed all orders of his superior in rank with more unquestioning alacrity. He was one man as a soldier, another as a politician.

The navy under Porter was all it could be, during the entire campaign. Without its assistance the campaign could not have been successfully made with twice the number of men engaged. It could not have been made at all, in the way it was, with any number of men without such assistance. The most perfect harmony reigned between the two arms of the service. There never was a request made, that I am aware of, either of the flag-officer or any of his subordinates, that was not promptly complied with.

The campaign of Vicksburg was suggested and developed by circumstances. The elections of 1862 had gone against the prosecution of the war. Voluntary enlistments had nearly ceased and the draft had been resorted to; this was resisted, and a defeat or backward movement would have made its execution impossible. A forward movement to a decisive victory was necessary. Accordingly I resolved to get below Vicksburg, unite with Banks against Port Hudson, make New Orleans a base and, with that base and Grand Gulf as a starting point, move our combined forces against Vicksburg. Upon reaching Grand Gulf, after running its batteries and fighting a battle, I received a letter from Banks informing me that he could not be at Port Hudson under ten days, and then with only fifteen thousand men. The time was worth more than the reinforcements; I therefore determined to push into the interior of the enemy's country.

With a large river behind us, held above and below by the enemy, rapid movements were essential to success. Jackson was captured the day after a new commander had arrived, and only a few days before large reinforcements were expected. A rapid movement west was made; the garrison of Vicksburg was met in two engagements and badly defeated, and driven back into its stronghold and there successfully besieged. It looks now as though Providence had directed the course of the campaign while the Army of the Tennessee executed the decree.

Upon the surrender of the garrison of Vicksburg there were three things that required immediate attention. The first was to send a force to drive the enemy from our rear, and out of the State. The second was to send reinforcements to Banks near Port Hudson, if necessary, to complete the triumph of opening the Mississippi from its source to its mouth to the free navigation of vessels bearing the Stars and Stripes. The third was to inform the authorities at Washington and the North of the good news, to relieve their long suspense and strengthen their confidence in the ultimate success of the cause they had so much at heart....

There was no time during the rebellion when I did not think, and often say, that the South was more to be benefited by its defeat than the North. The latter had the people, the institutions, and the territory to make a great and prosperous nation. The former was burdened with an institution abhorrent to all civilized people not brought up under it, and one which degraded labor, kept it in ignorance, and enervated the governing class. With the outside world at war with this institution, they could not have extended their territory. The labor of the country was not skilled, nor allowed to become so. The whites could not toil without becoming degraded, and those who did were denominated "poor white trash." The system of labor would have soon exhausted the soil and left the people poor.

The non-slaveholders would have left the country, and the small slaveholder must have sold out to his more fortunate neighbor. Soon the slaves would have out-numbered the masters, and, not being in sympathy with them, would have risen in their might and exterminated them. The war was expensive to the South as well as to the North, both in blood and treasure, but it was worth all it cost....

After we had secured the opening of a line over which to bring our supplies to the army, I made a personal inspection to see the situation of the pickets of the two armies. As I have stated, Chattanooga Creek comes down the centre of the valley to within a mile or such a matter of the town of Chattanooga, then bears off westerly, then north-westerly, and enters the Tennessee River at the foot of Lookout Mountain. This creek, from its mouth up to where it bears off west, lay between the two lines of pickets, and the guards of both armies drew their water from the same stream. As I would be under shortrange fire and in an open country, I took nobody with me, except, I believe, a bugler, who stayed some distance to the rear. I rode from our right around to our left. When I came to the camp of the picket guard of our side, I heard the call, "Turn out the guard for the commanding general." I replied, "Never mind the guard," and they were dismissed and went back to their tents. Just back of these, and about equally distant from the creek, were the guards of the Confederate pickets. The sentinel on their post called out in like manner, "Turn out the guard for the commanding general," and, I believe, added, "General Grant." Their line in a moment front-faced to the north, facing me, and gave a salute, which I returned.

The most friendly relations seemed to exist between the pickets of the two armies. At one place there was a tree which had fallen across the stream, and which was used by the soldiers of both armies in drawing water for their camps. General Longstreet's corps was stationed there at the time, and wore blue of a little different shade from our uniform. Seeing a soldier in blue on this log, I rode up to him, commenced conversing with him, and asked whose corps he belonged to. He was very polite, and, touching his hat to me, said he belonged to General Longstreet's corps. I asked him a few questions—but not with a view of gaining any particular information—all of which he answered, and I rode off....

**[He won the Battle of Chattanooga. Lincoln named him a lieutenant-general and gave him command of the armies of the United States.]**

Although hailing from Illinois myself, the State of the President, I never met Mr. Lincoln until called to the capital to receive my commission as lieutenant-general. I knew him, however, very well and favorably from the accounts given by officers under me at the West who had known him all their lives. I had also read the remarkable series of debates between Lincoln and Douglas a few years before, when they were rival candidates for the United States Senate. I was then a resident of Missouri, and by no means a "Lincoln man" in that contest; but I recognized then his great ability.

In my first interview with Mr. Lincoln alone he stated to me that he had never professed to be a military man or to know how campaigns should be conducted, and never wanted to interfere in them: but that procrastination on the part of commanders, and the pressure from the people at the North and Congress, *which was always with him,* forced him into issuing his series of "Military Orders"—one, two, three, etc. He did not know but they were all wrong, and did know that some of them were. All he wanted or had ever wanted was some one who would take the responsibility and act, and call on him for all the assistance needed, pledging himself to use all the power of the government in rendering such assistance. Assuring him that I would do the best I could with the means at hand, and avoid as far as possible annoying him or the War Department, our first interview ended.

The Secretary of War I had met once before only, but felt that I knew him better.

While commanding in West Tennessee we had occasionally held conversations over the wires, at night, when they were not being otherwise used. He and General Halleck both cautioned me against giving the President my plans of campaign, saying that he was so kind-hearted, so averse to refusing anything asked of him, that some friend would be sure to get from him all he knew. I should have said that in our interview the President told me he did not want to know what I proposed to do. But he submitted a plan of campaign of his own which he wanted me to hear and then do as I pleased about. He brought out a map of Virginia on which he had evidently marked every position occupied by the Federal and Confederate armies up to that time. He pointed out on the map two streams which empty into the Potomac, and suggested that the army might be moved on boats and landed between the mouths of these streams. We would then have the Potomac to bring our supplies, and the tributaries would protect our flanks while we moved out. I listened respectfully, but did not suggest that the same streams would protect Lee's flanks while he was shutting us up.

I did not communicate my plans to the President, nor did I to the Secretary of War or to General Halleck....

**[He planned the northern strategy of sending Sherman through Georgia to the sea while he kept the pressure on Lee's army around Richmond.]**

I have always regretted that the last assault at Cold Harbor was ever made. I might say the same thing of the assault of the 22d of May, 1863, at Vicksburg. At Cold Harbor no advantage whatever was gained to compensate for the heavy loss we sustained. Indeed, the advantages, other than those of relative losses, were on the Confederate side. Before that, the Army of Northern Virginia seemed to have acquired a wholesome regard for the courage, endurance, and soldierly qualities generally of the Army of the Potomac. They no longer wanted to fight them "one Confederate to five Yanks." Indeed, they seemed to have given up any idea of gaining any advantage of their antagonist in the open field. They had come to much prefer breastworks in their front to the Army of the Potomac. This charge seemed to revive their hopes temporarily; but it was of short duration. The effect upon the Army of the Potomac was the reverse. When we reached the James River, however, all effects of the battle of Cold Harbor seemed to have disappeared....

**[Grant held Lee's army in position while Sherman pushed out of Savannah and into the Carolinas.]**

On the last of January, 1865, peace commissioners from the so-called Confederate States presented themselves on our lines around Petersburg, and were immediately conducted to my headquarters at City Point. They proved to be

Alexander H. Stephens, Vice-President of the Confederacy, Judge [John A.] Campbell, Assistant-Secretary of War, and R. M. T. Hunter, formerly United States Senator and then a member of the Confederate Senate.

It was about dark when they reached my headquarters, and I at once conducted them to the steamer *Mary Martin,* a Hudson River boat which was very comfortably fitted up for the use of passengers. I at once communicated by telegraph with Washington and informed the Secretary of War and the President of the arrival of these commissioners and that their object was to negotiate terms of peace between the United States and, as they termed it, the Confederate Government. I was instructed to retain them at City Point, until the President, or some one whom he would designate, should come to meet them. They remained several days as guests on board the boat. I saw them quite frequently, though I have no recollection of having had any conversation whatever with them on the subject of their mission. It was something I had nothing to do with, and I therefore did not wish to express any views on the subject. For my own part I never had admitted, and never was ready to admit, that they were the representatives of a *government.* There had been too great a waste of blood and treasure to concede anything of the kind. As long as they remained there, however, our relations were pleasant and I found them all very agreeable gentlemen. I directed the captain to furnish them with the best the boat afforded, and to administer to their comfort in every way possible. No guard was placed over them and no restriction was put upon their movements; nor was there any pledge asked that they would not abuse the privileges extended to them. They were permitted to leave the boat when they felt like it, and did so, coming up on the bank and visiting me at my headquarters.

I had never met either of these gentlemen before the war, but knew them well by reputation and through their public services, and I had been a particular admirer of Mr. Stephens. I had always supposed that he was a very small man, but when I saw him in the dusk of the evening I was very much surprised to find so large a man as he seemed to be. When he got down on to the boat I found that he was wearing a coarse gray woollen overcoat, a manufacture that had been introduced into the South during the rebellion. The cloth was thicker than anything of the kind I had ever seen, even in Canada. The overcoat extended nearly to his feet, and was so large that it gave him the appearance of being an average-sized man. He took this off when he reached the cabin of the boat, and I was struck with the apparent change in size, in the coat and out of it.

After a few days, about the 2d of February, I received a dispatch from Washington, directing me to send the commissioners to Hampton Roads to meet the President and a member of the cabinet. Mr. Lincoln met them there and had an interview of short duration. It was not a great while after they met that the President visited me at City Point. He spoke of his having met the commissioners, and said he had told them that there would be no use in entering into any negotiations unless they would recognize, first: that the Union as a whole must be forever preserved, and second: that slavery must be abolished. If they were willing to concede these two points, then he was ready to enter into negotiations and was almost willing to hand them a blank sheet of paper with his signature attached for them to fill in the terms upon which they were willing to live with us in the Union and be one people. He always showed a generous and kindly spirit toward the Southern people, and I never heard him abuse an enemy. Some of the cruel things said about President Lincoln, particularly in the North, used to pierce him to the heart; but never in my presence did he evince a revengeful disposition—and I saw a great deal of him at City Point, for he seemed glad to get away from the cares and anxieties of the capital.

Right here I might relate an anecdote of Mr. Lincoln. It was on the occasion of his visit to me just after he had talked with the peace commissioners at Hampton Roads. After a little conversation, he asked me if I had seen the overcoat of Stephen's. I replied that I had. "Well," said he, "did you see him take it off?" I said yes. "Well," said he, "didn't you think it was the biggest shuck and the littlest ear that ever you did see?" Long afterwards I told this story to the Confederate General J. B. Gordon, at the time a member of the Senate. He repeated it to Stephens, and, as I heard afterwards, Stephens laughed immoderately at the simile of Mr. Lincoln.

The rest of the winter, after the departure of the peace commissioners, passed off quietly and uneventfully, except for two or three little incidents. On one occasion during this period, while I was visiting Washington City for the purpose of conferring with the administration, the enemy's cavalry under General Wade Hampton, passing our extreme left and then going to the south, got in east of us. Before their presence was known, they had driven off a large number of beef cattle that were grazing in that section. It was a fair capture, and they were sufficiently needed by the Confederates. It was only retaliating for what we had done, sometimes for many weeks at a time, when out of supplies—taking what the Confederate army otherwise would have gotten. As appears in this book, on one single occasion we captured five thousand head of cattle which were crossing the Mississippi River near Port Hudson on their way from Texas to supply the Confederate army in the East.

One of the most anxious periods of my experience during the rebellion was the last few weeks before Petersburg. I felt that the situation of the Confederate army was such that they would try to make an escape at the earliest practicable moment, and I was afraid, every morning, that I would awake from my sleep to hear that Lee had gone, and that nothing was left but a picket line. He had his railroad by the way of Danville south, and I was afraid that he was running off his men and all stores and ordnance except such as it would be necessary to carry with him for his immediate defence. I knew he could move much more lightly and more rapidly than I, and that, if he got the start, he would leave me behind so that we would have the same army to fight again farther south—and the war might be prolonged another year.

I was led to this fear by the fact that I could not see how it was possible for the Confederates to hold out much longer where they were. There is no doubt that Richmond would have been evacuated much sooner than it was, if it had not been that it was the capital of the so-called Confederacy, and the fact of evacuating the capital would, of course, have had a very demoralizing effect upon the Confederate army. When it was evacuated (as we shall see further on), the Confederacy at once began to crumble and fade away. Then, too, desertions were taking place, not only among those who were with General Lee in the neighborhood of their capital, but throughout the whole Confederacy. I remember that in a conversation with me on one occasion long prior to this, General Butler remarked that the Confederates would find great difficulty in getting more men for their army; possibly adding, though I am not certain as to this, "unless they should arm the slave."

The South, as we all knew, were conscripting every able-bodied man between the ages of eighteen and forty-five; and now they had passed a law for the further conscription of boys from fourteen to eighteen, calling them the junior reserves, and men from forty-five to sixty to be called the senior reserves. The latter were to hold the necessary points not in immediate danger, and especially those in the rear. General Butler, in alluding to this conscription, remarked that they were thus "robbing both the cradle and the grave," an expression which I afterwards used in writing a letter to Mr. Washburn.

It was my belief that while the enemy could get no more recruits they were losing at least a regiment a day, taking it throughout the entire army, by desertions alone. Then by casualties of war, sickness, and other natural causes, their losses were much heavier. It was a mere question of arithmetic to calculate how long they could hold out while that rate of depletion was going on. Of course long before their army would be thus reduced to nothing the army which we had in the field would have been able to capture theirs. Then too I knew from the great number of desertions, that the men who had fought so bravely, so gallantly and so long for the cause which they believed in—and as earnestly, I take it, as our men believed in the cause for which they were fighting—had lost hope and become despondent. Many of them were making application to be sent North where they might get employment until the war was over, when they could return to their Southern homes.

For these and other reasons I was naturally very impatient for the time to come when I could commence the spring campaign, which I thoroughly believed would close the war....

**[He met with Lincoln. Grant's siege of Lee's army was successful at Petersburg and he surrounded the Confederates near Appomattox Courthouse.]**

I had known General Lee in the old army, and had served with him in the Mexican War; but did not suppose, owing to the difference in our age and rank, that he would remember me; while I would more naturally remember him distinctly, because he was the chief of staff of General Scott in the Mexican War.

When I had left camp that morning I had not expected so soon the result that was then taking place, and consequently was in rough garb. I was without a sword, as I usually was when on horseback on the field, and wore a soldier's blouse for a coat, with the shoulder straps of my rank to indicate to the army who I was. When I went into the house I found General Lee. We greeted each other, and after shaking hands took our seats. I had my staff with me, a good portion of whom were in the room during the whole of the interview.

What General Lee's feelings were I do not know. As he was a man of much dignity, with an impassable face, it was impossible to say whether he felt inwardly glad that the end had finally come, or felt sad over the result, and was too manly to show it. Whatever his feelings, they were entirely concealed from my observation; but my own feelings, which had been quite jubilant on the receipt of his letter, were sad and depressed. I felt like anything rather than rejoicing at the downfall of a foe who had fought so long and valiantly, and had suffered so much for a cause, though that cause was, I believe, one of the worst for which a people ever fought, and one for which there was the least excuse. I do not question, however, the sincerity of the great mass of those who were opposed to us.

General Lee was dressed in a full uniform which was entirely new, and was wearing a sword of considerable value, very likely the sword which had been presented by the State of Virginia; at all events, it was an entirely different sword from the one that would ordinarily be worn in the field. In my rough traveling suit, the uniform of a private with the straps of a lieutenant-general, I must have contrasted very strangely with a man so handsomely dressed, six feet high and of faultless form. But this was not a matter that I thought of until afterwards.

We soon fell into a conversation about old army times. He remarked that he remembered me very well in the old army; and I told him that as a matter of course I remembered him perfectly, but from the difference in our rank and years (there being about sixteen years' difference in our ages), I had thought it very likely that I had not attracted his attention sufficiently to be remembered by him after such a long interval. Our conversation grew so pleasant that I almost forgot the object of our meeting. After the conversation had run on in this style for some time, General Lee called my attention to the object of our meeting, and said that he had asked for this interview for the purpose of getting from me the terms I proposed to give his army. I said that I meant merely that his army should lay down their arms, not to take them up again during the continuance of the war unless duly and properly exchanged. He said that he had so understood my letter.

Then we gradually fell off again into conversation about matters foreign to the subject which had brought us together. This continued for some little time, when General Lee again interrupted the course of the conversation by suggesting that the terms I proposed to give his army ought to be written out. I called to General [Ely S.] Parker, secretary on my staff, for writing materials, and commenced writing out the following terms:

> Appomattox C. H., Va.,
> Ap'l 9th, 1865

Gen. R. E. Lee,
Comd'g C.S.A.

Gen.: In accordance with the substance of my letter to you of the 8th inst., I propose to receive the surrender of the Army of N. Va. on the following terms, to wit: Rolls of all the officers and men to be made in duplicate. One copy to be given to an officer designated by me, the other to be retained by such officer or officers as you may designate. The officers to give their individual paroles not to take up arms against the Government of the United States until properly exchanged, and each company or regimental commander sign a like parole for the men of their commands. The arms, artillery and public property to be parked and stacked, and turned over to the officer appointed by me to receive them. This will not embrace the side-arms of the officers, nor their private horses or baggage. This done, each officer and man will be allowed to return to their homes, not to be disturbed by United States authority so long as they observe their paroles and the laws in force where they may reside.

> Very respectfully,
> U. S. Grant,
> Lt.-Gen.

When I put my pen to the paper I did not know the first word that I should make use of in writing the terms. I only knew what was in my mind, and I wished to express it clearly, so that there could be no mistaking it. As I wrote on, the thought occurred to me that the officers had their own private horses and effects, which were important to them, but of no value to us; also that it would be an unnecessary humiliation to call upon them to deliver their side arms.

No conversation, not one word, passed between General Lee and myself, either about private property, side arms, or kindred subjects. He appeared to have no objections to the terms first proposed; or if he had a point to make against them he wished to wait until they were in writing to make it. When he read over that part of the terms about side arms, horses and private property of the officers, he remarked, with some feeling, I thought, that this would have a happy effect upon his army.

Then, after a little further conversation, General Lee remarked to me again that their army was organized a little differently from the army of the United States (still maintaining by implication that we were two countries); that in their army the cavalrymen and artillerists owned their own horses; and he asked if he was to understand that the men who so owned their horses were to be permitted to retain them. I told him that as the terms were written they would not; that only the officers were permitted to take their private property. He then, after reading over the terms a second time, remarked that that was clear.

I then said to him that I thought this would be about the last battle of the war—I sincerely hoped so; and I said further I took it that most of the men in the ranks were small farmers. The whole country had been so raided by the two armies that it was doubtful whether they would be able to put in a crop to carry themselves and their families through the next winter without the aid of the horses they were then riding. The United States did not want them and I would, therefore, instruct the officers I left behind to receive the paroles of his troops to let every man of the Confederate army who claimed to own a horse or mule take the animal to his home. Lee remarked again that this would have a happy effect.

He then sat down and wrote out the following letter:

Headquarters Army of Northern Virginia,
April 9, 1865

General:—I received your letter of this date containing the terms of the surrender of the Army of Northern Virginia as proposed by you. As they are substantially the same as those expressed in your letter of the 8th inst., they are accepted. I will proceed to designate the proper officers to carry the stipulations into effect.

R. E. Lee,
General
Lieut.-General U. S. Grant.

While duplicates of the two letters were being made, the Union generals present were severally presented to General Lee.

The much talked of surrendering of Lee's sword and my handing it back, this and much more that has been said about it is the purest romance. The word sword or side arms was not mentioned by either of us until I wrote it in the terms. There was no premeditation, and it did not occur to me until the moment I wrote it down. If I had happened to omit it, and General Lee had called my attention to it, I should have put it in the terms precisely as I acceded to the provision about the soldiers retaining their horses.

General Lee, after all was completed and before taking his leave, remarked that his army was in a very bad condition for want of food, and that they were without forage; that his men had been living for some days on parched corn exclusively, and that he would have to ask me for rations and forage. I told him "certainly," and asked for how many men he wanted rations. His answer was "about twenty-five thousand": and I authorized him to send his own commissary and quartermaster to Appomattox Station, two or three miles away, where he could have, out of the trains we had stopped, all the provisions wanted. As for forage, we had ourselves depended almost entirely upon the country for that.

Generals Gibbon, Griffin and Merritt were designated by me to carry into effect the paroling of Lee's troops before they should start for their homes— General Lee leaving Generals Longstreet, Gordon and Pendleton for them to confer with in order to facilitate this work. Lee and I then separated as cordially as we had met, he returning to his own lines, and all went into bivouac for the night at Appomattox.

Soon after Lee's departure I telegraphed to Washington as follows:

Headquarters Appomattox, C. H., Va.,
April 9th, 1865, 4.30 P.M.

Hon. E. M. Stanton:
Secretary of War,
Washington.

General Lee surrendered the Army of Northern Virginia this afternoon on terms proposed by myself. The accompanying additional correspondence will show the conditions fully.

U. S. Grant,
Lieut.-General

When news of the surrender first reached our lines our men commenced firing a salute of a hundred guns in honor of the vicotry. I at once sent word, however, to have it stopped. The Confederates were now our prisoners, and we did not want to exult over their downfall.

I determined to return to Washington at once, with a view to putting a stop to the purchase of supplies, and what I now deemed other useless outlay of money. Before leaving, however, I thought I would like to see General Lee again; so next morning I rode out beyond our lines towards his headquarters, preceded by a bugler and a staff-officer carrying a white flag.

Lee soon mounted his horse, seeing who it was, and met me. We had there between the lines, sitting on horseback, a very pleasant conversation of over half an hour, in the course of which Lee said to me that the South was a big country and that we might have to march over it three or four times before the war entirely ended, but that we would now be able to do it as they could no longer resist us. He expressed it as his earnest hope, however, that we would not be called upon to cause more loss and sacrifice of life; but he could not foretell the result. I then suggested to General Lee that there was not a man in the Confederacy whose influence with the soldiery and the whole people was as great as his, and that if he would now advise the surrender of all the armies I had no doubt his advice would be followed with alacrity. But Lee said, that he could not do that without consulting the President first. I knew there was no use to urge him to do anything against his ideas of what was right.

I was accompanied by my staff and other officers, some of whom seemed to have a great desire to go inside the Confederate lines. They finally asked permission of Lee to do so for the purpose of seeing some of their old army friends, and the permission was granted. They went over, had a very pleasant time with their old friends, and brought some of them back with them when they returned.

When Lee and I separated he went back to his lines, and I returned to the house of Mr. McLean. Here the officers of both armies came in great numbers, and seemed to enjoy the meeting as much as though they had been friends separated for a long time while fighting battles under the same flag. For the time being it looked very much as if all thought of the war had escaped their minds. After an hour pleasantly passed in this way I set out on horseback, accompanied by my staff and a small escort, for Burkesville Junction, up to which point the railroad had by this time been repaired.

After the fall of Petersburg, and when the armies of the Potomac and the James were in motion to head off Lee's army, the *morale* of the National troops had greatly improved. There was no more straggling, no more rear guards. The men who in former times had been falling back, were now, as I have already stated, striving to get to the front. For the first time in four weary years they felt that they were now nearing the time when they could return to their homes with their country saved. On the other hand, the Confederates were more than correspondingly depressed. Their despondency increased with each returning day, and especially after the battle of Sailor's Creek. They threw away their arms in constantly increasing numbers, dropping out of the ranks and betaking themselves to the woods in the hope of reaching their homes. I have already instanced the case of the entire disintegration of a regiment whose colonel I met at Farmville. As a result of these and other influences, when Lee finally surrendered at Appomattox, there were only 28,356 officers and men left to be paroled, and many of these were without arms. It was probably this latter fact which gave rise to the statement sometimes made, North and South, that Lee surrendered a smaller number of men than what the official figures show. As a matter of official record, and in addition to the number paroled as given above, we captured between March 29th and the date of surrender 19,132 Confederates, to say nothing of Lee's other losses, killed, wounded and missing, during the series of desperate conflicts which marked his headlong and determined flight. The same record shows the number of cannon, including those at Appomattox, to have been 689 between the dates named.

There has always been a great conflict of opinion as to the number of troops engaged in every battle, or all important battles, fought between the sections, the South magnifying the number of Union troops engaged and belittling their own. Northern writers have fallen, in many instances, into the same error. I have often heard gentlemen, who were thoroughly loyal to the Union, speak of what a splendid fight the South had made and successfully continued for four years before yielding, with their twelve million of people against our twenty, and of the twelve four being colored slaves, non-combatants. I will add to their argument. We had many regiments of brave and loyal men who volunteered under great difficulty from the twelve million belonging to the South.

But the South had rebelled against the National government. It was not bound by any constitutional restrictions. The whole South was a military camp. The occupation of the colored people was to furnish supplies for the army. Conscription was resorted to early, and embraced every male from the age of eighteen to forty-five, excluding only those physically unfit to serve in the field, and the necessary number of civil officers of State and intended National government. The old and physically disabled furnished a good portion of these. The slaves, the non-combatants, one-third of the whole, were required to work in the field without regard to sex, and almost without regard to age. Children from the age of eight years could and did handle the hoe; they were not much older when they began to hold the plough. The four million of colored non-combatants were equal to more than three times their number in the North, age for age and sex for sex, in supplying food from the soil to support armies. Women did not work in the fields in the North, and children attended school.

The arts of peace were carried on in the North. Towns and cities grew during the war. Inventions were made in all kinds of machinery to increase the products of a day's labor in the shop, and in the field. In the South no opposition was allowed to the government which had been set up and which would have become real and respected if the rebellion had been successful. No rear had to be protected. All the troops in service could be brought to the front to contest every inch of ground threatened with invasion. The press of the South, like the people who remained at home, were loyal to the Southern cause.

In the North, the country, the towns and the cities presented about the same appearance they do in time of peace. The furnace was in blast, the shops were filled with workmen, the fields were cultivated, not only to supply the population of the North and the troops invading the South, but to ship abroad to pay a part of the expense of the war. In the North the press was free up to the point of open treason. The citizen could entertain his views and express them. Troops were necessary in the Northern States to prevent prisoners from the Southern army being released by outside force, armed and set at large to destroy by fire our Northern cities. Plans were formed by Northern and Southern citizens to burn our cities, to poison the water supplying them, to spread infection by importing clothing from infected regions, to blow up our river and lake steamers—regardless of the destruction of innocent lives. The copperhead disreputable portion of the press magnified rebel successes, and belittled those of the Union army. It was, with a large following, an auxiliary to the Confederate army. The North would have been much stronger with a hundred thousand of these men in the Confederate ranks, and the rest of their kind thoroughly subdued, as the Union sentiment was in the South, than we were as the battle was fought.

As I have said, the whole South was a military camp. The colored people, four million in number, were submissive, and worked in the field and took care of the families while the able-bodied white men were at the front fighting for a cause destined to defeat. The cause was popular, and was enthusiastically supported by the young men. The conscription took all of them. Before the war was over, further conscriptions took those between fourteen and eighteen years of age as junior reserves, and those between forty-five and sixty as senior reserves. It would have been an offence, directly after the war, and perhaps it would be now, to ask any able-bodied man in the South, who was between the ages of fourteen and sixty at any time during the war, whether he had been in the Confederate army. He would assert that he had, or account for his absence from the ranks. Under such circumstances it is hard to conceive how the North showed such a superiority of force in very battle fought. I know they did not.

During 1862 and '3, John H. Morgan, a partisan officer, of no military education, but possessed of courage and endurance, operated in the rear of the Army of the Ohio in Kentucky and Tennessee. He had no base of supplies to protect, but was at home wherever he went. The army operating against the South, on the contrary, had to protect its lines of communication with the North, from which all supplies had to come to the front. Every foot of road had to be guarded by troops stationed at convenient distances apart. These guards could not render assistance beyond the points where stationed. Morgan was foot-loose and could operate where his information—always correct—led him to believe he could do the greatest damage. During the time he was operating in this way he killed, wounded and captured several times the number he ever had under his command at any one time. He destroyed many millions of property in addition. Places he did not attack had to be guarded as if threatened by him. Forrest, an abler soldier, operated farther west, and held from the National front quite as many men as could be spared for offensive operations. It is safe to say that more than half the National army was engaged in guarding lines of supplies, or were on leave, sick in hospital or on detail which prevented their bearing arms. Then, again, large forces were employed where no Confederate army confronted them. I deem it safe to say that there were no large engagements where the National numbers compensated for the advantage of position and intrenchment occupied by the enemy....

After I left General Lee at Appomattox Station, I went with my staff and a few others directly to Burkesville Station on my way to Washington. The road from Burkesville back having been newly repaired and the ground being soft, the train got off the track frequently, and, as a result, it was after midnight of the second day when I reached City Point. As soon as possible I took a dispatch-boat thence to Washington City.

While in Washington I was very busy for a time in preparing the necessary orders for the new state of affairs; communicating with my different commanders of separate departments, bodies of troops, etc. But by the 14th I was pretty well through with this work, so as to be able to visit my children, who were then in Burlington, New Jersey, attending school. Mrs. Grant was with me in Washington at the time, and we were invited by President and Mrs. Lincoln to accompany them to the theatre on the evening of that day. I replied to the President's verbal invitation to the effect, that if we were in the city we would take great pleasure in accompanying them; but that I was very anxious to get away and visit my children, and if I could get through my work during the day I should do so. I did get through and started by the evening train on the 14th, sending Mr. Lincoln word, of course, that I would not be at the theatre.

At that time the railroad to New York entered Philadelphia on Broad Street; passengers were conveyed in ambulances to the Delaware River, and then ferried to Camden, at which point they took the cars again. When I reached the ferry, on the east side of the City of Philadelphia, I found people awaiting my arrival there; and also dispatches informing me of the assassination of the President and Mr. Seward, and of the probable assassination of the Vice-President, Mr. Johnson, and requesting my immediate return.

It would be impossible for me to describe the feeling that overcame me at the news of these assassinations, more especially the assassination of the President. I knew his goodness of heart, his generosity, his yielding disposition, his desire to have everybody happy, and above all his desire to see all the people of the United States enter again upon the full privileges of citizenship with equality among all. I knew also the feeling that Mr. Johnson had expressed in speeches and conversation against the Southern people, and I feared that his course towards them would be such as to repel, and make them unwilling citizens; and if they became such they would remain so for a long while. I felt that reconstruction had been set back, no telling how far.

I immediately arranged for getting a train to take me back to Washington City; but Mrs. Grant was with me; it was after midnight and Burlington was but an hour away. Finding that I could accompany her to our house and return about as soon as they would be ready to take me from the Philadelphia station, I went up with her and returned immediately by the same special train. The joy that I had witnessed among the people in the street and in public places in Washington when I left there, had been turned to grief; the city was in reality a city of mourning. I have stated what I believed then the effect of this would be, and my judgment now is that I was right. I believe the South would have been saved from very much of the hardness of feeling that was engendered by Mr. Johnson's course towards them during the first few months of his administration. Be this as it may, Mr. Lincoln's assassination was particularly unfortunate for the entire nation.

Mr. Johnson's course towards the South did engender bitterness of feeling. His denunciations of treason and his ever-ready remark, "Treason is a crime and must be made odious," was repeated to all those men of the South who came to him to get some assurances of safety so that they might go to work at something with the feeling that what they obtained would be secure to them. He uttered his denunciations with great vehemence, and as they were accompanied with no assurances of safety, many Southerners were driven to a point almost beyond endurance.

The President of the United States is, in a large degree, or ought to be, a representative of the feeling, wishes and judgment of those over whom he presides; and the Southerners who read the denunciations of themselves and their people must have come to the conclusion that he uttered the sentiments of the Northern people; whereas, as a matter of fact, but for the assassination of Mr. Lincoln, I believe the great majority of the Northern people, and the soldiers unanimously, would have been in favor of a speedy reconstruction on terms that would be the least humiliating to the people who had rebelled against their government. They believed, I have no doubt, as I did, that besides being the mildest, it was also the wisest, policy.

The people who had been in rebellion must necessarily come back into the Union, and be incorporated as an integral part of the nation. Naturally the nearer they were placed to an equality with the people who had not rebelled, the more reconciled they would feel with their old antagonists, and the better citizens they would be from the beginning. They surely would not make good citizens if they felt that they had a yoke around their necks.

I do not believe that the majority of the Northern people at that time were in favor of Negro suffrage. They supposed that it would naturally follow the freedom of the Negro, but that there would be a time of probation, in which the ex-slaves could prepare themselves for the privileges of citizenship before the full right would be conferred; but Mr. Johnson, after a complete revolution of sentiment, seemed to regard the South not only as an oppressed people, but as the people best entitled to consideration of any of our citizens. This was more than the people who had secured to us the perpetuation of the Union were prepared for, and they became more radical in their views. The Southerners had the most power in the executive branch, Mr. Johnson having gone to their side; and with a compact South, and such sympathy and support as they could get from the North, they felt that they would be able to control the nation at once, and already many of them acted as if they thought they were entitled to do so.

Thus Mr. Johnson, fighting Congress on the one hand, and receiving the support of the South on the other, drove Congress, which was overwhelmingly republican, to the passing of first one measure and then another to restrict his power. There being a solid South on one side that was in accord with the political party in the North which had sympathized with the rebellion, it finally, in the judgment of Congress and of the majority of the legislatures of the States, became necessary to enfranchise the Negro, in all his ignorance. In this work, I shall not discuss the question of how far the policy of Congress in this particular proved a wise one. It became an absolute necessity, however, because of the foolhardiness of the President and the blindness of the Southern people to their own interest. As to myself, while strongly favoring the course that would be the least humiliating to the people who had been in rebellion, I had gradually worked up to the point where, with the majority of the people, I favored immediate enfranchisement.

# TUNIS GULIC CAMPBELL
## 1812–1891

*Tunis Campbell often shared the stage with Frederick Douglass at abolition meetings in the North before the Civil War. After the war, Campbell talked with President Ulysses Grant about enforcing equal treatment for the people freed by the war but still living in the South. Grant helped a little, but at the end of Reconstruction, a sixty-four-year-old Campbell found himself wearing chains and a prison uniform working as a convict-laborer hired out on a Georgia plantation.*

*He was born free in New Jersey. In an age when few African-Americans had any formal education, Campbell spent twelve years in an otherwise all-white Episcopal school in New York. He trained to be a missionary for the American Colonization Society which hoped to return all blacks to the newly-established country of Liberia in Africa. When he opted to fight against slavery in America instead of taking African-Americans to a foreign land, he joined the Methodist Church, founded an anti-colonization society and preached abolition.*

*After working in hotels in New York City and Boston, Campbell wrote the first American-published book on hotel management,* Hotel Keepers, Head Waiters, and Housekeepers' Guide *(1848). When the Civil War began, Campbell was married, had three children (one an adopted son), and owned a partnership in a bread company in NYC. He offered to join the army, but the U.S. was not accepting black soldiers at that time. In 1862, he got a commission to go to Port Royal, South Carolina, where refugeed slaves were getting land. He was to help in resettling them.*

*With the establishment in 1865 of the Bureau of Refugees, Freedmen and Abandoned Lands, Campbell was appointed a Bureau Agent to five Georgia islands. He set up schools, parceled out land, formed militia companies, and taught the ex-slaves about democracy. Beginning in 1867, after Congress took charge of Reconstruction, Georgia voters elected Campbell to the Constitutional Convention, state senate, and state legislature, as well as vice-president of the state's Republican party and local justice of the peace.*

*Campbell used his state offices to further black equality through legislation and by his associations with national Republican politicians. He used his local office as a judge to protect citizens along the Georgia coast in Darien, where he lived. He became the political boss of McIntosh County's Republican party and counseled blacks on labor contracts and civil rights.*

*By so doing he angered resurgent white reactionaries who refused to accept changes in the Southern way of life.*

*After white Democrats and their militant arm, the Ku Klux Klan, forced Georgia's only-elected Republican governor to flee the state, Northerners tired of fighting the South, and Grant insisted "Let us have peace," Campbell became a target for removal. His house was burned, his wife and son threatened, and his legislative office stripped from him. Campbell was sentenced to the penitentiary from which he was hired out for one year as a convict laborer for eight dollars to a rich landowner. Released in 1877, Campbell moved to Washington, D.C., and wrote his memoirs. From there his life is obscure. He died in 1891 and was buried in Boston.*

Sufferings of the Rev. T. G. Campbell and His Family, in Georgia. *Washington, D.C.: Enterprise Publishing Co., 1877.*

I was born in Middlebrook, Somerset county, New Jersey, on the 1st day of April, in the year 1812. My father, (John Campbell, sr.,) was a blacksmith by trade. I had five sisters and four brothers. I was the youngest of all, except two sisters, and they were living near Middlebrook. When at the age of 5 years, a gentleman rode up on horseback and spoke to me, as I was playing with two of my sisters by the roadside. He inquired for my mother. We all knew him very well, for he lived in Middlebrook. He told my father and mother that he could get me in a school on Long Island, in the State of New York. I was subsequently sent to a school at Babylon, on Long Island. I was the only colored child in the school. The principal and assistants were very kind to me. At the age of 18 I returned home. I would not agree to go to Africa as a missionary, and from this period I commenced as an anti-slavery lecturer.

My father had removed to the city of New Brunswick, New Jersey. Here, in the year 1832, I formed an anti-colonization society, and then pledged myself never to leave this country until every slave was free on American soil—unless I went to learn something, or to get help to secure their liberation. I was brought up in (and intended to be sent out from) the Episcopal Church, but after leaving school I joined the Methodist Church; and except being mobbed many times while lecturing or preaching, and nearly killed once, there was nothing of note occurred, except that I was the first moral reformer and temperance lecturer that entered the Five Points, in the city of New York. After the work was begun, then noble-hearted white men stepped in; and where the old dens of thieves and pannel-houses stood, they have raised a mission house.

The mayor of Jersey City was kind enough to send a policeman down to the ferry, every Monday night, to protect me from the ferry, and back to the ferry, from the temperance meetings held in that city every Monday night; and through Divine Providence kind friends came forward and helped us to raise our school houses and churches in Jersey City during the years 1841, 1842, 1845, and 1846. I also, during the same time, labored in Brooklyn and Williamsburg in the same way.

I now pass to the year 1861. I was at this time a partner and general agent of the firm of Davies & Co., unfermented bread manufacturers, on the corner of Third avenue and Fourteenth street, in the city of New York....

This was the first year of the war. Myself and other colored men offered to aid the Government in putting down the rebellion, but our services were refused— Secretary Seward replying that we were premature. In 1863 I sent a personal petition to the President, but got no answer. An old friend of mine in the city of New York asked me if I had got any answer to my Washington letter. I told him no. He then said, "Write again, and I will try what I can do for you." I did write again to President Lincoln; and in about a month after this I called to see my friend, and he had that very day received a package from the Secretary of War, upon opening which, I found a commission ordering me to report forthwith to General Saxton, at Hilton Head, in South Carolina; and there I remained with General Saxton, and did whatever was entrusted to me, I think, to his satisfaction. After the fall of Charleston I requested to be sent to the Sea Islands, in Georgia, and had assigned to me Burnside, Ausaba, Saint Catharines, Sapelo and Colonel's Islands, with orders to organize and establish governments on the Islands; protect freedmen and refugees for thirty miles back from the seashore; and I remained for two years governor on these Islands. I had three teachers brought from the North at my own expense, and paid them. Under my policy-plan (that of President Johnson) I was removed by General Tilson, who was then placed as head of the Freedman's Bureau, and military commander-in-chief of Georgia.

The schools which I had established on the Islands were broken up, and the people driven off—unless they work under contracts which were purposely made to cheat the freedmen out of their labor. Rebels, who before had appeared humble and repentant, now insisted that all colored men and women should sign these contracts; and when they refused, they would waylay them and beat them, telling them that they would have them back when the Yankees left the State.

I went to General Tilson at the time his headquarters were in Augusta, and told him that I could not go on the Islands with safety. I showed him my certificate as an Elder of the Zion Methodist Episcopal Church in America, with my commission from Right Rev. J. J. Clinton as missionary for the States of Georgia and Florida. He said, "That is all right; but I cannot give you any protection!" I now returned back to Savannah. I sent down to a little village called Thunder Bolt and got a sail boat to take me to the islands. In it I went to see the people, to tell them that if they would come over on the main land I would try to get a plantation called Belleville, which was owned by a gentleman of the name of Hopkins, in McIntosh county. There was 1,250 acres of land in this plantation, and he would not sell it for less than $14.50 per acre. Looking at the pitiful condition of the people, I agreed to give it; on which I advanced $1,000. As the people had to move with what they could only take in small boats, I got one flat-boat; but what with rain and storm, when we got to Belleville, it was almost worthless—for everything was burned up during the war on the place.

As the people dare not stay there without me, I therefore moved my own family into a camp made of old boards on the side and ends, and a Palmetto roof—for I had to have one to cook in, and the other to sleep in....

Under the Reconstruction Act of Congress I was appointed one of the registrars for the Second Senaterial District of Georgia—Liberty, McIntosh and Tatnall counties,—and subsequently was elected a member of the constitutional convention; and upon the submission of the constitutions to the people for ratification, I was elected Senator for the Second District of the State of Georgia....

TUNIS GULIC CAMPBELL

[**After being expelled from office because of his color, he went to Washington, D.C., met with Senator Charles Sumner and others, protested the expulsion and lobbied for a new Amendment, the Fifteenth, to guarantee voting rights. The national government returned Campbell to his senatorial seat and he worked to keep Georgia under military Reconstruction until Georgia Democrats were willing to acquiesce in the results of the Civil War Amendments.**]

We all saw the danger of the State being admitted without some additional restriction, and this was brought by myself before the convention of colored men held in the city of Atlanta on February 3, 1871. I was by that convention elected a delegate at large to go to Washington and urge Congress to pass a law to protect loyal citizens in the Southern States. I arrived there in March, and found Congress just ready to adjourn; but, through the providence of God, the President issued his message to Congress, recommending to that body the consideration of the condition of loyal citizens in the Southern States, and the passage of some law looking to their protection. I had the honor of calling on the President at that time, and had assurance of his sanction to any bill passed by Congress for that purpose. The Ku-Klux Bill was passed, and of course my mission was accomplished.

Now the rebels became more enraged at me than ever. My friends informed me in Washington of plots layed to murder me on my way home, and advised me to stay in the North for a while; but without answering them, I came home before they thought I had left Washington, and went to work to find out, if possible, how they intended to kill me. The plan was this: Certain men were to come up from the country and watch for me going to or coming from the church at night, and kill me: then take my body a short distance in the woods, and leave something by it to make it appear that colored men from the country had done it. I pursued my inquiries until the statements made were fully corroborated by incidents that occurred at my own house and near the church. The parties were well known; and when they found that I was aware of their intentions, they had me arrested and taken to Savannah under the Ku-Klux Bill, before the United States Commissioner. It was another part of the programme to keep me in lawsuits, so as to compel me to leave the county to keep out of jail; or if I was put in jail, then break the jail at night and kill me in it. In any event, my life was to be taken.

I was compelled, on going up to the legislature last November, to leave my house at dusk, and go by land, to meet my son, who was waiting in Savannah for me. On my return, the captain of the steamer "Hardy" (a boat that stops at Darien coming and going to Savannah) refused to take me and another gentleman who was with me, and had my trunk put on the dock. After first taking our fare, he then came and gave it back to us, and ordered us on shore. All this was to get up a difficulty in Savannah; but being aware of their object, I at once ordered my things to be taken directly off the wharf, and crossed the country in a wagon, which took one day longer to get home. The only security that I now had for my life or property was this: The rebels knew that they would be held responsible by the loyal people of this country, both colored and white, for any injury that might be done to me....

[**Georgia Democrats surged back into office in 1872 and began a systematic campaign to remove all black officeholders. As a state**

**senator and a local justice of the peace (J.P.) in Darien, Campbell
was a prime target. He found himself facing charges of judicial
malfeasance in a case that had come before his J.P. court.]**

My case charged false imprisonment of a man named Rafe. This man was charged with breaking into a house in which two families lived, and threatening to kill the two men—both heads of these families. Upon the affidavits of said parties I issued a warrant for his arrest, and upon a hearing, he was ordered to give a bond of $50 in each case to keep the peace for six months as towards these families, and to pay the costs of court, which he agreed to do. He went to get bondsmen; but came back and said he would not give bonds; upon which, I ordered him to be locked up; but he went and made an affidavit that he had given bonds, and then ran away.

I was indicted without having a notice to appear before the grand jury, and that charges had been preferred against me. When the regular term of court came it was adjourned, and no time was set. I had business in Washington, and went there. Upon my return home I found my dwelling-house had been burned, and the grocery and dry-goods store of my wife and son was also burned. That day the court met, and I was arrested the next day....

**[After an all-white jury found him guilty but recommended "mercy,"
the judge sentenced him to jail. While his attorneys worked to appeal
the conviction, he spent time in a prison camp.]**

We then got papers ready while one of my counsel was speaking to move before Judge Hopkins, of the Atlanta Superior Court; and to do this, we had to dismiss it from before the Court of Ordinary. As soon as we dismissed it, irons were put upon me. I was then dragged to a covered wagon, and taken out of town, through by-roads, to a woods, when they made me get out and walk. Of course I took my time. When we got within a mile of a prison camp, two men came up on horseback and served papers upon the guard, ordering him to bring me back; but they not being officers, he refused. I was put in irons there, and that afternoon put to work, and the next day, until 2 o'clock, I worked, when I fell—being unable to work any longer.

The next morning it was raining. After they had breakfast I was taken by two men up to the guard tent, or headquarters, when they took off my chains. The captain of the guard showed me the order of court forbidding chains being put upon me, and ordering my return to Atlanta. After I had read it, he asked me when I expected my friends would send for me. "Why," I replied, "you are ordered by this to send me back, therefore they will not come." He then ordered a buggy to be brought, and ordered me put in, to be sent back to the Atlanta jail, in charge of a guard. I was carried to the jail by two men. When they laid me down upon the cell-floor, the men said, "He will soon die, for he is scarcely alive now." I asked one of the men to get me a little rice and milk. In about two hours he brought it. With difficulty I ate it, for I had not eaten anything for two days. The food given to prisoners was corn meal, mixed with water, without salt, made into an oval shape, and baked hard on the outside—but, as a general thing quite raw inside—and a piece of fat bacon, that eight persons to one would find raw. In going about they would pick up pieces of old-iron pots and kettles, and these were used for frying meat upon. Then they would break open the corn bread, and lay the pieces upon the coals and cook it—or rather burn it—so as to make it more palatable; but I could not eat it.

In the jail at Atlanta the food was better; but I had my meals brought from the hotel. As a general thing they kept them out in the office, until quite cold. I could never see the man who brought them. There were white prisoners who had their meals sent to them from some hotel, and the man would carry them in their cells.

Two or three days after my being brought back—I do not remember the day, for I was very sick—my lawyers brought me out again for a hearing before Judge Hopkins. I was carried up in a carriage....

**[Judge Hopkins put him in an Atlanta jail while he ordered the McIntosh County court to accept bond in the case. It took a month for the lower court to comply.]**

I was then brought out again, before Judge Hopkins, and gave bond. I now went down to Savannah, on my way home. I got to Savannah about 5 o'clock in the afternoon. The next day, at 2 o'clock p. m., I was arrested upon an old suit, which was not only out of date, but had been decided in my favor by the Supreme Court. In this case the judge refused to take bonds. I was then put in the jail in Savannah, which had been condemned by the grand jury on account of its unhealthiness. I was kept there for eight months and ten days. The first month I was kept in a cell down stairs, nine feet long and four and one-half feet wide. The prisoners were let out to walk in a hall six feet wide once in two weeks. Mr. Russell, after I had been there about four weeks, ordered me to go up stairs, and every day after that my cell was unlocked, and I was allowed to walk about the hall all day. My wife also made arrangement with a friend of ours to send me something to eat every day. She also sent me medicines, for her knowledge of the medicinal qualities of roots and herbs was very extensive.

I was attacked with a severe cough, and a swelling in my body, but was relieved of them by rubbing with a liniment and taking three doses a day of a syrup which was made by her.

I wrote a letter to President Grant, after I had been three or four months in jail, and, in answer, Attorney General Pierrepont informed me that he did not see how he could do anything for me. About three days after I got a communication from the Attorney General. I also received a letter from my wife, informing me of her having written to President Grant; and the same afternoon I received a communication from the Department of Justice, informing me that my wife (Mrs. Harriet Campbell) had written a letter to the President; and from statements made therein—said letter having been referred to him—that an immediate investigation should be made in my case. Just when I got through reading this letter I was ordered down to the office, and there I found the assistant attorney general for the State of Georgia—Colonel G. Thomas. He said that a dispatch had been received at Atlanta, ordering them to take my case into the United States Court. He had an affidavit drawn up, already for me to sign. He read it to me. I told him that was all right; but there was the other case before the Supreme Court of the State of Georgia, which ought also to be brought into the United States Court....

**[When the Georgia Supreme Court refused to hear the case because of a legal technicality in the way the appeal had been filed and when the federal courts refused to intervene, Campbell resigned himself to defeat.]**

On or about the 12th of January, 1876, the guard from the State prison came, about 7 o'clock a. m., and handcuffed me, and, with a chain about twelve feet long, dragged me along the streets of Savannah to the Central railroad, and then took me one hundred and forty miles from Savannah, to a prison camp on the plantation of Colonel Jack Smith's, in Washington county, State of Georgia. The weather was very cold, and they took me up in a wagon. I was helpless when we got there, at 1 o'clock in the night—my hands being chained together. I had a very bad fall in getting out of the wagon. I tried to get pen and ink, and finally did get pen, ink and paper, and wrote a letter to my wife. I suffered very much from my fall. They were clearing land, and ordered me to pile brush. It is impossible to describe the way in which prisoners were worked. They were taken out as soon as they could see—both winter and summer—and kept to work as long as it was light, with one hour for dinner. They had breakfast before daylight. If wood was to be cut, the strongest and most expert men with the ax were made leaders, and every other man had to keep stroke with him all day long; and if they failed to do so, they were beaten most unmercifully with a leather strop, or a buggy trace, and given from fifty to one hundred strokes, until they would keep up or die. I am well satisfied that four men in the camp where I was were whipped to death—and this was considered one of the best camps in the State. These beatings made men reckless, and they would rush here and there, like wild men, to get the favor of the guard. I must say that the guards were a low and brutal set of men, as a general thing. You could hear them all the time calling out to the men, "I don't hear those axs! Go in with those axs! Go in with those axs!" If a man could not stand the work, then he was reported, and of course beaten. Women were treated in the same manner. I was in this camp eleven months and twenty-one days.

Two women—one a prisoner and the other a hired woman (both colored)—had white babies—which shows the state of morals there. I preached in this camp. I was for three Sundays in chains; but the Monday morning after the third Sunday my chains were taken off, and I was put as overseer of the wheelwright and blacksmith shops. The keys of the store houses and cribs were given to me, as also the books for all accounts of work done on the place, or for our neighbors. Mr. and Mrs. Smith always, from that time, treated me very kindly. My meals came from their table. My wife sent me every month a box of nourishments and medicines—clothing, soda-crackers, sugar-cakes, pound-cake, strawberry and other preserves, pickled eggs, &c. Since I have been out of prison I found that my wife went to the principle keeper and stated my case to him, and through her statements he was induced to have my chains taken off. Yet I feel under many obligations to Colonel J. T. Smith and lady for their kindness to me.

My wife and daughter were, during my confinement, in the city of Atlanta; and every dollar that she had been able to collect from her customers was used up in trying to help me. She also made up medicine in the winter to sell; and in the summer, went into the woods around Atlanta and picked blackberries, and brought them to the city to sell; and from the fields brought strawberries in, and sold them. About three weeks before I got home—January 6, 1877—my little girl went out to work, so as to keep a room, that I might have a place to come once more, and be with them. She wrote all the letters sent to President Grant by her mother. In this connection, I must say that Mrs. Campbell (my wife) is a woman of remarkable good judgment, guided by firm Christian principles, and I have no language to express my thankfulness to God for both wife and child.

During the whole of this time I was in dread of the ku-klux, or parties of men who broke open jails and prison camps to get persons that they wanted out of the way.

# SELECTED BIBLIOGRAPHY

Adams, Timony Dow. *Telling Lies in Modern American Autobiography*. Chapel Hill: University of North Carolina Press, 1990.

Addis, Patricia K. *Her Story: An Annotated Bibliography of Autobiographical Writings by American Women*. Metuchen, N.J.: Scarecrow Press, 1983.

Andrews, William L. *Sisters of the Spirit: Three Black Women's Autobiographies of the Nineteenth Century*. Bloomington: Indiana University Press, 1980.

———. *To Tell A Free Story: The First Century of Afro-American Autobiography, 1760–1865*. Urbana: University of Illinois Press, 1986.

Banner, Lois. *Elizabeth Cady Stanton: A Radical for Woman's Rights*. Boston: Little, Brown, 1980.

Berry, J. Bill, ed. *Home Ground: Southern Autobiography*. Columbia: University of Missouri Press, 1991.

Borg, Mary. *Writing Your Own Life: An Easy-To-Follow Guide to Writing an Autobiography*. Fort Collins, CO: Cottonwood Press, 1992.

Braxton, Joanne M. *Black Women Writing Autobiography: A Tradition Within a Tradition*. Philadelphia: Temple University Press, 1989.

Brignano, Russell C. *Black Americans in Autobiography: An Annotated Bibliography of Autobiographies and Autobiographical Books Written Since the Civil War*. Durham: Duke University Press, 1974.

Briscoe, Mary L. *et al. American Autobiography 1945–1980: A Bibliography*. Madison: University of Wisconsin Press, 1982.

Brumble, H. David. *American Indian Autobiography*. Los Angeles: University of California Press, 1988.

Bruss, Elizabeth W. *Autobiographical Acts: The Changing Situation of a Literacy Genre*. Baltimore: Johns Hopkins University, 1976.

Burke, James Wakefield. *David Crockett: The Man Behind the Myth*. Austin, Texas: Eakin Press, 1984.

Bushman, Claudia. *"A Good Poor Man's Wife": Being a Chronicle of Harriet Hanson Robinson and Her Family in Nineteenth-Century New England*. Hanover: University Press of New England, 1981.

Butterfield, Stephen. *Black Autobiography*. Amherst: University of Massachusetts Press, 1974.

Coe, Richard N. *When the Grass Was Taller: Autobiography and the Experience of Childhood*. New Haven: Yale University Press, 1984.

Cooley, Thomas. *Educated Lives: The Rise of Modern Autobiography in America*. Columbus: Ohio State University Press, 1976.

Costanza, Angelo. *Surprizing Narrative: Olaudah Equiano and the Beginnings of Black Autobiography*. New York: Greenwood Press, 1987.

Couser, G. Thomas. *Altered Egos: Authority in American Autobiography*. New York: Oxford University Press, 1989.

———. *American Autobiography: The Prophetic Mode*. Amherst: University of Massachusetts Press, 1979.

Cox, James M. *Recovering Literature's Lost Ground: Essays in American Autobiography*. Baton Rouge: Louisiana State Press, 1989.

Culley, Margo, ed. *American Women's Autobiography: Fea(s)ts of Memory*. Madison: University of Wisconsin Press, 1992.

Duncan, Russell. *Freedom's Shore: Tunis Campbell and the Georgia Freedmen*. Athens: University of Georgia Press, 1986.

Eagan, Susanna. *Patterns of Experience in Autobiography*. Chapel Hill: University of North Carolina Press, 1984.

Eakin, John Paul. *Fictions in Autobiography: Studies in the Art of Self Invention*. Princeton: Princeton University Press, 1985.

Griffith, Elisabeth. *In Her Own Right: The Life of Elizabeth Cady Stanton*. New York: Oxford Unversity Press, 1984.

Hawke, David Freeman. *Franklin*. New York: Harper and Row, 1976.

Holte, James Craig. *The Ethnic I: A Sourcebook for Ethnic-American Autobiography*. Westport: Greenwood Press, 1988.

Huggins, Nathan Irvin. *Slave and Citizen: The Life of Frederick Douglass*. Boston: Little, Brown, 1980.

Jelinek, Estelle C. *Women's Autobiography*. Bloomington: Indiana University Press, 1980.

Kaplan, Louis. *A Bibliography of American Autobiographies*. Madison: University of Wisconsin Press, 1962.

Lofaro, Michael A. *Davy Crockett: The Man, The Legend, The Legacy, 1786–1986*. Knoxville: University of Tennessee Press, 1985.

Lee, Robert A. *First Person Singular: Studies in American Autobiography*. Totowa, N.J.: Barnes and Noble Books, 1987.

Leibowitz, Herbert A. *Fabricating Lives: Explorations in American Autobiography*. New York: Knopf, 1989.

McFeely, William S. *Frederick Douglass*. New York: Norton, 1991.

———. *Grant: A Biography*. New York: Norton, 1981.

Nicholas, Roger L. *Black Hawk and the Warrior's Path*. Arlington Heights, Ill.: Harlan Davidson, 1992.

Olney, James, ed. *Autobiography: Essays Theoretical and Critical*. Princeton: Princeton University Press, 1980.

———. *Metaphors of Self: The Meaning of Autobiography*. Princeton: Princeton University Press, 1972.

Pascal, Roy. *Design and Truth in Autobiography*. Cambridge: Harvard University Press, 1960.

Payne, James Robert. *Multicultural Autobiography: American Lives*. Knoxville: University of Tennessee Press, 1992.

Piercy, Joseph K. *Anne Bradstreet*. New York: Twayne Publishers, 1965.

Sayre, Robert F. *The Examined Self: Benjamin Franklin, Henry Adams, Henry James*. Princeton: Princeton University Press, 1964.

Seavey, Ormond. *Becoming Benjamin Franklin: The Autobiography and the Life*. University Park: Pennsylvania State University Press, 1988.

Simpson, Brooks D. *Let Us Have Peace: Ulysses S. Grant and the Politics of War and Reconstruction, 1861–1868*. Chapel Hill: University of North Carolina Press, 1991.

Smith, Sidonie. *Where I'm Bound: Patterns of Slavery and Freedom in Black American Autobiography*. Westport: Greenwood Press, 1974.

Spengemann, William C. *The Forms of Autobiography: Episodes in the History of a Literary Genre.* New Haven: Yale University Press, 1980.

Stepto, Robert B. *From Behind the Veil: A Study of Afro-American Narrative.* Urbana: University of Illinois Press, 1979.

Stone, Albert E., ed. *The American Autobiography.* Englewood Cliffs, N.J.: Prentice-Hall, 1981.

Taylor, Gordon O. *Chapters of Experience: Studies in Twentieth-Century American Autobiography.* New York: St. Martin's Press, 1983.

White, Elizabeth Wade. *Anne Bradstreet: "The Tenth Muse".* New York: Oxford University Press, 1971.

Wright, Esmond. *Franklin of Philadelphia.* Cambridge, Mass.: Belknap Press of Harvard University Press, 1986.